Soviet–East European
Survey, 1986–1987

Soviet–East European Survey, 1986–1987

Selected Research and Analysis from Radio Free Europe/Radio Liberty

edited by
Vojtech Mastny

Westview Press / Boulder and London

Copyright © 1988 by Westview Press, Inc.

Published in 1988 in the United States of America by Westview Press, Inc.; Frederick A. Praeger, Publisher; 5500 Central Avenue, Boulder, Colorado 80301

Library of Congress Cataloging-in-Publication Data
Soviet-East European survey, 1986-1987.
    Includes index.
    1. Europe, Eastern--Foreign relations--Soviet Union.
2. Soviet Union--Foreign relations--Europe, Eastern.
3. Soviet Union--Politics and government--1982-   .
4. Gorbachev, Mikhail Sergeevich, 1931-   .
I. Mastny, Vojtech, 1936-   . II. RFE/RL, inc.
DJK45.S65S67 1988   327.47   87-31619
ISBN 0-8133-7477-4

Printed and bound in the United States of America

The paper used in this publication meets the requirements of the American National Standard for Permanence of Paper for Printed Library Materials Z39.48-1984.

6   5   4   3   2   1

Contents

Foreword   ix

Editor's Acknowledgments   xi

Introduction: Progress toward Pluralization/
    Vojtech Mastny   1

Gorbachev Turns to Political Reform
1 Gorbachev's Changing Priorities/ *Elizabeth Teague*   19
2 Conflict of Interests and Ideas:
    The January Plenum/ *Elizabeth Teague*   24
3 Curbs on Arbitrary Behavior/ *Julia Wishnevsky,*
    Roman Solchanyk   33
4 Burlatskii on Democratization/ *Henry Hamman*   38
5 Experiment with Contested Elections/*Elizabeth Teague* 42

Glasnost Gains Momentum
6 The Tool of Restructuring/ *Vera Tolz*   47
7 Return of Forbidden Literature/ *Julia Wishnevsky*   52
8 Rediscovering Soviet History/ *Vera Tolz*   63
9 Criticism of the Afghanistan War/ *Bohdan Nahaylo*   68
10 Telebridges with the West/ *Viktor Yasmann*   72

Social Ills Exposed
11 Prostitution in the USSR/ *Valerii Konovalov*   79
12 Drug Abuse/ *Sergei Voronitsyn*   82
13 Faltering Health Services/ *Sophia M. Miskiewicz*   87
14 The Misery of Rural Life/ *Elizabeth Teague*   92

The Lackluster Economy
15 Little *Glasnost* on Economic Accomplishment/
    Philip Hanson   95
16 Social Justice and Economic Progress/ *Aaron Trehub*   99
17 Expansion of the Cooperative Sector/
    Elizabeth Teague   105

18 Approaching the Ecological Barrier/ *Vladimir Sobell* 112
19 Low Targets and Low Growth/ *Philip Hanson*   116

New Thinking on Security
20 Sources of Security Reconsidered/ *Charles Glickham*   119
21 The Reykjavik Watershed/ *Bohdan Nahaylo*   130
22 Wisdom of Soviet Missiles Questioned/
   Elizabeth Teague   133
23 Red Square Landing Shakes up Top Military/
   Alexander Rahr   135
24 Toward an INF Treaty and Beyond/
   Douglas Clarke, Vladimir Socor   138

Moscow's Foreign Policy and Public Relations
25 The Vladivostok Speech/ *Bohdan Nahaylo,*
   Kevin Devlin   155
26 Into Southeast Asia and the Pacific/ *Daniel Abele*   161
27 Iran and the Gulf War/ *Bohdan Nahaylo, Daniel Abele* 166
28 The Chautauqua Conference in Latvia/ *Dzintra Bungs*   175
29 Human Rights and Foreign Policy/ *Roland Eggleston,*
   Bohdan Nahaylo   177

Ferment Among Soviet Nationalities
30 The Kazakhstan Riots/ *Bess Brown*   189
31 Language Demands in Belorussia and the Ukraine/
   Roman Solchanyk   194
32 Nationality Discord in Estonia/ *Toomas Ilves*   203
33 Pamiat Takes to the Streets/ *Julia Wishnevsky*   208

Czechoslovakia: The Touchstone of Gorbachevism
34 The Springs of Prague and Moscow/ *Vladimir V. Kusin* 211
35 The Ultracautious Reformers/ *Vladimir Sobell*   216
36 The Trial of the Jazz Fans/ *Vladimir Sobell*   224
37 Gorbachev's Delayed Visit/ *Vladimir V. Kusin, Kevin* 229
   Devlin

East Germany, Hungary, and Reform
38 GDR: Complacency of the Unreformed/ *Barbara*   237
   Donovan
39 Hungary: Despondency of the Reformed/ *Ivan Volgyes* 242
40 East Germany's Restive Churches/ *Barbara V. Flow*   247
41 Hungarian Experiments Continue/ *Karoly Okolicsanyi*   250

Progress in Poland?
42 Amnesty at Last/ *Louisa Vinton, Roman Stefanowski,*
   Anna Swidlicka   265
43 New Consultative Council/ *Jan B. de Weydenthal*   270

44 Solidarity Attempts to Regroup/ *Anna Swidlicka*   272
45 Diplomatic Isolation Broken/ *Anna Swidlicka,*
   Roman Stefanowski   277
46 Special Relationship with Moscow/ *Roman Solchanyk,*
   Anna Swidlicka   281
47 The Pope's Visit/ *Jan B. de Weydenthal*   287

The Balkan Ways
48 Reform Albanian Style/ *Louis Zanga*   295
49 Ceauşescu and Gorbachev/ *Anneli Ute Gabanyi*   306
50 Greek-Bulgarian Friendship Treaty/ *Stephen Ashley*   318
51 Genocide in Kosovo?/ *Milan Andrejevich*   326

Dissension among Dissidents
52 Yugoslavia's Divided Opposition/ *Slobodan*
   Stankovič   335
53 Soviet Dissidents on *Glasnost*/ *Nancy A. Beatty*   342
54 Czechoslovak Opposition Ponders Reform/ *Vladimir*
   V. Kusin   344
55 The Fad of Oriental Religions/ *Saulius Girnius*   349

In Search of a New Europe
56 The Europeans of the East/ *Kevin Devlin*   353
57 A Comecon-Common Market Rapprochement/ *Jan Zoubek*   356
58 East Berlin Cultivates European Identity/ *Barbara*
   Donovan   361
59 Three Faces of Central Europe/ *Patricia Howard*   364

Whither the USSR?
60 Popular Dissatisfaction with Gorbachev/ *Elizabeth*
   Teague   369
61 Liberalization and Soviet Jewry/ *Julia Wishnevsky*   372
62 The Growth of "Informal Groups"/ *Vera Tolz*   374
63 The June Plenum: Too Far or Not Far Enough?
   Philip Hanson, Elizabeth Teague   379

Notes   391

Index   435

Foreword

Radio Free Europe/Radio Liberty is well-known for broadcasting news and information to millions of listeners in Eastern Europe and the Soviet Union. In order to be an effective surrogate home service, RFE/RL has built up over the years a large research capacity, where Western-trained specialists describe and analyze developments in Eastern Europe and the Soviet Union by drawing on radio and television monitoring, Soviet and East European print media, and Western scholarly publications. They also make use of RFE/RL's archives and library, which includes many samizdat publications as well as more than 120,000 volumes in 30 languages.

In short, RFE/RL is not only an international broadcaster, it is also one of the world's major research organizations on Eastern Europe and the Soviet Union. Its regular research reports are considered invaluable by scholars, journalists, and government officials. The work done by RFE/RL's able research staff not only helps to make RFE/RL's broadcasts accurate and incisive, it also provides useful information for those who, like myself, are involved in the formulation of U.S. foreign policy.

Several years ago, RFE/RL decided to make these reports more accessible to the general reader by having a distinguished scholar select the most important ones to be included in an annual volume. Last year's volume was introduced by my distinguished colleague in the Senate, Claiborne Pell. I am most happy to have been asked to provide a foreword for this volume, which I am certain will be just as helpful to me as the previous three volumes have been. As someone who has closely followed the activities of RFE/RL in my many years on the Foreign Affairs Committee, I am glad to see that this annual series is making RFE/RL's work more widely known.

Dante B. Fascell
Chairman
Foreign Affairs Committee
House of Representatives

Editor's Acknowledgments

The preparation of the fourth volume of *Soviet/East European Survey* posed several challenges that had not been present before.

First, as the reform movement under Gorbachev gained momentum, the sheer amount of events deserving close attention has vastly increased; at the same time, the space available in the book has diminished.

Second, a visit to the Soviet Union shortly after the start of the editing provided the editor with a first-hand experience of observing the "restructuring" in action and inaction--an added perspective which necessitated a partial restructuring of the book as well.

Third, the transfer of the publication from Duke University Press to Westview Press, which has resulted in a shortening of the production schedule by half, has meant more work, less time, and additional responsibilities for the editor and his staff.

That these responsibilities were discharged as required has been very much an accomplishment of Clodagh Devlin, an exemplary editor and excellent colleague. At the crucial stage when a complex new word-processing system had to be applied, Clari Kovacs contributed her unmatched three-year experience with the project as a typist while Claude Spiese supplied his special computer expertise; both were indispensable in ensuring a product of high technical quality.

My graduate students Maureen Gay, of Boston University, and Meredith Heiser, of the Johns Hopkins School of Advanced International Studies in Washington, helped most efficiently to expedite the proof-reading at very short notice. Evan A. Raynes, the author of the index to volume one, again deserves gratitude for compiling the index to the present volume.

In Munich, RFE's deputy director of research Vladimir Kusin consistently provided the necessary administrative support, as well as expert advice, during the editing

stage.   Chris Willcox, special assistant to the President
of RFE/RL, and Stephen Miller, the publications director in
Washington, played crucial roles   in implementing the
transition to the new publisher.

   An auspicious launching of the volume at Westview
Press has been made possible by the personal interest of
its director, Frederick A.   Praeger, and the careful
attention given to the project by Susan McEachern.

Vojtech Mastny
Boston

INTRODUCTION

PROGRESS TOWARD PLURALIZATION

Vojtech Mastny

During his second year in power as supreme Soviet leader, Mikhail Gorbachev proved the fallacy of the facile and seemingly safe assumption made by the majority of Western observers who had been predicting for years that "muddling through" would be the Kremlin's way for the fore-seeable future. By mid-1987, only a minority of Western conservatives, who shared with their Soviet counterparts a predilection for the familiar pattern of East-West confrontation, still preferred to believe that Moscow's quest for change was not genuine or sufficiently important.

Legitimate differences of opinion, to be sure, could be entertained about the manner and degree in which the Soviet leadership intended to reform the system to whose revitalization it was so obviously committed. It also remained unclear to what extent the intended changes could actually be implemented given both the subjective limitations in the minds of the reformers and the objective obstacles in the environment that surrounded them. But regardless of these uncertainties, prospects of the system's eventual pluralization appeared brighter than perhaps at any time since its inception. This sudden opening of new perspectives in a country long judged incapable of providing any transcending policies and personalities was enough reason for excitement but also for care in estimating the nature and pace of the prospective pluralization.

The impetus for change emanated almost entirely from above while the great mass of the Soviet people remained largely inert. Such a pattern of reform was in keeping with earlier Russian traditions, and therefore presumably well-suited to the country's needs. By the same token, it stood in contrast with the attempts at reform previously undertaken in Eastern Europe during which the people had typically played a more active role, often forcing the hands of their rulers. Moscow's example could not be readily replicated in its dependencies, and thus added new strains to the already complicated triangular relationship between the Soviet Union, the East European

1

regimes, and the East European peoples. At the same time, the absence of a foreign power capable of intervening and quashing the striving for change gave Gorbachev the one crucial advantage that all East European reformers lacked.

During his first year in office, Gorbachev had projected the image of a cautious, reluctant and somewhat disingenuous reformer, concerned with the appearance rather than the substance of change, and with the limits rather than the possibilities of reform. He had not seemed to see, or had not wanted to see, the urgency of truly radical changes that most outside observers agreed the country needed in order to function as a modern society. Although he had displayed impressive skill in consolidating his power, he had not given signs of having a clear concept of what to with it.

The subsequent year proved that the initial impression was incorrect, or at least misleading. It could not be immediately determined whether the General Secretary was being driven to assume more radical positions because of the pressure of circumstances, as his predecessor Nikita S. Khrushchev had often been. The regime understandably took pains to distance itself from this ill-fated reformer whose career had ended in his fall from power. More to the point, Gorbachev's style showed little affinity with Khrushchev's predilection for genial improvisation. And it suggested a greater capacity to keep potential opponents constantly off balance by having everyone guess what the next step would be. But this technique did not preclude a sufficiently clear concept of what was eventually to be accomplished.

Gorbachev's design could be gleaned from his numerous speeches, which cynics at first mistakenly dismissed as a substitute for action, and from what his regime did and allowed to happen. The design was in no sense of the Western liberal variety. It envisaged not less government, but a better government, founded on competence rather than popular will; it aimed at improving the society rather than the individual. It sought to transform the country's ruling establishment from an obstacle to change to an instrument of change, rather than to rely on generating popular enthusiasm for reform, which might initially be in short supply.

The vision implied in the flood of new legislation was not that of a free society but of a well-ordered society, where laws would set clear limits on both authority and individual freedom. In such a society, predictability would foster progress and the need for coercion would presumably diminish, thus resulting in a greater measure of general happiness. Enlightened legislation without any significant institutional changes was thus to pave the Soviet Union's path to the ranks of modern civilized nations.

Gorbachev's quest for a government based on the rule of law echoed the nineteenth-century German concept of a *Rechtsstaat*, which had been filtered into the Kremlin through Marxism. However, the indispensability of a supreme ruler, rather than reliance on the State as an institution, classified Gorbachev's approach as more specifically Russian. It was reminiscent of the kind of changes that had made late nineteenth-century Czarist Russia a much better place to live than before--even if not quite good enough by contemporary European standards. Nor was that period to be forgotten as one of impressive economic growth and great cultural achievement.

While the implementation of Gorbachev's design remained uneven, it was remarkable how much, not how little, was happening. Although the economic reform might be seen as the part of the program most suited to command the necessary minimum of consensus, the regime shifted its priorities toward the much more divisive area of political reform. It was in this area that the most startling developments occurred, many of them all but inconceivable only a few months before.

In molding the bureaucracy to his purposes, Gorbachev gave substance to the word "radical" which he frequently used to describe the kind of change he sought. His public statements dwelt on the clash of interests and ideas that his push for restructuring (*perestroika*) ignited within the Soviet establishment, particularly during the plenum of the party Central Committee in January 1987. Although the details of what happened were kept from the public, successive postponements of the meeting were as suggestive of the seriousness of the disagreements as Gorbachev's subsequent allusions to the plenum as a watershed were of their resolution on his terms. The cleansing of the government and party apparatus, resulting in dismissals, trials, even executions, may have merely touched the tip of an iceberg. It still served to impress on the officialdom that the abuse of power does not always pay and on the populace that justice could sometimes be done.

Not even the KGB, the notorious Soviet security agency, was exempt from the housecleaning, as exemplified by the publicity given in March 1987 to the punishment of its officials guilty of muzzling a reporter. This did not necessarily mean that the role of the organization was diminishing. Gorbachev, once a protégé of KGB chief Iurii Andropov, had benefited from its support during his rise to power. He also needed it for the present and the future because of its particular concern with efficiency and the gathering of accurate information--two pillars of successful restructuring. The agency tended to attract to its service some of the best and brightest people indispensable for a reform Gorbachev-style. And there was a special role for the KGB as a guardian of the rule of law--a conversion of the poacher into the gamekeeper indicative of the peculiar paths of progress in the Russian milieu.

The maintenance of instruments of totalitarianism did not preclude a reduction of the regime's totalitarian aspirations, as the Yugoslav party had done after its break with Moscow. Leading Soviet commentator Fedor Burlatskii explained that democratization meant less of the government's direct involvement in different areas of public life. And indeed, the authorities proved willing to tolerate unprecedented manifestations of spontaneity, such as the demonstration of Crimean Tatar activists in downtown Moscow in the summer of 1987. Yet the inability of the demonstrators to obtain the high-level hearing they sought, much less a redress of their grievances, served as a reminder that democratization was not democracy.

The difference underlay also the experiment with contested local elections, first implemented in June 1987. The availability of alternative candidates, who had to defend their records and justify their promises to their constituents, was certainly a striking novelty in the Soviet setting, as was the failure of some of the uncontested candidates to receive enough votes to get elected. Yet for the rank and file of the population, this was one of the less consequential innovations of Gorbachev's program. In a nation unaccustomed to genuine electoral process, the cumbersome and ostensibly haphazard selection of officials by popular vote held less promise of improvement than straightforward co-optation of competent individuals by well-meaning authorities acting on the people's behalf.

If the goal of democratization was not democracy, neither was the goal of liberalization liberty. Gorbachev's *glasnost*, not quite adequately rendered into English as "openness" or "transparency," differed in both concept and practice from the freedom of expression that was part of the Western political tradition. It was a policy, not a right; it was incremental, not given. It stemmed from the belief that matters affecting the public should proceed sufficiently in the public view to convince the people that the authorities cared. There was to be less secrecy and distortion of what was happening and more open discussion about what should be done. A tool of restructuring, *glasnost* was to revitalize the political process by exposing corruption and incompetence, by identifying problems and their solutions, and by keeping performance in the limelight.

Within the Soviet context, the limitations of *glasnost* were less significant than its potential. By 1987 the changes in what was allowed to be said publicly were the most impressive part of restructuring. And Gorbachev kept exhorting his audiences to be more outspoken rather than to mind the limits. After all, the limits were being tested less by the opponents of the regime--as would have been the case in Eastern Europe--than by its supporters, especially from among the intelligentsia. Applied deliberately rather than impulsively, *glasnost* lacked the explosive potential of Khrushchev's earlier liberalization policies--or so at least it must have seemed to a leadership more safely in power than he had ever been.

Without abandoning censorship, the regime granted editors a measure of discretion in deciding what to publish that they had not experienced since the nineteen-twenties--the vaunted "golden" years of Soviet rule. Much of what seemed daring probably still appeared on command; on a widening range of topics, however, editors could exercise their own judgment if they wished. Most of them did not, thus keeping the bulk of the Soviet press still excruciatingly boring. But growing numbers of them did, thus making some of it more interesting than anything that was being published in Eastern Europe, with the usual exceptions of Poland and Yugoslavia.

True to tradition, creative writers and artists were in the forefront of exploring the frontiers of *glasnost* in a country accustomed to addressing its big problems through the medium of art and expecting satisfying rather than conclusive answers. The removal of taboos on previously forbidden authors--Nikolai Gumilev, Boris Pasternak, Evgenii Zamiatin, Vladimir Nabokov--was therefore an intensely political event. Novelists and playwrights, rather than academic historians, were also the ones to pioneer the rediscovery of the myth-ridden Soviet history, even of such eminent nonpersons as Nikolai Bukharin and Lev

Trotskii. The result was not necessarily a complete or accurate picture; it was a liberating experience all the same.

In its willingness to air controversial issues, the Soviet leadership sometimes proved more tolerant than the Soviet people. It not only stopped jamming the broadcasts of the Voice of America and the BBC but also allowed unrehearsed television interviews with both ordinary Western citizens and outspoken Western statesmen, including British Prime Minister Margaret Thatcher and US Secretary of State George Shultz. The experiment proved controversial: some of the domestic audiences resented the use of the nation's media to convey Western views, particularly if the Soviet participants in the discussions failed to parry them effectively.

In acknowledging the dark sides of the system under which they lived, national pride and self-respect were much more at stake for the Russians than for most East Europeans; the system, after all, was their own rather than a foreign import. Many an ordinary Soviet citizen therefore tended to regard public admission that such social problems as prostitution, drug addiction, or violent crime existed and were getting worse as gratuitous disservice to the nation rather than the necessary beginning of its rehabilitation. The regime nevertheless proceeded to acknowledge severe deterioration even in such fundamental areas of socialism's alleged superiority over capitalism as free health care or collectivized agriculture--if only to emphasize that the fundamentals must not be abandoned.

While the alleviation of the Soviet Union's social problems depended very much on the progress of the radical economic reform Gorbachev had been enunciating, the economy seemed to be performing less than satisfactorily during his second year, although it was difficult to ascertain just how much. In particular, reliable statistics were still missing, thus suggesting that the previously advertised "acceleration" did not have enough results to show. Nor was the word itself being used so often any more. Some of the crucial reforms, such as decentralization of the state enterprise, could not possibly produce quick results. But others, which could have produced such results, notably the encouragement of private enterprise that had proved so eminently successful in China, simply did not go far enough in the Soviet Union. And there was a lingering suspicion that, in anticipation of the modest results, the targets may not have been set that high in the first place.

In some areas, more visible in Eastern Europe than in the Soviet Union, environmental destruction set an "ecological barrier" to further economic expansion. But the more fundamental obstacles to growth were other than economic--enough reason for Gorbachev to turn his attention to political reform. There was, however, an economic price for political reform, just as there was a political price for economic reform. In particular, the campaign against corruption disturbed the system of personal connection which had kept the economy before an adequate substitute could be provided. Yet political stability could be endangered by such imperative economic measures as the abolition of food subsidies and guaranteed wages. The faster pace of political rather than of economic change made the resulting tensions more dangerous still.

While the future of domestic reform thus remained in doubt, Moscow's "new thinking" in foreign affairs produced some of the most encouraging changes since Stalin's time. The Soviets seemed to have grasped that their massive investment in military power during the previous decade did not give them the security they desired and proved in fact counterproductive in provoking the Western rearmament that had reduced their earlier strategic gains. Dwelling on the importance of international rather than merely national security, Moscow accepted the notion of the interdependence of nations and postulated a growing role of the political rather than military aspects of security. These were risky propositions, considering the West's overwhelming supriority in nonmilitary attributes of power. Yet Gorbachev evidently decided to take the risks by becoming the first Soviet leader to propose radical reductions of the strategic arsenals along lines compatible with the prevalent Western thinking.

So radical and unexpected was Gorbachev's proposal to phase out both superpowers' long-range strategic missiles, submitted in October 1986 during the preliminary summit meeting at Reykjavik, that it caught US President Ronald Reagan unprepared. As if unable to differentiate between the proposal and the abolition of all nuclear weapons, which would have forced the West to abandon its long-established strategy of deterrence, the President inexplicably signaled his approval for the more sweeping option, thus prompting Gorbachev to play for the highest stakes. But by insisting that the United States discard the program of Strategic Defense Initiative, which Washington had made the centerpiece of its security policy, the Soviet leader overplayed his hand, causing the summit to eventually collapse without any agreement other than to continue negotiations.

By coming so close to, but not achieving, a landmark deal which would have greatly diminished the standing of the Soviet military, Gorbachev made himself vulnerable in a manner similar to that which had precipitated the downfall of Khrushchev two decades before. It was symptomatic of his tactical   skill,   as   well   as   of the relative insignificance of the Soviet military as an independent political force, that his position nevertheless suffered no perceptible damage.   Not only did Moscow continue to negotiate deep reductions of nuclear armaments but it also indicated a willingness to expand the talks to take into account its vastly superior conventional forces--for the West the acid test of Soviet intentions.   And when in May 1987 the young West German amateur pilot Matthias Rust humiliated the Soviet professionals by flying his tiny plane through their elaborate air defenses and landing it on Moscow's Red Square, Gorbachev used the embarrassment to assert his authority even more by replacing the Minister of Defense and shaking up other top brass as well.

By that time, the arms control negotiations had slowed down, raising new questions about Soviet willingess to make concessions.   But the delays were the result less of the Kremlin's reassessment of the desirability of an agreement than of the dissension within and among the NATO governments that provided it with tempting opportunities to exploit the differences to Soviet advantage. The belief nevertheless   prevailed   that   substantive   accords, particularly the total elimination of intermediate nuclear missiles, were well within reach.

With   the   notable   exception   of   arms   control, Gorbachev's foreign policy was so far still lacking the drama inherent in his domestic policies. In his July 1986 Vladivostok speech, the General Secretary re-emphasized his country's role as an Asian power. His conciliatory tone suggested tantalizing possibilities--growing likelihood of Soviet disengagement from Afghanistan, progress toward accommodation with China, settlement of the territorial dispute with Japan--but produced no tangible results.   Nor did Moscow's diplomatic penetration into Southeast Asia beyond Indochina and into the Pacific beyond Japan show signs of a major investment in power and prestige.

While the Soviet Union came nowhere near abdicating its superpower pretensions, clinging especially to the overseas client states it had inherited from the Brezhnev era, neither could it be fairly described as the world's

chief troublemaker. The distinction of arrogantly flouting
the accepted norms of international behavior passed onto
other countries, such as Iran. Using economic incentives,
Moscow tried to maintain and even expand its relations with
this truly revolutionary nation. However, it was
handicapped by being the main supplier of arms to Iran's
mortal enemy, Iraq, and by its own dirty war against Iran's
coreligionists in Afghanistan. Having also discovered that
it was not immune to the dangers of international
terrorism, largely manipulated from Teheran, Moscow was
being drawn to the side of the forces of order, seeking
termination of the Gulf war without a clear victory by
either side. Yet despite the coincidence of Soviet and
American interests in that regard, the well-founded
mistrust of Moscow's intentions in the region so far
prevented concerted action by the two superpowers.

In its quest for greater international respectability,
Moscow behaved as if it finally understood the connection
between its domestic practices and its acceptance as a
desirable partner abroad. At the Vienna follow-up meeting
of the Helsinki Conference on Security and Cooperation in
Europe (CSCE), Soviet representatives proved more amenable
than before to discuss specific human rights abuses in
their country. They even made the startling proposal to
hold a special CSCE conference on human rights in Moscow.
In all these innovations, it was sometimes difficult to
ascertain where public relations ended and serious business
began. When pressed about safeguards that would ensure
free access to the conference even to dissidents and
foreign critics, Soviet spokesmen were evasive, pleading
for patience lest excessive pressure jeopardize progress.

In view of the release from confinement of growing
numbers of Soviet dissidents, most notably Andrei Sakharov,
such pleas may not have been totally disingeneous. They
suggested that Moscow indeed wished to be rid of the
incessant embarrassing publicity brought about by its
repressive practices but was reluctant to do so in any
other way than its own. And the Soviet way was to dispose
of the most scandalous cases by administrative leniency
while introducing new legislation that would henceforth set
clear limits on both dissidence and its suppression. The
new law on foreign travel, which meant less capriciousness
but also reduced opportunities for applicants to exact
concessions, was a case in point.

Ferment among Soviet nationalities highlighted the
desirability, though not necessarily the feasibility, of
reforming cautiously. The outbreak of street violence in

the capital of Kazakhstan, Alma Ata, prompted by the replacement of its corrupt party boss by an ethnic Russian, attested to the explosive potential of Central Asia's demographic balance, increasingly unfavorable to the privileged Russian minorities. Although the opposite applied in the Baltic republics, there it was *glasnost* that encouraged the Estonians, Latvians and Lithuanians to reaffirm their Western-oriented national identities, protesting vigorously the Russianization of the public life and restrictions on native culture and religion.

Ostensibly linguistic and literary endeavors, expressed in proposals to institutionalize the primacy of the native languages in schools and public administration, had the deepest implications in Belorussia and the Ukraine, the Soviet Union's large non-Russian Slavic republics. With signs of support in the highest places, the demands for institutions "national in content and socialist in form," rather than vice versa, echoed Lenin's strictures against "Great Russian chauvinism." Any return to his policies, however, was bound to clash with the resurgent Russian nationalism whose occasionally quasi-fascist manifestations attested to the less attractive features of the nascent pluralization. In May 1987, several hundred adherents of "Pamiat," a group dedicated to promoting respect for the Russian past and also to blaming Jews and Freemasons for the country's ills, took to Moscow's streets and even gained a hearing from the city's party boss.

The Soviet Union aside, nowhere was the ambivalence of Gorbachevism more on display than in Czechoslovakia--the country that two decades earlier had pioneered a congenial attempt at a reform from above yet had since been ruled by a Moscow-imposed regime bent on its extirpation. Accustomed to toeing the Soviet line, the Prague leaders were now experiencing acute difficulties in adjusting to the new winds blowing from the East. They even went so far as to occasionally confiscate or censor Soviet press. And at the very time that Moscow was beginning to release its own dissidents, Prague defied international outcry by staging a show trial of nonconformist jazz musicians.

Although very Brezhnevian in other ways, Czecho-slovakia was not as extensively ridden with corruption and economically mismanaged as the Soviet Union. Its political stability and relative economic health made it imprudent for Gorbachev to interfere with its affairs too much. This gave the Prague leaders an exceptional opportunity to chart their own course--an opportunity, however, they were too timid to grasp. Having composed the relatively minor differences that divided them, they instead proceeded to apply the Soviet reform model in a minimalist fashion--by introducing a long-term structural reform of the economy but hardly any *glasnost*.

This clarification of the course paved the way to Gorbachev's visit in April 1987, though not without a last-minute delay. But the delay was the result of his momentary preoccupation with domestic priorities rather than of any disapproval of the ultracautious manner of the Prague reformers. Thus the spontaneous affection that much of the Czechoslovak populace showed the visiting Soviet leader was largely misplaced. It was still embarrassing enough for the country's rulers, putting the adequacy of their kind of reform in doubt.

If the habitually subservient Prague conservatives uttered but timidly the notion that socialism did not require the imitation of the Soviet model, their more assertive East Berlin counterparts said so more vocally. Not only were they presiding over the one country where the economic tenets of Gorbachev's domestic program had largely been accomplished; also some of the main objectives of the GDR's foreign policies that Gorbachev's predecessors had obstructed were now vindicated by being adopted as Moscow's own. This was particularly true about a reduction of both superpowers' nuclear arsenals in Europe as a necessary precondition of détente.

While Gorbachev paid tribute to his clients' prowess, he did not go so far as to suggest that their model was applicable to his homeland--and not only because it was German. There was a difference in kind between Soviet *glasnost*--a new, deliberate and positive policy--and the GDR's openness to Western ideas, which its regime had long been compelled reluctantly to tolerate as a deplorable consequence of its geographical location. As a result, *glasnost* did more to promote the spirit of critical inquiry in the USSR than in the GDR. And as far as the relevance of East Germany's economic success was concerned, that was greatly diminished by the extent of its dependence on the country's special relationship with West Germany.

Moreover, the success appeared no longer as impressive as it had been, yet the rapid expansion of the relationship was bound to raise expectations. There was a new restiveness among the young, articulated by the GDR's increasingly outspoken Churches more vigorously than anywhere in Eastern Europe except Poland. And even if the East Germans' mood seldom approximated the *Weltschmerz* of their West German counterparts, it was considerably more worrisome for a regime styling itself as a guardian of people's minds.

The most peculiar case of malaise in Eastern Europe afflicted Hungary. It surprised observers accustomed to regarding the country as the most liveable in the region because of its unique balance of relative freedom and relative prosperity--an achievement of the supposedly astute leadership of party secretary János Kádár and the reputed brilliance of Hungarian economists. That the aging, capricious, and increasingly ineffectual Kádár had dissipated much of the popular legitimacy he had earned and that the celebrated New Economic Mechanism had engendered expectations that could not be fulfilled, did not suffice to account for the depth of the spreading gloom. Indeed, comparisons were being drawn with the crisis that had preceded Hungary's collapse in 1956, except that this time there was no revolution in the making.

Unlike in 1956, the malaise permeating the nation was less political than social, or sociopathological. The economic downturn, attributable to excesses of both laissez-faire and regimentation characteristic of the hybrid Hungarian system, was conducive to dislocations painfully affecting the everyday lives of large numbers of citizens. The growing visibility of extremes of wealth and poverty in a supposedly socialist country was as demoralizing as was the rapidly rising crime rate in what was still, after all, a police state. Peculiarly Hungarian were also the feelings of outrage and helplessness at the oppression of the millions of compatriots by the contemptible Ceauşescu regime in Romania--a plight certain to traumatize a nation that had always regarded itself an embattled island in a sea of ethnically alien neighbors. The effect tended to be multipled among a people perhaps more susceptible to despair than others, as the Hungarians' exceptionally high suicide rates would seem to indicate.

Meanwhile, Hungary's economic experiments proceeded, more boldly than in the Soviet Union yet evidently with its blessing. They included unorthodox practices that Moscow still shunned, such as the issuance of govern- ment bonds to finance budgetary deficit or the bankruptcy of inefficient factories, which made unemployment inevitable. However, since the root causes of the nation's despondency were not solely, or even mainly, economic, not much could be accomplished by economic remedies alone. Indeed, the apparent lack of any effective remedies made the Hungarian crisis different--more elusive and intractable--from all the previous crises in the region.

In Poland, the perspectives were sharper though hardly brighter. Deadlock in the relations between the rulers and the ruled continued, though not for any lack of maneuvering for positions by the regime, the opposition, and the Church. In this regard, the government of Gen. Wojciech Jaruzelski did better than any time in its six years in power, but still not well enough. The release of all political prisoners after several partial amnesties was a daring calculation which succeeded in confusing the opposition. The return of its activists enabled the underground Solidarity to regroup but not to appreciably enhance its effectiveness amid an increasingly tired population. The opposition had to prepare for a long struggle.

The creation of a Consultative Council of appointed notables was to create a semblance of wider participation in the government's decisions. The regime's willingness to entertain a greater range of unbinding opinions of its choice defined the extent of pluralization it was ready to tolerate. This sort of "democratization" would have gone a long way to ameliorate what Gorbachev himself described as the "inadequate" Soviet political culture; it could hardly meet the needs of the more advanced Polish polity. Nor could the promotion of the rule of law, so innovative in the Soviet milieu, impress the Poles; it did afford their opposition new opportunities to exploit the legal system for political struggle.

Besides Moscow's dependence on Jaruzelski for keeping Eastern Europe's most profoundly anti-Soviet nation subdued and besides Warsaw's dependence on Soviet economic subsidies, the two regimes' affinity in matters of "democratization" helped to forge their special relationship. The official Polish media exuded particular praise for Gorbachev's reformism, while cooperation extended into previously sensitive areas. Warsaw was allowed to open a consulate in Lvov, the center of the vast territory Poland had lost to the Soviet Union in World War II. And the two governments vowed to fill the many "blank spots" in history that underlay the persistence of Polish-Soviet hostility.

The Jaruzelski regime's limited but real concessions sufficed to break its diplomatic isolation though not to open the flow of badly needed Western credits. The lifting of the American sanctions, on which Warsaw had been trying to blame the nation's economic plight, brought no

significant material relief. The effects were mainly
political, particularly in helping to prepare the ground
for the Pope's third visit to his native country--an event
to which both the government and the Church, not to speak
of the people, looked forward with great anticipation even
if not for the same reasons.

The government intended to use the visit as a
conclusive proof of "normalization" that would convince the
opposition of the hopelessness of its case. The Church's
intentions were not immediately clear but became more so
once the Pope, to the dismay of his official hosts, began
to publicly lecture the communist authorities about respect
for the people's rights as an indispensable foundation of a
truly peaceful society. Such pronouncements served to
establish the Church's claim to rule on the propriety of
the regime's actions--a position that could enable it to
exact from the government concessions without aspiring to
power, much as Solidarity had done in its early days.

Eastern Europe's evolving pluralization accentuated
the distinctions not only between it and the Soviet Union
but also between its northern and its southern parts.
Whether in their Byzantine preoccupation with appearances
or in their art of dissimulation learned during the Ottoman
experience, the Balkan politics were growing more Balkan
and less communist. Albania, still the most effectively
concealed from the public eye, further accelerated its
opening up to the outside world by means of commercial and
cultural contacts, without giving up its pretense as the
world's sole outpost of true revolutionary purity.
While professing abhorrence of the very notion of reform,
it quietly began to apply material incentives, rather than
merely the appeal to patriotism or crude coercion, to build
up its backward economy.

In another triumph of appearance over substance,
Bulgaria and Greece in August 1986 concluded an ostensibly
sensational treaty of friendship and nonaggression. Unlike
with the Romanian-Soviet relations, here the purpose of the
dissimulation by the two aspirants to greater regional role
was to conceal the divergence rather than the convergence
of their interests. On paper, the pact cast doubt on their
obligations to their respective alliances--only to state
expressly that this was not the case. In fact, no sooner
was it signed than the strange bedfellows proceeded
to discount its significance.

If much of the Balkan diplomacy was not what it
purported to be, the worsening ethnic strife in the area
was only too real. At least the Romanian-Hungarian

hostility over Transylvania and the Bulgarian-Yugoslav dispute over Macedonia were susceptbile to management by the respective governments; the Serbian-Albanian conflict in Kosovo, however, was getting out of hand. Fueled by the dynamics of democracy and economics, rather than by either Belgrade or Tirana, the clashes between the rising Albanian and declining Serbian communities turned vicious. Although the Yugoslav authorities at last perceived that the Kosovo problem threatened the nation's very integrity, they were yet to develop a concept, let alone a policy, toward its resolution.

Nor did Yugoslavia's vocal opposition, with its social base among the intelligentsia and its regional base in the most advanced republic of Slovenia, provide a coherent program of action beyond often penetrating analyses of the multi-ethnic state's impending crisis. In some ways, Yugoslavia's predicament resembled that of the Soviet Union; there, too, an oversized, incompetent, and largely corrupt bureaucracy obstructed reform while ethnic discord threatened to inhibit its orderly progress. Unlike in the Soviet Union, however, Yugoslavia lacked a central authority powerful enough to institute a reform from above Gorbachev-style. For better or for worse, it ultimately had to rely on the recuperative power of its already pluralized society.

The advent in Moscow of a regime more enlightened than its predecessors disoriented Soviet and East European dissidents, particularly the advocates of true democracy rather than mere democratization. Their disposition to dismiss *glasnost* as window dressing threatened to increase their isolation--whether because of being proven wrong or because of obstructing genuine improvement. Dissension among Soviet dissidents peaked when their hero Andrei Sakharov, freshly returned from exile after Gorbachev's personal intervention, distressed some of his admirers by his readiness to give the leadership the benefit of the doubt.

Nor were East European dissidents necessarily better equipped to judge. The Poles' ingrained mistrust of anything Muscovite was compounded by their resented rulers' newly found intimacy with the Kremlin. The Czechoslovak opposition, with its memories of the country's reform movement of 1968, wondered what the similarities between that false start and Gorbachev's current program presaged for the future. The signatories of Charter 77, proud to celebrate the tenth anniversary of their organization, pondered the need to adjust their strategy to the new

perspectives. This inevitably revived discord between
disillusioned former communists and the dissidents free
from such a burden of the past.

Ruminations about the future by men deprived of power
would have been of little more than academic interest had
the re-emergence of the issue of Europe's unity not given
them a special pungency. Far from eradicating the East
Europeans' identification with Europe as a whole, the forty
years of Soviet domination made it even stronger than in
Western Europe. There was also a new nostalgia for the
narrower concept of "Mitteleuropa," with or without
Germany, which cut across the East-West divide by invoking
a common past under the defunct central European empires of
the nineteenth century. In their own ways, the policies of
the communist states and even the Soviet Union now conveyed
the notion that Europe was one. To make his disarmament
proposals more attractive to Europeans, Gorbachev spoke
about "our common European home," while the GDR sought
added legitimation of its separate existence by proclaiming
its Europeanness. Efforts at a rapprochement between the
Common Market and Comecon, its Eastern counterpart, had so
far foundered on the asymmetry of the two organizations.
But at issue was now less the viability of Europe's
partition than the manner and degree of control that Moscow
should try to retain over the diverse countries of its
Eastern part.

The progressing pluralization of the Soviet orbit
belied the fact that Gorbachev's reform program posed many
more questions than it answered. Quite apart from the
formidable Soviet bureaucracy's resistance to change, his
leadership proved so far unable to generate solid popular
support--this at a time when such a support was finally
beginning to matter. Not surprisingly, the notoriously
apolitical Soviet worker remained less than enthusiastic
about a regime urging him to work more and drink less. And
the perennially abused Soviet peasant was not ready to be
won quickly by half-hearted incentives to individual
enterprise--if, indeed, anything short of decollec-
tivization could save Soviet agriculture. Thus the
intelligentsia and the new office holders that owed their
careers to Gorbachev formed the exceedingly narrow base of
his reform program.

If the probability of the program's failure exceeded
that of its success, after two years in power Gorbachev
nevertheless created the impression that the course he was
taking was irreversible. If there is any truth in the adage
that the status of the Jews is the best indication of the

direction in which a society is moving, the gradual removal of restrictions on Jewish culture, the prominence of Jews among Gorbachev's active supporters, even the greater number of Jews allowed to emigrate, were all harbingers of progress toward pluralization. So was the proliferation of citizens' associations outside the official establishment, but tolerated or even encouraged by it. These were able to pursue at least some specific and ostensibly nonpolitical interests--from the protection of the environment to the promotion of the cultural heritage--which were in broad agreement with the purpose of restructuring but no longer formulated exclusively by its managers.

The contentious plenum of the Soviet party Central Committee in June 1987, which approved a compromise version of the law on state enterprise as the centerpiece of economic reform, accentuated the open-endedness of the transformation that was taking place. As divergent views about its desirable pace persisted, the emphasis was more on the process of change than on its final goal. This was prudent enough, for the extrapolation of the existing trends into a more distant future indeed presaged eventual transition to something different from the familiar Soviet system of power, whether after further acceleration of the reform program or, more likely, after its failure--and this the leadership could hardly be expected to contemplate. Yet often in the past had statesmen been overtaken by unintended consequences of their actions. Winston Churchill vowed that he had not become His Majesty's Prime Minister to preside over the dissolution of the British Empire; he had presided over it all the same, though Britain survived. Warned by Gorbachev that there was no alternative to the course he was taking, the Soviet Union could do worse than to prepare for a similar prospect.

GORBACHEV TURNS TO POLITICAL REFORM

1
GORBACHEV'S CHANGING PRIORITIES

Elizabeth Teague

On being elected as head of the CPSU on March 11, 1985, Mikhail Gorbachev made it clear that his most urgent priority was to halt and reverse declining rates of economic growth. Unless the economy was made to work efficiently, he warned, the USSR's status as a military superpower could be at risk. The new leader blamed the country's problems on his predecessors' failure to modernize the antiquated system of central planning, or to allow the increasingly well-educated population any say in the running of society.

Gorbachev inherited a bloated bureaucracy and a demoralized work force. "We have forgotten how to work," he told an informal meeting in the summer of 1986. "Not just that, but [we have] forgotten how to work in democratic conditions."[1] The domestic policies of his first two years were aimed at shaking the population out of the inertia of the Brezhnev years and getting the country back to work.

Yet Another Discipline Campaign. As a first step, Gorbachev resorted to the time-honored method of mass mobilization. Immediately after his election, he launched a campaign for tighter discipline and order. A new twist was added by tough measures against alcoholism and, showing he meant business, he began a sweeping round of personnel changes. Officials of the Brezhnev generation were unceremoniously retired, their places going to younger, predominantly technocratic appointees.

Construction of a personal power base of loyal appointees is an essential first step for any Soviet leader. In this respect, Gorbachev's first two years were very successful. Personnel turnover was particularly high in the Politburo, the Council of Ministers and the Central Committee's Secretariat, the last of which Gorbachev seemed to be turning into his personal staff. Although not all the new appointees could be considered Gorbachev's protégés, the general secretary's political position appeared reasonably secure. For all his complaints about resistance to his policy of *perestroika* (restructuring), no organized opposition appeared, and he had no obvious rival as party leader.

Personnel turnover did not slacken during Gorbachev's second year. At the level of primary party organizations, for example, where only 23 percent of officials had been replaced by the end of Gorbachev's first year,[2] turnover had reached 33 percent by January 1987.[3] Building a power base was not an easy process, however. Gorbachev needed less than four months to oust his rival Grigorii Romanov from the leadership, but it required a dogged campaign of ten months to ease another opponent, Viktor Grishin, out of his post as party boss in Moscow, and it was nearly two years before Gorbachev was able to replace Dinmukhamed Kunaev as party leader in Kazakhstan. Brezhnev-era appointees remained a significant force in the Central Committee.

The new appointees were not just "Brezhnev clones in smart suits." Unlike their predecessors, they were unburdened by direct experience of the Stalin terror of the nineteen-thirties, and too young to have seen active service in World War II. Thus they seemed to have outgrown at least some of the fear and mistrust of the general population that characterized the Brezhnev leadership. Their career patterns were, however, very similar to those of their predecessors. This, plus the fact that there was almost no difference in institutional allegiance between the members of the Central Committees of the CPSU elected under Brezhnev in 1981 and those under Gorbachev in 1986, indicated that, though the faces had changed, neither the Soviet system nor the distribution of power therein had done so.[4]

Thinking about Economic Reform. Gorbachev understood that it would require more than personnel changes and calls for discipline to achieve sustained economic growth. Early on in his leadership, he pledged to streamline the system of economic management. Central planning, he promised, would be rationalized; the myriad ranks of middle-level bureaucracy would be pruned, and enterprises given greater independence. More effective incentives were to be introduced for workers and managers, while the enterprise work force was promised a greater say in decision-making.

Measures adopted during Gorbachev's first two years included encouragement of the cooperative sector and of small family businesses. In the teeth of strong opposition from ideological die-hards, a new law regulating "individual labor" was finally published in November 1986--preceded in the spring of 1986, however, by tough new restrictions cracking down on "unearned incomes." A new law defining the status of enterprises under state ownership was published in draft form.[5] It included some provisions that might, in the opinion of Western specialists, pave the way toward Hungarian-style market reform by increasing the independence of the enterprise vis-à-vis the branch ministry. "Customers' orders," for example, were to be part of the basis on which the enterprise would draw up its production plan; enterprises unable to make a profit would be threatened with closure; materials were to be obtained partly through "wholesale trade." The work force was to be consulted on the appointment of an enterprise director, and was also to have the power to recommend the dismissal of a manager whose performance proved unsatisfactory. At the same time, the law contained elements not compatible with a market reform. Thus, enterprises still required the approval of a higher authority--presumably a branch ministry--before making final decisions in such key areas as the setting of prices and production targets.

A common characteristic of all these new regulations was their ambiguity. They bore the hallmarks of a policy shaped by compromise between reform-oriented and conservative forces. Their thrust remained basically conservative, as they aimed to rationalize the centrally administered system, not to discard it. However, though they left existing political structures intact, they ran into formidable resistance.

The Strength of Resistance to Change. Gorbachev was aware, when he came to power in 1985, that even moderate decentralization of the economy would meet opposition. His early speeches indicated that he expected resistance to come from the middle levels of officialdom but that he believed this resistance would be relatively easy to neutralize. His plan was to appeal to the population over the heads of the bureaucrats, who were to be discredited in the public eye by charges of corruption and nepotism within their ranks. "Restructuring," Gorbachev stated on many occasions, "must be carried out from below and from above."[6]

Gorbachev may have underestimated the potential strength of the opposition. Evidence of policy disagreements within the top leadership began to accumulate in the winter of 1985-86 during the lead-up to the Twenty-seventh Congress of the CPSU. In the course of 1986, Gorbachev became increasingly outspoken about resistance to change, which he admitted existed not only among the middle strata of the bureaucracy but at every level of society, as virtually no group in Soviet society stood only to gain from the changes. On the contrary, almost everyone stood to lose, at least in the short run.[7]

Gorbachev favored a renegotiation of the "social contract" of the Brezhnev era--scornfully described by the workers as "they pretend to pay us, and we pretend to work." As an incentive, he envisaged a wage reform based on wider salary differentials. Those who worked hard would be paid well, but there would be sharp salary cuts for those who did not. There was much talk, too, of reducing the huge state subsidies for food and housing and of increasing differentiation in the pricing of consumer goods. Some of Gorbachev's advisers warned that shop-floor workers who worked poorly or who lacked skills could find themselves facing relocation or even temporary unemployment.[8] If implemented, the changes under discussion would enhance the role of personal incomes and increase the responsibility of the individual to care for himself, while reducing the role of state subventions to that of providing basic protection for members of society unable to take care of themselves.

Such measures were bound to be extremely unpopular with large segments of the population and were approached by the leadership only with the greatest caution. When strikes broke out in the summer of 1986 in the Ukraine and Belorussia in protest against meat price increases in certain areas of these republics, the price hikes were swiftly rescinded.[9]

Many Soviet citizens were skeptical about *perestroika*. For a year at least, Gorbachev seemed to get nowhere at all; people simply failed to respond or responded negatively. From mid-1986 on, his speeches expressed a sense of growing frustration, perhaps even of desperation. He seemed to become convinced that popular apathy was so strong that, until it was overcome, other changes would be impossible. Only when "a restructuring of people's thinking" had been achieved, Gorbachev told a meeting in September 1986, "shall we be able to tackle our tasks."[10] To activate "the human factor," he shifted his emphasis from economic to political reform.

The Switch to Political Reform. Lack of popular enthusiasm for his policies was not the only reason for Gorbachev's change of emphasis. The April 1986 disaster at the Chernobyl nuclear power plant also played a role. Attributed to human error and irresponsibility, Chernobyl destroyed the myth of the superiority of socialist society. It demonstrated the deep moral crisis brought about by the leaders' long neglect of the legitimate needs of the population.[11] Thereafter, Gorbachev's campaign for greater openness in the media gained momentum.

Early on in his leadership, Gorbachev indicated that he did not have time to deal with the treatment of culture or history--specifically, of the Stalin question--until the economy was sorted out.[12] It turned out, in fact, to be the other way around. By 1987, Gorbachev appeared convinced that the economy would not be restored to health without some relaxation of social and political controls.

In a speech in Krasnodar in September 1986, Gorbachev spoke for the first time of the "democratization" of Soviet society as his main priority.[13] The means chosen was *glasnost*, or "openness." On the principle that before a disease can be cured, it must be correctly diagnosed, the press was encouraged to focus public attention on the negative aspects of daily life in order to find solutions. Western observers noted that no criticism of the political system itself was tolerated. At the same time, a greater role was allowed to public opinion in certain areas--such as environmental protection--that did not impinge directly on the political sphere. A marked liberalization occurred in cultural life, and there were signs of a tentative reexamination of Stalin's role in Soviet history[14]. Some of those imprisoned under Brezhnev's leadership for their political or religious beliefs were freed, though their release fell short of a full amnesty. At a plenary meeting of the Central Committee of the CPSU in January 1987, Gorbachev made potentially significant proposals regarding the introduction of multiple-candidacy balloting for local government positions and, perhaps even more important, for party posts. Resistance to his proposals from within the party caused the plenum to be postponed three times between October 1986 and January 1987.

How Strong Is Gorbachev? Gorbachev had embarked on a risky endeavor. He had invested personal credibility in economic modernization, but understood that this could not be achieved without a relaxation of political and social controls. He had to maintain the momentum of change in order to prevent society from slipping back into the inertia of the Brezhnev years. Since no political leader would willingly place his own post in jeopardy, however, he was not prepared to countenance any reduction of the monopoly on power held by the CPSU. Instead he had to be prepared to restrain any social group that began to demand freedom from central party control. This applied to the creative intelligentsia and to certain of the national minorities, whose representatives began to use *glasnost* as a means to express grievances regarding language and culture.[15] The balancing act of within-system reform demanded all Gorbachev's political skills. To foster relaxation in certain areas while tightening controls in others, he required the support of a broad leadership coalition. Evidence of policy disputes within the leadership suggested that he did not command this kind of support. Gorbachev was a strong leader in a weak position.

2
CONFLICT OF INTERESTS AND IDEAS:
THE JANUARY PLENUM

Elizabeth Teague

The Emerging Ideological Platform. During a visit to the south Russian region of Krasnodar in September 1986, Gorbachev pointed the finger at those who opposed restructuring "because they understand what its consequences will be" and were concerned with retaining their privileges by preserving old and obsolete ways. He asserted that such people were to be found at every level of society "among workers, and peasants, and management workers, and workers in the apparatus, . . . [and] among our intelligentsia."[1]

Gorbachev quoted approvingly from an article in the weekly *Literaturnaia gazeta* by the well-known Soviet playwright Aleksandr Gelman.[2] That article referred to "the newly discontented," those for whom "restructuring" meant the loss of their privileges. These "newly discontented," Gelman said, "oppose every move toward greater independence and freedom" for the rest of the population.

In the same vein, an article in the newspaper *Sovetskaia kultura* reported that restructuring was "running into resistance from those who either `cannot or will not` discard outworn methods of thought and action."[3] The author of the article, Valentin Tolstykh, a senior staff member at the Institute of Philosophy of the USSR Academy of Sciences, charged that those who opposed the restructuring did so because it threatened their individual or group interests. Tolstykh wrote that the time had come to construct "a typology" of the supporters and opponents of restructuring and to lay bare "the material interests feeding the resistance of certain specific groups and individuals" to the policies adopted at the 27th Congress of the CPSU. Like Gorbachev, Tolstykh stressed that resistance was not only to be found in the upper ranks of Soviet society; rank-and-file workers, he said, were also unwilling to give up a system under which they received an adequate salary merely by pretending to work, in exchange for a system that would offer them good wages only in return for hard work.

As early as 1983, the sociologist Tatiana Zaslavskaia warned in what became known as the "Novosibirsk document" of potential resistance to economic reform. This opposition, she wrote, would have its roots in those social interests that would suffer if a reform were carried out. Zaslavskaia argued that, with its insistence on the harmony of interests of all classes and groups and on the monolithic nature of Socialist society, the orthodox Marxism of the Brezhnev era precluded all possibility of dealing effectively with such opposition.[4]

The influence of Zaslavskaia's ideas could be seen in an article published in *Pravda* on September 12, 1986. Written by Professor Vsevolod Davidovich, a little-known academic from the University of Rostov, the article was entitled "Soviet Society: Unity in Diversity."[5] This "unity" refers to the harmony of interests that supposedly existed between all social groups and classes within Soviet society. During the later years of the Brezhnev leadership, this concept came under attack from reform-oriented scholars such as Zaslavskaia and Anatolii Butenko, who argued that greater account had to be taken of real clashes of interest between different social strata.[6] These writers stressed that powerful group and individual interests persisted even under socialism; to pretend that they did not was fraught with extremely dangerous consequences. First, neglect of the legitimate material interests of the work force was leading to apathy and alienation, moral decay, and worsening labor discipline among the general population. Second, failure to curb powerful bureaucracies from pursuing their own selfish interests encouraged widespread corruption. During Brezhnev's declining years, certain areas of the country--the municipality of Moscow, the southern port of Rostov-on-Don, and the Central Asian republic of Uzbekistan, for example--escaped almost entirely from the control of the central party and state authorities.

Support for reform-oriented arguments had been given by Gorbachev in a speech to a meeting of propagandists in December 1984. Calling for "a clearer understanding" of the different interests of "individual social, socio-demographic, and professional groups," he stated that, "as long as such differences remain, it is necessary to take them into account."[7]

Davidovich's article focused on the "diversity" of Soviet society. Despite, he claimed, the existence of certain interests common to the whole of Soviet society (such as peace and the maintenance of a strong defense), there were significant differences between the aims and interests of various social groups and strata that, if ignored, could lead to "collisions" and social clashes. Like the authors cited above, Davidovich complained about "departmentalism," "localism," and "egoistic concerns" which, he said, were obstructing the party's strategy of "acceleration."

Davidovich seemed chiefly concerned with the possibility of even greater conflicts of interest if and when, as Gorbachev promised, greater decision-making powers were devolved from the central ministries in Moscow to individual enterprises and work collectives. To guard against the danger of "centrifugal tendencies," Davidovich called for "democratism" at the enterprise and work collective level to be combined with "effective and forceful centralization."

Thus, while Davidovich's appreciation of the existence of competing group and individual interests came as a welcome change from the traditional view of Socialist society as a monolithic unity, the blueprint he proposed was not the introduction of any kind of pluralism, but rather a stricter and more streamlined implementation of the principle of democratic centralism. The Communist party, Davidovich stated, was the unifying force of Soviet society; it was the duty of the party's local organizations to protect the general interest against the selfish interests of society's component parts.

Quest for Truth and Creativity. A two-day conference of social scientists from institutes of higher education opened in the Kremlin on October 1, 1986, and was addressed by Gorbachev and the CPSU's chief ideologist, Egor Ligachev. Both called for innovation in the social sciences, but their underlying message was of the urgent need for moral renewal. The leadership declared its intention "to restructure" economic and social life, and made no secret of the stubborn resistance this policy was encountering at all levels of society.

Opening the conference, Gorbachev remarked that "an acute, uncompromising struggle of ideas" was under way. He said that this struggle pitted old ways of thinking against the need for profound, revolutionary changes within society. The struggle was not always out in the open, and was one in which old ways "will not give up without a fight." Indeed, he warned, old ways were well capable of finding new forms of adaptation, subsuming new ideas within "outdated dogmas and stereotypes," and "emptying them of their novelty and revolutionary content."[8]

Gorbachev went on to say that "today's processes must not be altered to fit the old formulas." New ideas would have to be developed and this, he asserted, "can only be done in an atmosphere of creativity." The "search for truth" would have to be conducted through free discussion and the clash of different opinions; "dialogue," he said, would have to replace "monologue."

Gorbachev instructed the academics to train young people "to think independently and creatively." Deploring the "dogmatic" and "scholastic" way in which the social sciences were taught in the universities, he called for the preparation of new programs of study, new lectures, and new textbooks. Modern society, he said, did not need narrow specialists capable only of learning by rote, but well-rounded scientists and engineers capable of thinking independently and responsibly and of responding to the fast-changing demands of the modern age.

The state of the social sciences also came under attack from Ligachev.[9] In the recent past, Ligachev said, neglect of "the link between ideology and life and the unity of words and action" had led to "negative phenomena" in the economy, "flaws" in personnel policy, and an overall deterioration in "the moral atmosphere" in the country. The needs of the population as regards education, science, health care, and culture had all, he declared, been seriously neglected.

Philosophy, Ligachev charged, had departed even further from the real world than the other social sciences. He complained also about the failure of sociologists and economists to provide answers to the problems of the modern age, assailing them for "timidity of thought" and "lack of civic courage."

Like Gorbachev, Ligachev expressed alarm about the training of young specialists in higher education institutes. He accused teachers of being primarily interested in pushing students through, paying little attention to the quality of education provided. Indicating that poor teaching standards were leading to a decline in the prestige of the teaching profession, Ligachev complained of "a weakening of the influx of capable young people" into the profession.

Ligachev's words implied an elitist approach of the "better fewer, but better" variety to higher education for young people. His stress on the deterioration of moral standards in society echoed the words of Gorbachev, who had stated in opening the conference: "We know from experience that, if the spiritual and moral development of the individual and of society is neglected, consumerist attitudes and material greed inevitably grow." The same stark warning about the decline of moral standards was sounded in a program broadcast on October 1 by Radio Moscow. The commentator, Mikhail Antonov, warned of the decline in recent years of what he called "the quality of the individual."[10] "When a person loses his conscience," he said, "he ceases to be a human being, and becomes a living corpse." Antonov asked: "How was it possible to lose the spiritual and moral values that took centuries to build up?" Antonov charged that, because of "a prolonged lagging in the social sciences, people have for some time been deprived of clear moral guidelines."

The call for greater boldness and creativity in the social sciences dated back to the leadership of Iurii Andropov who, shortly after his election as general secretary of the CPSU, made what was a truly extraordinary admission for a Soviet leader: "We have not yet made a proper study of the society in which we live and work and have still not fully revealed the laws governing its development."[11] Andropov's call was taken up by Gorbachev even before his own appointment as party leader.[12]

Gorbachev's speech at the conference coincided with the publication of a very unusual resolution in which the Central Committee of the CPSU complained that the restructuring of economic and social life was proceeding too slowly and running into bureaucratic resistance and inertia. "The struggle of the new against the old," the resolution stated, was "facing difficult social, psychological, and organizational obstacles and meeting resistance from those who, in their own egotistical interests, seek to preserve obsolete rules and privileges."[13]

Resistance to Restructuring. The novelist Sergei Zalygin, chief editor of the literary journal *Novyi mir*, described Soviet society as split into "progressives and conservatives."[14] The party first secretary of Turkmenistan alleged that certain officials were practicing "direct political sabotage" of *perestroika*.[15] And a Moscow University economist wrote in *Pravda* that the most significant brake on the pace of "restructuring" was the lack of broad-based public support for change.[16]

An analysis of the different forms of resistance to changes was published in the weekly *Moscow News* by party philosopher Anatolii Butenko,[17] who restated many of the ideas for which he had been publicly censured two years earlier. Writing in the journal *Voprosy filosofii* in 1982 and again in 1984, Butenko had used the example of the crisis of 1980-81 in Poland to call for structural reforms in the USSR. The failure of Poland's Soviet-style system to adapt to changing circumstances, Butenko had argued, had led to the alienation of the workers from the political system. Unless Soviet leaders instituted economic and social reforms, the USSR would run the same risk. Butenko rejected the orthodox tenet that internally generated crises could no longer occur in the Soviet Union. Instead, he had concluded, the "nonantagonistic" contradictions inherent in socialist society might, if neglected by the leadership, turn into "antagonistic" ones; into acute social conflicts.[18]

In his article in *Moscow News*, Butenko wrote that Soviet society was experiencing "a heightened struggle of the new against the old, of the forces of progress and renewal against those of conservatism and bureaucracy." This conflict would intensify still further, he warned, as there was no one whose interests were not directly affected by *perestroika*.[19]

Butenko divided Soviet society into four separate groups. The first consisted of those who wholeheartedly embraced "restructuring" and were doing all they could to ensure its success. Butenko offered no estimate of the size of this group, but did not pretend that it represented a majority of the population. The second group he perceived as being made up of those who understood the necessity of working in a new way but did not know how to go about it in practice. Such people, Butenko said, were redeemable, since they were willing to be taught new ways.

Butenko's third group was made up of skeptics and cynics who believed neither in the good intentions of the party leadership nor in its power to make significant improvements. They had accordingly adopted a "wait-and-see" position. (This group was described by the editor of *Moscow News*, Egor Iakovlev, in an interview: "There are many people," he said, "who believe in nothing--neither in slogans nor in appeals. They are tired."[20])

Finally, Butenko described a fourth group--those actively opposed to the process of "restructuring" and doing everything they could to frustrate it. For such people, Butenko wrote, "reconstruction goes against the grain":

> Having learned to grab more from the state by means of "result-padding," as well as by "sitting around looking busy," by "taking a break for a smoke," by holding meetings instead of working, or simply by pilfering and profiteering, they are perfectly well aware of what the consequences of restructuring will be. If it is consistently implemented, they will have to work--and work hard--to earn their incomes honestly. They are not accustomed to this; nor do they want to get accustomed to it.

Butenko stressed that "the struggle between the old and the new" arose from the different and conflicting interests of the various social groups in society. Noting that it had often been said that the economy would have to be restructured so that the mass of the people would find it in their interest to work honestly and well, he continued that it was not usually pointed out that the reason why so many people worked badly and dishonestly was that it was in their interest to do so. It was not, however, in the general interest of society. He warned against the conventional view that this conflict of personal and public interests could be explained away as "a remnant of the tsarist past," blamed on the evil influence of Western imperialism, or viewed in purely personal terms as "a sum total of individual clashes or quarrelsome personalities." It must, he said, be understood as "a social struggle with solid social foundations." Butenko was careful to stress that this social struggle could not be reduced to class antagonism, but he argued that it was none the less real for all that. "Marxism-Leninism has never asserted," he wrote, "that social-class antagonism is the only source of clashes of social interests."

The January Plenum of the CPSU. Speaking at a plenary meeting of the CPSU Central Committee on January 27, 1987, Gorbachev went a good deal further in his dissection of the ills of Soviet society than he had previously done. For the first time he used the word "crisis" to describe the Soviet Union's social and economic predicament.[21]

Gorbachev indicated that his decision to speak more openly was prompted by the failure of attempts to stimulate economic growth in the two years that had elapsed since his election as party leader. "We see," he said, "that change for the better is taking place slowly, that the business of reorganization is more difficult, and that the problems that have built up in society are more deeply rooted than we first thought."

"There is still," Gorbachev went on, "some misapprehension in society and in the party of the complexity of the situation in which the country finds itself." He made it clear that party members were among those expressing doubts about the wisdom of the new course and added: "We are often asked if we are not making too sharp a turn."

Gorbachev painted a bleak picture of moral and economic decline. The economy, he said, was stagnant and impervious to innovation: "Most plan targets have not been met since the early nineteen-seventies." Even more seriously, the system had become "deaf to social issues." The need for housing, food, health care, and education had all been neglected. This "social corrosion" had had a profound impact on general morale. People had become, Gorbachev said, cynical, callous and skeptical; they had lost their "enthusiasm for work" and their "Soviet patriotism." The frequency of labor discipline infringements and industrial injuries, he revealed, had been rising since the nineteen-sixties. Alcohol and drug abuse had spread; the crime rate had risen.

Gorbachev stressed that it was essential to make a thorough analysis of the causes of this crisis, and showed himself willing to dig a good deal deeper than at the previous year's party congress. Then, he had seemed content to lay the blame on the "subjective" errors of the Brezhnev leadership. At the January plenum too, Gorbachev stated that the past leadership was guilty of "failing to see the need for change in time and in full," but he also indicated that the evil was rooted in "serious shortcomings in the performance of the institutions of socialist democracy." In a clear reference to the rule of Stalin (though not mentioning him by name), Gorbachev said:

The causes of the situation go back far into the past and are rooted in that specific historical situation where, by virtue of well-known circumstances, vigorous debates and creative ideas disappeared from theory and the social sciences, while authoritarian evaluations and opinions were turned into unquestionable truths.

The cornerstone of the remedies Gorbachev proposed was an attempt to "democratize" the way in which officials of the CPSU were appointed. He proposed that party secretaries, including first secretaries, should be elected by secret ballot at all levels from raion to republic. He further suggested that "members of a party committee would have the right to put on the voting ticket any number of candidates."

Gorbachev described the failures of the system in depressing detail: its lack of concern for ordinary citizens, the waste it engendered, and the corruption it encouraged. He spoke of "our mistakes," meaning the mistakes of the party and its leadership at all levels. At the grassroots level, he said, primary party organizations had tolerated nationalism, drunkenness, and nepotism. Senior party officials, he went on, had been accomplices or even organizers of criminal activities. They had regarded their high posts as sinecures and themselves as "above criticism." The Central Committee had become a mere rubber-stamp; its meetings brief and formal; many crucial problems were never even discussed and many members of the Central Committee had no opportunity to take part in debates or even to put forward proposals. In a burst of *glasnost*, Gorbachev said the capacity for work even of the Politburo and the Secretariat had been weakened. The CPSU was, in short, part of the problem, not part of the solution.

He listed five "lessons of the past" that the party must note in correcting its personnel policies.

1. There must be a constant influx of fresh blood into the upper echelons of the party, the Politburo and Secretariat.

2. Party bodies at enterprise or ministerial level must not be allowed to identify with the interests of the organization whose work they were supposed to be supervising.

3. There must be a stop to the nepotism within the party which had led to the promotion of inefficient

or dishonest people whose only qualification was that they were related to others in power.

4. There must be greater control over party officials, who should be made accountable for their actions.

5. Most important, Gorbachev declared that the "main cause" of the problems outlined above was neglect of "democratic principles" in the party. It was to correct this situation that he proposed the introduction of multi-candidate, secret balloting for party posts.

To sum up, Gorbachev's speech to the plenum contained several striking features: his grim description of the ills of Soviet society; his acknowledgment that these ills had brought the USSR to a stage of crisis; his admission that the legacy of the Stalin terror was still making its evil influence felt. His proposals, however, did not, nor were they intended to, challenge the fundamental characteristic of the Soviet system: the monopoly of power enjoyed by the Communist party.

3
CURBS ON ARBITRARY BEHAVIOR

Julia Wishnevsky and *Roman Solchanyk**

Corrupt Judiciary. In 1986, the Soviet newspapers began to acknowledge with unprecedented frankness that there had been miscarriages of justice in Soviet courts. Among the matters discussed at the session of the Politburo on October 2, 1986, was the need for "a consistent restructuring of the work of the prosecutor's office, the police, courts, and other law enforcement agencies." In its report on the session, Radio Moscow declared that reforms, the need for which was constantly being reiterated by the Gorbachev leadership, required "strict observance of the laws" to "ensure social justice and the inviolability of the constitutional rights of citizens." The Politburo was

---

* Author of the section on the Berkhin affair

also said to have underlined "the inadmissibility of any attempts by whatever party to interfere in the investigation and trial of specific cases."[1]

On September 24, *Literaturnaia gazeta* published an interview with Aleksandr Iakovlev, a section head at the Institute of State and Law of the USSR Academy of Sciences. In the interview, Iakovlev proposed several reforms to protect the citizens against criminal miscarriages of justice.[2]

Iakovlev's proposed reforms were in part reminiscent of those introduced in the eighteen-sixties by Tsar Alexander II, and in part approximated models existing in the West. He suggested, for example, that the number of people's assessors should be increased to five or seven. Previously there had been only two, and "frequently their participation in the court proceedings is purely nominal." He also suggested that the Soviet court be turned into "a court of people's assessors": "The primary task of the judge will be to provide a precise legal formulation of the verdict of the people's assessors." Iakovlev's use of the foreign word *verdikt* in this context connoted the idea of trial by jury.[3]

In the Soviet Union, the measure of restraint applied to the suspect for the duration of the investigation was at the discretion of the investigatory organs themselves. Iakovlev proposed that only a court should decide whether a suspect be remanded in custody or set free on bail. He pointed out that investigators and prosecutors were more inclined to choose custody, as "the suspect is more pliant, and the investigation goes more quickly." Iakovlev further suggested that a lawyer be involved in his client's case from the onset of the investigation.[4] Such reforms appeared designed to protect citizens against those crimes against justice committed by judicial officials in pursuance of their own career interests.

It seems that the authorities became aware of the vicious nature of the system when they began trying to stamp out the corruption that had assumed quite intolerable proportions during the latter part of the Brezhnev era. An article on this subject by Aleksei Buturlin, prosecutor of the Uzbek SSR, described the case of Uzbekistan, where theft, bribe-taking, and lawlessness had assumed "a most acute form." This involved a large proportion of the local party hierarchy, including republican party First Secretary Sharaf Rashidov. At that time, many prosecutors engaged in illegal practices and accepted bribes. At the same time, Buturlin pointed out, the efforts of other prosecutors in

Uzbekistan to carry out their duties conscientiously as regards both the investigation of crimes and the observance of legality in the courts "were regarded as circumvention of party control, with all the consequences that this entailed," although, according to Article 168 of the Constitution of the USSR, the organs of the Prosecutor's Office were subordinate only to the Prosecutor General.[5]

Similarly, according to Article 155 of the Constitution, "judges . . . are independent and subject only to the law." Yet many judges considered a telephone call from somewhere "at the top" to be more important than the law.[6] In his interview, Iakovlev related how a certain "raion leader" had arranged the dismissal of the woman chairman of a raion people's court who refused to agree to his demand that she acquit a manager who had permitted a blatant violation of safety regulations, resulting in a death.

In the course of the campaign against corruption, the press began to reveal other aspects of "telephone justice." By exploiting the dependence of judges and prosecutors on the local party leadership, highly placed bribe-takers managed not only to evade accountability for their own crimes but also to imprison people who, on account of their official position or at the behest of their conscience, attempted to expose them.[7]

The influential journalist Fedor Burlatskii explained why provincial authorities exploited the decree on combatting nonlabor incomes in order to prosecute an old gardener who sold a rare sort of flower that he had grown, while taking no action against a butcher who earned 150 rubles a day selling meat--a product in short supply--under the counter at an inflated price. According to Burlatskii "the old man is easy to catch--he's a toiler, whereas it's difficult to catch the butcher--he's a thief."[8]

Unpublished Directives. *Izvestiia* broke yet another taboo when it revealed material describing unpublished departmental directives known in legal jargon as "sub-legal acts." This phenomenon was described by two doctors of law from the All-Union Research Institute of Soviet Legislation, Ivan Kazmin and Albert Pigolkin, in an interview with *Izvestiia* correspondent Iurii Feofanov.[9]

According to Pigolkin and Kazmin, there were more than 200,000 sub-legal acts, of which 10,000 were generally binding--i.e., ones that affected not only the employees of a given department but other organizations and private individuals as well. These acts could be issued both by heads of departments holding the rank of minister and by heads of administrations or sections within these departments. As the interview revealed, in cases where a directive contradicted the law, it was the directive and not the law that was applied in practice.

Feofanov pointed out that many of these directives "are only departmental in form, but in practice limit, not always for good reasons, the rights of citizens." As an example he cited a hotel regulation forbidding guests to receive visitors of the opposite sex in their rooms after ten or eleven o'clock at night.

Further examples of sub-legal acts involved a directive from the Ministry of Internal Affairs concerning the internal regulations of corrective labor institutions[10] and the Ministry of Health's directive concerning the immediate hospitalization of mentally ill persons who represented a danger to society.[11] There was no law at the time governing the departure of Soviet citizens from the USSR for temporary or permanent residence abroad. The procedure for them to leave the country, like the procedure for Soviet citizens residing permanently abroad to enter the Soviet Union, was regulated exclusively by means of secret directives from the Department of Visas and Registration.[12] This was also responsible for the "Basic Rules of Behavior for Soviet Citizens Temporarily Abroad on Private Business."[13]

For Soviet managers, the abundance of unpublished rules carried a hidden danger of another sort. As Feofanov said, "because of these contradictory norms, particularly regarding financial matters, you're never far from landing in prison."

All three participants in the discussion agreed that any "real possibility" of a Soviet citizen obtaining the revocation of an illegal departmental prohibition was not great: "After all, in a dispute with a department, a citizen is, as a rule, powerless. In a legal sense he has no support." None of the participants mentioned the publication in September 1986, of a plan of the Presidium of the Supreme Soviet and the Council of Ministers of the USSR, to pass a law in the first quarter of 1987, "on the procedure for appealing against unjust actions by senior officials."[14]

The Berkhin Affair. The Ukrainian party daily *Radianska Ukraina*, reported in its January 8, 1987, issue that the Central Committee in Kiev had examined the materials relating to the illegal arrest in July 1986 by local authorities in Voroshilovgrad of Viktor B. Berkhin, a correspondent for the Soviet journal *Sovetskii shakhter*.

The Berkhin affair was given wide coverage in the Western press after Viktor Chebrikov, the KGB chief, disclosed on the front page of *Pravda* the same day--January 8--that Berkhin's arrest and interrogation had been ordered by the head of the Voroshilovgrad KGB. Western reports emphasized that this was perhaps the first time since the early nineteen-fifties that the security organs were being criticized in the press.[15]

The resolution adopted by the Ukrainian Central Com-mittee upon the conclusion of its investigation stated that "the violation of legality was made possible by serious shortcomings in the training of cadres in the organs of the Public Prosecutor's Office and of internal affairs of Voroshilovgrad Oblast and by a weakening of control and of meticulousness on the part of the Voroshilovgrad Oblast Party Committee, the Public Prosecutor's Office of the Ukrainian SSR, and the Ministry of Internal Affairs of the Ukrainian SSR." Rather than taking active measures to pro-tect the rights and interests of citizens, the newspaper said, "certain workers" in the Voroshilovgrad law enforce-ment agencies themselves "took the path of illegal activities."[16]

Severe reprimands were meted out to V. P. Shatalov, the Voroshilovgrad Oblast public prosecutor, and to H. M. Vetrov, the head of the Voroshilovgrad Administration of Internal Affairs, for irresponsible attitudes toward their official duties and for violations of the law. The entire staff of the Buro of the Voroshilovgrad Oblast Party Committee and "specifically its first secretary, Borys T. Honcharenko," were rebuked for laxity with regard to the cadres in the oblast's law enforcement organs. The Buro was also instructed to examine the reasons for the illegal actions of the individuals involved, resolve the question of their party responsibility, take measures that would preclude such activities in the future, and reinforce the law enforcement cadres with politically mature and professionally trained workers. On February 15, Ukrainian party leader Vladimir Shcherbitskii reported that the Central Committee in Kiev had adopted a decree releasing Honcharenko from his post.

The Berkhin affair acquired a new dimension when Chebrikov, the head of the KGB, revealed in *Pravda* that the reporter had been arrested on the orders of none other than the head of the local KGB.[17] Moscow, it seems, was determined to use the Berkhin affair as a political lesson. Thus, in mid-January, *Moscow News* wrote:

Pravda considers such steadfast conservatism typical of the first secretary of the Voroshilovgrad Regional Committee of the Communist Party of the Ukraine B. Goncharenko and his close associates to be the root of corruption. All those people have become adept at stifling criticism, democracy and openness. They are people who dislike the truth. In harassing the journalists, they are battling against the healthy reconstruction of our life, battling for their own cushy jobs and their welfare.[18]

Indeed, Gorbachev himself made an oblique reference to the Berkhin affair in his speech at the plenum of the Central Committee in January, suggesting that anyone who wanted to see for himself "that persecution of people for criticism is far from being a rare thing" should look at the "the materials in the national press in January."[19]

4
BURLATSKII ON DEMOCRATIZATION

Henry Hamman

On October 10, 1986, in Reykjavik, members of the group of experts accompanying Gorbachev to the talks with Reagan, held a briefing for the press on "the new realities" in the Soviet Union. Afterwards Fedor Burlatskii, political commentator for the influential weekly *Literaturnaia gazeta*, agreed to an interview in English with Radio Free Europe/Radio Liberty correspondent Henry Hamman and two other journalists, Patrick Cockburn of the London *Financial Times* and Fernando Mezzetti, Moscow correspondent for the Milan newspaper *Il Giornale*. What follows is an edited version of the transcript of that interview.

Burlatskii spoke frankly about the need for democratization in the Soviet Union.

Hamman: Could you discuss the restructuring of Soviet management? . . . There has always been a question about whether management should be chosen for political reasons or for the ability to manage. It seems to me that you suggested that the ability to manage and to make economic enterprises work is most important. Is that correct?

Burlatskii: Yes. Our official policy is that the process of democratization is a very important precondition for our economic success. This is the other side of the economic reforms, and without democratization there will be nothing in the reforms. Maybe this is the main thing that has been said by Gorbachev, especially in Krasnodar.[1] I have published some articles about this question. Maybe, if you are interested, you can read there about the question of economic reforms, of reforms in China,[2] and now some discussion between the first and second secretaries of an oblast party committee.[3] One is for the reforms, the other is against. I tried to compare their views, because, as you know, there are many difficulties with the reforms.

Hamman: It sounds like you are saying Mr. Gorbachev is going to challenge what has been described as the monolithic structure of the *nomenklatura* and to say that no longer can this work. Am I understanding you correctly?

Burlatskii: I don't remember that Gorbachev used this term, *nomenklatura*, but the economic and social reforms, the reforms in the political sphere need new men and new people.   This is a very old story--new policy needs new people. The same is in our country.   Therefore, as you see, there are many changes at the high political level, and on other levels, too.   Now may be the time for the second level, for the management in the economic and social spheres, in the different social organizations.

Mezzetti: Gorbachev in Krasnodar used for the first time the term "democratization."

Burlatskii: Yes.

Mezzetti: The term was repeated three or four days later by Ryzhkov, and by Ligachev to the social scientists. Would it be too strong to assume that the Soviet leadership recognizes that Soviet society isn't enough of a democratic society?   Ideologically, the official position was that there was the movement toward the perfection of socialist democracy. Now you say we need democratization.

Burlatskii: That is a little bit of a theoretical question, but a practical question too because, you know, we usually used before the term "the further development of democracy." But now, it is not enough. You must understand that we need a very big step and a very deep process in democracy in different fields. We need it. And maybe this is the reason why Gorbachev used the term "democratization."

The second reason is that this process must occur in different spheres: first in the party, then in the soviets. In social organizations like trade unions, in the economic sphere, in information. This is, I repeat, a precondition for our success in the economic and social spheres.

Cockburn: How would democratization be institutionalized within the party and within the soviets? How can this change from being rhetoric to being substantial organizational change?

Burlatskii: There are two possibilities, in my opinion. The first is to use the possibilities that are included now in our constitution and in the rules of the party, because there are very interesting and important chapters in these documents. We must use these practically. This is the first.

The second is new institutions. I don't want to forecast what kind of institutions, but I believe that there will be some. In the economic sphere, in the factories, in the cooperatives, something like soviets that will include representatives not only from administration but from trade unions and directly, *directly,* from the workers. This is my own opinion, but I believe a second step will be some new institutions.

Hamman: You have singled out two developments that were particularly interesting: the reversal of the plan to redirect the rivers and the ousting of the leadership of the Cinematographers' Union by the membership. Both of these changes indicate much more tolerance of nonofficial views, particularly the water project, since it had been approved in previous congresses. But there were still people writing and saying this is not a good idea. Are these signs of what you mean by democratization?

Burlatskii: Yes, of course. As you can remember, I talked first of all about the new role of public opinion, which depends on the new role of the press, the new role of social organizations, of writers, scientists, and other active people who will take part in discussions about very important government decisions. And now, it is a real factor. I used only one example. But there are other examples on different levels.

Hamman: Could you give some?

Burlatskii: First of all . . . the old films that have not had possibilities for demonstration. Then, our theaters; they now use new possibilities for staging some known dramas, and in the future they will have new possibilities to decide what to prepare. Their method of control will be criticism. The press will be the method for democratic control; not control from administration but control with the help of democratic institutions.

Mezzetti: An unofficial document has been published by

the Italian paper *l'Unità*. It is a transcript of the conversation Mikhail Sergeevich Gorbachev had with a group of writers a few months ago.[4] According to that document, Gorbachev says, "I know there is resistance in the *apparat*. The *apparat* has broken the neck of Khrushchev, but we shall not allow them to repeat it." Since you know Gorbachev personally, do you think this kind of statement can be wholly credible?

Burlatskii: I was not in on this meeting. Therefore, I cannot say yes or no.

Mezzetti: But do you think it possible? You know the man as we do not.

Burlatskii: I can explain only my own opinion, that Khrushchev had very big difficulties with the apparat. He tried to prepare some reforms. I was at the Central Committee and I remember the time. But the apparatus, and not only the apparatus but the whole population, the majority of the population of our country, were not prepared for radical reforms. For example, we know that the majority of our people believed in Stalin and his methods at that time. Khrushchev's problem was that he had good will but was not cultured enough--I mean political culture, and education, maybe--to understand the real possibilities of what to do, step by step.

Cockburn: How far would you say the relaxation of tension between the United States and the Soviet Union will have an impact on the restructuring? Do you think that better relations with the United States would speed up the pace of restructuring and that, on the contrary, worse relations would make it more difficult to change things in the Soviet Union?

Burlatskii: I believe that there is a connection between the internal and the international policy of the Soviet Union. You know, we usually use the words "new reality" when we talk about economic reforms and "new thinking" when we are talking about international policy. And these have the same basic connection: new policy. . . . I believe, and this is not my own opinion, that if we will have some success in the limitation of arms and have possibilities to use the money for our peace economy, it will help us in our reforms. It is very simple to understand. I believe that the United States and other countries need the same. We have difficulties, but this is not the main reason. Believe me, this is not the main reason. The main reason is reforms. We want . . . the new technology and to take part in the use of the new technological revolution in all fields. This is the main

Problem.   And   therefore there are very close   connections between our internal process of   reform and democratization and   our relations with the West, not only with the   United States, but with the Western countries in general.

Hamman: If I could put a political science question to you, you have talked about the role of public opinion, about allowing   more   debate   and   discussion,   about democratization, about opening economic reforms. You have talked about many things, but we haven't talked about how the leading role of the party fits in.

Burlatskii: . . . I believe that the party will concentrate its activities on main problems; not on the daily problems but on the strategic problems. . . . They will think about new conditions for all social and political organizations. This is the main problem for them.

5
EXPERIMENT WITH CONTESTED ELECTIONS

Elizabeth Teague

At the plenary meeting of the CPSU Central Committee which took place in January 1987, Mikhail Gorbachev made several proposals of considerable potential significance. Most striking was his call for the introduction of multiple candidacy and secret balloting both in local government and in party elections. Gorbachev spoke of

> the need to think of changing the procedure for the
> election of secretaries of district, area, city,
> regional and territorial party committees and the
> central committees of the communist parties of the
> Union republics. Comrades suggest that secretaries,
> including first secretaries, should be elected by
> secret ballot at the plenary sessions of the
> respective party committees. In that case, members of
> the party committee would have the right to enter any
> number of candidacies on the voting list.[1]

Gorbachev's proposals were clearly controversial. This could be seen from the fact that the resolution adopted by the Central Committee at the close of the meeting watered down his very explicit suggestions, and

called merely for "improving the mechanism for the
formation of elective party organs at all levels with the
aim of its further democratization." As far as party
elections were concerned, the resolution said nothing about
either multiple candidacies or secret balloting.

While the resolution omitted Gorbachev's enumeration
of the precise levels at which the post of party secretary
should be opened up to competitive election, it raised no
objection to the idea that lesser mortals should go through
that process. The resolution called for the work force to
be allowed to hold competitive elections in choosing
"managers of factories, production units, workshops,
departments, sections and farms, leaders of workers' teams,
and shift foremen." It also acknowledged Gorbachev's call
for procedural changes in the election of delegates to
local government bodies (the soviets), though it toned down
his proposal that pre-election meetings should discuss
"several candidacies, that elections be held in larger
electoral districts, and that several deputies be elected
from each of them," to an injunction that the voter "be
enabled to express his attitude toward a larger number of
candidacies and to participate effectively in the electoral
process at all its stages."

A senior editor at the Novosti Press Agency, Evgenii
Pozdniakov, told the Associated Press on January 29 that
Gorbachev's proposal really meant that more than one
candidate should be discussed before a nominee was chosen,
but that there would still be only one candidate on the
ballot.[2] The clear wording of Gorbachev's speech did not,
however, admit this interpretation.

Pozdniakov seemed to acknowledge that some of
Gorbachev's proposals ran into opposition. When the
election proposal was debated by the Central Committee on
January 28, he said, "the majority" approved of it.
Otherwise, he added, "it wouldn't have been mentioned in
the resolution in any form at all." His words suggested
both that a minority opposed some elements of the proposal
and that secret balloting was omitted because it was
opposed by the majority.

In Gorbachev's lexicon, democracy did not mean the
abolition of single-party rule, but it did envisage a
greater role for the general public in the selection of
candidates for official posts. The CPSU had traditionally
based its power on the exclusive right to make appointments
to key posts, the *nomenklatura*, and the maintenance of "the
cadre reserve," a list of people deemed suitable to be
appointed to such posts as they became vacant. Under this

system, all key appointments were made from above, and lower bodies merely acquiesced in the decisions of superior party organs.[3]

Gorbachev aimed to modify this tradition by introducing greater accountability of officials at the local level. The party would retain its control over the cadre reserve and the posts included in the *nomenklatura*, but party officials would also be required to consult at the local level prior to making an appointment. Gorbachev called for the opinion of the work force to be taken into account when making appointments to supervisory posts up to and including farm managers and enterprise directors. Experiments along these lines were carried in the late nineteen-sixties, when they proved popular with the work force but unpopular with managers.[4] In January 1987, the "RAF" bus factory in the Latvian capital of Riga dispensed with the cadre reserve and advertised for a new director in the pages of the national press. The management expected a few dozen applications; they were overwhelmed to receive 4,000 letters from people begging for a chance to show what they could do.[5]

Gorbachev also called for changes in the way deputies to local soviets were elected. Previously, a single candidate had been nominated in each constituency; now the authorities planned to experiment by holding multiple-candidate elections in some regions.

The authorities were driven to this measure by widespread disillusion over an electoral system that, according to émigrés, was leading to an increase in nonvoting on the part of the general public.[6] Data gathered during the course of the Soviet Interview Project, conducted among émigrés in the early nineteen-eighties, suggested that those who did not vote tended to be younger and better educated than those who did. Such people did not appear to be motivated by apathy; on the contrary, they tended to take a greater interest in public affairs than the voters did. Abstention seemed to have assumed the character of a political protest.[7]

The Komsomol led the way as regards multiple-candidate elections. From November 1986 on, a number of experiments were conducted whereby several candidates ran for election to posts in the youth organization.[8] The way in which elections were conducted openly, "not from any prearranged lists," at the congress of the Cinema Workers' Union in May 1986 and at the congress of the Theater Workers in December 1986 pointed in the same direction.[9] And at their congress in February 1987, the Soviet trade unions adopted new rules calling for the introduction of multiple candidacy in elections to official union posts.[10]

Gorbachev's most controversial proposal was that multiple candidacy and secret balloting should be introduced in party elections. Such elections had previously been carried out by a simple show of hands, even though the party rules explicitly stated that they were to be conducted by secret ballot. The rules said nothing about how many candidates could stand for each post but, in keeping with longstanding tradition, a single candidate was nominated from above and elected unanimously by the organization he was to lead.

Less than two weeks after Gorbachev's call for the introduction of multiple-candidate elections and secret balloting for party posts, a contested election was held in the Izhmorsky Raion party committee of Kemerovo Oblast in Western Siberia.[11] Press reports of the election provided detailed descriptions of both old and new voting methods and showed that the idea of a contested party election, conducted in secret, was in practice totally new. Indeed, many members of Izhmorsky Raikom expressed doubts about the experiment. Some asked whether party members were "psychologically ready" for such an election; others were worried the experience might put the candidates under intolerable nervous strain.

The two candidates for the post of party secretary in Izhmorsky Raion came from the party's cadre reserve. One was chairman of the raion soviet, the other manager of a local farm. They were almost identical in age and experience, and both were considered well qualified for the post. Commenting on the election results, the party first secretary of Kemerovo Oblast, N. S. Ermakov, raised a significant point. The similarity of the two candidates' qualifications and experience, he wrote, had perhaps made the election excessively personal. It might be better, he continued, if candidates were also judged on their plans for the future social and economic development of the region--"if you like, on their election platforms."[12] A proposal that candidates for elections to local soviets should support their cases on the basis of "electoral programs" was also made in an article in *Moscow News* by the chairman of the presidium of the Supreme Soviet of the Estonian SSR, Arnold Riuitel.[13]

Ermakov and Riuitel had put their finger on the weak point of Gorbachev's plans for electoral reform: however many candidates went forward, the electorate would be deprived of a real choice as long as all these candidates

represented a single party line.   Allowing candidates to
offer their own "election platforms," however, logically
presupposed the working out of quasi-independent political
programs   appealing   to different and even conflicting
interests within Soviet society.   As such, it raised the
specter of the development of factional tendencies in the
party, something that had been categorically prohibited
ever since the days of Lenin.

On   June   21,   local government   elections   were   held
throughout the USSR.   Deputies were elected to soviets in
district, city and rural areas.   For the first time, some
voters were given a choice of candidates; this happened in
four percent of the areas.   In other districts there had
been consultation about who the single candidate should be.
Soviet officials called the voting an experiment and said
the results would be taken into account in the elaboration
of new electoral procedures.   A month later, the newspaper
Izvestiia printed letters   from readers who expressed
disappointment about the way the elections had been held.
"We were all hoping to see a new approach," wrote one
reader from the Ukraine, "but it was just as it has been
for decades." Other readers complained about vote-rigging;
while some reported that party activists had loudmouthed
candidates chosen by work collectives and even, in some
cases, put pressure on them to stand down in favor of
candidates who had stood unopposed for years.[14]

GLASNOST GAINS MOMENTUM

6
THE TOOL OF RESTRUCTURING

Vera Tolz

After the initiation--shortly after Gorbachev came to power--of a campaign for more *glasnost* (openness) in the mass media, Western observers speculated as to how long the drive would last. Because there had traditionally been an increase in *glasnost* shortly before party congresses and a decrease thereafter, many expected the campaign to die a quiet death after the Twenty-seventh Congress of the CPSU in the spring of 1986.[1] The expected decline in frankness did not, however, materialize. On the contrary, as chief editor of *Pravda* Viktor Afanasev pointed out in an interview given to the Madrid newspaper *El País*, openness in reporting on negative phenomena in Soviet society entered a new phase after the congress.[2]

A Broader Spectrum of Problems Discussed. The Soviet media started to deal with issues such as drug abuse, the deteriorating quality of the health care system, moral decay in society, and excessive control exercised over the written word.[3] New taboos were being broken almost every day: on one day *Literaturnaia gazeta* objected to single-candidate elections to the soviets,[4] while on another day readers learned that the director of the Moscow State Institute of International Relations (MGIMO) had been expelled from the party for extending favors to the children of officials wishing to enroll in the institute.[5] Reports of new corruption scandals involving officials or about the nonfulfillment of plans no longer surprised anyone. There was also a new emphasis on the scope of existing social problems; the media readily admitted that cases of corruption or mismanagement were typical, rather than being the exception. With regard to the decline in moral standards, writer and literary critic Georgii

47

Kunitsyn stated in an interview on Radio Moscow that the process of moral decay had touched almost every person in the country.[6]

The Role of Public Opinion. Prior to the Twenty-seventh party Congress, the press had already been publishing an increasing number of readers' letters, many of which criticized various aspects of life. Only after the congress, however, did public opinion begin to play a truly new role. Attitudes and judgments expressed by the public were acknowledged to have been a major factor in the Politburo's decision to halt the projected diversion of northern and Siberian rivers into the southern regions, as well as in its decision to seek a new design for the controversial World War II victory monument to be erected in Moscow.[7] These debates were reflected in the media.[8]

The Limits of *Glasnost*. Media statements saying that no internal problems could avoid dissent were not fully warranted. On February 13, 1986, for instance--on the eve of the party congress--the privileges enjoyed by the party and government elite were fiercely criticized in a letter published in *Pravda*. At the congress, Egor Ligachev singled out *Pravda* for having made mistakes in selecting materials for publication.[9] After the congress, the sensitive topic of privileges for the elite was very rarely touched upon in the press. Indeed, when the subject arose, the right of the leadership to enjoy extra luxuries was upheld. In response to the complaint of some Komsomol members that leaders of the youth organization enjoyed such perquisites as chauffeured cars, leader Viktor Mironenko defended the custom.[10]

The top-level party officials still appeared safe from media criticism. In an unusual move on September 29, *Pravda* published Ukrainian party First Secretary Vladimir Shcherbitskii's admission that the newspaper's earlier criticism of the performance of party organizations in the Cherkassy Oblast had been justified. However, this admission was most likely prompted by the fact that the Cherkassy scandal had been brought to light by Gorbachev himself, at the June plenum of the CPSU Central Committee.[11]

Moreover, the coverage of domestic affairs in the media often remained shallow. In a samizdat article entitled "Notes on *Glasnost*", the well-known journalist Oleg Volkov noted that while attention was being called to all manner of defects, their root causes were not considered.[12] Almost simultaneously with the publication of Volkov's essay in the West, Radio Moscow carried an interview with Kunitsyn which indirectly confirmed Volkov's complaint; while vigorously condemning the moral decay in Soviet society, Kunitsyn merely noted the difficulty of finding answers.[13]

Reporting on international affairs underwent less change than the coverage of domestic affairs. In July 1986, Moscow Television nevertheless aired an unusually frank discussion of East-West relations with two prominent West European Social Democrats, David Owen and Egon Bahr.[14]

An unexpected result of the campaign for *glasnost* was criticism of the media for depicting only the Western world in a negative light. In May, *Pravda* complained that reports about the West in the television news program "Vremia" were "monotonous." According to the newspaper, "journalistic clichés migrate from broadcast to broadcast," and the program "shows mainly meetings, demonstrations, and protests" and "rarely tells about the achievements of science and technology."[15]

The Influence of Chernobyl. The accident at the Chernobyl nuclear power plant in April 1986, was a test of Gorbachev's campaign for openness. The initial Soviet delay in announcing the accident and the subsequent reluctance to release details made it appear that *glasnost* had failed that test.[16] About two weeks later, however, the media started to release what was by Soviet standards, a remarkable amount of information.[17] Moreover, the worldwide criticism of the initial secrecy appeared to prompt more informative reporting about several other disasters that followed. These included earthquakes in Moldavia, the sinking of the passenger ship *Admiral Nakhimov* in the Black Sea, and the fire on the Soviet nuclear submarine that subsequently sank near Bermuda.[18] In view of the military significance of the submarine disaster, the Soviet Union's prompt and forthright reporting of that event was seen in the West as an indication of a welcome change.[19]

Attitudes of Local Officials and Ordinary People. On the eve of the party congress, the central newspapers acknowledged that *glasnost* was running into difficulties in the provincial press.[20] Gorbachev himself pointed out that openness there might be even more important than in the central press, as the provincial press was the first source of information for the majority of the population.[21] More than half a year after the congress, however, the lack of *glasnost* in provincial newspapers seemed to indicate local officials as being the main bastion of opposition to reforms. Abundant articles were published in the press about provincial officials who gave direct orders for the withdrawal of critical material from issues of local newspapers or who punished journalists for practicing *glasnost*.[22]

Literaturnaia gazeta stated that local officials did not hesitate to punish journalists for openly reporting about shortcomings and corruption,[23] as officials were practically never brought to court for suppressing criticism. This occured even though a law had been passed in October, 1985, making suppression of criticism a crime. Even ordinary citizens, however, seemed reluctant to espouse the cause of *glasnost*, presumably because they were used to a different tradition and found it difficult to understand the value of free and open debate. During a Leningrad-Boston television link-up in the summer of 1986, the Soviet moderator of the program, Vladimir Pozner, tried to encourage the Leningrad women to criticize their country's shortcomings and thus show that candor was permitted in Soviet society. The women, however, aggressively persisted in praising every aspect of their lives.[24] Several public opinion surveys published in the press showed that many of those interviewed rejected *glasnost* on the grounds that not everyone would understand criticism of Soviet life in the right way.[25]

On the other hand, despite all the efforts of the leadership, the population still refused to believe media reports. In the wake of Chernobyl, newspapers admitted that, despite media assurances that the food in Kiev stores had been checked for radioactivity and found safe, they were not believed.[26] In a private letter that reached the West through unofficial channels, a Ukrainian stated that he did not believe a single word in the official press about radioactive levels in the Ukraine and that he was in a state of panic.[27]

Instructions to Journalists. On February 13, 1987, a meeting was held in the CPSU Central Committee with representatives of the mass media and of information and propaganda agencies.[28] In his speech at the meeting Gorbachev gave instructions to journalists on how to handle the campaign for *glasnost* and spelled out some of its limits.

Since the relative relaxation of censorship, *glasnost* had started to gain a momentum of its own, and many intellectuals had been trying to promote their ideas even without the open support of top officials.

In June 1986, Gorbachev met informally with a group of thirty Soviet writers. Talking about *glasnost*, he emphasized that, "if we start trying to deal with the past, we will dissipate our energy."[29] Despite these instructions, however, many journalists and writers raised the question of the Soviet Union's past, especially in the Stalin era. These discussions of Stalinism seemed to influence Gorbachev, and at the Central Committee plenum in January 1987, he admitted the need to analyze the past. At the meeting with representatives of the mass media, he said that he "agreed that there should be no forgotten names and blank pages in Soviet history and literature."

Calling for a dialogue between the press and readers, Gorbachev condemned "the prosecutor's tone" adopted by some journalists, pointing out that "nobody has the final word when it is a question of the truth." In his speech at the plenum, Gorbachev also touched upon the problem, saying that in the past, "authoritarian evaluations and opinions were turned into unquestionable truth."

In an apparent attempt to set limits on *glasnost*, Gorbachev called for portrayals of those whom he termed "the heroes of the restructuring of Soviet society." He claimed that the press was not active enough in this area. But he was less insistent than Egor Ligachev in an article in the journal *Teatr*, in which the latter demanded that playwrights should not let themselves be carried away by the desire to criticize, but should also praise the current societal changes, and depict the "heroes of our days."[30] In contrast with Ligachev, Gorbachev not only emphasized the need for criticism, assuring his listeners once more that *glasnost* was not a short-term policy, but even condemned "comrades who thought that criticism should be switched on and off."

<u>Why *Glasnost*</u>? Soviet officials made it clear that they regarded *glasnost* as an essential part of the restructuring, and a precondition for the success of economic reforms.[31] The restructuring could not be effected until the inertia and demoralization that were partly the result of a shortage of candid information on what was happening in the country were overcome. *Glasnost* was to build up trust in the official media and to improve morale.[32]

According to *Pravda*:

> The party views the press as a powerful instrument of progress, *glasnost*, and public control. . . . The press could help collectives to seek and find a positive solution to problems that arise. . . .

Strict control over plan fulfillment is also one of the main tasks of the press.[33]

Thus, by writing to a newspaper, ordinary citizens could help end corrupt practices or expose mismanagement at their places of work.

A further cause for the policy of *glasnost* was concern over the influence of information from abroad. Facts about Soviet life that had previously been brought to the attention of the people only by Western radio stations, could be relayed to them by the domestic mass media in a form more in keeping with the party's propaganda goals.[34]

7
RETURN OF FORBIDDEN LITERATURE

Julia Wishnevsky

A Thaw Begins. In his speech at the Eighth Congress of Writers, held in Moscow from June 24 to 28, 1986,[1] poet Andrei Voznesenskii said that even well-known Soviet writers often spent only 10 percent of their time writing books and 90 percent trying to get them published. Following the congress, a report appeared in the Western press about a decision to limit the role of the state's organ of censorship, *Glavlit*, to its real task--the guarding of state secrets--and to forbid its bureaucrats to interfere in the literary process.[2]

"By way of an experiment," Soviet theaters were allowed to choose their own repertoires.[3] The Union of Cinema Workers elected a new leadership and created a commission to investigate films banned by the censor.[4]   A campaign was launched to exhibit classics by the early twentieth-century Russian avantgarde such as Pavel Filonov, Kazimir Malevich, and Vasily Kandinsky.[5] Finally, there was a complete change of party personnel responsible for culture; putative conservatives were replaced by more enlightened party functionaries, including the new head of the Propaganda Department of the CPSU Central Committee, Aleksandr Iakovlev.[6]

The nostalgia expressed for the late editor of the journal *Novyi mir*, Aleksandr Tvardovskii, who had been removed from his post in 1970, was a clear sign of change.

On June 14, an article on him appeared in *Izvestiia* by Vladimir Lakshin, a close colleague. At the congress, the essayist Gavriil Troepolskii devoted almost his entire speech to Tvardovskii, while the Leningrad prose writer Daniil Granin, having declared from the rostrum that the Writers' Union lacked "a creative spirit," exclaimed: "We don't have enough editors like Aleksandr Trifonovich Tvardovskii!"

In March 1967, Tvardovskii had called censorship "an organ of our literature that is a relic of the past." At the same time, he had voiced his concern about the foreign publication of Soviet manuscripts that had been rejected in the USSR. He said:

> Can this be permitted? How can we fight it? By quietly confiscating manuscripts and stacking them away in a safe? I am not sure, I fear that this would simply be adding fuel to the fire. . . . This can be eliminated only by publishing at home, with appropriate cuts and editing.[7]

Evgenii Evtushenko made the same point in his famous speech about *glasnost* at the Sixth Congress of Russian Writers in December 1986. On that occasion he urged that the whole truth about the country's past and present be written about and published. He said that half the transmissions from Western radio stations were based on issues that the Soviet media "concealed and kept quiet."[8]

Soviet newspapers began publishing statements for which people, who expressed the same opinions in samizdat or in the Western media, had previously been persecuted. Evidently this was the result of a deliberate policy intended to arouse hope of reform among Soviet citizens by expressing ideas that on Western radio or in samizdat would have a very different psychological effect. At any rate, the "thaw" was considerable in both form and scale.

There was a considerable change of tone when referring to prominent Soviet cultural figures who had been forced to emigrate under Brezhnev and Andropov.[9] Some of them--the cellist Mstislav Rostropovich, the former director at the Taganka Theater Iurii Liubimov, the film director Andrei Tarkovskii and the writer Viktor Nekrasov--were unofficially approached by former colleagues traveling abroad, who hinted that, under the present regime, they could return home either permanently or for a visit.[10]

The Writers' Congress. Under Gorbachev, the authorities began primarily to demand mastery of the craft from the artist, and not "uninspired eulogies in rhyme and prose."[11] No longer was the writer obliged to be a toady; suffice that he be simply loyal and not speak out directly against the regime. At the same time a slow but steady change was occurring in attitudes toward the literature of the past.[12]

Customarily before a writers' congress, one of the union's older members would write a curtain-raiser in *Literaturnaia gazeta*. The task was entrusted to Veniamin Kaverin, who in 1967 had fervently supported Aleksandr Solzhenitsyn in the latter's protest against censorship of the Fourth Congress of Soviet Writers.[13] In the article, Kaverin stated that "dishonor has been discovered."[14] And in later evaluating the results of the congress he said that he had not heard "such frank, direct, straightforward, honest speeches" for a long time.

The congress examined problems ranging from the destruction of nature to nationality conflicts, from shortcomings in the teaching of literature in schools to falsification of the election results in the Union of Writers, from mistrust of young writers to the burden of bureaucrats who did not write books but influenced the atmosphere of the union.

The problem of censorship was raised at the congress not only by isolated "individuals" but also by such establishment figures as the first secretary of the Moscow Writers' Organization, Feliks Kuznetsov, the party poet Robert Rozhdestvenskii, and the chairman of the State Publishing Commission, Mikhail Nenashev. The latter admitted:

> For the authors of new and daring ideas, for pioneers in literature, science, and culture, our publishing houses are often bleak and uninviting. Conservatives and opportunists feel more comfortable there.

Critics complained about "the table of ranks," by which the contents of critical articles, literary prizes, and the size of editions were made dependent on the writers' official position. Between 1976 and 1980, Soviet libraries received 700 million new books, of which 500 million were never checked out.[15]

Unlike the Union of Cinema Workers,[16] which had elected as its new leader the talented film director Elem Klimov, who had suffered under censorship his whole life,[17] the Writers' Congress reached a compromise decision. It elected Vladimir Karpov as first secretary--a man with a relatively good reputation but more of a literary functionary than a writer.[18]

In his speech, Vosnesenskii listed fourteen of the most famous poets, prose writers, and dramatists who were not present in the congress hall. As a result, four of them--Bella Akhmadulina, Bulat Okudzhava, Viacheslav Kondratev, and Iurii Chernichenko--were elected to the new board of the Union.

Voznesenskii, Granin, and Academician Dmitrii Likhachev spoke at length about the necessity of publishing the works of banned writers of the past, including the works of émigré Russian writers such as Evgenii Zamiatin, Vladislav Khodasevich, and Dmitrii Merezhovskii.[19]

Poet Evgenii Evtushenko presented the presidium of the congress with an appeal signed by forty delegates calling for the creation of a museum devoted to the poet Boris Pasternak in his house in Peredelkino. Evtushenko pointed out that Pasternak's house and grave had become "a place of pilgrimage" for the youth. Voznesenskii also proposed that the union "should concern itself with masterpieces and the fates of sacred literary works"--*i.e.*, with the publication of "the full works of Akhmatova and Pasternak."

After these speeches it seemed that the ban on Pasternak's novel *Doctor Zhivago* was being reviewed. At the Twenty-seventh party Congress in March 1986 the then first secretary of the Union of Writers, Georgii Markov, had told foreign journalists that *Doctor Zhivago* would never be printed in the Soviet Union.[20] After the Eighth Writers Congress, however, the head of the RSFSR Writers' Organization, Sergei Mikhalkov, and the new editor of the journal *Ogonek*, Vitalii Korotych, hinted that "Soviet publishing houses were considering the possibility" of publishing Pasternak's novel.[21] More problematic was Voznesenskii's demand to publish "in full" the works of Akhmatova, among them the poem *Rekviem* [Requiem]--a powerful portrayal of the terror during the Stalinist purges.

Voznesenskii also called on the union "to defend the honor of writers." He described Mikhail Zoshchenko and Anna Akhmatova as "classics," calling for an official repeal of the notorious "Zhdanov" decree of August 14, 1946, "On the Journals *Zvezda* and *Leningrad*," under which Zoshchenko--who had been hounded almost to the point of lunacy--and Akhmatova were expelled from the Writers' Union.[22]

For Freedom on the Stage. The Union of Theater Workers of the RSFSR came into being during the October

1986 Congress of the All-Russian Theater Society. This was
thrown into disarray when the chief director of the Moscow
Arts Theater, Oleg Efremov, made a speech proposing that
the All-Russian Theater Society be immediately disbanded
and replaced by a creative union which would protect its
members from arbitrary treatment by theater censors.[23]
Efremov's proposal was supported by a majority of the
delegates at the congress and a resolution was adopted
recognizing the Fifteenth Congress of the All-Russian
Theater Society as the First Congress of the Union of
Theater Workers of the RSFSR. In the following five weeks,
theater workers in the Soviet Union fought a tough battle
but managed to score a major victory. In December, 1986,
instead of the creation of a Union of Republican Theater
Societies as originally desired by the authorities, a Union
of Theater Workers of the USSR was set up,[24] and this was
followed by corresponding changes in the other Union
republics.

At the end of November, *Sovetskaia kultura* published a
lengthy open letter from nine prominent figures in the
theater world entitled "What Sort of Union?"[25] The list of
signatories revealed the identities of the disturbers of
the peace in the theater: the chairman of the board of the
Union of Theater Workers of the RSFSR, actor Mikhail
Ulianov; the Leningrad stage director Georgii Tovstonogov;
Oleg Efremov; actors Iuliia Borisova, Rufina Nifontova, and
Vladimir Vasilev; stage directors Andrei Goncharov and Mark
Zakharov; and the well-known playwright Mikhail Shatrov.

The authors of the letter answered the question "What
Sort of Union?":

> The union must also defend the actual creators of art
> against, among others, certain incompetent petty
> officials in the field of art in whose hands both
> "legislative" and "executive" power has been entirely
> and completely concentrated.

The nine bemoaned the fact that every theater in
Russia was obliged to have its repertoire endorsed by
Moscow and that the cultural department of an oblast
executive committee might ban the performance in "its"
theater of a play that was running successfully in other
cities.[26] The Koltsov Drama Theater in Voronezh was, for
example, banned from staging Aleksandr Misharin's play *The
Silver Wedding*,[27] which even Politburo member Egor Ligachev
cited as "a major contribution . . . to the nationwide and
partywide cause of restructuring."[28]

Tovstonogov described the history of the production of Liudmila Razumovskaia's play *Garden Without Earth* at the Bolshoi Drama Theater in Leningrad, where he was director. A three-man commission dispatched by the Ministry of Culture introduced 164 changes--not political but artistic ones. Finally, regardless of the opinions of both playwright and stage director, even the title of the play was changed, becoming *The Sisters*.[29] Mark Zakharov, chief stage director of the Lenin Komsomol Theater in Moscow, battled for four years with various ministerial commissions for the chance to perform his production of Liudmila Petrushevskaia's play *Three Girls in Blue*,[30] which later became the sensation of 1985.[31]

Zakharov wrote in *Sovetskaia kultura*:

> The "censor" can do his job anywhere; it is all the same to him what and whom he is running. Today he may be in charge of culture, tomorrow of an agricultural exhibition.
>
> These jolly vampires demanded and continue to demand of artists a superficial and declaratory cheerfulness, while maintaining a categorical ban on any opinions that they cannot understand.[32]

The draft statute of the Union of Theater Workers of the RSFSR, published in February 1987, was a document reflecting the efforts of members of the Soviet intelligentsia to seize the initiative from below. Paragraph 4 of the new draft statute provided for the protection of theaters from the tyranny of petty officials, who in the past had had the power to decide the fate of a production, a theater collective, or even of an entire trend in dramatic art.[33] It gave the union the right to make decisions concerning the theater. To safeguard against bureaucratization, the draft statute stipulated that the chairman and members of the Secretariat of the union could be elected for no longer than two terms, and the chairmen of the boards of local branches of the union for no more than four terms in succession. In order to safeguard the union against protectionism and corruption, the draft statute barred the secretaries of the board from recommending candidates for union membership. The draft represented the first attempt to furnish a legal foundation for the changes that had taken place as a result of the liberalization of cultural policy under Gorbachev.

Gumilev, Nabokov and Zamiatin. In September 1986 the newspaper *Sovetskaia kultura* published an article by the

philologist   B.   Egorov   about   the   arbitrariness   of
censorship. Egorov wrote:

> For example, for many years it was not only
> impossible to print Gumilev's poetry, even his name
> could not be mentioned (on occasions when it was
> impossible to get round mentioning him, he was
> referred to indirectly as "one of the leaders of
> Acmeism," "a certain poet," or even--the shame!--"the
> husband of Anna Akhmatova"). And now, at last,
> articles are being written to mark the hundredth
> anniversary of his birth, and a volume of his works
> is being prepared in the series "Poets' Library."[34]

The works of Nikolai S. Gumilev, a poet who was shot
in August 1921 by the Bolsheviks, were thus being given
back to readers with an unprecedented degree of honor.
Meanwhile *Shakhmatnoe obozrenie*, a journal devoted to
chess, published for the first time in the Soviet Union an
excerpt from Vladimir Nabokov's *Drugie berega* [Speak,
Memory].[35]   Apart from two collections of poetry written
during his adolescence and published before the Nabokov
family left Russia in 1919, the Soviet press had never
published a line of Nabokov's works other than in abusive
articles urging that this "amoral" writer be stigmatized.[36]
The limited circulation of *Shakhmatnoe obozrenie*, in
which the excerpt from Nabokov's memoirs appeared, bore no
comparison with that of *Literaturnaia Rossiia*, where a
selection of Gumilev's poetry first appeared after nineteen
years of being banned.[37]   It did not compare either with
the illustrated journal *Ogonek*, intended for a mass
readership, in which another collection of Gumilev's poetry
was republished.[38]   Several months later, *Novyi mir* printed
some of Gumilev's correspondence with Akhmatova as well as
a number of his poems.[39]   *Ogonek* also took the
unprecedented step of publishing an essay about Gumilev by
Vladimir Karpov.[40]
This was surprising for a number of reasons. First,
it was extremely rare for *Ogonek* to publish such a long
piece--seven pages of small print. Second, this organ of
mass culture had never before published a piece of literary
criticism on such an elevated intellectual level. Third,
it had not been accepted practice for the biography of a
recently posthumously rehabilitated author to be presented
to the population by a first secretary of the USSR Writers'
Union. Thus the publication represented a rehabilitation of
not only Gumilev but also of *Ogonek*, which for thirty-three

years had been edited by the notorious Stalinist
obscurantist, Anatolii Sofronov.

At the end of 1986, the ban was lifted on the works of
Evgenii Zamiatin, the author of the novel *My* [We] and
father of the twentieth-century anti-utopian novel. *My*
preceded by many years the appearance of Aldous Huxley's
Brave New World and Nabokov's *Priglashenie na kazn*
[Invitation to a Beheading], and later influenced George
Orwell's *1984*,[41] and, through him, the anti-utopian novels
of Anthony Burgess.[42]

My was written in 1920 and was never published in
Russia. In 1924, it appeared in English translation in the
United States, and in 1927 it was published in Czech in
Prague. The émigré journal *Volia Rossii* then translated it
back into Russian from Czech and published it in
installments. Two-and-a-half years after its publication
in Russian, the Soviet literary establishment vented its
rage upon Zamiatin in the press in a manner unprecedented
at that time. In June 1931, Zamiatin appealed to Stalin to
allow him to go abroad. His appeal was supported by Maksim
Gorkii, and in November 1931, Zamiatin and his wife left
the Soviet Union.

The ban on Zamiatin was lifted with the publication of
a collection of his short novels and short stories in
Voronezh in the "Otchii krai" series. The last 1986 issue
of *Literaturnaia Rossiia* published three of Zamiatin's
Nechestivye rasskazy [Profane Tales] accompanied by an
article in praise of him by Oleg Mikhailov,[43] who wrote:

> Zamiatin's most important work in those immediate
> postrevolutionary years was indisputably his
> fantastic novel *My*, which was interpreted by his
> contemporaries as a malicious caricature of a
> Socialist society of the future. Although the novel
> was never published, the critics analyzed it in some
> detail, quoting at length from it and engaging in
> sharp polemics with its author.

Mikhailov's interpretation of the ideas behind
Zamiatin's novel, however, was at variance with the
generally accepted version. He wrote of Zamiatin's stay in
England, where he was working as an engineer and
shipbuilder:

> It was from there, from bourgeois England, that
> Zamiatin got the idea for his fantastic utopia *My*

(1920). Here, in England, he saw how the foundations
of an accursed "machine paradise" were being laid.

The treatment of Zamiatin's novel was reminiscent of
the metamorphosis that took place in the Soviet
interpretation of Orwell's *1984*,[44] now seen as giving
"grounds for comparing modern Britain with the gloomy
prophecy of thirty-five years ago." Thus the cultural
revival was sometimes used also for the purposes of
anti-American, antibourgeois, or otherwise anti-Western
propaganda.

Re-emergence of the "Men of the Sixties". A careful
perusal of Soviet newspapers reveals that the people behind
the changes that had been taking place in a wide range of
fields represented a numerous but nevertheless fairly
closely linked group. At the beginnng of 1987, for
example, the legal commentator Arkadii Vaksberg gathered a
score of writers and lawyers in the editorial offices of
Literaturnaia gazeta for a discussion on the need for a
radical reform of Soviet justice and an end to the
indictment of innocent people.[45] Among the speakers were
essayist Iurii Chernichenko, who had long been a proponent
of economic reform in agriculture, journalist Oleg Volkov,
who became known for his championship of Lake Baikal, and
the new editor of the journal *Novyi mir*, Sergei Zalygin.
Also present were playwrights Mikhail Shatrov and Aleksandr
Gelman, both actively involved in setting up the Union of
Theater Workers in October 1986 to protect Soviet theater
against the arbitrary actions of the official cultural
censors,[46] and theater critic Aleksandr Svobodin, who
provided a description of what happened on that
occasion.[47] In addition, Shatrov and Svobodin had been
active in calling for the elimination of the consequences
of Stalinism in Soviet historiography.[48]

Most of those primarily involved in Gorbachev's
restructuring belonged to the generation whose attitudes
were formed in the years of the Khrushchev "thaw" in the
nineteen-sixties and were often known as
"*shestidesiatniki*," or "men of the sixties." Moreover,
quite a number of people whose names were remembered for
their writings in that period, but had been obliged to take
up other work in the nineteen-seventies and early
nineteen-eighties, had returned to journalism. These
included the critic Vladimir Lakshin, who had been a
leading contributor to *Novyi mir* in Tvardovskii's time and
was now deputy chief editor of *Znamia*,[49] theater critic Len
Karpinskii and economist Otto Latsis, who had been expelled

from the party in 1976 for criticizing the Brezhnev regime from a eurocommunist position,[50] and feuilletonist Leonid Likhodeev.

At a meeting of four poets of the nineteen-sixties in the editorial offices of the journal *Ogonek*, Evgenii Evtushenko listed the basic principles that he and his colleagues shared: first, negation of Stalin and Stalinism; second, rejection of all proscriptions on art; and third, "an aversion to 'tub-thumping' patriotism and national narrow-mindedness."[51]

In the course of the same meeting, poet Andrei Voznesenskii stated that the nineteen-eighties were much freer than the nineteen-sixties: many films, books, and stage shows that were now appearing would have been unthinkable previously, let alone some of the items that were printed in the newspaper *Moscow News* in later years.[52] While in the nineteen-sixties any criticism of Stalinism had to be from the standpoint of official ideology--"true Leninism"--that was no longer obligatory.

Religion and Nationalism. There was a nostalgia among the Soviet intelligentsia for religion and the Judaic-Christian ethic. In an article entitled "On Mercy," writer Daniil Granin complained that the years of the Stalin terror had destroyed compassion for the fallen, the sick, the poor, the dying, and the persecuted. Mercy, Granin said, was preserved only among believing Christians.[53]

Whereas under Brezhnev it was only Russian nationalists who could display their interest in Christianity, now people such as Granin, who was profoundly opposed to nationalism, were doing so.[54] Evtushenko published an article in *Komsomolskaia pravda* in which he defended religion as a source of morality,[55] and in his review of the film *Repentance*, writer Boris Vasilev declared that "the bouts of vomiting of Great Russian chauvinism" were a result of many years of religious persecution.[56]

At the plenum of the board of the USSR Union of Writers, the disputes between Russian nationalists and their opponents flared up once again.[57] Despite Gorbachev's appeal at the January 1987 plenum to repulse all manifestations of nationalism, chauvinism, Zionism, and anti-Semitism, the proponents of these "-isms" (with the exception of Zionists) continued to express their views freely. True, they were begining to encounter opposition, some of their critics countering the views of the nationalists, for example, with Lenin's theory of the existence of "two cultures" (bourgeois and proletarian) in every national culture.[58] Others put forward the argument that nationalism is destructive of all cultures, not least its own.

Academician Dmitrii Likachev defined nationalism as an evil engendered "by hatred of other peoples and of the part of one's own people that does not subscribe to nationalist views"-- that is, the intelligentsia.[59] Likhachev was supported by such people as poet Bella Akhmadulina[60] and historian Iurii Afanasev,[61] who explained their rejection of nationalism not with references to Lenin, but by citing the traditions of the Russian intelligentsia, to which, they claimed, nationalism was always an alien concept.

Opponents of *Glasnost*. Several speeches delivered at the meeting of the Secretariat of the Board of the RSFSR Union of Writers on March 17, 1987,[62] attacked literary critics and scholars who were seeking to replace the entrenched hierarchy of Soviet literary officialdom. The people who came under attack most frequently were those authors who wrote with excessive enthusiasm about the leading personalities of the Silver Age of Russian culture--Pasternak, Akhmatova, Mandelshtam, Tsvetaeva, and Bulgakov, and especially about such writers as Nabokov, Gumilev, and Khodasevich, who had not been published in the Soviet Union before Gorbachev came to power.

A second target of attack was any attempt to criticize the works of those in high positions in the Union of Writers. For example, Hero of Socialist Labor and Chief Editor of the conservative journal *Oktiabr* Anatolii Ananev complained about "a conspiracy of silence" against his epic *Gody bez voiny* [Years Without War], which dealt with a rural raion party committee in the Brezhnev era. Ananev went so far as to demand that "the leadership of the Union of Writers take appropriate administrative measures" against these silent critics.[63]

At the writers' meeting, the chairman of the Board of the RSFSR Union of Writers, Sergei Mikhalkov, called for an end to the practice of "simply ignoring" holders of important Soviet awards including "People's Artists of the USSR."[64] In his opinion, *glasnost* was being exploited by "time-servers, speculators, people without talent and of dubious character." The speakers who followed Mikhalkov went even further. Nikolai Shundik resurrected the Stalinist label "our enemy," while Iurii Bondarev spoke of "the pseudodemocrats of literature," and Mikhail Alekseev of "demagogy" and "phrase-mongering." Petr Proskurin described as "hooliganism" the methods used by *Moscow*

News[65] (in reference to that newspaper's criticism of a novel by Belov) and *Ogonek*. Bondarev, compared the activities of "the totally destructive ranks of our critics" with the victories of Adolf Hitler's armies in July 1941, "when progressive forces, offering unorganized resistance, retreated under the impact of shattering attacks by civilized barbarians." In his opinion, "restructuring must not be turned into an imitation of the West."[66]

8
REDISCOVERING SOVIET HISTORY

Vera Tolz

In the course of the campaign for *glasnost*, writers and historians called for more truth about the dark periods of Soviet history. It had been stated in the press that the rewriting of Soviet history had become commonplace, resulting in a credibility crisis in the work of Soviet historians.[1] The history of the revolution in 1917 was especially topical in 1987, the seventieth anniversary of that event.

Leadership and the Past. It had been noted in the West that "anti-Stalinism is becoming a major factor in official Soviet politics."[2] However, it was not the Soviet leadership but rather Soviet cultural figures who used the campaign for *glasnost* as an opportunity to emphasize the need to reveal some truths about Soviet history, especially Stalinism. More than a year after coming to power, Gorbachev was reported in June 1986 as having said at a meeting with writers that "if we start trying to deal with the past, we will dissipate our energy."[3] At that time, however, Soviet cultural figures had already emphasized the need to analyze mistakes of the past in order to understand and improve the present. Despite Gorbachev's clear indication that he saw no purpose in talking about history, the debates on Stalinism and other historical problems continued.

At the plenum of the Central Committee of the CPSU in January 1987, Gorbachev appeared to have changed his approach. He reiterated what had already been said by such "enthusiasts of restructuring" as Evgenii Evtushenko and

Mikhail Shatrov, and others, namely, that "the causes of the situation go back far into the past."[4] At a meeting with journalists in February 1987, Gorbachev said that "there should be no forgotten names and blank pages in Soviet history" and that those people who made the revolution should "not be pushed into the shade."[5]

It was not Gorbachev, however, but the second man in the Politburo, Egor Ligachev who, in connection with the upcoming anniversary of the revolution, presented more specific guidelines for how history should be presented. He made it clear that Soviet history should not be depicted as "a chain of errors." He said that no secret should be made of the fact that the Soviet people had lived through "the bitterness of temporary setbacks, difficult and complex stages," but also emphasized that this year should be above all "a time of triumph for the socialist system."[6] He thus suggested that criticism of certain periods in Soviet history was to be accompanied by praise for the socialist system in general.

The Position of Historians. Calls for frank portayals of the three men who had led the USSR for over half a century, Stalin, Khrushchev and Brezhnev, had been evident in Soviet literature, especially since 1986. Many journals carried a great number of works that dealt relatively frankly--by Soviet standards--with the most difficult historical periods--mainly Stalin's. Novels and stories by such writers as Iurii Trifonov, Daniil Granin, Aleksandr Bek, Mikhail Dudintsev, and Anatolii Rybakov and verses on Stalin by such poets as Alexandr Tvardovskii and Anna Akhmatova appeared in *Novyi mir*, *Znamia*, *Druzhba narodov*, and other literary journals.

Several historians also published interviews and articles calling for the reevaluation of history in accordance with calls for more openness. First to spell out the need for a more objective approach was the director of the Moscow State Institute of Historical Archives, Iurii Afanasev. On the eve of the Twenty-Seventh party Congress in February 1986, he published an article entitled "Proshloe i my" [The Past and Ourselves] in the CPSU Central Committee journal *Kommunist*.[7] In the article, Afanasev said that a truthful disclosure of history was necessary for the activization of the population and that the past played a major role in the understanding of current problems. From early 1987, Afanasev moved away from stressing the importance of history for solving current problems to criticizing existing historiography.[8]

Afanasev singled out the periods between 1917 and 1929

and from 1956 until 1965 as being most important. He emphasized that the legacy of the Twentieth party Congress in 1956, at which Khrushchev delivered his famous secret speech on Stalin's crimes, should be analyzed in detail and that historians should go further in the de-Stalinization campaign than was the case under Khrushchev.

Afanasev said it was not enough to pass off what he called "the mass repressions" in the nineteen-thirties as a mistake or shortcoming. He criticized the leading Soviet expert on Stalinism, V. Kasianenko, for not having revealed enough about Stalin's terror, and complained that Western historians had produced far more research about Stalin than their Soviet counterparts.[9] Afanasev said that in past decades historians who had attempted to say something new were often removed "from the horizons."

Academician Aleksandr Samsonov, best known for his works about World War II, also addressed the subject. The propaganda weekly *Argumenty i fakty* (No. 10, 1987) carried a talk with Samsonov, in which he criticized the existence of "blank pages" in Soviet history, particularly those about Stalin's mistakes on the eve of the war, which resulted in defeats immediately after the German invasion.[10] He also complained that the fate of Soviet armies surrounded by Germans during World War II had not been adequately analyzed and that there was no Soviet book studying the plight of General Andrei Vlasov, whose army had been encircled and captured by the Germans. Vlasov became a commander of former Soviet POWs who had fought on the German side. Introducing a 100-minute television documentary dealing with the battle of Moscow in 1941, Samsonov said that "the repressions of the nineteen-thirties, besides being inhumane and immoral, also caused a great setback to our combat readiness."

The doyen of Soviet historians, ninety-two-year-old Academician Isaak Mints, also spoke out against "blank pages" in history. Although himself one of those most responsible for falsifying and rewriting history, Mints complained in an interview with TASS that the names of certain old Bolsheviks purged by Stalin were not known to the public.[11]

In May, Stanislav Tiutiukin, a Doctor of History, called in *Izvestiia* for a proper evaluation of Stalin, Khrushchev, and Brezhnev, saying that the credibility of Soviet historiography had been undermined.[12]

Afanasev suggested republishing the materials of all party congresses and conferences and restructuring the work of the Soviet archives. He also called for the publication of a new journal on Soviet history.

Revelations from the Archives. In spring 1987
Afanasev sponsored a series of lectures on Stalinism in
various official venues in Moscow, which provoked a good
deal of interest. The first lecture, delivered by the
historian Professor Iurii Borisov on March 27, repeated
what had already been said in numerous articles on the
subject, namely, that the negative sides of Stalin's
character had been described by Lenin in his famous
"Testament" but that other leaders (Trotskii, Bukharin, and
Kirov) had their own shortcomings and that therefore the
party had practically no choice but to promote Stalin.

Another lecture by Borisov took place on April 13. "A
bespectacled young scholar" took the podium after Borisov
and disclosed the results of his own research work in the
Moscow archives. He was twenty-two-year-old Dmitrii
Iurasov, a student at Afanesev's Institute. His comments
contained hitherto undisclosed information on the Stalin
purges. Iurasov said that he had been able to work for a
time in Moscow in the Central State Archives of the October
Revolution and the National Economy and the Archives of the
USSR Supreme Court and its Military Collegium. According
to a samizdat transcript, Iurasov said:

Between 1935 and 1940, the military collegium
sentenced 50,000 people in all. Between 1953 and
1957, it rehabilitated 48,000, including 31,000 who
had been shot. The most complete information is kept
in the card-index of the First Special Department of
the USSR Ministry of Internal Affairs (MVD), where
all anti-Soviet crimes commited since 1929 are on
record. Of course, I didn't have access to it. . . .

I saw the files on Meierkhold's case,[13] also from the
oversight materials. The investigator in the
Meierkhold case was Senior Lieutenant Boris
Veniaminovich Rodos, who later became a lieutenant
general in State Security and was himself shot in
1955.[14] There is a letter from the already sentenced
Meierkhold to Vyshinskii.[15] It's a striking document.
Meierkhold listed all the "impermissible methods of
conducting an investigation" that Rodos had used on
him: for instance, he broke Meierkhold's left hand
(so that he could sign with his right) . . . Rodos
gave him urine to drink. . . . Meierkhold cried,
humiliated himself, literally crawled on his knees,
but . . . he had to sign everything. There are two

dates   for   Meierkhold's   death, . . . The   real
date . . . was in 1940. . . . He was shot.

And here's an unknown fact: Marshal of the Soviet
Union Kulik was also shot. First he was demoted, in
1942 or thereabouts. They arrested him in 1946. He
was kept in Kuibyshev military prison until 1950. In
that year they shot him. The Soviet Military
Encyclopedia says only that he was stripped of the
title marshal, and that's all.

Incidentally, oversight material from the late
nineteen-thirties has been partly destroyed, as the
term of preservation has run out. It has been
decided to transfer more recent materials to the KGB,
because there's nowhere to store them. . . . Still,
there's a lot of material in the archives of the
military collegium on the trial of the
nineteen-fifties, the trials of Beria's men. . . ."

Iurasov was asked whether he was not afraid of the
consequences for him of making such revelations. He
replied: "At least it will show whether *perestroika* has
really started in the USSR or whether it is just words."
    <u>Non-historians in the Forefront</u>. Playwright Mikhail
Shatrov did more than anybody else to publicize the
executed revolutionaries in the official media. In his
play *Brestskii mir* and in interviews with the press,
Shatrov presented a charming portrait of Nikolai
Bukharin,[16] which provoked criticism in *Sovetskaia kultura*.
In it, historian Vladimir Gorbunov said that Shatrov
had selected Lenin's statements on Bukharin in such a way
that only his positive characteristics were included while
negative ones were omitted.[17]
    As late as the spring of 1987, the proposed changes in
Soviet historiography were being put forward by writers and
journalists and only occasionally by historians themselves.
One reason was that the rewriting of Soviet history was, or
had been, a fairly common chore for Soviet historians.
Moreover, the process of reevaluation had always been
unpleasant, with many historians having to confess to past
mistakes. Evidence of dissatisfaction with the calls for a
reevaluation of Soviet history was provided by a letter
published in *Moscow News* No.19.[18] The letter, signed by
four Soviet historians, attacked Afanasev for his call to
reevaluate the approach to the past.

In conclusion it should also be mentioned that while many of the articles on Soviet history marked a great departure from previous taboos, some of them also demonstrated that the lifting of the ban on mentioning certain names or events did not necessarily mean that the truth would emerge.

9
CRITICISM OF THE AFGHANISTAN WAR

Bohdan Nahaylo

The January 15, 1987, issue of the Ukrainian Komsomol daily *Molod Ukrainy* published what was probably the most outspoken criticism of the war in Afghanistan and its portrayal yet to have appeared in the Soviet media. The condemnation consisted of extracts from a letter to the newspaper by S. Berezovska, mother of two sons serving in the military, who lived in the Western Ukrainian city of Ivano-Frankovsk. She wrote:

Today is Sunday. I opened your paper and saw the long article "A Step into Eternity" by O. Klymenko. I've read it, and this is what I want to say to you: the article greatly upset me and ruined my mood.

This is not the first time I've read an article about soldiers-internationalists. I see that for you they have become like plays or films that are interesting to watch. But no mother who has sons can read such an article calmly. You always think: this is not the Great Motherland War, where our people died defending their land.

I also have two sons. Both are soldiers right now. One of them is serving on the border near Afghanistan, and my heart aches for him all the time. And on top of this you write, or remind us on television, about how people are dying over there. There's no need to rankle our spirits. All the more so, because only the children of simple workers take part in the battles; there are no children of officials there.

I understand that it's necessary to help the Afghans,
but at such a costly price . . . ?

Not only did this mother castigate the media for the
coverage of the war in Afghanistan and question the high
cost in human lives; she also pointed out that this was not
the same kind of war as had been fought in defense of the
homeland against the Fascist invaders and alleged that a
disproportionate burden of the fighting had been imposed on
the offspring of the workers.

The article that prompted Berezovska's protest
appeared in *Molod Ukrainy* on December 14, 1986, in which
its author, Oleksandr Klymenko, praised the heroism and
sacrifice of a young soldier killed in Afghanistan. Under
the rubric "Heroes of Our Generation," Klymenko paid
tribute to Valerii Arsonov, a teenager from the Donbas,
posthumously decorated for giving his life "while
fulfilling his internationalist duty."

The publication of Berezovska's protest was
accompanied by a long response from Klymenko, noteworthy as
probably marking the first time a Soviet journalist
publicly apologized for dealing with the Afghanistan theme
in a glib and insensitive manner. Although trying to
justify himself, the correspondent admitted that he and his
colleagues were only just beginning to learn how to deal
with such a sensitive theme.

The correspondent opened his comments by suggesting
that Berezovska's letter reflected a generally "negative
reaction" on her part to all articles dealing with the
theme of Soviet boys dying in Afghanistan and that for her
his article was simply the last straw. He therefore felt
compelled to reply "not only on my own behalf but also for
all those who have written, are writing, or will write on
this theme."

Defending the increase in press coverage of the war,
Klymenko argued that even without it, "you would still know
that some return as invalids and some do not return at
all." In the absence of press coverage, however, he pointed
out, the "heroes" who fell in Afghanistan would be "buried
and forgotten." Furthermore, he continued, it was due to
newspaper pressure that veterans of the war, especially
those who had been wounded or crippled, had finally
received "rights and privileges comparable" to those given
to veterans of World War II.

Klymenko attempted to convince Berezovska that there
really were "boys" like Valerii who had actually asked to
be sent to Afghanistan, though he conceded that she would

probably not believe him. He was unable, however, to come
up with any detailed rebuttal to Berezovska's allegation
that "they take only the children of workers to serve in
Afghanistan."

Berezovska's protest reflected the beginnings of a new
candor in the press in discussing popular attitudes toward
the war. *Sobesednik*, the weekly supplement to
Komsomolskaia pravda acknowledged that there was
considerable antipathy among the youth toward what was
happening there.[1] Significantly, this development
coincided with increased emphasis by the Kremlin on the
desirability of withdrawing Soviet troops from Afghanistan
as soon was feasible.

On February 1, *Moscow News*, a weekly publication
mainly for foreign audiences and one of the flagships of
glasnost, published a statement by Evgenii Ambartsumov
arguing the case for a speedy political settlement of the
Afghanistan problem. This, he wrote, would "make it
possible to bring the humanitarian principles of Soviet
foreign policy to fruition" in this region. Furthermore,

> reconciliation in Afghanistan would mean the early
> return of our troops . . . awaited with such
> impatience and such concern at home. Our boys would
> stay alive, and "death notifications" would no longer
> bring untold grief to Soviet families. Lastly, we
> would be able to release additional forces and means
> which are so needed by our economy. I do not know
> how much internationalist aid costs our people, but I
> think the price is not small.

Ambartsumov not only attempted to refute the view
that in pulling out of Afghanistan the USSR would be
"playing into the hands of our adversaries in the West" and
that the withdrawal of Soviet troops would have an adverse
effect on international prestige, but also mentioned that
"the introduction of a military contingent into
Afghanistan" had not met "with the support of the majority
of UN members."[2]

Early in January 1987, a powerful new documentary
film, "Is It Easy To Be Young?" opened in Moscow. It
presented an honest picture of the tragedy of the
Afghanistan war, complete with forthright interviews with
disabled and embittered Afghanistan veterans, or *Afgantsy*,
as they were called.[3]

On January 31 and February 7, 1987, the writer
Aleksandr Prokhanov was shown on television speaking with a

number of Afghanistan veterans about the the frustrations
and difficulties they faced in readjusting to civilian
life.   Back home it was "considerably more difficult" than
in Afghanistan, Prokhanov was told by one *Afganets* named
Foteev, as "there are no extreme conditions" and
"relations with people are much more complicated."
Afghanistan veterans were considered "dangerous," Foteev
complained.   "Some do not understand us at all, others call
us fanatics, still others understand us but cannot support
us because they do not feel up to it."

The media began to acknowledge criticism of their
one-sided and incomplete coverage of the war. According to
a Soviet commentator:

> The war in Afghanistan has been portrayed in terms of
> a handful of renegades and bandits waging an
> undeclared war against their own people, while the
> Soviet internationalist servicemen are "protecting"
> the women and children of Afghanistan from the
> bandits; there has been no mention of the fact that
> the so-called *dushmany* are not just a handful of
> bandits but [comprise] vast numbers of the Afghan
> population; nor of the fact that tens of thousands of
> Afghan families have left Afghanistan and are living
> in Iran and Pakistan. . . .   Let's look at the
> origins of the war. As everyone knows, the *dushman*
> resistance forces began receiving aid from the West
> in the form of weapons and military hardware only
> after the Soviet Union moved its troops into
> Afghanistan. Which intervention came first and which
> came second is obvious.

Moreover, the double-edged nature of *glasnost* was
highlighted by the frank criticism of the Soviet occupation
of Afghanistan uttered by US Secretary of State George
Shultz during an interview shown on Soviet television on
April 16. On that occasion he said:

> You have come into conflict with the people of
> Afghanistan.   The Afghan people want you to leave
> their country; they do not want your armed forces to
> be in their country. How many soldiers do you keep
> there--120,000?

It seems that at this point Shultz may have overstepped the limits of *glasnost*, for his following two sentences were not translated:

> It is a very devastating war, and they do not want you there. They want peace with you, but they do not want you occupying their country.

The Soviet media may also have broken with custom early in 1987, by acknowledging that Afghan guerrillas had been making raids across the border into Soviet territory. On April 2 *Pravda* confirmed that the Afghan resistance had launched a rocket attack into Tajikistan. On April 18, TASS admitted that Afghan guerrillas had carried out a second raid on to Soviet territory and killed two border guards.

The greater candor brought home the scale of the fighting and of the social problems that the war created at home. It may well have been that *glasnost* was raising more questions than it was providing answers on this tricky topic. Yet having gone so far, there seemed to be no going back.

10
TELEBRIDGES WITH THE WEST

Viktor Yasmann

Television came to be the most popular media form in the Soviet Union; for more than 86 percent of the people, television became the prime source of information about world events.[1] From its inception, television had been allocated a special role in Gorbachev's campaign for *glasnost*.[2] While press and radio were supposed to make the citizens believe that their leadership was pursuing a policy of "renewal," television was to allow them to see for themselves that this was so. After the adoption of the new party program, Central Television replaced more than 25 percent of its programs.[3] Many newspapers adopted the Western practice of regularly including pages of television criticism.

Television became more prominent than ever when the Soviet leadership realized that, in the era of the information revolution, official propaganda and ideology would be faced with increasing competition from external ideas. At a meeting of ideologists on the subject, Central Committee Secretary Aleksandr Iakovlev, considered to be the architect of *glasnost*, stated quite frankly:

> Today's world is becoming ever smaller . . . ever more interconnected. . . . To think that it is possible to create some sort of niche or cloister cut off from external influences and to sit in timid resignation is not only to indulge in illusions but also to [condemn] ourselves to defeat. We need to be active, to adopt an offensive stance; one that guarantees not only absolute priority in our own house but also a steady strengthening of our . . . influence on the outside world.[4]

Use of Western broadcasting techniques and the consideration of viewers' interests transformed Soviet television. It acquired an uncharacteristically dynamic, topical, and aggressive style that was particularly noticeable in news programs--watched by some 90 percent of the viewers[5]-- and in telebridges with the West.

Telebridge with Tokyo. In January 1987, Soviet television broadcast a discussion between Soviet and foreign studio audiences via a satellite link, connecting Moscow and Vladivostok with Tokyo.[6]

In each country there was a studio audience of about 200 people. The discussion opened with the question: "What do the citizens of the two countries know about one another?"

The Soviet audience generally had positive things to say about Japan, while the Japanese perceived the Soviet Union as being a dismal, bureaucratic country. The Soviet people, on the other hand, were believed to be sympathetic as individuals, but dull en masse, and identical when speaking in an official capacity. The Russian audience responded by accusing the Japanese media of presenting a distorted image of Soviet life.

This prompted further Japanese questions about whether the Soviet people could criticize their government through the media and whether it was possible to set up independent television companies in the Soviet Union and make critical statements through them. The most pointed question was: "Can critical remarks be directed against Gorbachev and the Central Committee, and can they express a point of view opposed to the official one?" One of the Soviet participants replied: "Gorbachev and the CPSU Central

Committee represent common interests, so if someone is defending my interests, what do I have to protest about?"

A considerable proportion of the discussion, clearly on Japanese insistence, centered on the question of four of the Kurile Islands occupied by the Soviet Union since the end of World War II. The first Japanese question on this subject was: "Do the Soviet people know of the existence of Japanese territorial claims against the Soviet Union?" Almost all members of the Soviet audience raised their hands, provoking laughter from the Japanese audience. Soviet answers to other questions concerning this problem were received with even greater skepticism. Without even pausing for thought, the Soviet participants in the telebridge answered the most complex questions, giving details about Soviet-Japanese relations that normally only a specialist would know. One man in his early thirties, for example, began to quote, without reference to notes, from the San Francisco Treaty of 1951 and the Yalta and Potsdam agreements. He claimed that Japan herself agreed to the Soviet occupation of the four islands in the Kurile chain.

Although representatives of TBS (Tokyo Broadcasting Systems) were able to select participants for the program in Moscow, the Soviets had sufficient time to "prepare" them beforehand. Furthermore, Soviet television transmitted the telebridge a week later than TBS. Consequently, Soviet propagandists already knew the Japanese reaction to the program and were thus better able to calculate its propaganda effect.[7]

Evidently, Soviet propagandists had counted on the Western audience being unprepared and on "their" people having become accustomed to "dialectical" casuistry. Thus awkward questions were permitted as long as the "correct" answers scored points for the Soviet side. In the Moscow-Vladivostok-Tokyo telebridge, the Soviet audience answered general questions by focusing on details and questions about specifics with generalizations.

Donahue, Pozner, and the KGB. The first Soviet-US telebridges organized by US television figure Phil Donahue and Soviet television commentator Vladimir Pozner, were regarded as a triumph for the Soviet Union:

> In telebridges as well as in other broadcasts with foreign audience participation, our arguments always look more solid. The propagandistic effect of such broadcasts is very high . . . [8]

Most of the questions posed by Phil Donahue were either "not offensive" to the Soviet audience or the subject of private or public discussion in the Soviet Union anyway. It would have been naive to expect Soviet participants in telebridges with the United States to "bare their souls" in front of Donahue's microphone. Thus, in a discussion about family problems broadcast on Central Television on March 14,[9] two members of the Soviet audience complained that they could not have children because of their poor living conditions and low wages. These questions had, however, already been discussed in the Soviet press and therefore, by raising them, they may have hoped the authorities would do something about their cases. The posing of difficult questions, including political ones, by the US audience, was seen by the Soviet organizers as a way of getting their audiences accustomed to such questions, of reducing social tension, or, as Soviet propagandists said, "of inducing ideological immunity to the effects of hostile propaganda."

That such immunity can be induced is beyond doubt. On the day the telebridge was shown, *Izvestiia* published a letter from an outraged reader seeking KGB protection against the "gangs of anti-Soviet and anti-Russian 'denouncers'" entrenched, the letter suggested, in television and the press.[10] The author of the letter, V. Bochevarov from Leningrad, called the Soviet-US telebridges "a dirty anti-Soviet show" and wrote of "the patriotic anti-American feelings" that such broadcasts aroused.

> Since when have you begun to cultivate . . . an unconcealed sympathy for an imperialist land that has been raised in a spirit of unbridled anti-Sovietism, in an animal hatred for all things Russian, by the power of darkness that rules there?

"Should we love America for its attitude toward us?" he continued, answering his own question with a series of anti-American clichés. Bochevarov perceived the US as "a country that has cold-bloodedly and maliciously worn us out in Afghanistan, Poland, Angola, Mozambique, Cambodia, and Vietnam." All his anti-American clichés were, incidentally, still to be found in abundance in that same Soviet television he cursed for its "liberalism."

Bochevarov wrote of the Soviet patriots' "burning hatred" for "the political provocateur Phil Donahue" and his collaborator Vladimir Pozner. Then, evidently appealing directly to the KGB, he proclaimed: "We do not need these telebridges, which are harmful to our country and our people."

   <u>Interview with Margaret Thatcher</u>.   In the opinion of Soviet television viewers, Margaret Thatcher inflicted a painful defeat on three leading Soviet journalists questioning her in a late-night televised interview on March 31, 1987.[11]   One of the participants, Vladimir Simonov,[12] admitted that, as had been expressed in viewers' letters, he and his two colleagues "looked like village chess players up against world champion Kasparov."[13] Appearing on the new music and information program "Before and After Midnight,"[14]   Simonov said that some viewers had felt that the interview had "provided the propagandists of world imperialism with a free tribune" and that Mrs. Thatcher "was not adequately rebuffed on Soviet television." Others, according to Simonov, criticized the journalists for behaving in an unmannerly way, fidgeting and interrupting the prime minister while she was speaking.

   Simonov tried to explain what had taken place in the television studio at Ostankino.   He pointed out that never before had such "a wide-ranging, uninhibited interview with a Western leader" been broadcast in the Soviet Union and that the interview with Mrs. Thatcher was "an unprecedented experiment by Soviet television in the field of *glasnost*." He also unwittingly admitted that when *Izvestiia* published an interview with President Reagan in 1985,[15] the main object of the Soviet newspapermen had been not to inform their readers, but to deal the president "an ideological rebuff." This they did, albeit in an exceedingly clumsy way:

> True, our journalists had already conducted an interview with the American president, but that interview was accompanied by commentary almost as long as the interview itself. Reagan was "rebuffed," so to speak, retroactively.

   Attempting to justify his own lackluster performance, Simonov said that he and his colleagues were following the rules of the journalist's craft in trying "to get their interlocutor's point of view across." Addressing Vladimir Molchanov,[16] the moderator of "Before and after Midnight," Simonov asked him:

> Do you have a better idea of the British prime minister now? Of how intelligent, strong-willed and

resolute a person she is, but one who nevertheless holds views that are dangerous for mankind?

Molchanov duly responded in the affirmative (it might be noted that loaded questions like this are a favorite device of journalists taking advantage of *glasnost*). Simonov continued:

> Why, then, do we journalists feel . . . that it was a failure and that the audience was dissatisfied? I think that the problem lies in ourselves, that we are not yet ready for the level of *glasnost* to which we were exposed.

"The feeling of failure," he concluded, "comes from the fact that no lecturer appeared after the interview with a briefcase and a pointer to explain what had been good and what bad."

The fact that Soviet television returned to the Thatcher interview a few days later underlined the broad response it had evoked among viewers. The object of the "self-criticism" indulged in by one of the participants was evidently to neutralize the effect as far as possible. The authorities were seeking, before it was too late, to "co-opt"[17] information not to their liking, that Soviet citizens would in any case have obtained from other sources, Western radio broadcasts in particular.

SOCIAL ILLS EXPOSED

11
PROSTITUTION IN THE USSR

Valerii Konovalov

In late 1985, the Soviet press began to broach the subject of prostitution, albeit with considerable caution and characteristic prudishness.

Literaturnaia gazeta was the first publication to touch on the matter.[1] A piece called "The Girls in the Bar" described girls who visited a bar every day in the hopes of being "picked up." They sat waiting for some "crooked fellow"--usually a black marketeer--to approach them, snap his fingers, and nod casually toward the exit. The confessions of Lialka, one of "the bar girls," were quite interesting. Although she was only sixteen and her girlfriend Katerina somewhat younger, they already referred to each other as being "worn out." To them, going to the bar every day was like going to work. "In order to buy 'Banana' jeans and other brand-name clothing, you need money. But where to get it?," Lialka asked. She had already been hauled in to the police station for having had a fistfight with a certain "citizen" who she claimed had harrassed her. The life of the girls revolved around the bar, commented the newspaper, and when they spoke of being "picked up" by a different man every day, it was as if they perceived themselves as being objects for rent.

Further revelations about prostitution appeared in *Sobesednik*, the weekly illustrated supplement to *Komsomolskaia pravda*.[2] Here a letter from two girls named Marina and Galia was published together with a commentary by Professor Igor Bestuzhev-Lada, a well-known psychologist. Marina and Galia revealed a number of interesting facts about themselves--that they collected lovers, for example, competing to see who could have the most. Nearly half of these lovers, the girls noted, they had known for only a few hours. They usually met them, had

79

dinner in a restaurant, and then spent the night together. Both girls wrote that they had recently undergone abortions. They explained that their lovers were all of a specific type; nearly all worked in the retail trade, and every one of them had a car. After spending the evening with their "escort," the girls proceeded to an apartment that had been held free for this particular purpose. They admitted to having few interests in life other than funny but vulgar anecdotes, picnics with shashlik, lots to drink, expensive presents, and so-called free love. They did not believe in true love and spoke of having banished all virtue from their characters.

The girls did not describe themselves as prostitutes, nor did Bestuzhev-Lada refer to them as such in his commentary. He chose instead to use the term "fallen woman," noting in this connection that the times were long past when society stigmatized such people, rejecting them with contempt. Personally, the psychologist added, he was prepared to extend a helping hand and give them counseling. It was evident from his words that Bestuzhev-Lada was also prepared to admit, if only through the euphemism of "fallen woman," that prostitutes did exist in Soviet society.

An article in *Sovetskaia Belorussiia* on violations in currency transactions, attested to the existence of a special "foreign-currency" [*valiutnyi*] variety of prostitution, but cautiously avoided discussing the problem of prostitution itself.[3] The newspaper reported on foreign currency speculation in Minsk, noting that "restaurant girls" were one of the money changers' sources of hard currency. These girls had received it from their clients as a reward for certain "services."

The same article reported that an illegal institution, run by a certain Nina Gunina, had once existed on Vostochnaia Street. Here foreign tourists seeking relaxation and entertainment could, for the appropriate sum in hard currency, count on "a cup of coffee" and "company until the morning." The police and the public prosecutor quickly put a stop to the activities of the "*valiuta* girls."

Latvian Komsomol newspaper *Sovetskaia molodezh,*[4] wrote about women in the harbor cafés, bars, and restaurants of Riga. No one called them by their real names; they all had nicknames, such as "Lucky Strike" (*Nakhodka*), "Intourist Girl," or "Piglet." Their gathering places were mainly frequented by foreigners. Most evenings followed a similar pattern for these women: they would meet a sailor, dance a bit, have a few drinks, name a price, and leave together, either for home or for "a hang-out." One woman named Irina, known as "the Fly," told the newspaper that she started going out with foreign sailors eleven years ago; she was now thirty years old. Not all of her customers paid in hard currency, she recounted; sometimes she was given clothes sporting a Western brand name, or a bar of fancy soap. *Sovetskaia molodezh* noted that "the Fly" and women like her had a circle of acquaintances who traded in foreign currency and acted as their procurers. The dollars and marks the women received for their services ended up in the pockets of these "brokers." This milieu, the newspaper commented, had its own laws and its own methods of punishing the uncooperative.

   Sovetskaia molodezh reported that a small number of women who supplied their services in exchange for foreign currency had even acquired an international reputation. One Dzintra Revalde, for example, was familiar not only to the police of Riga's Kirov Raion but to the readers of a Finnish smut magazine, where her address and photograph had appeared. The article concluded with a report on a trial of foreign-currency speculators that had just been held in Riga. Many were sentenced to lengthy prison terms but, the newspaper added regretfully, not all of the women involved in the case were penalized.

   Indeed, the Criminal Code of the RSFSR and the analogous codes for the Union republics carried no penalty for prostitution. The number of articles in the criminal code that might have been used to bring charges against a woman practicing prostitution were quite limited.

   The fact that prostitution was not officially admitted to exist also ruled out criminal proceedings against prostitutes on charges of acquiring non-labor income through the practice of an illegal trade. It was not always possible for the law enforcement authorities to bring criminal charges against prostitutes for parasitism either. According to A. Grishchenko, the chief of the Latvian Ministry of Internal Affairs' Administration for the Struggle against Misappropriation of Socialist Property, all of the women in Riga who earned hard currency by night could be found in the employment records as working in an ordinary job by day--as medical assistants, cleaning ladies, or "extra help".[5]

   Grishchenko believed designating prostitution as a criminal act to be the most effective way of solving the problem that had developed. The tendency of the authorities to punish as criminal any activities they considered undesirable, was not new. The real cause for concern, however, was the evident lack of alternative measures to criminal repression in the arsenals of the organs responsible for curing social ills. This was the case with alcoholism, parasitism, and the problem of so-called "non-labor incomes"; there was little reason to expect a different treatment of prostitution.

Two small steps in the direction of *glasnost* were taken: the existence of prostitution was openly admitted on the pages of an official press organ, and the word "prostitute" was finally allowed to appear in print, without the usual recourse to euphemisms.

12
DRUG ABUSE

Sergei Voronitsyn

For many years, official publications and spokesmen in the USSR insisted that the problem of drug abuse did not and could not exist under the conditions of Soviet society, arguing that to bring the matter to public attention would only arouse an unhealthy interest in drugs and a desire to taste forbidden fruits. In 1983, in a discussion with correspondents of *Argumenty i fakty*, the weekly information bulletin for *agitprop* workers, the leading narcologist, Eduard Babaian, firmly stated that the problem of drug abuse was virtually nonexistent in his country; there were merely "individual cases of addiction."[1] He had previously been quoted in the journal *Novoe vremia* as claiming that the USSR had about 2,700 "registered addicts undergoing treatment,"[2] for the most part invalids and people dependent on pain killers; the number of these cases, he said, was steadily declining.

In contrast with such periodic assurances that all was well, Soviet newspapers and journals carried a number of articles on drug addiction in 1986, along with indications that the problem was being discussed at the highest levels. It was raised at the Twenty-seventh Congress of the CPSU[3] and at a meeting of the Bureau of the Moscow City Party Committee[4]; and the Procurator General, Aleksandr Rekunkov, addressed the issue in an interview in *Zhurnalist*. He told the journal's correspondent that cases of drug addiction "are not all that rare" in the Soviet Union, adding that reticence about drug abuse led to underestimation of the danger it presented and that miscalculations could be fraught with very serious consequences.[5]

In addition to these official pleas to pay heed to a growing threat, the press began revealing the relative ease with which the essential raw ingredients for narcotics could be illegally obtained. *Komsomolskaia pravda*, for example, published a lengthy article about the illegal harvesting of poppies on plantations in Kuibyshev Oblast. Every year people interested in the crop flocked there from all over the country.

> The poppies have hardly started to bloom, and "tourists" begin appearing in the villages. That's what the *kolkhozniks* call the drug addicts. They arrive by car, in groups. On motorcycles. From Orenburg, Orel, Krasnodar. They even drive down from the Baltic republics.[6]

Around the time this article appeared, *Izvestiia* reported on a police operation to search out secret poppy plantations in the Karakalpak ASSR and to cut off hashish distribution channels. The *Izvestiia* correspondent also noted that drug abuse among teenagers was increasing:

> Recently, adolescent toxin addicts [*toksikomany*], who sniff various chemical substances, have appeared on the scene. There have been cases where groups of children have died from poisonings of this kind. People are introduced to the needle, to the "cigarette with a high"--*i.e.*, hashish--in various ways. Sometimes it's simple curiosity.[7]

Chingiz Aitmatov's novel *Plakha*, the first part of which appeared in the literary journal *Novyi mir*, played a special role in the campaign against narcotics. The excerpt described how the main character secretly joined an expedition of "couriers" traveling to the distant steppes of Kazakstan to procure hashish so that he might study at first hand the origins of the spreading evil of drug abuse. As the hero strove to understand how such a vice could have made its way into a Socialist society, his burning desire was to reach others with the publication of his insights:

> Why is this happening, why is something like this possible in our life, in our society, which has proclaimed to the whole world that our social system

is immune to vices? Oh, if only I could succeed in writing such a piece, make it such that many people, ever more people, respond to it as they would to an urgently personal matter, a fire in their own home, harm to their own children; only then might this word, taken up by many people who are not impartial, overcome [the power of] money and defeat vice. God grant that it has this effect, that it is not uttered in vain, that--if it is true that "In the beginning was the Word"--this word has kept its original strength.[8]

The decision to replace the policy of silence about drug abuse with a campaign of enlightenment in the press, was possibly the result of pressure from the creative intelligentsia and the medical community--as had been the case with the anti-alcohol campaign.[9]

However, accurate and reliable information on the numbers of addicts was hardly available, as virtually no one gave these problems serious study during the years of silence. Thus medical workers, police officials, and employees of administrative bodies for youth affairs found themselves unprepared to deal with the tasks they now faced in connection with the new policy on drug abuse.[10]

At the same time, the pool of young drug users grew as young soldiers returned from Afghanistan, where, according to accounts of war prisoners who turned up in the West, the use of drugs had become widespread. Those addicted to alcohol contributed to yet another influx of drug addicts. Limitations on the sale of alcohol led to a desperate search for substitutes. Among the substitutes mentioned in the press were perfumes and toilet water,[11] various potent medicines,[12] and chemical opiates, an intermediate product in the manufacture of true narcotics.[13] Small comfort could be drawn from the fact that alcoholic beverages were in little danger of being replaced by narcotics on a large scale due to the particular social role played by drink, both in an intimate setting and on family and holiday occasions.

By 1987, the authorities had launched a long-term public information campaign, chiefly in the Komsomol newspapers of the union republics, but also on central television and in the central newspapers. *Uchitelskaia gazeta* carried two copies of a leaflet with the words "Stand like a wall against drug abuse," which the newspaper urged its readers to cut out and give to older children.[14]

Alongside the public information campaign, authorities

launched an offensive against the cultivation of plants used in the preparation of narcotics--plants previously relatively easy to obtain. Efforts were being made to limit the areas cultivated, to increase vigilance over plantations of hemp and opium poppies, and to find a means of destroying wild hemp, particularly in Kazakhstan. As this plant grew wild over vast expanses of land from Khabarovsk to Transbaikal, the task of eradicating it was not without its difficulties. Using herbicides to destroy wild hemp had a harmful effect on the environment, while plowing it in was impossible in some areas owing to the contours of the land and also entailed the danger of erosion. Finally, experience had shown that curtailing the cultivation of one or another crop from which narcotics could be made did not necessarily lead to a reduction in the number of drug addicts; they rather turned to other means of intoxication.

Closely linked with the restriction of access to the raw materials for producing narcotics was another, more difficult task--namely, the blocking of channels by which narcotic substances reached the user. The Minister of Internal Affairs, Aleksandr Vlasov, stated in an interview that, in one operation alone, 300 couriers and more than 4,000 "manufacturers" of drugs had been arrested,[15] while the newspaper *Sotsialisticheskaia industriia* carried reports on the discovery and "neutralization" of a network of drug dealers that had been operating in several cities with the arrest of forty-three people.[16]

According to Vlasov, there were 46,000 registered drug addicts,[17] probably only a fraction of the true number. The overwhelming majority of addicts did everything possible to avoid being registered, particularly in those republics (Kirgizia, Uzbekistan, and Georgia) where it was a criminal offense not only to prepare, acquire, and sell drugs but also to use them. In other republics, the use of narcotic substances that had not been prescribed by a doctor was an administrative offense (punishable with a fine or administrative arrest). In practice, however, the local authorities often employed a variety of arbitrary sanctions against drug addicts. As a rule, school doctors and administrations, workers' collectives, and the friends and relatives of drug addicts tried to conceal cases of addiction.

RSFSR Minister of Health Anatolii Potapov admitted: "We do not know the true number of people suffering from drug addiction."[18] According to expert calculations,[19] there were 30,000-50,000 drug addicts in Hungary (0.3-0.5

percent of the population); in Poland there were 200,000-600,000 (0.5-1.6 percent of the population); while in the Soviet Union there were only 46,000 (about 0.016 percent of the population) according to the official figure. Of course, Hungary and Poland were more open to temptations imported from the West. In the Soviet Union, on the other hand, there were vast, fairly accessible supplies of the raw materials needed for making drugs and some republics where the use of drugs was traditional.

To judge from the large (albeit fairly subjective) body of data that had appeared in the press since the policy of silence on the problem of drug abuse was lifted, drug addiction affected every social group in one way or another. Drug addicts were to be found among workers, in the countryside, among the intelligentsia, schoolchildren, students, and among the children of both well-off and problem families. The greatest proportion of drug addicts were under thirty, while the maximum age seemed to be forty. These facts led some of those studying the problem to conclude that drug addicts did not live to be very old. Among the main reasons for young people taking drugs was a desire to imitate peers, the wish to experience new sensations, or just plain curiosity. As in the West, some young people took drugs in order to escape from the difficulties and contradictions of everyday life.

Another obstacle hindering the implementation of an effective campaign against drug abuse was the unresolved question of whether a drug addict should be regarded as a criminal or a sick person? The absence of clarity over this question resulted in legal uncertainty and made particularly difficult the task of creating a system whereby addicts could be treated anonymously. What might be called a "double-track" approach to this question emerged in 1986, in which a drug addict was seen in a medical context as a sick person but in a social context as a criminal. Thus, if a drug addict agreed to cooperate with the medical authorities and accept treatment he was freed of criminal liability. If, on the other hand, he refused treatment, he was liable to be subjected to compulsory measures and administrative (or criminal) penalties. Medical workers, police officials, lawyers, sociologists, and addicts themselves, spoke in favor of anonymous treatment. As the emergence of similar problems in the campaign against alcoholism have demonstrated, however, the resolution of such questions under the conditions of an authoritarian system will take time.

13
FALTERING HEALTH SERVICES

*Sophia M. Miskiewicz**

Increased life expectancy, reduced infant mortality, and an overall decreasing death rate are generally accepted as measures of the well-being and health of a nation. The increased prosperity and technological progress that accompany the industrial development of a modern state are expected to stabilize and reduce death rates and increase life expectancy. Yet in the years prior to 1986, indicators of the health conditions in the Soviet Union and Eastern Europe ran counter to this trend. Nicholas Eberstadt of the Harvard Center for Population Studies reported that:

Progress in reducing mortality virtually ceased during the nineteen-sixties in most of these countries. By the early nineteen-seventies, life expectancy at birth for men and women was unmistakably falling in some of them.

Eberstadt elaborated on the evolution of this trend:

Like the Soviet Union, Eastern Europe enjoyed rapid improvements in health in the nineteen-fifties and early nineteen-sixties, when life expectancy at birth rose by nearly six years. By contrast, life expectancy in the twelve European NATO states rose less than 3.5 years. In the early nineteen-fifties, life spans were nearly six years shorter in Warsaw Pact Europe than in NATO Europe. By the later nineteen-sixties, the gap had been narrowed to 2.5 years. Since that time, however, the gap has once again

*This is the general introduction to a longer piece on the health services in Eastern Europe. The full paper was published in *Survey* (London), Volume 29, No. 4(127) of August 1987, and will appear in a forthcoming book entitled *Social and Economic Rights in The Soviet Bloc* (Transaction Publishers: New Brunswick, New Jersey, 1987). For details about individual countries, see RAD 161/86, "Health Service in Eastern Europe," and RL 289/86, "Quality of Soviet Health Care Under Attack."

widened; by the early nineteen-eighties, life spans
were nearly five years longer in NATO Europe than in
Warsaw Pact Europe. In part this spoke [of] health
improvements in the West, but the rapidly growing gap
was also due to Eastern European trends. After rapid
strides, health improvements had come to a halt, and
for the region as a whole, life expectancy has
actually dropped.[1]

According to figures submitted to the World Health
Organization, the age-standardized death rate for males
from all causes rose after 1970 in Bulgaria, Hungary, and
Poland. In seven others countries worldwide--Cuba,
Uruguay, Czechoslovakia, Denmark, Ireland, Romania, and
Sweden--the rate declined by less than 10 percent after
1970, although in Denmark and Sweden it had already been
relatively low at the beginning of the nineteen-seventies.
Canada and the USA belonged to the next group of countries
in which the mortality rate had declined by between 10
percent and 20 percent over the same period; and Puerto
Rico, Hong Kong, and Japan had lowered their mortality
rates by more than 30 percent from 1970 on.[2]
Female death rates fell universally after 1970. But
in Cuba, Bulgaria, Hungary, and Poland, the size of the
decline was less than 10 percent. Czechoslovakia, Romania,
and Yugoslavia, along with Canada, Denmark, France, Norway,
Sweden, the United Kingdom, and New Zealand all registered
falls of between 10 percent and 20 percent from 1970 on,
while Japan, Finland, Chile, Costa Rica, and Puerto Rico
lowered their female mortality rates by more than 30
percent during the same period.[3]
There were numerous factors that could have
contributed to this picture of deteriorating health
conditions in Eastern Europe vis-à-vis the West. The
stress accompanying modern industrialization, introduced at
a faster pace in Eastern Europe than in the West,
undoubtedly contributed to an increase in heart and
circulatory problems. Also, inadequate concern was shown
for the environment during this period of intensive
industrial growth, and industrial pollution is likely to
have added to the health hazards in Eastern Europe. The
incidence of respiratory diseases, in particular, is likely
to have been raised by such pollution, as well as by
increased cigarette smoking. Between 1965 and 1985
cigarette use per adult rose nearly a third in Poland, over
a third in Hungary, and over 50 percent in East Germany.
The consumption of alcohol also rose sharply in Eastern

Europe during the nineteen-sixties and nineteen-seventies. Average per capita consumption of distilled spirits was already slightly higher in Eastern Europe than in Western Europe in 1960; and by 1980 it was estimated to be more than 70 percent higher.[4]

New health risks, therefore, seemed to emerge in Eastern Europe; but as Eberstadt observed:

> Increased health risks . . . do not necessarily lead to deterioration in national health conditions. State social policies can prevent health deterioration when properly framed and implemented, even during periods of seriously increased health risks. The public health programs of the East European countries are, in varying degree, replicas of the Soviet system. These are characterized by relatively high ratios of medical personnel and hospital beds to population, and provide extensive services that are nominally free of charge. However, the relationship between the availability of medical personnel and the health level of the national population, in fact, appears to be negative: countries with the greater number of medical personnel per 10,000 people generally seem to have lower levels of adult life expectancy. This illustrates that in these countries' labor-extensive health care programs priority is given to the quantity of "doctors" fielded rather than to the quality of training or equipment.[5]

Statistically, public health care in all of the countries of Eastern Europe, as in the Soviet Union, appeared impressive. There had been steady increases in the numbers of doctors, nurses, pharmacies, hospitals, hospital beds, clinics, dentists, and specialized care centers. The mass media repeatedly announced the authorities' concern for public health and the many new advances made in medical research and technology; they reported on the numerous national decisions to update, modernize, and add to the country's medical facilities. But these new facilities were often slow to materialize and sometimes never completed on account of shortages in material, funds, and manpower or simply because of poor planning.

Soviet and East European medical care was, in principle, financed directly and virtually entirely by the state; thus, the quantity and quality of these services, and the policies regarding them, were determined not by the consumers, but by state leaders according to political priorities. In the centrally planned economies of Eastern Europe--where there was no need for prices to respond to scarcities, and income did not necessarily provide access to goods or services--the patterns of state expenditure did not give a reliable picture of the quality or quantity of resources allocated. It was, moreover, difficult to separate health-care expenditure from outlays on other social welfare programs, as it was usually listed together with pensions and disability outlays as well as research and construction costs.

Health care, like other social services, remained low on the East European governments' lists of priorities. When cutbacks were required in, for example, investment or modernization programs, the health-care service was the first area to be affected. Auxiliary medical institutions were also repeatedly neglected. It seemed that more attention was paid to raw statistics and to presenting an image of ever-rising expenditure and uninterrupted technological advance, than to the actual services provided. New housing projects with inadequate sewage-disposal facilities, or new factories that did not comply with the proper safety standards or possess the necessary waste-disposal facilities were examples of this blind preoccupation with a purely statistical picture of progress. (In 1986, Warsaw still did not have a single sewage treatment plant; two plants were under construction, but work on the first of these had already dragged on for 11 years).[6]

As shortages abounded in all areas of health care, from beds and pills to doctors and nurses, those who had friends in the right places or were willing to pay a bribe or gratuity tended to be treated first. Party functionaries and other members of the ruling elite were given priority in the use of scarce medical facilities; special facilities were even provided for party and military personnel and sometimes also for fee-paying patients from abroad. Those not belonging to the elite, or who were unwilling or unable to pay gratuities (often amounting to several months' salary), simply went without treatment, joined the long waiting lists, or were "processed" by medical personnel compelled to be more concerned with meeting quotas and filling out forms than with diagnosing and treating an illness. Moreover, responsibility for slackness was difficult to assign, as patients might have been treated by different doctors on each visit to the same treatment center.

The level and extent of the medical service also varied geographically. The differences between the provisions in large urban centers as compared with rural areas (where it was difficult to attract well-qualified medical personnel on account of poorer living conditions and inadequate technical support) were particularly marked. Part of the cause of the unevenness of the medical treatment within each East European country was the shortage of personnel, leaving staff little time in which to update and upgrade knowledge and skills. Moreover, given the shortage of doctors, those whose knowledge and practices became outdated were not likely to be fired or demoted. The quality of treatment provided often depended simply on the amount of time and effort the doctor could afford to devote to a given case, the overworked doctor being much more likely to pass on more difficult cases than take on the responsibility himself. Even the most dedicated and best qualified doctors were liable to become discouraged when forced to work without the minimum required supplies, equipment, and medications.

Patients in Poland and Romania were granted a limited choice in their doctor in later years, and were also able to pay for certain optional treatment and services. But these reforms came dangerously near to transgressing the ideological concept of the right of all citizens to free health care. Thus further substantive reforms were avoided, even though these might have affected the population's health.

While each of the East European regimes repeatedly voiced concern for the nation's welfare, and trumpeted the great benefits secured for the citizen by socialism, it was highly questionable whether the statistics and reports published in the state-controlled media in those one-party systems gave a full and balanced picture of health matters. The information presented to the public on issues such as pollution, environmental damage (such as the Chernobyl accident), and later on public health dangers (such as AIDS or drug abuse), seemed at the very least inadequate--a situation that was bound to have serious and irreversible repercussions in the future.

The fact that certain deficiencies and difficulties were common to all the health-care services of Eastern Europe indicated that these were not the accidental shortcomings of one or two mismanaged health-care programs but were problems rooted in the very concept of "free" health care in a centralized system. Indeed, these health services, all aspects of which (including medical research, drugs, treatment, and equipment) were subject to strict central planning, merely illustrated many of the weaknesses of the wider social and economic system in which they operated. Great effort went into compiling and presenting statistics showing the effort and money being spent on health care. But no amount of statistics were able to hide the frequent shortages of the most routine items resulting from the habitual failure of the centralized system to coordinate supply and demand. And when they were available, the equipment and medications on offer lagged far behind Western standards, since the sector suffered from the same obsolescence, stagnation, excessive bureaucracy, widespread corruption, and isolation from the rest of the world that afflicted East European economies at large. Meanwhile new strains of bacteria and viruses developed immunities to older drugs, paying no heed to the slowness of medical research in the East in developing new ways to combat them. Patients tended to lack confidence in their doctors and domestically produced medicines. Indeed, doctors were often forced to prescribe Western-made medications available only for hard currency. When state budgets could not or would not allocate funds for this purpose, the patient had to pay or do without.

Central planning in Eastern Europe generally led to excessive bureaucracy, inefficiency, and constant shortages. This meant that health facilities tended to lag behind the population's needs; there was nothing to suggest that the gap could be closed without major systemic changes.

14
THE MISERY OF RURAL LIFE

Elizabeth Teague

In an open letter to an imaginary peasant, Ivan Vasilev painted a dismal picture of life in the Russian countryside. Occupying half a page in the issue of *Pravda* for December 7, 1986, the letter berated the peasantry for their "mindless" attitude toward the land. Vasilev described the destruction of the natural environment, saying that forests of pine and birch had been turned into vast rubbish tips, into storage dumps for manure, and into swamps by the unnecessary diversion of streams.

Worse than the destruction of nature was the loss of human sensitivity from which it sprang. Removed from the traditional small villages dotted across the Russian countryside into big rural settlements, the peasantry had lost its traditional sense of community and self-help. "Nobody thinks about anyone else any more," Vasilev wrote, "only about himself." The local authorities were too preoccupied with meeting production targets--and feathering their own nests--to heed the needs of society's weaker members.

Children and old people suffered most from the uncaring attitudes of the local bosses. Vasilev told of officials who pretended to care about education, yet built the local school on unhealthy marshland, saving the best land for grazing cattle. He bemoaned the fate of the elderly, living alone with no one to help them unless they could offer a bottle of vodka as a bribe, or unable to find the provisions they needed in poorly stocked local stores. Officials were interested only in able-bodied workers who could help meet production targets. "If you are old and cannot work," they would shrug, "don't expect us to worry about you. That's what social security is for." All the while, these same officials were siphoning off farm funds to build themselves comfortable homes--complete with double garages, storerooms, and verandas.

Addressing his imaginary peasant in the familiar second person singular, Vasilev reproached him in the bluntest possible terms for his mindlessness. "You just live from one day to the next," he wrote. "You get up, put on your harness, drag your load from one place to the next, get out of harness again and then . . . you stick your face in the trough. Excuse me for saying so, but that's how horses live. People are supposed to *think*."

Vasilev blamed the bad habits of the past for contemporary problems, specifically indicting the system established under Brezhnev, whereby the peasants became entitled, for the first time, to a guaranteed minimum wage. That change meant, according to Vasilev, that peasants were thenceforth assured of a living wage regardless of how little or how badly they worked. But Vasilev was so eager to lay the blame for all the present woes on the Brezhnev leadership that he made no reference to the fact that the destruction of the way of life of the Russian peasantry could be traced back even earlier--to the break-up of the traditional peasant smallholdings and the collectivization of agriculture carried in the nineteen-thirties under Stalin.

Vasilev blamed an economic system that laid sole responsibility for meeting plan targets on local party leaders and set no store by "collective wisdom" and "collective energy." The past twenty years, he complained, had seen the "bureaucratization" of the countryside: "conscience has been usurped by edict." The local party leaders, he said, were themselves dehumanized and had lost touch with the people.

The introduction of a system of self-financing in the agricultural sector might, Vasilev said, assist the recovery of what had been lost--"community, collectivism, and conscience." He called on the party to "root out individualism" and overcome "the present lack of communal feeling." But Vasilev was not optimistic on this score. Local party committees, he said, tended to identify not with the people but with the party secretary. It was unimaginable, he said, that a party committee should find itself disagreeing with the party secretary; the committee had become a servant of the secretary, instead of the other way round, and no longer had an independent life of its own.

The secretary himself was a slave to the plan, which had to be fulfilled at any cost. He had neither the time nor the energy to leave his office and go out into the countryside to talk to the peasants and enquire after their needs and concerns. In this way, the party had lost touch with the inhabitants of rural areas.

THE LACKLUSTER ECONOMY

15
LITTLE *GLASNOST* ON ECONOMIC ACCOMPLISHMENT

Philip Hanson

The official plan fulfillment report for 1986 showed a clear improvement in all the main indicators of Soviet economic growth.[1] National income produced was 4.1 percent up on 1985, as compared with a 3.5 percent average growth rate in 1981-85; national income utilized was up 3.6 percent (versus 3.1 percent in 1981-85); gross industrial output was up 4.9 percent (as opposed to 3.7 percent); gross farm output was up 5.1 percent (versus 2.1 percent); and investment was up about 8 percent (versus 3.5 percent).[2]

Customarily, a new Soviet leadership would report that it was doing better than its (routinely discredited) predecessors. Thus, skeptics both inside and outside the USSR, tended to look for signs of statistical chicanery on these occasions. In the case of the 1986 report, however, the evidence for a genuine improvement was strong. Western analysts accepted that the official Soviet presentation of major national and sectoral output totals reported in rubles could be misleading, but agreed that industrial product figures reported in tons, cubic meters, and kilowatt-hours, had usually been reliable--at least concerning their rates of change over time. The 1986 report contained forty-seven such items (excluding subcategories) for the industrial sector, including food-processing. Of those forty-seven, twenty-three showed a growth of more than 4.0 percent over 1985, while only four showed a drop in output, and only ten revealed a growth between zero and 2.0 percent.[3] The unweighted average for these forty-seven items was 4.2 percent. This was clearly better than 1985, when ten of fifty such items had shown a decline in output, a further fifteen had increased by not more than 2.0 percent, and the unweighted average growth had been only 1.8 percent. Certainly good weather must have contributed in part, through increased inputs into the food-processing industry's contribution to this growth. But even if food-industry items were excluded, the improvement between 1985 and 1986 was clear. (Industrial growth in 1985, though most of it took place after Gorbachev's accession to power, was close to the average for 1981-85, thus serving as a basis for comparison.)

The output of main farm products also showed strong growth after two years of stagnation. The livestock sector benefited from the fact that the harvest had not been too bad in 1985, so that feed supplies were reasonable in 1986. In addition, relatively good weather conditions contributed to sharp increases in the grain and potato crops.

To judge by physical indicators, transport and construction also seemed to have performed moderately well. Therefore, unless there had been an unusual amount of report-padding in physical output figures, the performance in general had to be considered a real improvement.

A major social achievement was claimed in the campaign against alcohol: it was said to have contributed to a fall in the crude death rate, and an increase "for the first time in ten years" in average life expectancy (to sixty-nine).

More important for the future, perhaps, was the whole approach to economic policy-making adopted by the new leadership. The report threw some intriguing sidelights on Gorbachev's economic policies and their public presentation which suggested that the approach had hitherto been traditional, with no real departure from the previous pattern.

First of all, there continued to be strange goings-on when reporting figures for the national income.[4] In 1986, the Soviet Central Statistical Administration switched, in its quarterly reports, from reporting the national income utilized, to reporting the national income produced; the plan target for 1987 was also given for the latter.[5] Previously, published plan targets and fulfillment reports had given only the national income utilized. The report for the year suggested a possible presentational reason for this change. National income produced was then reported as having exceeded the increase forecast in the 1986 annual plan (it was said to have been up 4.1 percent, as against a planned rise of 3.9 percent), while the national income utilized grew less than planned (3.6 percent, as against

3.8 percent). This switch was irritating as a 1986 plan target for the national income produced was published for the first time (to show that it had been exceeded), while there was no reference in the report to the original target for national income utilized, nor to the fact that it was not fulfilled. For the original target, the seeker after truth had to refer back to the *Gosplan* chairman's speech in 1985, on the plan for 1986.[6] If this was *glasnost*, it was *glasnost* of a kind tediously familiar from the speeches of Western politicians when scoring party points. Official statistical reporting in most Western countries was less partisan.

There appeared to be another, more serious, problem in connection with the reported growth of national income. If the national income utilized grew less than had been planned, while the national income produced grew more than (allegedly) had been planned, the reason probably was that export volume was more than had been planned or import volume less than had been planned, or both. How these particular national income figures were derived was, however, unclear. As in 1985, they seemed to have been oddly manipulated. The national income produced was said to have totaled 590 billion rubles at 1986 prices, only 2.2 percent above the 1985 current-price figure.[7] If "real" growth was 4.1 percent, the average price level should have fallen by 1.9 percent in 1986. Thus, the story on prices looked a little implausible.

Once again, at least part of the explanation may have had to do with the demon drink: the further cuts in official alcohol production and sales (cuts reported at 35 and 37 percent respectively between 1985 and 1986) may have had an unwelcome effect on the statistics, and that effect may have been fudged. Retail sales of "other food goods" (which seems primarily to have been an alcoholic category) were equivalent to just over 10 percent of national income utilized in 1984.[8] Insofar as cuts in alcohol sales were not offset by increases in official supplies of other items, they could have had quite a damaging short-run effect on the national income statistics. Though one could not be certain, the fact that a 4.1 percent "real" increase in national income produced was somehow obtained from a 2.2 percent increase in national income in current prices, may have been related to this.

Another sidelight concerned priorities. The new leadership had raised the priority given to investment vis-à-vis consumption in the annual and five-year plans. The system's deeply ingrained tendency to give informal priority to investment might have been expected to reinforce such a shift. Thus, even if a plan were feasible and internally consistent, the informal priority system might have made the squeeze on consumption greater than the plan would indicate. There were some signs in the report that this happened in 1986. The percentage increase in the output of industrial producer goods (industry group A) was greater than planned (5.2 percent as opposed to 4.3 percent), while that in the output of industrial consumer goods (industry group B) was less than planned (4.0 percent versus 4.4 percent). According to the figures, 1986 was nonetheless not a bad year for the consumer--at least for the nonalcoholic consumer--but a large element in this improvement was the rebound in farm output due to better weather. If the tendency (and implementation) of these policies to squeeze consumption were to coincide with poor weather, the consumer might well feel the pinch.

The informal priority given to investment was probably all the more important because the plan had not, in fact, been feasible and consistent. The targets for increases in machinery output and investment had been extravagant. The plan fulfillment report showed that the 1986 targets for percentage increases in one year for new capacity installed, were in many cases bizarre: 34 percent for the metallurgy complex, 36 percent for the machine-building complex, 37 percent for the construction complex, and 42 percent for the chemicals-and-timber complex. (The report gave percentage actual, reported increases over 1985, and percentage fulfillment of the 1986 plan, from which these targets could be deduced.) The increases actually reported were: metallurgy, 11 percent; machine-building, 5 percent; construction, 19 percent; and chemicals and timber, 2 percent.

The report also contained evidence that the private sector of agriculture may have suffered from the campaign against "nonlabor incomes." Increases were reported both for total output of meat, milk, and eggs and for the output of these items from socialized agriculture only. In percentage terms, they amounted to 3.5, 2.5, and 3.9, respectively, for total output and 8, 5, and 6, respectively, for the socialized sector. Given the 1985 totals for the private and socialized sectors,[9] it appeared that private-sector meat output had been estimated as being down by 11 percent and private sector output of milk and of eggs as each being down by a little over 1 percent. The reason for this was not clear; it was probably the result of inconsistent and initially hostile policies adopted by the leadership toward the private sector.

These observations are not meant to suggest that the improvement in Soviet economic growth in 1986 was not real or that, even if it was real, it reflected no credit on the new leadership. There did appear to have been a genuine improvement, achieved in part by energetic new leaders. They were prepared to put more pressure on officials and managers for results, and this pressure, rather than being counterproductive, seems to have elicited more output. The plan report also revealed, however, that Gorbachev had thus far been proceeding in an old-fashioned way. Overly taut investment plans and conflicting signals being passed down, the hierarchy had apparently damaged the private sector. There had also been something that looked suspiciously like a cooking of the books--and that could hardly be called nouvelle cuisine.

16
SOCIAL JUSTICE AND ECONOMIC PROGRESS

Aaron Trehub

Two important articles, one by the Doctor of Philosophical Sciences V. Z. Rogovin and the other by Academician Tatiana Zaslavskaia, shed some light on Gorbachev's concept of "social justice" (*sotsialnaia spravedlivost*).[1]

What Is "Social Justice"? According to Rogovin, "the strict implementation of the principles of social justice is an important condition for the unity and political stability of a society, for its dynamic development."[2] Zaslavskaia viewed what she termed "socialist justice" (more on this below) as a precondition for "the effective functioning of the human factor."[3] She even linked neglect of "social justice" and "the human factor" during the Brezhnev years with the accident at the Chernobyl power station.[4]

The essence of "social justice" evidently lay in the principle `From each according to his ability, to each according to his work.` This simple formula, however, contains many ambiguities. An especially knotty problem is the relationship between "social justice" and social equality (*ravenstvo*). It is generally agreed that the two concepts are closely related. But are they identical?

Rogovin claimed that they are not: "The concepts of social justice and social equality, while closely linked, are far from identical."[5] To support this view, he cited the infamous practice of "leveling" (*uravnilovka*), or equality in wages.[6] Leveling, he said, achieved social equality, but only at the expense of "social justice."

Zaslavskaia solved the problem of reconciling social equality and "social justice" by consigning it to the future. "In the long-term development of a socialist society," she wrote,

> social justice is understood to mean the establishment of the political, social, and economic equality of social groups--*i.e.*, the guaranteeing of the social equivalency (*ravnotsennost*) of their situations, while preserving differences in their concrete manifestations.[7]

Thus, "social justice" and social equality would coincide at some distant point on the road to communism. In the meantime, the main task facing the Communist party was the achievement of "socialist justice" (*sotsialisticheskaia spravedlivost*), which Zaslavskaia defined as "the consistent realization of the principle, 'From each according to his ability, to each according to his work.'"[8]

Zaslavskaia's approach appears to have been inspired by Lenin's thoughts on the relationship between justice and equality, as set forth in *The State and Revolution* (1917):

> The first phase of communism cannot provide justice and equality: differences in wealth, including unjust differences, will remain, but the *exploitation* of man by man will be impossible, because it will be impossible to seize *the means of production*-- factories, machines, land, etc.--and convert them into private property. In smashing Lassalle's petit-bourgeois, murky phrase about "equality" and "justice" *in general*, Marx shows *the course of development* of a communist society, which is *forced* in the beginning to destroy *only* the "injustice" that lies in the seizure of the means of production by separate persons and which is *incapable* of destroying

immediately the further injustice that consumer goods
are distributed "according to work" [not need].[9]

For Zaslavskaia, "social justice" referred to the
establishment of social equality; according to Lenin,
however, justice and equality could not be achieved during
"the first phase of communism"--*i.e.*, socialism.
Therefore, it would be incorrect to speak of establishing
"social justice" in a country that still had to implement
"the basic principle of socialism." By making a distinction
between "social justice" and "socialist justice,"
Zaslavskaia preserved ideological consistency while
simultaneously avoiding the troublesome question of
equality.

How To Achieve "Social(ist) Justice". The task, then,
was "the consistent realization of the principle 'From each
according to his ability, to each according to his work.'"
Rogovin focused on the second half of this formula viewing
the problem of achieving "social justice" primarily as a
problem of distribution. Zaslavskaia was as concerned with
the first half of the formula--*i.e.*, with the creation of
conditions that would permit people to work to the best of
their ability--as she was with the second. Both, however,
agreed that a program for "social justice" should include
the following areas:

Incomes. The most prominent aspect of the campaign
for "social justice" was the struggle against "nonlabor
incomes" (*netrudovye dokhody*). These were incomes earned
outside the official economy, in what Zaslavskaia called
"the shadow economy," often as a result of speculation (in
housing, deficit goods), bribery, moonlighting (with
materials and equipment filched from the state), and even
gambling.[10] Rogovin applauded anti-"nonlabor incomes"
legislation; he argued, however, that it did not go far
enough and suggested establishing "a system of direct,
immediate control over the processes of formation and use
of incomes and personal property"[11]--a Soviet version of
the Internal Revenue Service. He also suggested using
expropriated "nonlabor incomes" to supplement the state's
social consumption funds.[12] Zaslavskaia was more moderate
and less specific, calling merely for "the eradication of
all illegal incomes and [the establishment of] a socially
just income level in the individual production sector."[13]
What about those earning large sums legally? Rogovin's
treatment of this question was revealing. Citing a study
that had discovered that more than half of the total sum of

all bank deposits in the Latvian SSR was concentrated in 3
percent of the accounts, he concluded that:

> even if it is assumed that the amount of savings
> owned by the 3 percent and the remaining 97 percent
> of the population was identical and that such a
> significant disparity was not tied to the existence
> of illegal nonlabor incomes, even then, in my view,
> it should not exist in a socialist society.[14]

In other words, to earn (or save) a lot more than
one's neighbors, violated "social justice." Zaslavskaia
agreed; discussing "people who are ready to work very hard,
not under group conditions but rather 'on their own'--for
example, as family contract workers, in the private
auxiliary economy, in seasonal construction brigades, and
in other types of piecework," she warned that

> too large a difference in income per unit of labor in
> comparison with social [*i.e.*, state] production can
> lead to the formation of a social stratum that is
> distinguished by a disproportionately large share of
> society's wealth in relation to the remaining mass of
> workers.[15]

Like Rogovin, she advocated the establishment of a
strict income-monitoring system.

Taxation. Rogovin repeated his earlier call for an
inheritance tax (such a tax existed in the first decades of
the Soviet state, but was greatly reduced or, in the case
of money inheritances, abolished entirely in the
mid-nineteen-forties).[16] He also favored raising taxes on
incomes derived from the private auxiliary economy (from
the sale of flowers or vegetables grown on private plots,
for example); in this connection, he borrowed an idea
advanced by Zaslavskaia in an interview in April 1986[17] and
proposed levying an additional tax on those owning private
plots in certain areas (*e.g.*, the northern Caucasus,
Transcaucasus, and Central Asia) with especially good
climatic conditions. Finally, he called for a progressive
tax on royalties (*gonorary*), paid to authors and artists
for the publication, performance, or "other use" of their
works.[18] Zaslavskaia favored a progressive income tax for
those working in the private sector.

Subsidies. Soviet citizens enjoyed cheap housing,
meat, and dairy products, thanks to state subsidies
amounting to over 8 billion rubles a year for housing and

between 40 and 50 billion rubles a year for meat and dairy products.[19] According to Zaslavskaia, however, housing (separate apartments), meat, and dairy products were all deficit items. This meant that people with access to those goods were, in effect, living on "nonlabor incomes." She suggested raising the prices of meat and dairy products to reflect their real cost, thereby reducing or even eliminating the enormous state subsidies on these goods and "putting all social groups on an equal footing with regard to obtaining [them]."[20] On the question of housing, she favored, together with Rogovin, increasing the difference in rent for living space exceeding the state-established "sanitary norm" of nine square meters per person, and a rent system which reflected differences in apartment quality and location.[21]

So much for the areas addressed by both Rogovin and Zaslavskaia. Rogovin also raised the touchy issue of privileges--"preference in health care, housing, dachas, trips to holiday homes, and services of a cultural, day-to-day, and provisioning nature"--for members of "the administrative apparatus."[22] He approvingly quoted Moscow Party Chief Boris Eltsin's call at the Twenty-seventh Congress of the CPSU to abolish "unjustified" privileges for the elite,[23] and cited a legal expert to the effect that such privileges "undermine the workers' faith in justice and thereby give rise to lawlessness." For her part, Zaslavskaia emphasized the need to look after "the millions of unskilled workers" who would be "freed" (thrown out of work) by the modernization of Soviet industry:

> It is already necessary, first, to construct reliable quantitative predictions regarding the freeing of certain categories of workers, their distribution by region and branch [of industry], and, second, to look for the most effective way, in the economic and social sense, of using them further.[24]

She foresaw that this fundamental change in "the conditions of employment" in the Soviet Union would require "a psychological restructuring" (*psikhologicheskaia perestroika*) among "groups of workers that have historically been distinguished by a high degree of stability." In other words, workers would have to accept that they may find themselves out of a job, possibly for a long time. Here Zaslavskaia was repeating a point made by Professor V. Kostakov in an article that unleashed speculation about the emergence of mass unemployment.[25]

Analysis. The program outlined by Rogovin and Zaslavskaia implied profound social consequences. The public had become used to paying nominal amounts for food and housing; attempts to get them to pay more could only aggravate social tensions. And in flirting with the idea of using the threat of unemployment to stiffen labor discipline, Zaslavskaia was treading on dangerous ground.[26]

However, even though the measures proposed by Rogovin and Zaslavskaia entailed a serious revision of the Soviet "social contract" and were bound to arouse discontent in some quarters, they probably reflected the mood of a growing number of Soviet citizens. When Gorbachev raised the issue of revamping rents at the 27th Congress of the CPSU, he was interrupted by applause.[27] A press debate on the feasibility of increasing the number of pay-for-service polyclinics revealed widespread dissatisfaction with the free health care system.[28] And many Soviet citizens seemed to be in favor of the fight against "nonlabor incomes."[29]

This last was an important point. Despite their ritualistic denunciation of "leveling," Rogovin and, to a lesser extent, Zaslavskaia shared the popular distrust of the well-off. This was revealed in Rogovin's statement that "significant disparities" in wealth, even if legally amassed, "should not exist in a socialist society", and in Zaslavskaia's insistence that incomes in the private sector be limited to a "socially just" level. Indeed, Rogovin called for "an active state policy of redistribution," which sounded rather like a euphemism for expropriation of the well-to-do.[30]

Rogovin's vehemence may have been due to the fact that his article was, in part, a response to the economist Gennadii Lisichkin, who had previously attacked him in *Literaturnaia gazeta*.[31] Contributing to a series of articles which posed the question "Is It Shameful To Earn a Lot?," Lisichkin offered a spirited defense of enterprise and thrift, savaging Rogovin and other proponents of "an active state policy of redistribution." Lisichkin spoke of the need to "teach [people] how to make money" and praised "those healthy people who want not merely to receive more, but to earn more." Lisichkin's comments had a certain historical resonance: they brought to mind Stolypin's "wager on the strong"[32] and Bukharin's exhortation to the peasantry to "enrich yourselves."[33]

In any case, they clearly nettled Rogovin, who repeated them in support of his call for the creation of "a 'barrier psychology'" against "the carriers of an enterprising spirit far removed from socialism."[34] It would seem that such a psychology was already rather wide-spread in the Soviet Union, where, as the émigré writer Alexander Zinoviev stated, "prevention"--that is, the habit of dragging enterprising individuals down to "some average social level"--was "the main form of social struggle."[35] Ironically, Rogovin lent credibility to Zinoviev's theory; he quoted an office worker with "a modest lifestyle," who said of a prosperous former classmate, "I don't want to live like her; I want her to live like me." This, Rogovin claimed, "revealed a correct understanding . . . of the requirements of social justice."[36]   One might ask whether it was not precisely this attitude, and the official encouragement of it, which made the "restructuring" of Soviet society necessary in the first place.

The articles by Rogovin and Zaslavskaia confirmed that "social justice" occupied an important place in Gorbachev's overall strategy for the "restructuring" of Soviet society. The program they advanced for the achievement of "social justice" contained many new and even daring elements (*e.g.*, abolishing special privileges for the administrative elite, raising rents and food prices).   It also appeared to legitimize the suppression of enterprising people, and the expropriation of prosperous ones. In this sense, it was a wager on the weak, and seemed likely to guarantee political stability at the cost of economic progress.

17
EXPANSION OF THE COOPERATIVE SECTOR

Elizabeth Teague

At the Twenty-seventh Congress of the CPSU in February 1986, Gorbachev called for "a fresh look" at "certain theoretical concepts," including "socialist property and the economic forms of its implementation." Cooperative property, he asserted, had "far from exhausted its potential," and support must be given to the creation and development of cooperative enterprises, which should play a greater role in "the production and processing of goods; in housing, orchard and garden construction; and in the provision of consumer services and trade." Gorbachev followed this call for expansion of the cooperative sector with a denunciation of prejudice against "commodity-money relations," that is, nonstate economic activity. Market relations, he declared, should not be considered incompatible with socialism.[1]

Agricultural and Manufacturing Cooperatives. A new edition of the party program adopted at the Twenty-seventh Congress promised "further development" of the consumer cooperative system, which was called upon "to improve trade in the countryside and to organize the purchase from the population and the marketing of agricultural products." The collective farm market, the program added, "will retain its significance."[2]

Gorbachev raised the subject of manufacturing cooperatives in a speech delivered in July 1986 in Khabarovsk. Letters to the central authorities in Moscow, he said, showed there was wide popular support for a return to the system of manufacturing cooperatives, "which were eliminated in the fifties and sixties, evidently prematurely."[3] The topic was also discussed at a meeting of the Politburo on August 14. Manufacturing cooperatives should be created, it was reported, with the aim of "more fully satisfying popular demand for consumer goods, household wares, and various services by making use of local resources, secondary raw materials and waste materials." As a first step, the Politburo approved a government proposal "to set up cooperatives in a number of Union republics for the procurement and processing of secondary raw materials."[4]

Two Forms of Socialist Ownership. In his speech to the Twenty-seventh party Congress, Gorbachev lamented that there were many who saw "any change in the economic mechanism as a virtual abandonment of socialist principles."[5]

Having devoted the bulk of their energies to thinking about overthrowing the systems into which they were born, the founding fathers of Marxism-Leninism were notoriously vague about the new society they wished to create. Marx merely described the society that would follow the proletarian revolution as consisting of two stages--the "first" and "second," or "higher," phases of communism. He and Engels envisaged the new society as one of limitless material abundance without classes or private property, markets, prices or wages.

Lenin elaborated on this two-period scheme. Predicting *three* periods of development, Lenin distinguished "socialist" from "communist" society. First, he added a period of "building socialism" to designate the phase of transition from capitalism to socialism. Next, Lenin gave the name of "socialism" to Marx's "first phase of communism." Finally, he equated Marx's "higher phase" with true communism.[6]

The system that took shape under Stalin in the nineteen-thirties bore little relation to Marx's predictions. While private ownership of the means of production was eliminated in the Soviet Union, two distinct forms of ownership, "state" and "cooperative", coexisted within the framework of a single planned economy. Ordinary workers were employed and paid directly by the state. But, because the collective farms were organized as cooperatives that owned their own equipment and divided their incomes among their members, collective farm peasants were officially held to constitute a separate class.[7]

Soviet leaders inherited Marx's distrust of the peasantry, and traditionally viewed cooperative property as a lower form of social and economic organization than state property. The sooner the collective farm sector was merged into the state sector, it was assumed, the better, and the faster would be the transition to communism. The party program of 1961, adopted under Khrushchev's exuberant leadership, promised that the Soviet Union would reach full communism by the early nineteen-eighties. By that time, *kolkhoz* cooperative property would gradually have been transformed into "public property," and the peasants would themselves have voluntarily relinquished their private plots.[8]

By the late nineteen-sixties it was clear to Brezhnev and his colleagues that Khrushchev's promises could not be met, and party ideologists began to look for ways of explaining this to the population. Adapting some vague remarks of Lenin's,[9] they declared that the Soviet Union had reached the "qualitatively new" phase of "developed socialism"--said to be "a fully formed socialist society in which the main conditions have matured for the full-scale building of communism."[10] They stayed well clear, however, of rash predictions about when the "historically lengthy" period of developed socialism might give way to full communism. Utopia, in short, was indefinitely postponed.

Debate Over Policy Options Gets Under Way. As the long years of the Brezhnev leadership wore on, the USSR found itself facing serious and mounting difficulties. The decline in the rate of growth of national income that had plagued the economy for many years became increasingly acute, and was exacerbated by a succession of poor harvests. The population sank into apathy and depression.

Calls for a change of economic policy became louder and, behind the scenes, a debate began over the need for structural reform of the Soviet economy.

Much of this debate was conducted under the guise of an argument over what stage of "development" or "maturity" Soviet socialism had reached. The debate got under way well before Brezhnev's death and was clearly in evidence during the nationwide discussion of the new constitution in 1977. At that time, calls were made to speed up the progress toward communism. Proposals included the introduction of equal pay and pensions for all workers, regardless of length of service, skills, or qualifications. Calls were also made for the elimination, or at least the sharp reduction, of private plots. These and similar suggested amendments to the constitution were rejected, Brezhnev said, because they "run too far ahead, failing to realize that the new constitution is the Fundamental Law of a state that, although developed, is still socialist, and not communist."[11]

The dominant opinion during the late Brezhnev period was that of the "conservative" school, represented by Brezhnev himself and his close associate Konstantin Chernenko. They adopted a complacent attitude to the development of Soviet society which, they argued, was well along the road to the final goal of communism. To be sure, there were several areas needing improvement, but the party's policy was deemed basically correct and required no fundamental change.

"Integral Socialism" Enters the Fray. At the same time, a good deal of influence was wielded by a purist wing of opinion whose spokesman was Richard Kosolapov--chief editor of the journal *Kommunist* until early 1986. Kosolapov and his colleagues extolled the role of the working class and warned of the dangers of "exaggerating the significance of the intelligentsia" or of "idealizing the socio-moral foundations of rural life."[12] Bitterly opposed to any idea of decentralizing market-oriented reform for the economy, they warned that private plots represented a vestige of private enterprise and a potential threat to the socialist system, and they were appalled by proposals seeking to increase the role of private enterprise. But Kosolapov and his colleagues were by no means conservatives; they advocated a radical restructuring of Soviet society that would, by merging the collective farms into the state farm sector, "integrate" the peasantry into the working class and lead to the long-awaited establishment of a classless society.

Kosolapov called for the elimination of the "bifurcation" of society into two forms of ownership and two separate classes, and for the establishment of what he called an "economy of the whole people." He divided "developed socialism" into two substages. The first, he said, would see the merging of state and cooperative property into one; to this end, he persistently advocated the phasing out of the collective farm sector by means of the "industrialization" of agriculture.[13]

Then, said Kosolapov, the second and higher stage of developed socialism would begin. Borrowing a phrase from Marx, he spoke of the "integrity of socialism" to urge the elimination of all vestiges of the division of labor and the establishment of "full social homogeneity."[14] Later, he and party theoretician Petr Fedoseev began to use an obscure reference of Lenin's to "integral socialism" (*tselnyi sotsializm*) to denote the kind of collectivist society toward which they thought the Soviet Union should be moving.[15]

Kosolapov and his colleagues won an important victory in 1981 when, in his report to the Twenty-sixth Congress of the CPSU, Brezhnev stated that the Soviet Union would see the establishment of a classless society "within the historical framework of mature socialism."[16] Kosolapov interpreted this as a green light for the accelerated elimination of class and property differences.

The Advocates of Economic Reform Speak Up. At the same time, calls for modernization and restructuring of the Soviet economy were becoming more insistent. Those advocating economic reform were a loosely-knit group; though not without influence, many of them wielded little if any political power. They called for decentralization of state planning, the granting of greater decision-making powers to enterprises, and, to reward workers and managers who showed a flair for innovation and were not afraid to use initiative, wider wage differentials and greater use of material incentives. Pointing to the example of small-scale private enterprise in Hungary and East Germany, some reformers called for the extension of private agriculture and trade, citing with especial approval Lenin's introduction, in 1921, of the New Economic Policy (NEP)--Soviet Russia's experiment with a mixed economy.

In stark contrast to Kosolapov's call for the integration of Soviet society, the well-known sociologist Tatiana Zaslavskaia called for social and economic reforms to enable greater account to be taken of individual and group interests.[17] Such proposals met with impassioned opposition from Kosolapov. "Socialist society," he protested, "is a society of labor, not a consumer society!"[18]   Market-oriented reforms he denounced as "incautious commodity-monetary romanticism."[19] Even the very limited experiment introduced by Iurii Andropov, granting increased autonomy to enterprises in certain industries and regions, was too much for Kosolapov.[20] And he warned against the idea that concessions made to private farmers and traders during the NEP period could produce more than "tactical" results:

> But what happened when they were adopted uncritically, . . . when the specific nature of the socialist reorganization of society was slurred over and a lighter interpretation of its essence was given? The result was the strengthening of the contradictions of the transition period, of the "NEP" with all its consequences, and the hindering of social progress that this entailed.[21]

Among the most vocal advocates of expansion of the private sector was Anatolii Butenko of the Institute of Economics of the World Socialist System--the Moscow think-tank specializing in the study of Eastern Europe. In a series of articles published over a number of years, Butenko argued that the entire socialist formation (that is, both the earlier and the later "developed" stages) was characterized by the existence of two classes (the working class and the peasantry) and by both state and cooperative property. Moreover, he continued, commodity production and market relations--by which Butenko indicated he meant not just the sale by peasants of surplus vegetables from their private plots but also small-scale private trade by individual craftsmen--far from being alien to the nature of socialism and mere "vestiges of capitalism," as Kosolapov argued, were essential characteristics of it.[22]

<u>Andropov Enters the Debate</u>. During the struggle for the Brezhnev succession, culminating in 1982, Andropov advanced the thesis that the Soviet Union was only at the very beginning of the "developed socialist" phase and that substantial changes were necessary, particularly in the economy but also in the political sphere, before it could advance further.[23] Later, Andropov cautioned against "exaggerating the level of progress toward the higher stage of communism" and stated that the USSR faced "outstanding problems left over from yesterday," as well as "difficulties of growth." It would, he warned, "take some

time to draw up the straggling rear and forge ahead."[24]
Andropov's stress on the existing shortcomings of Soviet
society distanced him from both the "purists" and the
"conservatives," aligning him rather with the "reformers."
     The Polish Factor.   The Polish crisis of 1980-81
profoundly shook the confidence of the Soviet leadership in
the viability of their own social and economic system. The
different sides drew different conclusions. More pragmatic
leaders used the Polish events to underline the dangers
awaiting a system of government that appeared not to care
for the needs of the people. Kosolapov, on the other hand,
argued that Poland's toleration of "privately owned
agriculture" and a "capitalist sector" was a principal
cause of its social unrest; it was a historical
inevitability, he argued, that private commodity production
would be in conflict with socialist production. He
redoubled his calls for the merger of state and cooperative
property, the socialization of labor and the integration of
the economy.[25]
     Kosolapov rejected Butenko's arguments as "clearly
incompatible with the idea of developed socialism as a
social formation realizing its own integrity."[26] Since
communism would be classless and characterized by the
existence of only one form of property, and since the
foundations of communism must be built in the course of the
developed socialist phase, it stood to reason, Kosolapov
argued, that socialism must already be tending in that
direction.
     The Tide Turns.   After Brezhnev's death, there were
indications that Kosolapov was losing the battle. Writing
in the summer of 1984, Fedor Burlatskii, one of the most
outspoken advocates of political and economic reform,
defended Butenko's thesis that socialism was characterized
by both state and cooperative property and stated:

> The notion that there are "higher" and "lower" forms
> of ownership and that forms of ownership such as
> cooperative property must gradually be transformed
> into state property has recently been overcome.[27]

     Writing at about the same time, Vladimir Dmitrenko of
the Institute of History commented that, in the past,
progress had mistakenly been seen as a matter merely of
"eliminating the birth marks of capitalism, . . . by
restricting market relations, turning collective farms into
state farms, and liquidating manufacturing cooperatives."[28]

Kosolapov did not go down without a fight. Writing in *Pravda* the following month, he complained that "the socialization of labor and production" was being "pushed to one side" and advocated, once again, the "transformation of agricultural labor into a variety of industrial labor."[29] The concept of integral socialism was even included in the draft of the party program published in October, 1985,[30] but was shot down during the public debate that preceded the program's adoption at the Twenty-seventh party Congress in the spring of 1986. Its opponents pointed out that Lenin had described integral socialism as a society that would be built "by the revolutionary collaboration of the proletarians of all countries."[31] The concept therefore had international connotations that rendered it unsuitable to describe *internal* Soviet developments. It was dropped from the party program without further explanation and was not heard of again.

Kosolapov suffered a similar fate. He was not reelected to membership of the Central Committee at the party congress in March 1986, and his post as chief editor of *Kommunist* was soon thereafter assigned to a new appointee. In July, the activity of the journal was extensively discussed by the Politburo, which "pointed to the need for changing the forms and methods of the journal's work."[32] Finally, the Gorbachev leadership abandoned the whole concept of developed socialism. It had, in Gorbachev's words, become bogged down in "bookish pedantry and playing with definitions."[33]

18
APPROACHING THE ECOLOGICAL BARRIER*

Vladimir Sobell

Poor Environmental Record. East European propaganda and theoretical writings maintained that environmental abuse was yet another inherent flaw of capitalism and that the socialist, centrally planned economic system guaranteed that such abuse would not occur. These claims were mainly based on the notion that only the centrally planned systems

---

*For details on individual countries, see RAD Background Report 42, "The Environment and Eastern Europe."

could act in the interests of society as a whole (interests that included environmental conservation), whereas individual firms were said to pursue their own narrow self-interests under capitalism. An objective verdict on the relative damage inflicted under the two types of systems to the environment is hard to make, for there were, unfortunately, plenty of examples of ecological disasters in both communist and noncommunist countries to be considered.

Whatever the exact balance, however, there was clearly little to support the claim that the communist economies had a vastly better record on environmental issues. One Western study of the Soviet Union concluded that: "There can be no question of the Soviet economic order's being structurally superior to market economies in combating ecological problems."[1] Another author concluded that "the degree of environmental pollution in the major industrial centers [in the USSR] is certainly approaching that of the industrial regions of Western Europe and North America, although the overall level of pollution [in the USSR] is lower."[2] It should be added that the extent of environmental damage to the European parts of the Soviet bloc, especially in Czechoslovakia and the GDR, was nothing short of catastrophic, both by Eastern and Western standards.[3]

The East European claims to a superior environmental record were flawed on another account. A comparison between the industries of Western and Eastern Europe suggested that the latter used significantly more fuel and and raw material than did the Western manufacturing industries per unit of production; moreover, this inefficiency was no accident but was imbedded deeply in the centrally planned system.[4] The corollary was that the industries of the CMEA could achieve the same production levels while causing less pollution if they operated according to Western-style, market-based systems and did not pursue a Soviet model of industrialization. Viewed from a different angle, it could be argued that the Western economies at least obtained "value for pollution" by being less wasteful and more consumer-oriented than their Eastern counterparts, thereby securing a generally higher standard of living than would have accompanied comparable pollution levels if generated by centrally planned economic activity. Eastern economies brought disproportionately small benefits to the citizen for the level of pollution created.

Little Awareness of the Ecology. In fact a closer look at the way in which both systems functioned suggested that communism was worse rather than better equipped to protect the environment. The central planners may theoretically have been better placed to command protection, but in practice, environmental considerations figured little in their plans. When the production requirements clashed with those of environmental protection, as they often did, it was the former that usually took precedence. In this way the planners behaved just as the "selfish capitalists" they condemned.[5]

The difference was that as capitalism tended to go hand in hand with an open and democratic society, information on ecological damage was more difficult to suppress, independent environmental pressure groups could openly protest, and there was room for a constructive relationship between the electorate and the lawmakers. Under these circumstances the profit motive was less able to wreak havoc, being more answerable to common interests.

In the East, the societies were more closed. The citizen was able to voice environmental concern so long as it posed no real challenge to those with a vested interest in the status quo. Environmental "protest" was by and large restricted to officially sponsored organizations; independent activity in this field was generally treated as harshly as any other form of dissent. The media did publish a good deal of information on the issue, but such coverage was subjected to far greater state control than pollution itself. Under no circumstances was blame allowed to be attached to those in high places. Not that there was no legislation to protect the environment; there was, but it profited no authority to see that it was implemented. On the contrary, it was usually in the interests of those highly placed to turn a blind eye to any transgression. And there was no way for the ordinary citizen to ensure that the rules were not ignored in this way, or that exemption after exemption was not granted in the name of plan fulfillment. In short, in Eastern Europe the state was both polluter and protector, and there was consequently little incentive for environmental concerns to be promoted over industrial ones.

The "Ecological Barrier". Does this mean that there were no checks at all on environmental damage in Eastern Europe? How far were the CMEA states prepared to go before acting against pollution? The answer was, unfortunately, very far indeed, given the lack of incentive for planners to slow down production for environmental reasons. But the Soviet-type economic leviathans were plodding toward a point at which the waste exuded began to impede their own industrial progress. The "ecological barrier" loomed; that point at which any advantages to be gained by a small increase in production (along the lines of the current output mix) would be outweighed by the inordinately great damage caused to the environment, the health of the population, and to the economy itself.

It is impossible to determine precisely where such a barrier lies. The criteria for judging the critical point vary according to one's point of view; they are different for the citizen living in the shadow of a large industrial plant and for a government official in some remote office. However, there is a point at which the damage wrought poses a threat to further economic growth itself. That point might be reached when the population in an economically vital and badly affected area begins to migrate and a labor shortage results; or when forests cease to regenerate; or when agricultural land cannot absorb any more chemical fertilizers.

Learning Slowly. There were many signs that the CMEA countries, and especially the worst polluters among them (the GDR and Czechoslovakia) were about to reach this ecological barrier. So costly had the additional disruption of new growth in production become, due to the damage inflicted on the ecological balance by industrial pollution, that the regimes were forced to take environmental factors into account. The Czechoslovak government at long last embarked upon a long-term program of ecological rehabilitation, and increased concern was also shown by the East German and other East European regimes.[6] For example, the issue figured unprecedentedly high on the agenda at the Eleventh SED Congress in March 1986. Both countries also became more responsive to international pressure and signed agreements obliging them to reduce emissions of sulfur dioxide by 30 percent by 1993 (taking 1980 as the base year).

Despite the heightened concern and the evidence of greater resolve in dealing with the pollution, it would have been unrealistic to expect any major improvement in the short term. The ecological barrier may have been imminent--it may in some areas even have been reached--but time was needed for its educative effect to prod the East European regimes into changing their course. To have perceived and indirectly acknowledged the existence of such a barrier was no more than the first step toward effective change. A period commenced in which the regimes and their planners were likely to be made increasingly aware of the folly of disregarding the environment. Unfortunately, the systemic deficiencies of communism made this learning process a longer one in Eastern Europe than in the West. Things might have to get even more painful and more costly in economic and human terms before a real change of heart could occur.

19
LOW TARGETS AND LOW GROWTH

Philip Hanson

Soviet industrial output in the first four months of 1987 was reported to have been 2.8 percent higher than in the same period in 1986.   There was some improvement in May, so that the corresponding figure for the period January-May was given as being 3 percent.[1] That was a very modest performance in view of the annual plan target for industry in 1987 of a 4.4 percent increase and actual reported growth in 1986 of 4.9 percent.[2] And the real growth of industrial output was probably slower than the official total indicated.

What happened? Gorbachev's acceleration program really seemed to be working during 1986.   Had the engine cut out while the planners were still stepping on the gas? Or had they slowed down deliberately to negotiate a particularly tight bend in the road? Or was something else going on that would overextend this motoring analogy?

The official explanation, given in earlier reports in 1987 by the Central Statistical Administration, stressed two factors. First, unusually severe winter weather caused some setbacks. Second, there was large-scale rejection of output under the newly strengthened quality control system. The report for April said merely that some of the earlier retardation had been made up but that various shortcomings continued, particularly in the engineering sector.

There were some signs suggesting a deliberate, temporary slowdown. The monthly reports showed percentage plan fulfillment as well as percentage change from the same period of the previous year. From the first it was possible to work out what the plan targets were. For the items publicly reported in physical terms, the apparent targets for January-April were generally low. In nine out of 38 cases, output was planned to fall. In several of these cases, the planned reductions were substantial. There were eight items whose output fell.

The reductions in output were heavily concentrated in the engineering sector (including consumer durables). Most of the engineering-sector reductions were planned--or so the plan report figures indicated. The evidence, therefore, was of a more or less planned cut in the reported output of a number of engineering products. The question is why such a cut should have been planned.

The intention seems to have been to make only very short-term cuts in output. The published plan for 1987 provided few details, but it did call for a 7.3 percent increase in total engineering output, with faster growth (at an unspecified rate) for machine tools and computer equipment. The growth in the output of those engineering products for which data were published was clearly well below that rate. Indeed, the total of what might be called "published engineering output" in the first four months of 1987 was probably below the level of January-April, 1986. Such a cutback was apparently not planned to last much longer.

Three possible explanations could be advanced. First, there could have been an abrupt shift of resources from civilian products, the output of which was reported, to military products, the output of which was kept secret. This interpretation is plausible because a number of the items, the output of which was planned to fall, were produced in part as a sideline by military plants. The trouble with this explanation is that military production is believed to have been included in the reported total of industrial output, and that total was also growing slowly.

Second, the effects of the new quality-control regime on total officially acceptable output were at least partly anticipated. The plans for the first few months of the year were therefore set low to allow for a sharp but short-lived fall.

Third, the plan targets implied in the monthly reports had been adjusted down as problems arose. In other words, they were not real plan targets at all. That would be in line with the general character of Soviet planning in the past.

The second and third explanations are more likely than the first. If the second explanation was correct, the leadership was managing to plan with some flexibility to accommodate the effects of organizational changes. Nonetheless, the high targets for 1987 as a whole--not to mention the high targets for the whole five-year plan--still indicated a conflict between an old-fashioned push for growth through pressure from above and a reform approach that would require the setting of slack targets to allow more scope for initiative on the part of enterprises. There was even a conflict between high annual targets and the centrally imposed quality control arrangements that began in 1987; it is doubtful whether a few months would have been enough to enable radical adjustments to product quality to be made. If the third interpretation were correct, the leadership would have been making no progress at all in tightening planning procedures.

NEW THINKING ON SECURITY

20
SOURCES OF SECURITY RECONSIDERED

*Charles Glickham**

In the opening moments of his Political Report to the Twenty-seventh Congress of the CPSU, Mikhail Gorbachev noted:

> A turning point has arisen not only in internal but also in external affairs. The changes in the development of the contemporary world are so profound and significant that they require a rethinking and comprehensive analysis of all its factors. The situation of nuclear confrontation calls for new approaches, methods, and forms of relations between different social systems, states, and regions.[1]

"New Political Thinking". Gorbachev brought a renewed sense of vigor and dynamism to the conduct of foreign policy. Numerous acts bore witness to this dynamism: the unilateral moratorium on nuclear explosions, official expressions of willingness to consider on-site inspections as a means of verifying various arms-control agreements, the announced withdrawal of a limited number of Soviet troops from Afghanistan, and the apparent concession on the demarcation of the Sino-Soviet border along the Amur River. Soviet spokesmen referred to these and other initiatives, as manifestations of "new political thinking."

Two major policy statements from the top leadership provided the key to understanding this new thinking-- Gorbachev's report to the Twenty-seventh Congress of the CPSU and an article by Anatolii Dobrynin published

*The author would like to thank Elizabeth Teague and Martha Snodgrass for their helpful comments and suggestions.

in *Kommunist* in June 1986. While Gorbachev's speech presented no details of the "new political thinking," it did include several innovative statements on foreign policy and security issues:

1. a recognition of the existence of "global problems" that could only be resolved by "cooperation on a world-wide scale";

2. a new--and surprising--stress on the inter-dependence of states;

3. the elaboration of a set of "principled considerations" derived from an examination of the present world situation;

4. a recognition that if the nuclear arms race were to continue, "even parity will cease to be a factor of military-political restraint"; and

5. a harsh condemnation of the rigidity of previous Soviet foreign policy.

The statement on global problems--that is, those problems whose resolution required some degree of international cooperation--was brief but nonetheless suggestive of the attention that such problems were receiving at high levels.
Gorbachev noted that

> The real dialectics of contemporary development are [to be found] in the combination of competition and confrontation between the two systems and in the growing tendency toward interdependence of the states of the world community. This is precisely how...a contradictory but interdependent and, in many respects, integral world is taking shape.[2]

Gorbachev broke with tradition by emphasizing interdependence. He further elaborated on a set of "principled considerations" which he said were drawn from a discussion of the nuclear threat conducted at the CPSU Central Committee plenum in April 1985:[3]

1. Defense by military-technical means alone was not possible. Ensuring national security was increasingly becoming a political task.

2. In the context of US-Soviet relations, security could only be maintained if it was mutual.

3. While the United States remained "the locomotive of militarism," it was important to recognize that it had "genuine national interests" that were not the same as those pursued by the "military-industrial complex."

4. The world was a dynamic place, in which no "eternal" status quo could be preserved.[4]

Gorbachev noted the decreasing efficacy of parity as "a factor of military-political restraint,"[5] thus reinforcing the impression that the Soviet leadership was reconsidering how best to ensure national security specifically in an age of strategic nuclear parity. Distancing himself from Brezhnev's policies, Gorbachev seemed to be searching for a more perceptive and effective foreign policy with which to enter the nineteen-nineties:

> Of course, it is not possible to solve the problem of international security with one or two peace offensives, even very intensive ones. Only consistent, systematic, and persistent work can lead to success. . . .Firmness in defending principles and positions, tactical flexibility, and a readiness for mutually acceptable compromise are needed--the aim being not confrontation, but dialogue and mutual understanding.[6]

The article by Dobrynin, placed prominently in *Kommunist*, was more explicit and frank in outlining six basic principles of "the new political thinking":

1. The "interdependence of survival" had acquired "cardinal significance" in the nuclear age;

2. The level of military confrontation had to be lowered, while observing the principle of "equality and equal security"[7];

3. Security through military-technical means alone was impossible;

4. The concepts of national and international security had become "indivisible," and therefore

security for the US and the USSR could only be
mutual;

5. There was a need for a "qualitatively higher
level of flexibility in foreign policy [and] a
readiness   to   move   toward   reasonable
compromises"; and

6. The resolution of problems of international
security required a   multi-faceted   approach,
containing military, economic, political, and
humanitarian elements.[8]

Although Dobrynin essentially reiterated that which
Gorbachev first laid out in his address to the party
congress, there were two interesting aspects to his
article.   The first was his call for scientists and
academics to conduct more research on military-political
problems and for more scientific analysis of "the technical
aspects" of the verification of arms-control agreements and
of the destruction of nuclear and chemical weapons.[9]
Dobrynin   proceeded to make an even more   intriguing
proposal, calling on scientists to join scholars of world
politics and economics in order to study and elaborate "the
particulars of transferring the military economy to the
rails of civilian production."[10]

"The new political thinking" yielded three basic
components. The first was a revitalization of foreign
policy by means of both explicit rejection of certain
aspects of previous policy under Brezhnev, and appeals for
flexibility in the implementation of foreign policy.   The
second was the placement of at least two innovative
concepts--global   problems and interdependence--on   the
agenda of the top leadership.   The third was an apparent
reevaluation,   at the highest level, of the sources of
national security. Three of the conclusions produced by
this reevaluation were:

1. Parity would soon cease to be a factor of
political-military restraint.

2. National and international security had become
indivisible.

3. A multifaceted approach to problems of international security had to be employed. (This
last point seemed to suggest that, in the past,

the USSR had relied too heavily on the military factor alone in its foreign policy.)

The Genesis of the "New Political Thinking".   A comparison of Gorbachev's speech at the Twenty-seventh Congress of the CPSU with Brezhnev's speech at the party congress five years earlier and a brief survey of Soviet academic writing on foreign affairs since 1981 established two facts. With respect to programmatic party documents, several of Gorbachev's statements on foreign and security policy were unprecedented. Second, virtually all the ideas expressed by Gorbachev were being studied at academic levels in the period between 1981 and 1986.[11]

The foreign-policy sections of Gorbachev's and Brezhnev's respective reports differed in style as well as substance. In their presentation, Brezhnev's remarks had gone into great detail on specific countries (particularly in the discussion of the Third World) and fell into five sections. Gorbachev had less to say about specific countries (with the exception of the United States and China) and did not subdivide the foreign policy section of his report.[12]

While Brezhnev had clearly seen many difficulties and complexities in the world situation, his view of the operation of Soviet foreign policy in the world was a complacent one. Missing was a sense of urgency implicit--and at times explicit--in Gorbachev's analysis of the world and Soviet foreign relations.

More important for the purpose of this discussion were the facts that there had been no passages in Brezhnev's speech analogous to Gorbachev's remarks on interdependence, parity, and global problems and that Gorbachev, unlike Brezhnev, omitted any reference to "equality and equal security." In contrast with Gorbachev's prediction that even parity could soon cease to be a factor of military-political restraint, Brezhnev had noted that the existing equilibrium between the USSR and the United States "objectively serves the maintenance of peace on our planet."[13] When discussing issues such as conservation of natural resources, issues Gorbachev labeled "global problems," Brezhnev had used other terms.[14] Where Gorbachev avoided the phrase "equality and equal security" in his discussion of arms control, Brezhnev had noted that negotiations could be conducted only on the basis of this principle.[15] In sum, the two men, speaking five years apart, projected world views that, while having much in common, clearly diverged in their evaluation of some important precepts of foreign policy as practiced under Brezhnev.[16]

If a comparison of the 1981 and 1986 party congresses lends itself to highlighting discontinuity in the leadership's treatment of certain foreign and security policy issues, a brief survey of academic writing in the early nineteen-eighties on the same issues can be used to document a continuity of ideas--in this case from the theoretical analysis of scholars to the policy statements of party leaders. A good example of an academic analysis which clearly foreshadowed Gorbachev's innovative statements on security issues was the book *Novoe myshlenie v iadernyi vek* [New Thinking in the Nuclear Age], written by Anatolii Gromyko and Vladimir Lomeiko and published in 1984.[17] Not only did its title sound similar to "the new political thinking" of Gorbachev; its last three chapters contained an analysis of interdependence and security issues similar to those he advanced at the party congress. The authors had asserted confidently that, given the realities of the nuclear era, "no social system" could ignore another country's vital interests, adding that security could only be mutual. They seemed less confident, however, on the topic of interdependence. "The growing interdependence of our world" was presented as an idea of Western scholars; while the authors did not challenge the idea, they also did not forthrightly endorse it.

Evidence that analyses like those of Gromyko and Lomeiko were being considered at higher levels as early as 1984, can be found in an article in *Voprosy filosofii* of May of that year.[18] Entitled "The Logic of Political Thinking in the Nuclear Era," the article had been written by G. Shakhnazarov, one of four deputies to the head of the Central Committee's Department for Liaison with Communist and Workers' Parties of Socialist Countries for many years. Shakhnazarov, described as one of the more reform-minded ideologists in the Central Committee apparatus,[19] discussed many of the issues raised by Gromyko and Lomeiko and came to similar conclusions.[20] He noted that a "formal interdependence" of security had arisen in the nuclear age and that security could only be collective.[21] He gave his analysis a tentative flavor, however, by noting in the penultimate paragraph, that it made use of "a general system that had been designated conditionally 'the logic of political thinking in the nuclear age.'"[22]

Because the term "new political thinking" suggested that "global problems" transcended class and economic rivalries and that their solution required a nonclass approach, it was an ideologically divisive term. Furthermore, once the existence of global problems was admitted, ideological rivals like the United States and the Soviet Union logically had to work together to solve them.[23]

Increasing attention had been devoted to such problems in academic and official circles in the years prior to 1986. Writing in the lead article in *Voprosy filosofii* for September 1983, G. L. Smirnov, then Director of the USSR Academy of Sciences' Institute of Philosophy and later rumored to be an advisor to Gorbachev, noted the tremendous impact of so-called global problems on the fate of mankind, urging that they be studied further and explained "to the broad masses of working people."[24]   Later, Fedor Burlatskii, head of the philosophy department in the CPSU Central Committee's Institute of Social Sciences and a well-known political maverick, began an article with the orthodox claim that the "social-class" criterion was still the main one through which to view the contemporary world but proceeded with an extensive discussion of global problems, which he said could only be solved by the "joint efforts" of the entire world community—taking, in other words, a "nonclass" approach.[25]

In February 1986, Vadim Zagladin, first deputy head of the International Department of the CPSU Central committee, contributed the lead article in *Voprosy filosofii*.[26] Entitled "The Programmatic Goals of the CPSU and Global Problems," the article provided a definitive and, given Zagladin's position, authoritative treatment of the issue of global problems. Despite their inclusion in the new party program, Zagladin used the phrase "global problems" cautiously—in his statement, for example, that as an initial thesis for further discussion, it could be argued that global problems constituted "a kind of unified system."[27] Perhaps he remained noncommittal about the validity of the concept, because the first page of his article identified prevention of nuclear war as a global problem.[28] At any rate, Gorbachev did not include the prevention of nuclear war among the global problems mentioned in his report to the party congress.[29] In one other respect Zagladin appeared to break new ground: in his statement that global problems were a manifestation of "the growing interdependence of states."[30]

Thus Gorbachev's "new political thinking" had a history. The ideas were not his own, nor were they spontaneous, untested dreams. More important, such thinking appeared to have acquired a constituency, in academic circles and perhaps within the Central Committee apparatus, before Gorbachev presented his version of it at the party congress in February 1986.

Flexibility. Gorbachev's words produced deeds: major organizational changes occurred in both the Foreign Ministry[31] and the Central Committee's International Department. Particularly significant was the creation of a Directorate for Arms Control and Disarmament, headed by veteran arms-control negotiator Viktor Karpov and entrusted with broad oversight over all arms-control talks.[32] Previously, such oversight had not been centralized in any one department within the ministry.

The organizational change within the Central Committee's International Department had potentially more far-reaching implications. It involved the formation of an arms-control sector, headed by Major General Viktor Starodubov.[33] Among the responsibilities of this new sector was oversight of the technical and military aspects of all arms-control agreements.[34]

The effect of these organizational changes, Andrei Gromyko's removal from the post of foreign minister, and Dobrynin's appointment to head the International Department, had been to shift the locus of foreign policy decision-making away from the Foreign Ministry and into the Central Committee. In addition, these changes provided both the state and the party with a more streamlined decision-making apparatus, particularly in the all-important area of arms control. With the creation of a more effective central apparatus, an initial step toward flexibility had been taken.

Innovative Ideas. Gorbachev was successful in demoting, retiring, or otherwise removing from office some of the leading representatives of the old-style thinking, such as Gromyko (the former foreign minister, made chairman of the Presidium of the Supreme Soviet), Boris Ponomarev (the former head of the Central Committee's International Department), Konstantin Rusakov (the former head of the Central Committee's Department for Liaison with Communist and Workers' Parties of the Socialist Countries), and Andrei Aleksandrov-Agentov, (for many years an adviser on security issues attached to the general secretary's personal staff).

At lower levels, those disposed to "new" ways of thinking were moved into more responsible posts. Among them, Vladimir Petrovskii, one of the nine deputy foreign ministers from May 1986 on,[35] played a prominent role in articulating Soviet foreign and arms control policy in various forums.[36]

Petrovskii was an unusual combination of an academic and bureaucrat who in the summers of 1984-1986 had contributed to leading academic journals on foreign policy.[37] In a later article, in the issue of *MEMO* for June, 1986, he presented an analysis quite consonant with the views on foreign and security policy articulated by Gorbachev. In the past, he had written under a pseudonym in the central press on nonproliferation issues,[38] and presented what could be called a "soft-line" view. In the period prior to the conference in 1985 to review the Nuclear Nonproliferation Treaty, when there had been a dispute within the Foreign Ministry over whether to continue the pattern of cooperation with the United States on nonproliferation issues established in the past, Petrovskii was known to have sided with those favoring such cooperation.

Another rising man was Evgenii Primakov. The director of the USSR Academy of Sciences' Institute of Oriental Studies for many years, he had been promoted in 1986 to head the Academy's Institute for the World Economy and International Relations (IMEMO).[39] After he accompanied the Soviet delegation to the US-USSR summit in the fall of 1986, reports began to appear in the Western press describing Primakov as a close adviser to Gorbachev on international affairs.[40] A month before the party congress, Primakov published an article in *Pravda* foreshadowing Gorbachev's innovative statements on foreign and security policy. Ten days after the party congress, Primakov again contributed an extensive article to *Pravda* on the ideas articulated by Gorbachev at the congress,[41] which he referred to as "the philosophy of security."

In broaching certain sensitive topics, Gorbachev—unlike Khrushchev—was thus in no sense propagating "hare-brained schemes." His new thinking had a history, and it had advocates.

The Sources of National Security. A re-examination of the sources of national security included an increase of emphasis on the arms control process as a means to regulate the costs and risks of the military competition with the United States. There were also indications of a move away from heavy reliance on the military factor in foreign policy.

In 1985, there was a striking change in the attitude toward verification of arms control agreements. Gorbachev himself voiced some of the most important modifications of the Soviet position.[42] The difference concerned two issues: on-site inspections and the question of when, in the negotiating process, to address issues of verification.

Previously, Soviet spokesmen and negotiators had for the most part scoffed at the idea that on-site inspection could serve any useful purpose; instead, they accorded absolute priority to "national technical means" (satellites and electronic listening posts) in the verification of arms-control treaties.[43] Only later did the USSR express its willingness to consider on-site inspections.[44] It accepted them in the accord reached at the Stockholm Conference on Disarmament in Europe.[45]

In the past, Soviet spokesmen had insisted that verification procedures be considered only when an "unambiguous mutual understanding" on the basic content of an arms control agreement had been reached.[46] In March 1986, Gorbachev stated that, in the context of negotiations for a ban on nuclear explosions, verification issues could be addressed "from the very start of the negotiations."[47] Ten days later, his statement was echoed by Deputy Minister of Defense Vitalii Shabanov in an important article in *Izvestiia*.[48] These statements foreshadowed a substantive change in Soviet negotiating policy at the Nuclear and Space Arms talks in Geneva.[49]

The creation of a special sector for arms control within the Central Committee's International Department was an even stronger indication of change in attitudes toward arms control. The appointment of General Starodubov gave the civilian leadership access to more information on the technical aspects of arms control and, if so desired, greater flexibility in seeking arms-control agreements.

The importance of the military factor in Soviet foreign policy was often blurred by two mistaken ideas about the relationship between the civilian leadership and the military. The latter was neither completely subordinate to the political leadership, nor in any sense an autonomous political force.[50] If it enjoyed some independence in developing its strategy and tactics, this was lost when it came to the broader questions of national security, such as that of resource allocation to the military. While any change in resource allocation policy would most likely have been justified by the civilian leadership on economic grounds, it could also have provided an opportunity to advance what Gorbachev called a "multifaceted" approach to questions of international security--by way of signaling that the military factor in foreign policy would thenceforth be accorded a less central role. In this context, a connection could be postulated between, on the one hand, Gorbachev's domestic priorities and his statements about national security and, on the other, a change in official pronouncements on military allocations.

Traditionally, a highly ritualistic phrase was employed in speeches by officials, both military and civilian, on important occasions such as party congresses, Armed Forces Day, or Revolution Day to describe the party's commitment to provide resources to the military: "Everything necessary to reliably defend" the Soviet homeland was made available to the armed forces.[51] In the 1986 edition of the party program, however, it was declared that the armed forces were maintained "at the level that excludes strategic superiority by the forces of imperialism."[52] Defense Minister Sokolov used this formulation in his speech to the party congress, and it was used on several occasions--by Deputy Defense Minister Shabanov, in a lengthy article in *Krasnaia zvezda*, for example.[53]

The main difference between the two phrases was that the new one seemed to imply a discreet limit on the resources allocated to the military.

At the very least, official introduction of the new phrase at a time when Gorbachev was calling for a "multifaceted" approach to foreign policy and security issues--an approach including economic, political, and humanitarian elements--indicated that the role of the military in Soviet foreign policy was under review.

Conclusions. Three conclusions emerge from the foregoing analysis. First, the leaders began to talk about security and other global issues in a way qualitatively different from that of their predecessors. They seemed more concerned with attaining practical results than with maintaining ideological propriety.

Second, the "new political thinking" was only new for the top political leadership. It had already been elaborated in academic circles, and had gradually gained advocates at various levels.

The third point involves the correlation between words and deeds. Changes were occurring in several important areas, including organizational structures, personnel appointments, arms control, and the military. The articulation of Gorbachev's new ideas was not simply an attempt to gain a propaganda victory at home and abroad. While the propaganda component was certainly present, it went hand in hand with a desire, on the part of the Soviet leadership, for a more perceptive and effective foreign policy with which to enter the nineteen-nineties.

In early May 1986, a major conference at the Ministry of Foreign Affairs was the setting for some frank and unusually forceful remarks by Gorbachev. The conference, attended by Foreign Minister Shevardnadze and Central Committee Secretaries Dobrynin, Medvedev, and Iakovlev, addressed "The Tasks of the Central Apparatus and the Institutions of the USSR Foreign Ministry Abroad in Implementing the Decisions of the Twenty-seventh Congress of the CPSU in the Field of Foreign Policy."[54] Gorbachev delivered a speech that, according to reliable diplomatic sources in Moscow, stressed three points: 1) there was a growing interdependence in the world; 2) the Soviet leadership considered its arms control proposals to be serious ones and demanded flexibility from its negotiators; and 3) the Foreign Ministry would not be immune to the ongoing campaign against corruption.

21
THE REYKJAVIK WATERSHED

Bohdan Nahaylo

From the time it was announced on September 30, 1986, that a US-Soviet summit meeting would be held in Reykjavik, Moscow was quite clear on what it was seeking from the talks. As a precondition for a visit by Gorbachev to the United States, the Kremlin wished to obtain assurances of the Reagan administration's willingness to break the existing deadlock in arms control. It stressed that the meeting had been proposed by Moscow and depicted the proposal as yet another Soviet peace initiative.

Soviet spokesmen emphasized that Moscow wanted the Reykjavik meeting to deal primarily, though not exclusively, with arms control issues. According to the Soviet media, the Reykjavik meeting was to give the entire US-Soviet arms control process a jolt in the hope that the impasse could be overcome.

For a week after the summit, Moscow was clarifying, justifying, and promoting the stance it had assumed. Gorbachev appeared on television to expound on the state of US-Soviet relations and the prospects for ending the arms race in the light of what happened at Reykjavik.[1] The message was that Moscow was anxious to pursue the US-Soviet dialogue and, was ready to make bold compromises on nuclear disarmament, but that the Reagan administration's Strategic Defense Initiative (SDI) remained a stumbling block.

Gorbachev's statements gave a fuller picture of the manner in which the Kremlin had approached the summit. While, beforehand, Soviet spokesmen had played down expectations of what could be achieved, and had been careful to describe the forthcoming talks as a "preparatory" or "working" meeting between the two leaders, and not a real summit as such, elaborate preparations were being made behind the scenes to ensure that the meeting would become something more than a "working meeting" and that the American side would be put on the spot. In his speech on Soviet television on October 14, Gorbachev disclosed that

> We, the Soviet leadership, carried out extensive preparatory work ahead of the meeting, even before we received President Reagan's agreement to attend. Taking part in this work, apart from the Politburo and the Secretariat of the CPSU Central Committee, were the Ministry of Foreign Affairs and the Defense Ministry, other organizations, representatives of science, military experts, and specialists from various branches of industry.[2]

This "preparation" evidently entailed a major reevaluation of Soviet positions on arms control and disarmament issues. As Gorbachev said in the same speech, "we freed ourselves from obstructions that had formed, from petty things, from stereotypes that fettered new approaches in that important area of our politics."[3] As a result, the Soviet leader was able to take a package of important new proposals and concessions with him to Iceland . He later stressed this, and claimed that the American representatives "came to the meeting unprepared" and "with the same old baggage," while the Soviet team came "with constructive arms reduction proposals that are the most radical in the entire history of US-Soviet negotiations."[4]

The offers and compromises that Gorbachev made in Reykjavik were certainly a bold departure from the former rigid negotiating position. They included a proposal to reduce all strategic arms by half; an accord on the complete elimination of American and Soviet intermediate-range missiles in Europe (the deal not being dependent on the inclusion of British and French nuclear arsenals), which, as Gorbachev himself admitted, amounted in effect to an acceptance of President Reagan's earlier "zero option" proposal[5]; and agreement on a radical reduction in the number of Soviet intermediate-range missiles deployed in Asia.

Nevertheless, Moscow backtracked on the cardinal issue of SDI. At the November 1985 US-Soviet summit in Geneva, Gorbachev had introduced an element of flexibility into the Soviet stance precisely by appearing to waive the Kremlin's precondition for progress in the arms control process--the abandonment of SDI.[6] Until the Reykjavik summit, Moscow had been voicing opposition to SDI but had made it clear that it was nevertheless prepared to work toward reaching agreements with Washington in other areas of arms control and disarmament. At Reykjavik, however, Gorbachev again insisted that unless the Reagan administration gave way on SDI, the Kremlin would not sign any agreement on reducing numbers of long-range and intermediate-range weapons.

In his speech of October 22, Gorbachev specified that all the proposals and concessions offered at Reykjavik were part of an "integrated package" including provisions for the scuttling of SDI. "No package," he explained, "no concessions."[7] On the same day, military spokesman Colonel General Nikolai Chervov told his Swedish hosts that "the question is either SDI or arms control, because there is no way to have both."[8]

SDI thus once again became the central focus of Soviet public diplomacy. Gorbachev depicted it as "a question of principle, a question of our national security,"[9] and "the main obstacle to a nuclear-free world."[10] In calling on peace forces throughout the world to redouble their efforts, he was in effect urging them to concentrate on opposing SDI. Interestingly enough, after the Reykjavik summit, relatively little attention was paid by Gorbachev and the media to a total ban on nuclear weapons testing. Previously, this issue had been accorded even more weight by the Kremlin than SDI, but the emphasis seemed to shift.

Significantly, Gorbachev's speech of October 22 had a slightly defensive ring to it. Indeed, the fact that he decided to make a second nationally televised speech on the summit so soon after the first, was in itself intriguing. The explanation offered was that the meeting had led to "a new regrouping of forces in the camp of the enemies of disarmament and détente," and that consequently, "feverish efforts are being made to put up obstacles to check the process set in motion at Reykjavik." In particular, he charged that "quarters linked with militarism" were organizing a media campaign to sabotage the disarmament process.[11]

To judge from Gorbachev's speech, several things seem to have irked the Kremlin. Moscow resented the fact that the Reagan administration was claiming some credit for progress made in Reykjavik. From Gorbachev's two televised speeches on the summit, it would appear that only the Soviet side was prepared to make concessions and come up with new proposals. On the issue of SDI, Gorbachev castigated those who had rallied to its defense and blamed Moscow for the failure of the Reykjavik summit, charging that they claimed that the Soviet demand that SDI be renounced, was presented in the form of an ultimatum. Furthermore, Gorbachev expressed his frustration with West European leaders who had expressed concern about the implications of some of the accords initially reached in Reykjavik. He claimed that "what was being thoroughly disguised previously, is now becoming more clear: in US and West European ruling circles, there are powerful forces that seek to frustrate the process of nuclear disarmament." He also referred to those who were again asserting "that nuclear weapons are almost a boon."[12]

Moscow described the Reykjavik summit as "an important political event" that ushered in a "qualitatively new situation" in the arms control process, and stressed that the USSR had been more than forthcoming in this sphere and that the onus was now on the United States to accept what Fedor Burlatskii described in *Literaturnaia gazeta* as "the great historic compromise" that Moscow was offering.[13] Having in effect revitalized its long-standing peace offensive, Moscow was both warning that time was running out if the world was to be saved from the menace of nuclear war and, at the same time, affirming that the Soviet Union had the patience and perseverance to wait for Washington to yield on the SDI issue.

22
WISDOM OF SOVIET MISSILES QUESTIONED

Elizabeth Teague

Soviet foreign and defense policies had long been exempt from public criticism. There had been some signs of dissatisfaction in military circles with Gorbachev's moratorium on nuclear testing, and the press had begun to hint at popular concern over the war in Afghanistan, but the main tenets of foreign policy and strategic doctrine had remained unchallenged.

They had remained unchallenged, that is, until March 1987, when a polemic broke out between an influential Soviet journalist, Aleksandr Bovin, and a member of the General Staff, Major General Iurii Lebedev. The debate concerned both history--the deployment by the Soviet Union of SS-20 missiles targeted on Western Europe--and existing Soviet arms control policy. Publication of the discussion marked a new stage of *glasnost*, and suggested that there was disagreement within the Soviet leadership over the future conduct of arms control negotiations with the USA.

Soviet deployment of the SS-20 missiles in 1977 had caused considerable anxiety among the West European members of NATO. In 1983, after two years of unsuccessful US-Soviet negotiations over the "Euromissile" issue, the United States responded by deploying its cruise and Pershing-2 missiles in Western Europe. The USSR retaliated by installing medium-range missiles in Czechoslovakia and the GDR. On February 28, 1987, Gorbachev issued a statement offering to negotiate along the lines of an earlier American proposal, the "zero option," involving the withdrawal of all medium-range missiles from both Western and Eastern Europe and from the European part of the USSR. He thus abandoned the stand adopted following the Reykjavik summit, when the Soviet government stated that it would come to no agreement with the United States on any aspect of nuclear arms control until the American government agreed to confine its research on the Strategic Defense Initiative to the laboratory.

Writing in the weekly *Moscow News* on March 8, Bovin questioned the wisdom both of the original SS-20 deployment and of the Reykjavik "package." Regarding the 1977 deployment, which had been part of the massive Soviet arms build-up undertaken in the nineteen-seventies under the Brezhnev leadership, Bovin asked:

> The building and deployment of hundreds of new missiles must have cost a huge amount of money. And if we agree to destroy these missiles: why then were they built? Why were they deployed? It is not only me who is asking these questions. It would be very good to have competent answers to these questions.

Bovin also criticized later Soviet arms control
policies:

> And every time Moscow made a step forward, sparked
> hopes, politicians appeared who put a brake on the
> process. After Reykjavik, for example, the "package"
> came into play.[1]

The "politicians" denounced in this deliberately
ambiguous passage seemed to be Soviet, not American.
Major-General Lebedev certainly interpreted the remark in
that sense in his reply to Bovin's article, which appeared
in *Moscow News* on March 15:

> That the Soviet Union is today offering to eliminate
> medium-range missiles from Europe does not mean at
> all that this country created a problem and is now
> seeking a way out of it.[2]

Lebedev restated the standard Soviet position that the
deployment of SS-20s posed no fresh threat to Western
Europe. First, he said, it was a measure to counter
American weapons already in place in Western Europe.
Second, it represented merely a modernization of the SS-4
and SS-5 missiles previously deployed on Soviet territory.
Western specialists had shown both claims to be untrue.
That the subject was being discussed in the Soviet press
was in itself a new departure. The fact that Soviet policy
had reversed itself over the "package" negotiating posture
showed that there had been discussion, and probably
disagreement, within the leadership.   Significantly,
Lebedev's article was reprinted almost immediately in *Rudé
právo*[3]; the Czechoslovak Party newspaper, however, did not
afford Bovin the same honor.

23
RED SQUARE LANDING SHAKES UP TOP MILITARY

Alexander Rahr

On May 28, 1987--Border Guards' Day in the Soviet
Union--a nineteen-year-old West German, Matthias Rust,
completed an unsanctioned and unintercepted flight from
Finland across some 700 kilometers of Soviet territory and

flamboyantly landed the light aircraft he was piloting, a Cessna 172, in Red Square. Only the day before, at a ceremonial meeting in Moscow, the chief of the Political Administration of Border Guard Troops, who were under the jurisdiction of the KGB, had assured the Soviet population that it could rest easily insofar as the security of its national borders was concerned.[1]

By coincidence, on the day these assurances were made, a Soviet citizen took off from an airfield in Latvia in a crop-dusting airplane and escaped undetected to Sweden, where he requested political asylum.[2] Thus the flight of the young West German marked the second apparent failure of the Soviet air defense system in only two days. Furthermore, on the day of Rust's flight, at least 100 border guard troops were arrested for drunkenness in Gorkii Park in Moscow. Many of them had to spend the night in sobering-up stations.[3]

Gorbachev was in East Germany while these unusual developments were taking place, but he lost no time in turning them to his advantage when he got back to Moscow on May 29. In a move that displayed his astuteness as a politician, he called an emergency session of the Politburo within hours of his return and managed to bring about the dismissals of two top military leaders--Sergei Sokolov, the minister of defense, who had been a member of Gorbachev's delegation in East Berlin, and Aleksandr Koldunov, the commander in chief of the air defense forces. The Politburo, in a conspicuous assertion of civilian authority over the military, adopted a decision to strengthen the leadership of the Ministry of Defense. In a single stroke, Gorbachev was not only able to rid his administration of the seventy-six-year-old Sokolov--a holdover from the Chernenko period who had been widely seen as a transition figure and an obstacle on the path of Gorbachev's modernization program--but also to put in his place the sixty-three-year-old Dmitrii T. Iazov--a man who, to judge from his background, seemed to be a loyal ally of the general secretary. Western observers described the dismissals of Sokolov and Koldunov as the most dramatic humiliation of the Soviet military by a political leader since Nikita Khrushchev ousted Marshal Georgii Zhukov from the Ministry of Defense thirty years earlier.[4]

The dismissals of Sokolov and Koldunov resembled the punishment of Army General Aleksandr Altunin, who had been replaced as chief of Civil Defense after the Chernobyl disaster in 1986. Since Gorbachev's rise to power there had been several personnel changes in the senior ranks of

the Soviet defense establishment.   They included the
appointments of a new first deputy Minister of Defense,
Petr Lushev;   a   new   chief   of   the   Main   Political
Administration of the Soviet Army and Navy, Aleksei
Lizichev; a new commander in chief of the Soviet Navy,
Vladimir Chernavin; a new chief of Civil Defense, Vladimir
Govorov; a new commander in chief of Strategic Rocket
Forces, Iurii Maksimov; a new chief of the Main
Inspectorate, Ivan Tretiak, who later became commander in
chief of Air Defence; a new chief of the main inspectorate,
Mikhail Sorokin; and a new chief of the main personnel
directorate, Dimitrii Sukhorukov.

Iazov's appointment was unexpected.   His selection
bypassed several more senior military officers, such as
First Deputy Defense Ministers Sergei Akhromeev, Viktor
Kulikov, and Lushev, as well as several distinguished
deputy ministers of defense, all whom had been in the line
for promotion for many years.

Iazov was born on November 11, 1923, in the small
village of Iazovo (from which his surname was derived) in
the region of Omsk.[5] His father, a peasant, died in 1934,
during the period of collectivization. In the summer of
1942, he joined the army and fought on the Volkhov and
Leningrad fronts.   After the war, he served in various
command positions.

After graduating from the Academy of the General Staff
in 1967, Iazov assumed command of a division in the
Transbaikal Military District.   From 1972 to 1974 he was
commander of an army unit in the Transcaucasus Military
District.   In 1979, he was assigned to the post of
commander of the Central Group of Forces in Czechoslovakia,
and a year later was appointed commander of the Central
Asian Military District.

According to rumors in Moscow, Gorbachev was impressed
by Iazov when he met him while touring the Soviet Far East
in the summer of 1986.[6] In December 1986, Iazov was
transferred to Moscow to take over a position as Deputy
Defense Minister, replacing Ivan Shkadov as head of the
Main Personnel Directorate of the Ministry of Defense.

In an article published in *Krasnaia zvezda* in July,
1983, Iazov called for *glasnost* in the army. He criticized
the prevalence of corruption in the ranks of the military,
mentioning in particular the practice of sending
conscripted soldiers to do construction work on farms,
where in his view they were being exploited as a source of
cheap labor by private individuals.   Some officers, Iazov
also charged, were using military labor to build private

dachas and saunas.[7] Thus, as early as 1983, Iazov was already projecting the image of a leader in the Gorbachev mold. In January, 1987, *Krasnaia zvezda* published an account of various changes that had been carried out among the ranks of the military in Khabarovsk since Gorbachev's visit to the Far East,[8] which laid particular stress on Iazov's concern for tight discipline.

Gorbachev resolutely refused to take any responsibility for the embarrassing events of May 1987. Instead he laid the blame unequivocally on the military and exploited the situation both to rid himself of Sokolov, and to appoint a man of his own choice to a key post. The events therefore marked an important stage in Gorbachev's consolidation of his own position.

24
TOWARD AN INF TREATY AND BEYOND

Douglas Clarke and *Vladimir Socor**

Following the Soviet decision to come to an agreement on limiting intermediate range nuclear forces (INF) independently of the negotiations on strategic and space weapons, American and Soviet diplomats in Geneva began to formulate the details of an eventual treaty. The basic terms of this treaty were agreed at the abortive Reykjavik summit in October 1986; the negotiators now had to agree on the fine print.

At a press conference in Paris on March 6, 1987, Soviet First Deputy Foreign Minister Iulii M. Vorontsov, head of the Soviet negotiating team at the Nuclear and Space Talks in Geneva, said that "technical" details could constitute serious stumbling blocks. He also hinted at a dramatic shift in the Soviet approach to arms control verification.[1]

The Framework and the "Details". Spokesmen for both sides disclosed that each supported the elimination of longer-range missiles from Europe within five years. Each side would be allowed to retain 100 warheads on such weapons, but these would be based outside Europe. There

---

*Author of the final section

would be constraints on some shorter-range missiles in the treaty itself and a commitment to quickly begin more detailed negotiations on shorter-range missiles.

The unresolved details included the allowed locations for the residual force of 100 longer-range missile warheads, the disposition of the excess missiles, launchers, and warheads that would be eliminated from Europe, and the verification measures to prevent cheating.

NATO governments had long been concerned with both the range and mobility of the Soviet SS-20 missiles. When stationed just to the east of the Ural Mountains--the traditional boundary between Europe and Asia--the 5,000-kilometer-range SS-20 could strike most of the European NATO countries. Missiles further east could be quickly moved to within threatening range, either on their own truck-launchers or by rail. Yet simply moving the missiles farther to the east would create a separate problem for the United States. Responding to concern in Asia, particularly in Japan, the Americans assured their friends and allies in that region that any eventual INF treaty would not merely move the Soviet SS-20 threat from Europe to Asia.

The Soviets did not wish to see an American missile threat in Asia where none had previously existed. Accordingly, they initially proposed that the Americans not be allowed to station any of their 100 remaining missiles in Alaska, from where they could threaten Soviet military installations on the Kamchatka Peninsula. While the United States authorities had no plans to station Pershing II or ground-launched cruise missiles in Alaska, they wished to retain the right to do so in principle. Gorbachev's proposal that the 100 residual missiles be stationed outside Europe on the "national territory" of each side seemed to meet the American requirements.[2]

When the US negotiators placed their draft INF treaty on the table in Geneva, it reportedly contained a requirement that the Soviets station all their 100 allowed SS-20 warheads at a single base near Novosibirsk in Siberia. From this location, some 1,300 kilometers east of the Urals, they would not be able to reach most of the European NATO countries or Japan.

Concerning the disposal of the missiles, launchers, and warheads to be reduced by the treaty, Vorontsov made it clear that the Soviet Union would insist on their physical destruction. United States military planners were known to be considering the possible conversion of Pershing II missiles to a shorter-range version. NATO governments on both sides of the Atlantic voiced concern about the

Soviets' virtual monopoly in the shorter-range INF category, a superiority that would become more significant once NATO had given up its longer-range weapons in Europe. Conversion of some of the Pershing IIs could be an economically and militarily effective way to offset the Soviet advantage--although fraught with political difficulties.

Verification. Effective verification of the destruction of nuclear warheads was bound to be hampered by their small size and weight, often less than 100 kilograms. The radioactive material at their heart could only be processed at a very few nuclear weapons factories in some of the most sensitive and secret locations in both the United States and the USSR. By hinting at verification measures which would open up these plants to foreign inspectors, Vorontsov introduced a subject previously regarded as all but unthinkable.

While accepting the idea that a treaty limiting missiles must be verifiable, the NATO countries where missiles were based were not keen to have Soviet inspectors poking around at will on their territories. "We want to be able to go anywhere and see anything that interests us on missiles," said Vorontsov, adding that Soviet inspectors would demand the right to go "anywhere in NATO Europe, except France," to ensure that all the American mobile missiles had been removed.

Vorontsov's enthusiasm for verification was not limited to Europe. He warned that the United States might have to pass special legislation to open up the factories of its private military contractors to Soviet inspectors. Stating that "we can order our factories to open their doors," Vorontsov cautioned that the verification measures in an eventual treaty would be founded on strict reciprocity.

On March 12, 1987, the US delegation in Geneva presented the American verification proposal. According to a US State Department spokesman, this proposal had six elements.[3] The first four dealt with more traditional verification methods, including a ban on encoding the performance data radioed back to a control center from test missiles in flight and any other interference with National Technical Means. The final two provisions broke new ground. They required the stationing of inspectors from one side on the territory of the other and called for a "permanent presence" of both sensors and on-site inspectors at certain missile production, repair, and storage facilities.

The Dispute Over Shorter-Range Missiles. Soviet and American negotiators wound up their special session on March 26 without coming to an agreement. The regular seventh round of the Nuclear and Space Talks between the two countries, which as usual included sessions on strategic forces and space weapons as well as the Euromissiles, adjourned on March 6.

The principal stumbling block was the shorter-range INF missiles, those with ranges of between 500 and 1,000 kilometers. The US insisted on holding the USSR to the Reykjavik understanding that there would be a limit placed on these weapons in an INF treaty. The Soviets had approximately 130 missiles falling into this category, the 900-kilometer-range SS-12s and the 500-kilometer-range SS-23s. The USA had no similar missiles. The Americans also wanted the right to match any Soviet level of shorter-range missiles.

The Soviet position was that all discussion of shorter-range missiles should be deferred to follow-on negotiations, although Gorbachev had promised that the 50 or so SS-12 missiles placed in the GDR and Czechoslovakia would be brought back to the USSR once an INF treaty were signed. The Soviets adamantly opposed the USA's suggestion that some of the American Pershing II missiles might be converted to shorter-range missiles.

Some of the European NATO allies had long been concerned that the removal of American Pershing II and cruise missiles would leave NATO vulnerable to the overwhelming Soviet superiority in shorter-range missiles. Taking into account the tactical missiles that were not being discussed at Geneva, the Soviet missiles known to NATO as the SCUD, SS-21, and FROG, NATO was at a nine-to-one disadvantage. The only NATO missiles with ranges of less than 1,000 kilometers were the 72 Pershing I missiles fielded by the West Germans and some 90 American and allied missiles. The French and the British had been the most outspoken in insisting that at least some of the shorter-range missiles be constrained in an INF agreement. French Prime Minister Jacques Chirac said that an agreement on medium-range missiles "must not award an advantage in short-range missiles to the Soviets." In her meetings in Moscow, British Prime Minister Margaret Thatcher was reported to have conveyed a similar message to General Secretary Gorbachev.

NATO-Warsaw Pact Talks on Conventional Forces. In Vienna, the weekly informal meetings between NATO and Warsaw Pact representatives began on February 17, 1987.

They aimed at establishing the framework for a new conference on reducing conventional forces in Europe to supersede the moribund MBFR (Mutual and Balanced Force Reductions) talks.

Warsaw Pact Meeting. At a news conference summarizing the two-day meeting of Warsaw Pact Foreign Ministers, which ended in Moscow on March 25, a Soviet spokesman said that the ministers had unanimously agreed that the removal of shorter-range nuclear weapons from Europe had to be kept separate from a treaty on what the Soviets called medium-range missiles. These were the Soviet SS-20s and older SS-4s and the American Pershing II and ground-launched cruise missiles, which would be removed from Europe under the terms of the so-called "zero option."

The United States made it clear from the beginning of the negotiations in Geneva that it wanted constraints on at least some of the Soviet shorter-range Euromissiles. They singled out the SS-12 (Scaleboard) and the SS-23. In 1984 the Soviets moved several brigades of mobile Scaleboard missiles into the GDR and Czechoslovakia from their peacetime garrisons in the Soviet Union. They announced that this was one of their responses to the NATO deployment of US Pershing II and cruise missiles. According to the US Department of Defense, the USSR had more than 100 of these missiles.

Gorbachev said that the USSR would remove these missiles from the GDR and Czechoslovakia once an INF agreement were signed. In their communiqué following the Moscow meeting, the Warsaw Pact Foreign Ministers repeated this pledge.

The second Soviet shorter-range missile of concern to the United States was the SS-23. This 500-kilometer-range missile--which, like the Scaleboard, was carried on a highly mobile truck launcher--was far more accurate and had a much greater range than the older SCUD missile, which it would replace. In Geneva the USA proposed that the Soviet inventory of SS-12s and SS-23s be frozen at its existing level, believed to be roughly 130 missiles. The USA would then have the right to match this level.

New Soviet Offers. Earlier at the Geneva negotiations, the Soviets had indicated that they might accept a freeze on these shorter-range INF missiles but that the freeze would have to apply to both sides. They subsequently dropped their offer of a freeze.

Only four days after a speech in Prague in which he outlined initiatives on European missiles, conventional forces, and chemical weapons, Gorbachev made several even

more dramatic proposals in Moscow to visiting US Secretary
of State George Shultz.

He offered to eliminate all the "battlefield" nuclear
missiles. NATO claimed that the Soviets held a nine-to-one
advantage in these short-range systems. Gorbachev also
said that the Soviet Union would agree to include in any
treaty on INF missiles an obligation to eliminate its
shorter-range Euromissiles "within a relatively short and
clearly defined time frame."[4] He was referring to the 130
to 150 SS-12 and SS-23 missiles.

In his speech in Prague on April 10, Gorbachev offered
to hold simultaneous negotiations on these shorter-range
Euromissiles. He also repeated an earlier Soviet pledge to
remove the 50 or so SS-12s deployed in the GDR and
Czechoslovakia if an INF accord was signed. Gorbachev now
expanded on this proposal by offering to nail down the
result of these simultaneous negotiations in an INF treaty.
The Soviet inventory would be eliminated within a specific
time frame, which, according to TASS, might be "within a
year."

Within hours of the meeting between Gorbachev and
Shultz, TASS issued a lengthy statement describing the
substance of the discussion and including what seemed to be
a verbatim account of the Soviet offers. This immediate
publicity annoyed and embarrassed the Americans, who had
agreed with the Soviets not to discuss the substance of
Shultz's meetings with Soviet leaders until the conclusion
of his visit. It highlighted the Soviet inclination to
appeal directly to the Western public on arms control
matters rather than confine them to the negotiating table.

Gorbachev's proposals were shrewd public gestures.
Both Britain and France were beginning to expand their own
nuclear forces significantly, but there was a large and
growing antinuclear movement in Western Europe, fueled by
the Chernobyl accident in 1986. Moreover, the opposition
Labour Party in Britain was avowedly against nuclear
weapons; and although France was less divided politically
on this issue, the French government recognized that public
opinion could affect its nuclear modernization plans. One
of the French programs was the development of a
truck-mounted, 350-kilometer-range nuclear missile known as
the Hades. French leaders acknowledged that a US-Soviet
agreement to do away with shorter-range Euromissiles would
make it very difficult for them to go ahead with the Hades.

Soviet Nuclear Testing Offer. During Shultz's visit
to Moscow, Soviet Foreign Minister Eduard Shevardnadze
proposed that the USA and the USSR conduct nuclear tests on

each other's territories as a means of calibrating the seismic instruments used to monitor nuclear explosions. Before the Moscow talks ended, however, the Soviets appeared to back away from their own offer.

According to the head of the US Arms Control and Disarmament Agency (ACDA), Kenneth Adelman, the Soviets "started walking back" from some of the nuclear testing provisions that had been agreed by the two delegations. The American official believed, however, that the Soviet suggestion for exchanging tests remained on the table.[5] Soviet uneasiness about their own proposal could explain why so little was said about nuclear testing in the Soviet accounts of the Shultz visit. While TASS was very explicit in reporting on the Soviet proposals in other arms control areas, only two sentences were devoted to nuclear testing. These made no direct mention of the test exchange idea. Later, both Soviet and American sources said the Soviet proposal was "just an idea."[6]

The tests would have given the two sides greater confidence in the accuracy of the seismic instruments used to detect nuclear explosions and to measure their strength. This could have paved the way for ratification of two treaties signed in the nineteen-seventies that limited underground nuclear explosions: the 1974 Threshold Test Ban Treaty and the 1976 Peaceful Nuclear Explosions Treaty. The Threshold Treaty barred tests of underground nuclear weapons with an explosive force greater than 150 kilotons. Under the second treaty, this limit would also have applied to underground nuclear explosions for peaceful purposes.

The Geneva Nuclear Testing Talks. These talks, which both sides stressed were not negotiations, began in July 1986 and continued on an intermittent basis. From the beginning it was clear that the two sides had different agendas in mind. The Soviets wanted to establish the ground rules for early negotiations on a treaty banning all nuclear weapons tests. The USA, USSR, and the UK had carried on negotiations for such a Comprehensive Test Ban Treaty from 1977 through 1980 but failed to reach agreement on several major issues, including verification. Subsequently, the United States decided not to resume these negotiations. The American position was that while such a treaty remained a long-term goal of the United States, nuclear testing would be required as long as nuclear weapons played such an important role in the strategy of deterrence of the USA and NATO.

At the end of the fourth round of the talks between Soviet and American nuclear testing experts, the head of the Soviet delegation, Andronik Petrosiants, blamed the lack of progress on the USA for "not demonstrating the political will to put an end to nuclear tests." He said that the Soviet Union wanted to begin full-scale negotiations on "the entire range of issues related to the total termination of nuclear testing." These issues included, he said, verification measures for the two unratified treaties, interim measures that would limit the number of nuclear tests and perhaps lower the 150-kiloton ceiling, and ultimately a complete ban on testing.[7]

By listing the Soviet agenda in this order, Petrosiants seemed to be moving toward the USA's step-by-step approach. The Americans, however, wanted to concentrate exclusively on the first step and were very reluctant to make any commitments regarding the other topics of interest to the Soviets, such as limiting the number of tests, lowering the 150-kiloton ceiling, or resuming the talks on a comprehensive test ban.

Soviet Draft INF Treaty. On April 28, 1987, the day after he had handed a Soviet draft treaty on medium-range missiles to his American counterpart, Soviet arms negotiator Aleksei Obukhov discussed this latest Soviet arms control initiative at a press conference in Geneva. He described the Soviet text as a "compromise document" in response to the lengthy American draft treaty that had been tabled in early March.

The Soviet diplomat said that his delegation's draft provided for:

> verification and inspection everywhere--on missile dismantling sites; on the sites of their elimination; at ranges and military bases, including third countries; at depots and factories regardless of whether they are private or state-owned.[8]

All of these measures were without precedent in arms control; they were among those the US had insisted must be included in any eventual agreement limiting intermediate-range missiles. In mentioning "third countries," Obukhov was referring to the UK, FRG, Italy, and Belgium, where American Pershing-II and ground-launched cruise missiles were based. These countries eventually accepted the American position that any treaty dealing with mobile missiles, like the Soviet SS-20, required such on-site inspection if it was to be effective.

One significant omission in the Soviet verification list was any reference to so-called "suspect sites." The US did not want to limit its inspectors only to facilities that had been associated with the banned weapons. The American verification proposals would give each side the right to demand to look at any facility, for instance, a factory that normally produced strategic rockets but could be easily converted to producing smaller intermediate-range missiles. Some of America's NATO allies were particularly leary of this idea, since they felt the Soviets could demand to examine their most sensitive military facilities for the purpose of gathering intelligence under the guise of looking for illegal American missiles.

Obukhov also discussed the issue of what the Soviets called "operational-tactical" missiles--those with ranges between 500 and 1,000 kilometers. He said that the Soviet Union was calling for the elimination of these missiles in Europe, with the US and the USSR allowed an equal number of such missiles outside Europe. Such an agreement could be included in the medium-range treaty or could be a separate accord. The approximately 130 Soviet SS-12s and SS-23s were in this category. The Americans had no comparable missiles, although they did supply the nuclear warheads for 72 German Pershing-I missiles that could strike targets up to 720 kilometers away.

The Soviet proposals on the shorter-range missiles were not included in their draft treaty itself but had been presented orally to the American negotiators.

Efforts to agree on a NATO response to the Soviet proposal for eliminating the shorter-range, as well medium-range class, missiles in Europe had been underway since Gorbachev first broached the idea in Moscow earlier in April. The proposal sparked a fierce debate in NATO capitals, with many expressing the fear that the total elimination of shorter-range nuclear systems would make NATO too vulnerable to the superior Warsaw Pact conventional forces. The issue threatened to create a crisis in the West German government, where Chancellor Helmut Kohl had so far been unable to reconcile the views of his Foreign Minister, Hans-Dietrich Genscher, who was in favor of accepting the Soviet offer, and his Defense Minister, Manfred Wörner, who opposed it. The Americans said that they would leave the decision on shorter-range missiles up to their European allies, who were most directly effected by the threat of these weapons.

The Jaruzelski Plan. On May 8, Polish party First Secretary Gen. Wojciech Jaruzelski presented a proposal for the gradual reduction of "operational and tactical kinds of nuclear arms" in a nine-nation area astride the boundary between NATO and the Warsaw Pact. To the east, it was to encompass the GDR, Poland, Czechoslovakia and Hungary, while the FRG, Belgium, the Netherlands, Luxembourg, and Denmark would be included on the NATO side.

The Polish initiative also called for the gradual reduction of conventional weapons in this same area, beginning with those most suitable for offensive purposes--what the Polish leader referred to as those with "the greatest strength and strike precision." In addition, Jaruzelski looked beyond the question of weaponry to propose a fundamental change in the character of military doctrines, rendering them strictly and recognizably defensive in nature. Finally, he proposed a continued search for new security and confidence-building measures and the implementation of strict verification methods.

The Poles wanted their proposals to be considered within the context of the Helsinki Conference on Security and Cooperation in Europe (CSCE) process. Polish Foreign Minister Marian Orzechowski left Warsaw on May 10 for Vienna to present the Polish initiative to the CSCE review conference. The CSCE was composed of 35 nations, including all the European states except Albania, and the United States and Canada. The NATO allies--with the notable exception of France--wanted to limit conventional arms reduction talks to the members of the two opposing military blocs. The two sides had been holding informal discussions in Vienna to seek agreement on such talks. Orzechowski met with this informal gathering of NATO and Warsaw Pact military experts on May 11 and addressed the full 35-nation Helsinki review conference on May 12. The Polish proposal, which introduced what was essentially a regional plan into the broadest possible forum, including the many neutral and nonaligned members of the CSCE, was likely to complicate the effort to establish a new East-West forum for conventional arms reduction talks to replace the stalled Mutual and Balanced Force Reductions negotiations.

Jaruzelski's idea about radically changing military doctrines was bound to be dismissed as utopian. Modern armies--and especially that of the Soviet Union--subscribed to the maxim that "the best defense is a good offense." The line between offensive and defensive weapons had become so blurred as to be almost indistinguishable. Most military analysts would argue that only countries with the kind of geographic, political, and historical traditions peculiar to Switzerland, for example, could gain any security from a strictly defensive military doctrine. Yet the idea had some appeal to certain unorthodox thinkers

on defense in the West, particularly in the opposition
parties in the FRG and Denmark. This might explain why
Jaruzelski included Denmark, which had no nuclear weapons,
in his proposed zone.

The West German Concerns. The broad outline of a
Soviet-American INF agreement had been set since the
abortive Reykjavik summit. All of the longer-range nuclear
missiles were to be removed from Europe. These were the
270 Soviet SS-20s, each carrying 3 warheads, and the 112
older Soviet SS-4 missiles, as well as the 316 American
Pershing II and ground-launched cruise missiles (GLCMs).
They had maximum ranges of between 1,800 and 5,000
kilometers. Each side was to be able to keep 100 warheads
on such missiles, but not in Europe. The subsequent debate
was sparked by Gorbachev's additional proposal to eliminate
nuclear missiles in Europe with ranges as low as 500
kilometers. This became known as the "double zero" option;
the first zero for the longer-range missiles and the second
for the shorter-range ones.

At first glance this might have seemed to be a
tempting offer for the Americans, since they had no
missiles in this category while the Soviets fielded some
130-150 of these weapons in Eastern Europe and the western
USSR. Yet the long-held American position was that, while
they could welcome a reduction in the Soviet inventory,
they reserved the right to match the numbers of Soviet
missiles that would remain following such a reduction. No
one had anticipated that the Soviet Union would be willing
to give up both longer- and shorter-range INF missiles.

Faced with just such an offer, many in NATO expressed
the concern that such a wide gap in nuclear capabilities
could weaken the alliance's strategy of flexible response.
They argued that neither the threat of an American
strategic nuclear response to a Warsaw Pact conventional
attack nor the possibility of using very short range
nuclear weapons--such as nuclear artillery--was a
convincing deterrent. The United States made a commitment
to consult with its NATO allies before responding to the
latest Soviet offer, since the European members of the
alliance would be directly affected by the outcome of these
negotiations. The Americans, however, favored accepting
the Gorbachev offer, since they felt that they could still
retain ample nuclear forces in Europe to deter any
conventional aggression by the Warsaw Pact. Their position
also reflected a recognition that it would be politically
very difficult to introduce any new American nuclear system

into Europe. Thus, any theoretical right to match Soviet SS-12s, for example, would be a hollow one.

Bordering directly on the Warsaw Pact, West Germany had long been concerned that NATO's preoccupation with the longer-range nuclear missiles masked the threat from shorter-range systems. For example, the Soviet armies in East Germany and Czechoslovakia possessed hundreds of 300-kilometer-range SCUD missiles with nuclear warheads. These weapons could strike targets anywhere in the FRG just as easily as the SS-20s or SS-12s. It was with this concern in mind that Chancellor Kohl suggested on May 15 that any agreement on shorter-range nuclear weapons take into consideration those with even the very shortest range.[9] Contrary to some interpretations of Kohl's remarks, he was not proposing a third "zero," as he was fully aware of the disadvantages to NATO of a denuclearized Europe.

With the United Kingdom and most of the other members of NATO--as well as his own Foreign Minister--supporting the new American position, Kohl became increasingly isolated. In a clarification of his remarks on May 15, Kohl repeated that attention had to be paid to the shortest range nuclear weapons, as well as conventional and chemical weapons, but that these issues should not impede a US-Soviet accord on the SS-20s, Pershing IIs, and GLCMs.[10]

NATO's Nuclear Planning Group Steps In. As if the debate over shorter-range missiles were not enough, the Defense Ministers from NATO countries belonging to the alliance's Nuclear Planning Group muddied the waters on the central issue of longer-range missiles themselves. As stated in the communiqué from the semi-annual meeting of this group, held on May 14-15 in Stavanger, Norway, the Foreign Ministers "stressed the requirement to eliminate all United States and Soviet LRINF missiles [longer-range Euromissiles] and called upon the Soviet Union to drop its demand to retain a portion of its SS-20 force."[11]

Spokesmen for both the US State Department and the White House were quick to reaffirm the US commitment to its draft treaty on longer-range missiles formulated after the Reykjavik summit, which included the 100 warhead limit.[12]

If the response from Washington was cool, Gorbachev was quick to come up with a counteroffer. Claiming that the Soviet SS-20s in Asia served as a balance to the American nuclear weapons in that region, the Soviet leader said on May 19 that the USSR would agree to do away with these weapons if the United States "agreed to eliminate its nuclear weapons in Japan, South Korea, and the Philippines

and also to withdraw its aircraft carrier flotilla beyond
agreed lines."[13]   This could hardly have been taken as a
serious arms control proposal, since the United States had
no Pershing II or ground-launched cruise missiles in Asia.
It was like comparing apples with oranges. Most Western
analysts felt that the Soviet Asian SS-20 force served to
counter the Chinese nuclear capability.   The US nuclear
weapons in Asia, mainly aircraft bombs and naval weapons,
as well as some nuclear artillery and short-range missiles
based   in   South Korea, were types that had   been
specifically   excluded   from   the   Geneva   talks on
intermediate-range nuclear forces. Reacting to this offer
from Gorbachev, a State Department spokesman indicated that
the US was not prepared to make concessions on these other
types of weapons in order to reach an accord in the INF
negotiations.[14]

   East Berlin Summit. At the Warsaw Pact summit meeting
in East Berlin on May 28 and 29, 1987, the Soviet bloc
leaders called for consultations with NATO on military
doctrine and "disparities that have arisen in arms and
other forces" between the two sides. These talks, to be
held at "an authoritative expert level," could be held in
Brussels or Warsaw or in each of these cities alternately
and could start in 1987.[15]   In the long term, the seven
East   European   leaders called for   the   simultaneous
dissolution of the North Atlantic alliance and the Warsaw
Treaty itself.

   The leaders of the Warsaw Pact thought enough of these
proposals to separate them   from the regular meeting
communiqué. They were published in an accompanying document
setting out the fundamental provisions of their military
doctrine. The appeal for an East-West dialogue on military
doctrine could be seen as a follow up to one of the four
points in the "Jaruzelski Plan."

   The Soviets had long maintained that the military
forces of the two sides are "essentially equivalent," both
in nuclear and conventional forces. In their eyes, any
apparent Warsaw Pact advantage in one area, such as tanks
and artillery, was counterbalanced by a NATO advantage in
another, such as aircraft carriers.   Yet NATO's concern
about the conventional balance, particularly in the case of
sharp reductions in nuclear weapons, was being recognized
as such in Moscow.

   Immediately prior to the Warsaw Pact summit in East
Berlin, Soviet Foreign Ministry spokesman Boris Piadyshev
voiced some of the Soviet concerns in this area. He stated
that the   proper   solution   would   be   to reduce any

inequalities through reductions by the stronger side, rather than a build-up by the weaker side.[16] Along this line, the Warsaw Pact leaders decried the recent NATO Defense Ministers' appeal for an increase in NATO spending on conventional defense.

While NATO leaders might have welcomed such a solution in theory, they were sure to be leary about how it would work out in practice. They made it clear that they felt that the continuing discussions in Vienna between representatives of NATO and Warsaw Pact countries was the proper forum for developing subsequent conventional forces negotiations between the two sides. The Warsaw Pact communiqué stated that the member governments "attach great importance" to the informal discussions in Vienna but that they placed more emphasis on the full 35-country Conference on Security and Cooperation in Europe. They called for a meeting of the Foreign Ministers of the CSCE states to lay the groundwork for talks on reducing conventional and tactical nuclear weapons.[17]

The many Eastern arms control proposals--from a ban on nuclear testing, to nuclear free zones in several parts of Europe, to the prohibition of an arms race in space--were reviewed and supported in the lengthy communiqué. Each Warsaw Pact "sponsor" of a particular proposal was acknowledged; and as an indication that the Soviet Union's Eastern European allies would continue to play a role in proposing new arms control ideas, the communiqué announced the creation of a new consultative body. A "special commission" would be established to exchange views on arms control and to discuss "the initiatives of Allied States and the working out of joint proposals in this field." Representatives of the Ministries of Defense and Foreign Affairs would participate. This new commission appeared similar to a NATO consultative body known as the "Special Consultative Group", which had been coordinating the NATO position on European arms control matters since 1979.

Hardening Soviet Stance. Expected progress toward an INF treaty on intermediate-range nuclear forces (INF) was slowed down in June and July by new or extraneous issues raised by Moscow that complicated the negotiations. The Soviet moves appeared to be aimed at retaining unilateral military advantages acquired through the USSR's unmatched INF deployments and at using these as trump cards to obtain concessions in other areas outside the purview of the INF negotiations.

Both sides agreed on the principle of eliminating the US and the Soviet longer-range INF (LRINF) missiles and the

Soviet shorter-range INF (SRINF) missiles from Europe within five years of signing a treaty; the USA, which had no missiles of its own of this latter class in Europe, would under the double zero solution implicitly renounce the right to deploy them. Following the acceptance of this "double zero" solution for Europe, however, efforts by the US with strong support from its allies to extend the zero solutions to INF in Asia were countered by Soviet demands for reductions in US military assets specifically excluded from the mandate agreed upon for the INF negotiations.

Soviet Asian Missiles. The USA and its allies in NATO and the Far East, as well as China, all agreed that a continued Soviet INF monopoly in Asia after the double-zero solution was implemented in Europe would endanger the security of both Western Europe and the Far East. Owing to their mobility, the Soviet missiles could easily be shifted around from one theater to another and be brought within striking range of Europe or the Far Eastern countries. Moreover, it was generally accepted that the retention of a residual INF arsenal and infrastructure in Asia would greatly complicate verification. Consequently, the USA, with strong support from its European and Far Eastern allies and from China as well, was seeking Soviet agreement to extending the double-zero solution to Asia.[18]

The Soviets, however, insisted on the tentative solution outlined at Reykjavik in 1986, under which the USSR would keep 100 SS-20 warheads in Asia while the USA would have the right to deploy 100 warheads at home. The Soviets agreed to concentrate this force in an area just east of 80 degrees longitude, out of range of both Western Europe and the Far East, provided that the USA gave up the right to deploy its 100 warheads in the state of Alaska within range of Kamchatka. No agreement was reached on this point, however, mainly because, as noted above, pledges to confine Soviet INF missiles to a given deployment area were of little value in view of their high degree of mobility. With regard to SRINF missiles in Asia, Moscow similarly opposed extending the zero solution there, offering instead to negotiate equal levels between its SRINF missiles in Asia and the US nuclear deterrent capabilities in the Far East and the Pacific; these US forces were, of course, not equivalent to INF and were, in fact, by definition outside the agreed scope of the INF negotiations. Soviet officials from Gorbachev down elaborated on this proposal both publicly and in the negotiations with the USA, offering to eliminate both their LRINF and their SRINF missiles in Asia if the USA were to remove US nuclear and dual-capable systems from Japan, South Korea, and the Philippines; renounce INF missiles in the USA itself; and withdraw aircraft carriers in the Pacific behind a line to be agreed upon. The USA responded that it would not sacrifice nonequivalent systems in areas explicitly excluded from the INF negotiations and would continue to advocate the zero solution for INF in Asia.[19]

Moscow also gave the impression of backtracking from its long-standing pledge to remove its SRINF missiles from the GDR and Czechoslovakia as soon as a zero solution was reached for LRINF in Europe. Soviet officials, including Foreign Minister Shevardnadze, were now publicly saying that the removal of Soviet missiles from the two countries may be made conditional upon renunciation of the nuclear warheads of the dual-key SRINF Pershing I-A missiles in the Federal Republic of Germany.[20]

The USA was seeking in the negotiations with the USSR to establish the right to convert Pershing II and cruise missiles into systems that would be permitted once the contemplated INF treaty had taken effect. The Soviets publicly rejected all conversion options, insisting that systems limited by treaty must be destroyed and that this must apply to the nuclear warheads of Pershing I-As as well.

The sides also appeared deadlocked with regard to the timetable for eliminating missiles. In the US view, the lopsided superiority enjoyed by the Soviets meant that they would have to proceed first and reduce their force until equality was reached reached in the number of warheads; thereupon the two sides would proceed with equal and parallel reductions. The Soviets, however, reportedly maintained that the first stage of missile elimination should involve equal cuts of 50 percent by each side, a position obviously unacceptable to the USA.[21]

The USA proposed a verification plan centering on on-site monitoring and intrusive inspection of INF missile sites. The Soviets neither endorsed the US plan nor presented one of their own; they did not enter into detailed discussion of verification; they spoke mainly of inspection of the declared rather than of the suspected sites and of regular inspections rather than the more effective inspections upon challenge; and they referred to inspections "when necessary," appearing to reserve a right of veto, and advocated settling the terms of the treaty first and dealing with verification afterward.

MOSCOW'S FOREIGN POLICY
AND PUBLIC RELATIONS

25
THE VLADIVOSTOK SPEECH

Bohdan Nahaylo and *Kevin Devlin**

At Vladivostok, on July 28, 1986, Gorbachev delivered an important speech, of which half was devoted to the economic development of the Soviet Far East and the rest to Soviet foreign policy in the Asian and Pacific regions. The address represented the Gorbachev leadership's most comprehensive statement thus far on its approach to issues of international security and cooperation in Asia and the Pacific zone.

The Soviet Union, Gorbachev stressed, "is also an Asian and Pacific country" that "realizes the complex problems of this vast region." Indicating that the time had come for Moscow to embark on a broader and more active role in those areas, he stated that the USSR would seek "to give more dynamism to its bilateral relations with all countries situated here, without exception." He mentioned the friends and allies of the Soviet Union, the ASEAN countries, and then a whole range of states from Australia to Kiribati. China was singled out as a Socialist country that, together with the USSR, "has been entrusted by history with an extremely responsible mission"; he praised India as "the recognized leader" of the nonaligned states; and mentioned the mutual benefits of greater economic cooperation between the Soviet Union and Japan.

Among the topics Gorbachev dwelt upon, though adding little to what had previously been proposed, was the need for a joint and comprehensive approach to security and confidence-building in Asia and the Pacific region. He continued to promote the idea of a conference along the lines of the Helsinki Conference on Security and Cooperation in Europe, presumably in order to gain

* Author of the section on Sino-Soviet talks.

155

international recognition for the status quo in Indochina
and to further the USSR's influence in that part of the
world. Gorbachev suggested Hiroshima as a possible venue
for such an Asian-Pacific conference.

Much of the speech amounted to an indictment of
Washington's policies.   Switching momentarily to a more
conciliatory tone, Gorbachev reiterated that the Soviet
Union sought "peaceful, good-neighborly relations" with the
United States. He went out of his way to stress that the
USSR both recognized the United States as "a great Pacific
power" and realized that "without the United States,
without its participation, it is impossible to resolve the
problem of security and cooperation in the Pacific Ocean in
a way that would satisfy all nations in the region."
Gorbachev referred to "the considerable opportunities" for
"mutual   beneficial   cooperation"   between   Moscow and
Washington in that area.   Having said this, though,
Gorbachev indirectly acknowledged that the interests of the
two superpowers in Asia and the Pacific hardly overlapped.
He stressed that Washington paid insufficient attention to
Moscow's collective security schemes for Asia and the
Pacific, and insisted on the USSR's right to see to "the
minimal requirements of our defenses and the defenses of
our friends and allies, especially in the light of the
American military activity not far from our and their
frontiers."

Specifically,   Gorbachev   accused   Washington of
attempting to extend "NATO's 'competence' to the entire
world, including Asia and the Pacific Ocean"; of building
up its forces in the Pacific Ocean; of foisting the
establishment of "a militarized 'triangle' of Washington,
Tokyo, and Seoul" on Japan and South Korea and of deploying
nuclear weapons in those countries. The Soviet Union, on
the other hand, he claimed, "is a convinced advocate of
disbanding   the   military   groupings,   renouncing   the
possession of military bases in Asia and the Pacific Ocean,
and withdrawing troops from the territories of other
countries." Gorbachev chose not to mention the three Soviet
bases in Indochina (in Camranh Bay, Da Nang, and Kompong
Som); nor did he elaborate on the nature and extent of
Soviet "aid" to Vietnam, Laos, Cambodia, Mongolia, and
Afghanistan.

Attempting to break the ice, Gorbachev made
conciliatory proposals that for the first time dealt with
Peking's preconditions for a Sino-Soviet reconciliation.
He disclosed that the USSR and Mongolia were jointly
examining "the question of withdrawing a substantial part

of the Soviet troops from Mongolia," and also announced that Moscow would withdraw six regiments from Afghanistan before the end of the year. Turning to the Vietnamese occupation of Cambodia, the Soviet leader seemed to be at pains to create the impression that Moscow was unable, rather than unwilling, to exert leverage in connection with an issue it considered to be largely dependent "on the normalization of Sino-Vietnamese relations." Moscow for the first time implicitly acknowledged "the three obstacles" that the Chinese claimed stood in the way of normalization, (Soviet support for Vietnam's occupation of Cambodia, Soviet military intervention in Afghanistan, and the concentration of Soviet troops on China's northern border) and showed readiness to take steps toward removing at least two of them.

Gorbachev was careful not to admit that the moves connected with Mongolia and Afghanistan were in any way linked to the Sino-Soviet rift. Instead, for the express purposes of "creating an atmosphere of good-neighborliness" and boosting economic cooperation, he threw in several direct and tantalizing proposals. Emphasising the great potential for joint cooperation in developing the border regions and the Soviet Far East, Gorbachev offered concessions on a long-standing dispute over the demarcation of the Sino-Soviet border along the Amur River and suggested the renewal of joint water management projects in the Amur River basin begun in the nineteen-fifties as well as the resumption of construction of a railway from the Xinjiang Uigur Autonomous Region to Kazakhstan. He also proposed cooperation with China in the field of space exploration, including the training of Chinese astronauts. In short, Gorbachev's message was that the world's two leading socialist states shared the same priorities--"those of accelerating social and economic development"--and therefore "why not support each other?"

Gorbachev's Vladivostok speech brought no major concessions, but nevertheless created the impression that Moscow was willing to be more accommodating. Furthermore, it was followed up by the important announcement made on August 6 by Deputy Foreign Minister Mikhail Kapitsa at a press conference,[1] and by political commentator Fedor Burlatskii writing in *Literaturnaia gazeta*, saying that the USSR was ready "to discuss with the Chinese People's Republic commensurate cuts in Soviet and Chinese troops stationed along the border." This offer, according to Kapitsa, had been made by Moscow after the last round of Sino-Soviet normalization talks had ended in the spring.

Surprisingly, Gorbachev did not mention the proposal in his speech.

Peking's reaction was guarded. The first public response came on July 30, when Chinese Foreign Ministry spokesman Yu Zhizhong dismissed Gorbachev's announcement about the withdrawal of six Soviet regiments from Afghanistan before the end of the year, calling for the "prompt and complete" withdrawal of Soviet troops from the country.[2]

The Chinese refrained from heralding Gorbachev's speech as a breakthrough, but acknowledged that it contained some positive factors requiring careful study.[3] On August 6, Yu Zhizhong reflected this more favorable assessment when he told reporters: "We believe that he [Gorbachev] has made some new remarks on the improvement of Sino-Soviet relations which have not been said before. . . . We are studying the speech."[4]

Peking lost no time in tacitly underscoring its desire to find ways of reducing its differences with Moscow. Within days of Gorbachev's speech, China let it be known through Prince Norodom Sihanouk that it had formally offered major economic assistance to Vietnam if the latter were to withdraw its troops from Cambodia.[5] Furthermore, on August 7, Chinese Deputy Foreign Minister Liu Shuqing paid a surprise visit to Ulan Bator, becoming the highest-ranking Chinese official to visit Mongolia in twenty years. His trip resulted in the first consular treaty between the two states.[6]

Sino-Soviet Talks. Neither the visit of Deputy Prime Minister Nikolai Talyzin to Peking in September nor that of Deputy Foreign Minister Igor Rogachev in October brought any breakthrough in Sino-Soviet relations, although the latter talks did reach agreement on resuming frontier discussions after a seven-year lapse. On the basis of "authoritative leaks" from both the Chinese and Soviet delegations, veteran Peking correspondent of the Italian Communist Party newspaper l'Unità Siegmund Ginzberg provided a blow-by-blow account of the markedly tough discussions between Rogachev and his Chinese counterpart, Qian Qichen.[7]

Ginzberg quoted Rogachev as having said after the talks that in his view there was "not a single international problem on which there are antagonistic contradictions between China and the USSR," except for what the Chinese called the "three obstacles." While two of the three obstacles (Afghanistan and Soviet forces on the

frontier) had become "secondary," negotiations had stalled over the third one, the Cambodia-Vietnam issue.
On this, the Chinese stand was as follows:

We are ready to reach a compromise on everything else but not on the principle that Vietnam must withdraw from Cambodia. You know that Vietnam could not remain even one day in Cambodia without your political, military, and economic support. If we do not tackle this issue, there is no question of signing agreements on other matters.

To this, Ginzberg gave the Soviet reply:

In that case, you do not really want to reach an agreement but only to slow down the process of normalization. You have said that you want gestures on one or two of the obstacles in order to speed up normalization. Well, you have had Gorbachev's speech at Vladivostok. Now, instead of discussing those proposals, you say that the Cambodian issue must be settled first. At this point, how can we be sure that, even if we agreed to a compromise on that, you would not then bring up a fourth obstacle?

Qian reviewed "all the positive developments" in Sino-Soviet relations, beginning with Gorbachev's Vladivostok speech, and expressed appreciation for them.

He also, however, produced a list of negative phenomena, on which the Chinese had so far refrained from public comment. These included the emergence in Moscow, both in public and in private, of restrictive "interpretations" of the Gorbachev speech, which in the Chinese view contradicted its spirit, the continuation of frontier incidents, violations of Chinese airspace (according to them, there had been 37 reconnaissance flights from the [time of the] Vladivostok speech until mid-October), and other initiatives (espionage, etc.) which "hurt Chinese national feelings," because "such things are done only among enemies." In short, it was a way of insinuating that "while Gorbachev is saying certain things, are there not some on your side who are working in the opposite direction?"

In reply, Rogachev urged the Chinese not to dramatize matters, suggesting that they concentrate on points of agreement, not disagreement. He proceeded to disclose specific proposals that he had brought with him: the balanced reduction of troops on both sides of the frontier, new agreements on the level of interstate relations, and specific consultations on regional and international problems, beginning with a meeting on Cambodia, to be held in Moscow by the end of 1986, and a second one on Afghanistan, to be held the following year in Peking.

From that point on, the discussion was confined to the Cambodian issue. On this question, the Chinese were awaiting a "gesture" from Gorbachev. This should not have been so difficult, considering that "it all began under Brezhnev," so that the Gorbachev leadership could "take an initiative to get rid of this heavy inherited burden."

In reply, Rogachev advanced the Soviet view, that the way to solve the problem was through direct negotiations between Peking and Hanoi. "We cannot order them to withdraw from Cambodia," he remarked righteously. "Vietnam is a sovereign socialist state: why should you want us to act as a superpower and give them orders?" Instead, the Soviet suggestion was that China should normalize relations first with Vietnam and then with Laos, "leaving time to bring a solution to the Cambodian problem." Making everything dependent on Cambodia would be understood as a desire to hinder Sino-Soviet normalization and would mean that the Chinese still held to the old idea that the principal threat to China came from the USSR and its "encirclement" of the former.

Qian Qichen noted that there was talk in Hanoi of "friendship" with China, but stressed that to accept the idea of direct Sino-Vietnamese negotiations before the basis for a settlement of the Cambodian issue had been reached would mean accepting the *fait accompli* of the Vietnamese occupation, which China simply would not do. Once this issue had been settled, however, the rest would be easier: "We are ready to reach compromises on everything else, but not on the principle that one country cannot occupy another."

The session showed, however, how much "mutual suspicion" remained. The Chinese, Ginzberg said, suspected that the Soviets wanted to impose on them acceptance of the "irreversibility" of the situation in Indochina and, "probably even more important, that they wanted to speed up normalization so as to obtain unilateral advantages, and perhaps create difficulties in Sino-US relations." The

Soviets, on the other hand, saw the Chinese as trying to hold things up, perhaps with the aim of exacting a higher price for normalization.

26
INTO SOUTHEAST ASIA AND THE PACIFIC

Daniel Abele

Vanuatu and Kiribati. In June 1986, the USSR established diplomatic relations with Vanuatu, an island republic in the South Pacific. It also created a Pacific Ocean Department within the Ministry of Foreign Affairs. These developments followed the conclusion in 1985 of a fishing agreement with another island republic in the South Pacific, Kiribati. The Soviet economic and political initiatives being taken in this part of the world came at a time when the US influence in the region was in jeopardy due to disagreements over fishing rights and apparent American indifference to French nuclear testing in the region.

The USSR made use of the nuclear issue to further its political involvement in the South Pacific. In February 1986, Moscow hosted a delegation of representatives from the South Pacific to discuss the Ratatonga Treaty, which banned the stationing, production, and testing of nuclear weapons in the region. Soviet officials suggested an amendment to the treaty banning the transit and visits of nuclear-armed warships and aircraft throughout the nuclear-free zone.[1] In March, Soviet Foreign Minister Eduard Shevardnadze stated in a letter to the prime minister of the Cook Islands that the USSR would accept a nuclear-free zone in the South Pacific if other nuclear powers did the same.[2]

The creation of a new department in the Ministry of Foreign Affairs with responsibility for the South Pacific reflected the growing Soviet interest in the area. The existence of a Pacific Ocean Department was first noted in *Izvestiia* on June 29, 1986.[3] Liudvig Chizhov, formerly an advisor-envoy to the Soviet Embassy in Japan, was named head of the department.[4]

The Soviet Union signed a fishing agreement with the tiny island republic of Kiribati in August 1985. The USSR agreed to pay Kiribati as much as $1.7 million in return for the right for sixteen Soviet trawlers to fish for a year within the republic's exclusive economic zone. Although the Soviet representatives had requested access to onshore facilities for fish processing, ship repair, and replenishment of supplies, the final agreement did not provide for landing rights, and the Soviet trawlers were excluded from the countries 12-mile territorial zone.[5]

Kiribati's president, Ieremia Tabai, defended the fishing pact as "simply a commercial deal," likening it to the sale of wheat to the Soviet Union by the United States.[6] Tabai had stated that he would not allow Kiribati to be used for military purposes and that his country was only interested in the economic benefits of the agreement.[7] He refused, however, to rule out the possibility of an expansion of the contractual provisions at a later date.[8]

Analysts suggested that the sum of $1.7 million to allow sixteen Soviet vessels to fish for tuna in Kiribati's waters was not in line with the anticipated value of the fish. The Soviet offer was said to be double that which US and Japanese fishing fleets had offered for exclusive rights to fish in Kiribati's waters. A US State Department official contended that "there is a political component in the fee, and clearly, in our assessment, the Soviets are trying to establish a presence."[9] A number of observers noted that increasing dependence on Soviet hard currency could eventually lead Kiribati into a situation in which the USSR might demand onshore privileges and rights to bases. Others saw the hefty Soviet payment as having given Kiribati greater economic independence without yielding any political or military advantage in the region to Moscow.[10]

There was also concern that Soviet vessels might make use of their fishing privileges around Kiribati for the purpose of conducting surveillance of US military operations in the area and intercepting communications traffic between the United States and important allies such as Singapore, the Philippines, and Australia.

The fishing agreement was not renewed after it expired in October 1986. The Soviet Union argued that its tuna catch during the year did not match expectations and wanted to lower the $1.7 million license fee it paid. Kiribati refused to accept the proposed Soviet price and severed the arrangement, bluntly stating that the Soviet boats should no longer be in their exclusive economic zone. The Kiribati minister of natural resources and development,

Babera Kirata, suggested that the Soviet Union badly needed a fishing operation in the Pacific and that Soviet officials would eventually return with a better offer. By August 1987, however, there had been no further meetings.[12]

The Soviet Union established diplomatic relations with the South Pacific island of Vanuatu on June 30, 1986. A week before official ties were made, the two countries ended their first round of negotiations on a fishing pact. An agreement was reached in Vanuatu on January 26, 1987, whereby the Soviet Union was to pay $1.5 million for one year's rights for as many as eight vessels to fish in Vanuatu's 200-mile economic zone and stop on the island for food, fuel and other supplies. Soviet requests for permission to establish shore facilities to support its fishing fleet and have landing rights for civilian aircraft were refused, and the Soviet trawlers were not allowed to fish within 12 miles of the coastline.[12]

Vanuatu's prime minister, Walter Lini, an Anglican priest, insisted that the fishing agreement was "a purely commercial and economic deal." He declared that Vanuatu would not allow foreign powers to use its territory for military purposes and explained that only non-nuclear Soviet boats would be allowed into Vanuatu's 200-mile economic zone.[13] Refering to diplomatic relations with the USSR, Prime Minister Lini asserted that these ties did not indicate a shift away form Vanuatu's nonaligned and independent foreign policy, and that there was no danger of Vanuatu drifting toward communism.[14]

ASEAN. In his speech at Vladivostok, Gorbachev suggested that the countries of ASEAN and Indochina establish "mutually acceptable relations," and that given "good will" and noninterference from outside, they could settle their problems for the good of general Asian security." Gorbachev also noted the "positive value" of Soviet-ASEAN bilateral relations and called for stronger economic cooperation.[15]

Statements made during the subsequent visit of a high-ranking Soviet parliamentary delegation to four ASEAN countries shed some additional light on Soviet-ASEAN relations. The delegation, headed by a deputy chairman of the USSR Supreme Soviet, Akil Salimov, toured Indonesia, Singapore, Malaysia, and Thailand in early June meeting with the leaders as well as with foreign ministers and parliamentary representatives of each of the four states.[16]

The Salimov delegation tried to portray the Soviet Union as an Asian country with a vital role to play in solving regional matters and as a state that wished to be seen as a peace-loving neighbor opposed to outside interference and potential military alliances in the region. At a press conference in Singapore, Salimov, an Uzbek, referred to "a common Asiatic heritage" binding the USSR and Southeast Asia and emphasized that "the Soviet Union is an Asian country." He called upon the states of the region to draw on Soviet help to resist the danger of Japan and the United States using their economic dominance to build "a military axis" in the area.[17]

The emphasis of the mission was, however, clearly on developing better relations between the USSR and the ASEAN states, especially Indonesia and Thailand. Salimov suggested that "a wall of suspicion and mistrust" could be penetrated by means of increased economic and cultural cooperation. He repeatedly declared that USSR's interest in Southeast Asia was primarily of an economic nature and that it sought "mutually beneficial business relations".[18]

In Indonesia in May 1986, Soviet representatives offered aid and technology to Jakarta in return for more trade. An agreement was signed to exchange economic information and conduct joint studies on areas in which Soviet technology could be used in Indonesia. The Soviet side also offered commercial loans and technical assistance, and agreed that chamber-of-commerce offices should be set up in each other's capitals. A Soviet proposal to provide shipping of Indonesian products to the Soviet Union, Europe, and other parts of the world was also discussed.[19]

In seven years of occupation in Cambodia, the Vietnamese army had managed to destroy most of the resistance fighters' camps in Cambodia and to strengthen the Thai-Cambodian border against further incursions. The Soviet Union tried to persuade the ASEAN states that their security interests lay in accepting Hanoi's *fait accompli* in Cambodia and creating a peaceful relationship with a Soviet-backed Indochina.[20] Moscow stated its willingness to be a guarantor to a peace accord worked out between the countries of Indochina and ASEAN, but it seemed that any agreement acceptable to the USSR would have had to assure future Vietnamese dominance in Cambodia, which in turn lent security to the Soviet presence in Vietnam.

The ASEAN states, for their part, repeatedly urged the USSR to pressure Vietnam into negotiating the Cambodian issue, suggesting that Soviet influence in this matter would improve Moscow's status and image as a peace-maker in the region.[21] The USSR, which provided Vietnam over $1 billion annually in economic and military aid and maintained   naval bases at Camranh Bay and Da Nang, did not apparently use its leverage to persuade Hanoi to compromise with the ASEAN states on the Cambodian issue.

Indonesia   opened a dialogue with Vietnam   and   showed its willingness   to   reach   a   political   settlement   over Cambodia.   Because Indonesia's position had been relatively conciliatory toward   Vietnam,   the USSR strongly endorsed an Indonesian-Vietnamese   dialogue   in   the   hopes   that   a bilateral agreement would   lead to a reconciliation between the   ASEAN states and Vietnam over the Cambodian issue.   At a press briefing   in   August   1986,   Kapitsa   described   as positive   the   fact that "the ASEAN countries, if not all, then some of them, were maintaining contacts and conducting a   dialogue, in one form or another with the   countries   of Indochina".[22]

On the   other   hand,   Thailand,   which   confronted Vietnamese   soldiers   on its borders and suffered   repeated incursions into its   territory,   still   supported all three Cambodian   resistance   factions.   Bangkok insisted on   the withdrawal   of Vietnamese   troops   from   Cambodia   and   on internationally   supervised   free elections   in   which   the resistance   groups   would   be   represented.   Moscow   saw Thailand's support for the resistance coalition as a   major impediment to a settlement of the Cambodian issue.

The Soviet Union tried to   use   friendly persuasion to move   Thailand toward   a reconciliation with Vietnam on the Cambodian issue.   During   his   visit   to   Bangkok in June, Salimov emphasized that both the USSR and Thailand "can and should play a constructive role"   in strengthening peace in the   region.[23] There was no indication, however,   that   the USSR was willing   to   compromise   on Vietnam's control over Cambodia,   a   point particularly threatening to   Thailand's own security interests.   Kapitsa claimed in August that "a people's democratic system is consolidating in Cambodia and that developments there are   irreversible." It   seemed unlikely that the Soviet Union could expect much diplomatic success among the ASEAN   states   as long as it continued to back Vietnam's military aims in the region.   Much   depended on Moscow's willingness   to   pressure Hanoi   to   reach a political   agreement   with   the ASEAN states over   the Cambodian   issue.   Until   that   occurred,   it   seemed, Soviet-ASEAN relations could   only   be limited to "mutually beneficial" ties.

27
IRAN AND THE GULF WAR

Bohdan Nahaylo and *Daniel Abele**

In the course of 1986, Moscow continued to seek better relations with Teheran while at the same time continuing to supply Iran's enemy, Iraq, with arms. Although measured progress was made in restoring Soviet-Iranian economic ties, the political and ideological differences between the two neighbors continued to rule out any genuine rapprochement. Two major stumbling blocks remained: Moscow's position on the Iran-Iraq war and Teheran's condemnation of the Soviet occupation of Afghanistan. The issue of the pro-Moscow Communist, or Tudeh Party, on which Teheran cracked down in the spring of 1983, lost in importance. Also, the disclosures about the covert supply of US weapons to Iran, while apparently irking Moscow, did not result in any noticeable policy shift toward Teheran.

Progress in Economic Relations. Despite their chilly political relations, Moscow and Teheran acted to improve their economic and trade ties. The ice was broken with a visit to Teheran in February, 1986, by USSR First Deputy Foreign Minister Georgii Kornienko.[1]

Important visits to Moscow were made in August first by the Iranian Deputy Foreign Minister for Economic and International Affairs Mohammad Javad Larijani and later by Iranian Petroleum Minister Gholamreza Aqazadeh. On his return to Teheran, Larijani described his meetings as "positive and constructive." He confirmed that Iran was interested in resuming the export of natural gas to the USSR, which had been stopped soon after the Iranian revolution due to disagreements over prices.[2] Two weeks later, Aqazadeh was notified by his Soviet hosts that the USSR would abide by an Iranian-engineered decision by the Organization of Petroleum Exporting Countries (OPEC) to cut oil production in September and October in order to help OPEC boost falling world oil prices. The oil minister subsequently announced that Iran would shortly resume deliveries of natural gas to the USSR and that the two sides would examine possibilities for joint cooperation in the exploration and exploitation of oil and natural gas resources in the Caspian Sea.[3]

On August 28, Radio Moscow's Persian service stressed

---

* Author of the last three sections.

that it had been "the Iranians" who had "brought up the topic of resuming gas exports to the Soviet Union" and added that "the quantity of gas burned and wasted" by Iran when it stopped deliveries to the USSR "could have brought in enough money to build two other steel mills similar to the the one built in Esfahan with Soviet help." The broadcast also told listeners in Iran that Aqazadeh's visit had given "new impetus" to Soviet-Iranian economic relations and assured them that "the Soviet Union, as a good neighbor, [would] happily accede to Iran's wishes and establish its relations with Iran on the basis of mutual respect, nonintervention in each other's affairs, and, of course, mutual interest."[4]

At a meeting in Teheran in December of the Iran-Soviet Joint Economic Commission, a new protocol was signed, providing for expanded cooperation in commerce, banking, transport, fisheries and technology and for regular consultations. Iranian News Agency IRNA also indicated that the Soviets had agreed not only to send back the technicians building a steel mill in Estafan and two power plants, but also to cooperate in building a dam on the Aras river on their border.[5] However, although the document mentioned that an agreement had been reached on the question of natural gas, no specific date was given for the resumption of Soviet purchases of Iranian natural gas.[6]

Afghanistan. Teheran continued to insist on the unconditional withdrawal of Soviet troops from Afghanistan, while Moscow continued to accuse Iran of inflaming the conflict by sheltering and arming the mujahidin.[7]

The strongest Soviet criticism of Iran's position on Afghanistan appeared in *Izvestiia* on December 2, shortly after it was revealed in the Western press that part of the secret American arms shipments to Iran was destined for the Afghan resistance. The newspaper claimed that a group of Iranian "clergy" had crossed the Afghan border "with the aim of assisting the counterrevolutionaries." After insinuating that the Iranian authorities were in league with the CIA, the newspaper concluded that "the present leadership of Iran . . . pays lip service to its anti-imperialist goals, but in fact . . . is aiding the forces of imperialism to wage an undeclared war against the Democratic Republic of Afghanistan."

The Iranian stance on Afghanistan showed no sign of weakening. On December 15, Iran's minister of the interior, Ali Akbar Mohtashami, said that there were over two million Afghan refugees in his country. Iran was providing them with "economic, cultural, and military assistance." He added that if they wanted military training, "we shall provide that too."[8] Iran had evidently not been impressed by the Kabul regime's declaration of a unilateral ceasefire at the beginning of January, for TASS on February 2 again accused the Iranian authorities of preventing Afghan refugees from returning home to take advantage of the Kabul government's policy of so-called national reconciliation.

In February 1987, the visit to Moscow by Iranian Foreign Minister Ali Akbar Velyati,[9] the highest-level Iranian official to make a trip to the Soviet Union since the Iranian revolution, highlighted the delicate and limited nature of the ties between Moscow and Teheran. Evidently it was not all that successful. At the end of his visit Velyati merely said that his Soviet counterpart, Eduard Shevardnadze, had accepted an invitation to return the visit at some future date and mentioned bilateral agreements dealing with economic cooperation that had in fact already been announced a few months earlier. The visit confirmed that neither side was willing to budge on political differences, and revealed that, if anything, the Soviet Union had started toughening its tone.[10]

On April 9, Moscow Radio's Persian service implicitly blamed the Iranian authorities for an armed raid that had been carried out on the residence of the acting Afghan chargé d'affaires in Teheran. It said that Afghan officials had "strongly protested to Iranian officials about the trampling of accepted norms of international law, demanding that the criminals be punished."

The Iran-Iraq War. The USSR wanted to appear neutral but feared the consequences of an Iranian victory. Moreover, it was tied to Iraq by a treaty of friendship and had been supplying the Iraqis with arms. On the other hand, the USSR did not want to alienate Iran. Consequently, although it had long described the Iran-Iraq war as a "senseless" conflict that only serves the interests of "imperialism, Zionism [and] world reaction," and had called for a prompt political settlement, the Kremlin nevertheless had permitted arms to be transferred to Iran through Syrian, Libyan, and North Korean intermediaries. It had also allowed Iran to move its imports over Soviet territory and thereby circumvent the war-torn Persian Gulf. For these reasons Iran too, could not afford to sever the Soviet connection.[11]

On January 9, 1987, the Soviet government strongly appealed to both Iran and Iraq to end the Gulf war. However, the appeal was addressed more to Teheran than to

Baghdad. It reiterated that the Soviet Union "has consistently stood for the earliest termination of the Iranian-Iraqi armed conflict and for the solution of disputed questions between Iraq and Iran at the table of political negotiations and not on the battlefield." Furthermore, by insisting that a return to prewar borders was essential, the statement effectively called on Iran to withdraw from the Iraqi territory it had captured.

Soviet condemnation of Teheran's secret dealings with the United States was stepped up after various Iranian officials again publicly criticized the USSR and when one of them, the speaker of Iran's Islamic Consultative Assembly, Ali Hashemi Rafsanjani, defended his country's actions and criticized the USSR's response to the affair. On December 9, IRNA quoted Rafsanjani as saying that Moscow should have described the US arms shipments to Iran as "a great victory by a third-world country" and as asking why the USSR continued "strengthening Iraq" despite knowing "it is the aggressor country."

On December 24 *Izvestiia* countered with a strongly worded article claiming that "the hostile attacks on the Soviet Union intensified in Iran after the major political scandal over secret military deliveries to Iran erupted in Washington." The newspaper complained that "many high-ranking Iranian officials" were attempting "to 'equate' the USSR and the United States in the eyes of ordinary Iranians and to put their policies toward Iran on a par."

Iran had been concerned for some time about growing Soviet interest in the Gulf region. In 1986, Moscow established diplomatic relations with two more Gulf states--the United Arab Emirates and the Sultanate of Oman. In February 1987, the Kremlin stepped up its diplomatic activity in the Gulf region by sending First Deputy Foreign Minister Vladimir Petrovskii on visits to Kuwait, Oman, and the United Arab Emirates, as well as Iraq.[12]

Moscow attempted, with some success, to persuade Iran's only Arab supporter-Syria--to move closer to the Soviet position on this question.[13] On May 1, the Iranian Foreign Ministry criticized the Soviet policies in the Gulf, claiming that Moscow was encouraging Iraq by supplying it with military aid, while at the same time seeking an opportunity to increase its influence in the region.[14]

The Soviet-Kuwaiti Tanker Deal. During their seven-year conflict, both Iran and Iraq had been attacking neutral shipping in the Gulf in order to prevent the other side from receiving supplies and continuing its trade. Iran began targeting Kuwaiti-bound vessels, charging that the oil-rich state supported Iraq in the war. Consequently, Kuwait sought help from both the Soviet Union and the United States to protect its merchant shipping in the Gulf, evidently on the assumption that Iran would be reluctant to attack ships flying the flag of one of the superpowers. Both superpowers offered their assistance, but the stricter US maritime regulations made it more difficult for Kuwait to charter American vessels or reregister Kuwaiti ships to fly the American flag.[15]

On April 14 Soviet Foreign Ministry spokesman Gennadii Gerasimov announced Moscow's decision to lease three oil tankers to Kuwait for a three-year period and to offer naval protection for them "if necessary."[16] An Iranian Foreign Ministry spokesman condemned the Soviet- Kuwaiti deal as a "plot" by Iraq's supporters and a "dangerous" move that would exacerbate tensions in the Persian Gulf. Describing the Soviet move as "surprising," he stressed that Teheran regarded only the Persian Gulf states themselves as entitled to intervene in regional issues and that the superpowers should be kept out of the area.[17]

Teheran charged that Moscow, apart from favoring Iraq in the war, was seeking "an excuse" to obtain a foothold in the area, because it "wishes to fulfill the old dreams of the Russian Empire and expand toward the warm seas." The Iranian press dwelled on the theme of an anti-Iranian plot whereby Moscow and the United States were alleged to have acted in collusion, with the result that "Communist tankers, escorted by a Marxist navy fleet, will carry Persian Gulf oil to the capitalist West."[18]

Iranian Attack on a Soviet Vessel. On May 6, the Soviet freighter *Ivan Koroteev* was attacked and damaged in the Persian Gulf by unidentified launches that were almost certainly Iranian.[19] Two days later, TASS confirmed that a Soviet merchant ship had been subjected to "an act of piracy."

Teheran did not directly admit that it was responsible for the attack, but on the day the incident occurred, the Iranian Prime Minister Mir Hossein Mousavi reiterated Iran's opposition to any external intervention in the Gulf region and warned Kuwait to cease bidding for "the protection of the superpowers."[20] Two days later, Iranian President Ali Khameini accused Moscow and Washington of coordinating their policies to favor Iraq. He added that Teheran would not ignore Moscow's "unacceptable" support for Iraq.[21]

The Soviet response was surprisingly restrained. On May 11, Deputy Foreign Minister Petrovskii confirmed that Moscow believed Teheran to be responsible for the attack on the freighter and disclosed that the Kremlin had sent a memorandum to the Iranian government drawing its attention to the incident. Petrovskii reaffirmed the Soviet Union's committment to defending freedom of navigation in the Gulf.[22]

Moscow's Initiative. A visit by Soviet First Deputy Foreign Minister Iulii Vorontsov to Teheran and Baghdad in June shed some light on Soviet diplomatic initiatives in the Persian Gulf region. According to Soviet officials who accompanied Vorontsov, a draft plan was submitted to both Iranian and Iraqi officials calling for a truce in the tanker war and for negotiations between Iranian and Iraqi delegations in Moscow to discuss conditions for ending the seven-year war. Furthermore, according to the Soviet plan, the United Nations was to be asked to arrange international financial aid for reconstruction in the two countries, and OPEC was to be called on to raise Iran's and Iraq's oil output quotas. Other clauses were said to be very secret and were not revealed.[23]

The Soviet sources claimed that the Iranians had disagreed among themselves about some points in the plan but asserted that the results of Vorontsov's trip to Teheran were sufficiently positive for Moscow to send him to Baghdad.[24] One positive outcome of the trip was a statement made after Vorontsov's departure by Prime Minister Musavi that Iran would stop attacking shipping in the Gulf if Iraq did the same.[25]

Moscow's intiatives continued, shortly after Vorontsov's visit, with separate talks in the Kremlin between Soviet President Andrei Gromyko and officials from Iraq and Iran. Gromyko met with Iraqi First Deputy Prime Minister Taha Yassin Ramadan on July 2 and called for negotiations between Iraq and Iran. Subsequently, Gromyko reiterated his appeal to Iranian Deputy Foreign Minister Larijani, saying "the sooner representatives of the two countries sit down at the negotiating table, the better it is for Iran, Iraq, and the international situation as a whole".[26]

Vorontsov returned to Iraq and Iran in the first week of August and paid a visit to President Assad in Syria as well. Soviet Foreign Ministry spokesman Gerasimov noted that the trip was a "continuation of Soviet efforts" to end the Iran-Iraq war "in accordance with a resolution of the UN Security Council." Gerasimov told reporters that in

Teheran Soviet and Iranian officials had discussed reopening a gas pipeline and a possible second rail link between the two countries, but that no formal agreement had been reached.[27] Such facilities would have allowed Iran to reduce its dependence on the Gulf should its oil shipments by that route be disrupted.

An end to the fighting, especially if it came as a result of Soviet efforts, was apt to help the Kremlin in several ways. First, a negotiated end to the war would strengthen the improving ties between Moscow and Teheran. Second, peace in the region would strengthen Arab unity, regarded by Moscow as necessary to counter American influence in the area and Israeli military power. In addition, a Soviet-brokered peace settlement would bolster the standing of Moscow among the more moderate Arab states. Finally, such a settlement would prevent an Iranian victory over an ally of the USSR--an eventuality that could reinforce the growth of Islamic fundamentalism and have repercussions among the Muslim population of the Soviet Union.

The United Nations Resolution. On July 20, the United Nations' Security Council unanimously approved a resolution demanding an immediate ceasefire in the Iran-Iraq war. A companion resolution imposing an embargo on the country that failed to comply with the ceasefire, was to be considered within two months. Significantly, Soviet and American officials worked closely together on the ceasefire resolution and held high-level talks in Moscow, Geneva, and New York. In a letter to President Reagan the day after the resolution was passed, Mikhail Gorbachev noted that the "prerequisites for joint actions by the USSR and the USA at the Security Council" existed and said that he shared Reagan's opinion that there were "good prospects for constructive cooperation."[28]

Nevertheless, there were conflicting signals about Moscow's stance on the embargo resolution. It was reported that Gromyko had affirmed to Iraqi officials in Moscow that "serious measures should be adopted by the Security Council against the party that does not comply with its resolution".[29] On the other hand, Vorontsov was said to have told Iranian officials in Teheran that, if Iran stopped attacks on Soviet ships, Moscow might shun a resolution calling for an embargo.[30] Responding to a call by British Prime Minister Margaret Thatcher for a UN Security Council meeting to discuss an arms embargo, Gorbachev replied that he would "rather we take a slower course than a faster course" on the embargo issue.[31]

Moscow repeatedly called on the United Nations to play a greater role in resolving the Iran-Iraq conflict. In talks at the Kremlin with UN Secretary General Pérez de Cuéllar on June 30, Gorbachev had emphasized the importance of the United Nations in bringing to an end the "protracted and senseless war." He assured the UN Secretary General that the USSR "will act with a sense of responsibility. Let us consider what we can do in the existing situation and what can be done by the Security Council." For his part, Pérez de Cuéllar appealed for cooperation between the Soviet Union and the United States in view of expansion of the war.[32]   Indeed, much depended on the support of all five permanent members of the Security Council for the sanctions resolution. The USSR and China were now the major arms suppliers to Iraq and Iran, so their cooperation was critical to the resolution's success.

On August 5, the Soviet weekly *Literaturnaia gazeta* carried a sharply worded article by Igor Beliaev, chief of the newspaper's foreign policy department and expert on the Middle East. After expounding on the importance of the United Nations resolution of July 20, Beliaev criticized Iran for continuing the war, thereby "deliberately and stubbornly setting itself against the international community." He accused Iran of doing this "demonstratively and even as a challenge," and asked if Teheran was aware of the consequences of its "anti-peace" stance. Furthermore, the author criticized the "provocations" by Iranian pilgrims in Mecca and the burning down of the Kuwaiti embassy in Teheran as "ultimately calculated to wreck the implementation of the resolution of July 20."[33]

The Soviet Stance on the Gulf. Moscow was outspoken in its criticism of the escorting of reflagged Kuwaiti oil tankers through the Persian Gulf by US warships and labeled it an "obvious cause of tension in the region." Soviet Foreign Ministry spokesman Boris Piadyshev warned after the American operation began that US naval escorts "could become the detonator for a major conflict" in the Gulf.[34] A separate TASS analysis accused the United States of using the escort operations as an excuse for a "large-scale military action spearheaded against the countries of the region."[35]

The Soviet Navy had at least four warships in the Gulf accompanying Soviet merchant ships leased to Kuwait.[35] A TASS statement in English on July 3 claimed that the Soviet warships "have nothing to do with the heightening of tension in the area." The statement called on all "states not situated in the area" to withdraw their warships from the Gulf, but it did not say whether this applied to Soviet warships.   Four days later TASS announced that, if the warships of the United States, Britain, and France withdrew from the zone, "the Soviet naval ships will be unconditionally withdrawn."

Soviet Admiral Nikolai N. Amelko, an inspector-advisor in the Ministry of Defense, told reporters on July 17   that "the Soviet Union would oppose any military buildup in the Gulf," adding that the Kremlin's response "would be most negative." Alluding to the American operation, he claimed that Soviet naval policy in the Gulf was "not based on operations against the shore, but to prevent a seaborne attack against the Soviet Union." He also stated that the Soviet Navy had a frigate and three minesweepers in the Persian Gulf, adding that they "constitute absolutely no threat to the countries of the Persian Gulf or the nine US ships deployed there."[37]

While Moscow was quick to voice opposition to the US military presence in the Gulf, it deliberately kept a low profile regarding its own presence there.   The Soviet escort operation received little attention in the Soviet press and was usually mentioned only in contrast to the American involvement. The Soviet naval contingent, which included three minesweepers, was designed not to appear as any threat.

The major obstacle to Soviet efforts to find peace in the Persian Gulf remained the Iranian theocracy's determination to fight the war until the government of Iraqi President Hussein was brought down.   Unilaterally, Moscow could exert little leverage on Teheran to make it relinquish its goal. Moreover, the ceasefire resolution proposed by the UN Security Council could do little good if not supported by strong sanctions to assure compliance. Moscow may have been in a unique position to talk to both sides but, if it hoped to end the fighting, it would have to cooperate with other world powers and stop supplying weapons to the area.

28
THE CHAUTAUQUA CONFERENCE IN LATVIA

Dzintra Bungs

The Chautauqua Institution-Eisenhower Institute Conference on US-Soviet Relations held in Jūrmala, Latvia, on September 15-19, 1986, provided a forum for unprecedented public debates on the state of relations between Washington and Moscow, arms-control issues, regional conflicts, international terrorism, and the role of the media in influencing public opinion.

Although not on the agenda, one of the two recurring themes throughout the meeting was the arrest by the Soviet police of American journalist Nicholas Daniloff, head of the *US News and World Report* bureau in Moscow, on August 30. The second recurring theme was the forcible annexation of Estonia, Latvia, and Lithuania by the USSR during World War II.

When the Soviet Union proposed a Latvian seaside resort near Riga as the venue of the conference, the American side was confronted with the dilemma of holding a conference attended by high-ranking US officials on territory Washington did not accept as lawfully belonging to the USSR. Misgivings were also expressed by Baltic organizations in America.

Each side was represented by a 20-member delegation. The American delegation consisted of US government officials, prominent journalists, and representatives of private organizations devoted to fostering improved international relations and institutions of higher learning. The Soviet delegation included Georgii M. Kornienko, deputy chief of the CPSU Central Committee Department of International Affairs, Deputy Foreign Minister Vladimir Petrovskii, Gennadii I. Ianaev, head of the USSR-USA Society, and other government or party officials; a few delegates represented the media. There was only one delegate from Latvia, Žanis Zakenfelds, Chairman of the Presidium of the Society for Friendship and Cultural Ties between Latvia and Foreign Lands.

It had also been agreed that private citizens could attend the conference. Some 270 Americans traveled to the USSR expressly to do so; they included seven young Americans of Latvian extraction. The less than 2,000 private Soviet participants were all hand-picked by the authorities and had to show special entry tickets. Thus, the ordinary citizen from Riga or Jūrmala had no opportunity to attend what had been envisaged by the American organizers as a "town-hall meeting."

Although the issue of the Soviet Union's forcible annexation of the Baltic States in 1940 was not officially listed on the conference agenda, the matter was raised on the first day by Jack Matlock, a Senior Adviser on Soviet Affairs at the National Security Council and formerly chargé d'affaires in the US embassy in Moscow. After an opening statement in Latvian, Matlock presented a very critical review of US-Soviet relations, particularly in the postwar years. He condemned the USSR for attempting to impose its ideology and system of government on its Eastern and Central European neighbors and Afghanistan, and forcefully reiterated that the United States continued to withhold recognition of the legality of the incorporation of the Baltic States into the USSR. The essence of Matlock's statement was reported by the Soviet Latvian media, and on the following day all of Latvia was abuzz.

Once Matlock had breached the issue, the Baltic question became a regular part of the debates at the conference. An American delegate asked why the USSR did not allow Latvians to exercise the right of self-determination and secession from the USSR--a right that they theoretically possessed. Kornienko, the head of the Soviet delegation, chided the Americans for bringing up the Baltic question and urged them to look at the visas in their passports to find out what country they were in.

In the course of the conference, Soviet security officers declared that they could no longer guarantee the safety of the American Latvians at the conference. This warning was interpreted as intimidation and elicited an official protest from Mark Palmer, US Ambassador Designate to Hungary and a member of the US delegation.

Most of the American participants wore name plates and a lapel pin depicting the stars and stripes of the United States and the maroon-white-maroon colors of independent Latvia. The pin with the two flags became a sought-after souvenir among the local population and figured in the warning issued by the Soviet security agents.

In compliance with the accords reached beforehand, the Soviet Latvian press, radio, and television reported regularly and quite extensively on the political discussions and cultural events comprising the meeting. The conference was described as a unique forum for the open discussion of bilateral issues and as a step in the much longer process of improving relations between Moscow and

Washington. The most complete coverage was provided by Riga Television; the audience could see and hear Matlock deliver his speech in Latvian and Russian, watch the seven young Latvian-Americans taking part in the conference, and catch sight of the controversial lapel pins. In the principal Soviet Latvian newspapers, however, caution and ideological orthodoxy prevailed in the treatment of US-Soviet relations, particularly the US nonrecognition of the Soviet annexation of the Baltic States.

29
HUMAN RIGHTS AND FOREIGN POLICY

Roland Eggleston and *Bohdan Nahaylo**

Helsinki Review Conference Opens in Vienna. The Soviet Union attempted to use the first days of the Helsinki review conference, which opened in Vienna on November 4, 1986, to present a new image to the Western press. By the end of the week most Western journalists were still of the opinion that the reality behind the show was unchanged, but they were intrigued by the intensity of the Soviet public relations efforts.

Soviet diplomats held six public press conferences during the week. The first three were devoted to the main issues of the Helsinki Final Act--human rights and humanitarian affairs, military security, and economic and trade cooperation. The other three, on more varied subjects, followed the speech given by Foreign Minister Eduard Shevardnadze and his meetings with US Secretary of State George Shultz.

Most of the Soviet briefings were conducted by former Soviet Foreign Affairs Spokesman Vladimir Lomeiko, now ambassador-at-large. His partners at the press conferences varied according to the subject. On one occasion, they included his successor as foreign affairs spokesman--Gennadii Gerasimov--and First Deputy Foreign Minister Anatolii Kovalev. Among those at other press conferences was Oleg Grinevskii, who had led the Soviet delegation at the Stockholm security conference. All these officials were in the special team accompanying Shevardnadze, and they left with him.

_____

* Author of the sections on the Shevardnadze speech and the Moscow Peace Forum.

In addition to the press conferences, Lomeiko, Gerasimov, and other members of the Soviet delegation were always ready to talk to press representatives from the Western and the nonaligned countries. Lomeiko, who had once been a correspondent himself, was often to be found in the press room. He and other members of the delegation also had discussions with Western human rights activists and with American women trying to win exit permits for their Soviet husbands.

This willingness to respond to any and all questions gave the Soviet delegation in Vienna a refreshing "new look"; at the previous Helsinki review conference in Madrid, a senior Soviet diplomat had stormed out of a press conference in anger when asked a question about dissidents. In Vienna, all questions received an answer of some sort, even when they concerned repression in the Baltic states, emigration restrictions, Andrei Sakharov, or the invasion of Afghanistan.

By the end of the week, however, many Western journalists were beginning to feel that the new public relations approach was all show; wordy answers were being offered that frequently contained no concrete information. Questions about human rights, for example, usually won a soothing response along these lines:

> We are changing our administrative practices, as we promised at the Bern human contacts conference this year. We have already changed the regulations so that people applying for permission to travel abroad get an answer within a month. In urgent cases, the time has been cut to six days. This will become effective at the beginning of next year. Other measures are in preparation, such as publication of the regulations governing permission to travel abroad. But you must be patient. It takes time.

Soviet spokesmen often confided to journalists: "You know, things are changing since the bad old days." For the first day or two, this satisfied the journalists, but then they began pointing out that it was one thing to be assured of receiving an answer within a month to an application for travel abroad and another thing to know that the answer would be positive.

Western human rights activists spoke to several members of the Soviet delegation about exit permits for Ida Nudel, Vladimir Slepak, Iosif Begun, and Viktor Brailovskii. The Western activists said that they were always given a hearing but that, in the end, the answer was always: Yes, we know about these cases; they are under study, and we are sure they will be settled soon.

The new approach of the Soviet delegation was also found wanting when delegates were faced with hard questions about the persecution of members of churches or congregations not registered with the state or the imprisonment of human rights activists. In answer to such queries, Lomeiko fell back on the old formulation that

> no one is arrested or sentenced for his political views. The only people punished are those who violate the Criminal Code. I can only remind you that every country has its own laws and the right to implement them.

At one press conference, Lomeiko dodged questions about individuals by replying: "If we begin discussing individuals, we will be here for hours."

These and similar answers left many Western reporters doubtful that there was much new in the "new" Soviet information policy. Soviet spokesmen now replied to questions on any subject, but whether the replies really answered the questions was another matter.

Shevardnadze Proposes Conference in Moscow. Shevard-nadze's speech on November 5 brought a surprise: He announced that the USSR was proposing a conference of the thirty-five states that signed the Helsinki Final Act to be held in Moscow to discuss "humanitarian cooperation."[1]

Shevardnadze stressed that Moscow saw "the goals" of the Helsinki process "as promoting more democratic relations between states and greater democracy in public life within each country." He did not spell out what Moscow meant by the word "democracy" but did allude to the fact that the term was understood differently in the East and in the West. "Notions of democracy and freedom are not static," he argued. "What is more, there can be no monopoly on their interpretation and practical implementation."

The Foreign Minister explained that the proposed conference in Moscow should be convened to consider the whole range of problems "in the field of humanitarian cooperation," including "human contacts, information, culture, and education." Here he adhered to what had been the standard Soviet practice of using the term "humanitarian" in preference to "human rights." He did, however, make an exception in one of his numerous barbed references to Washington, alleging that "violations of fundamental human rights are of a systematic and massive nature" in the United States.

Shevardnadze also gave a further assurance that the Kremlin was working to improve its handling of some "humanitarian" questions. "Major legislative and administrative measures are at present being adopted in our country," he said, "to develop international contacts and resolve in a humanitarian spirit problems of family reunification and mixed marriages."[2] The week before, Iurii Kashlev, the head of the Soviet delegation, who also headed the department for humanitarian and cultural contacts of the USSR Ministry of Foreign Affairs, stated at a press conference in Moscow that the Kremlin was reviewing its emigration and travel procedures.[3] Furthermore, on October 29, Konstantin Kharchev, the chairman of the Soviet Council for Religious Affairs, said at the end of a visit to the United States that a review aimed at "democratizing" Soviet life was under way and that the process might extend to the religious sphere.[4]

Soviet Delegates Evade Questions. The message the West was trying to convey to the Soviet Union was that a turn for the better in East-West relations was contingent on an improvement in the Soviet human rights record. Western diplomats said, however, that the Soviet Union and some of its partners remained reluctant to accept respect for human rights as a factor influencing relations between states.

During November there had been daily expressions of concern by the United States, Canada, Britain, and West Germany over Soviet breaches of the human rights and humanitarian commitments in the Helsinki Accords and the Madrid Document. Czechoslovakia and, to a lesser extent, Romania and Bulgaria also came under fire, but the main target of the complaints was the USSR.

The Western criticism of Soviet human rights violations was totally ignored by the Soviet Union. Diplomats attending the daily closed sessions said the Soviet delegation listened to the speeches and the questions but offered no response--perhaps because there was no acceptable answer.

Efforts to start a dialogue on human rights issues were not so much rebuffed as ignored. The Soviet tactic was to counter questions from Western delegates about human rights with a barrage of inquiries about Western problems with unemployment, housing, and similar social issues. Every Western country attacked in Vienna responded a few days later with detailed replies to the Soviet questions.

They all admitted that unemployment was indeed a serious problem, and some acknowledged that they were experiencing difficulties in related areas. They explained what was being done to combat the problems. When the Soviet delegation was asked for equally detailed replies to questions about human rights violations, however, none was forthcoming.

Not surprisingly, the political atmosphere at the Vienna conference began to deteriorate. The conference opened when the optimism created by the meeting in Reykjavik between Reagan and Gorbachev had just begun to ebb. At that time, the atmosphere was neither good nor bad. Subsequently, however, it distinctly worsened. The Soviet Union began to show anger over the daily catalogue of human rights victims presented by US negotiators, over Britain's probing questions about unpublished laws or interruptions of postal and telephone communications, and over the sharp-tongued remarks of Canadian delegate William Bauer.

Western diplomats reported that at times anger seemed to get the upper hand altogether. In one heated session, the USSR said that Britain could only have obtained its information about unpublished laws by espionage or other clandestine means. As Britain pointed out, however, the government newspaper *Izvestiia* discussed some of these unpublished regulations in October, and much of Britain's information was provided by émigrés who had been victims of such laws.

Soviet delegation leader Kashlev usually remained on the fringe of the disputes, but there were sharp exchanges with his deputy, Gennadii Evstafev, who was said by Western diplomats to be a KGB official. He came to the Vienna conference from the United Nations Secretariat. Quickest to anger was Viktor Shikalov, who had years of experience at meetings held in connection with the Helsinki process. Diplomats said that just the mention of the word "Afghanistan" unleashed a torrent of abuse from Shikalov.

Diplomats from both East and West said they wanted to stop the atmosphere from worsening in the remaining weeks before the Christmas recess. The East European countries remained aloof from most of the disputes, though Czechoslovakia and Bulgaria intervened occasionally on the Soviet side. Poland was active in the general debate in the working groups and addressed several questions to Canada and the United States about problems with entry visas. Turkey continued its long-running fight with Bulgaria about the forced assimilation of the ethnic

Turkish minority in Bulgaria. Romania was generally quiet but intervened occasionally to reject allegations that it was mistreating its ethnic Hungarian minority. Czechoslovakia did respond to a British question about a Charter 77 member, but only to say that he had been convicted of theft in the past.

The daily discussions of human rights cast into the shade the sessions devoted to military security and those on improving East-West economic cooperation. The West had little interest in the military discussions, because it was waiting for a report from a high-level group in Brussels on all aspects of Western military policy. Diplomats said the economic discussions were still at the stage of reviewing the situation. Czechoslovakia said it was interested in hosting a meeting on economic problems in Prague, but gave no details.

The Soviet proposal to host a gathering in Moscow to discuss humanitarian problems was formally presented by Kovalev to a plenary session of the conference and later to the press. Kovalev said the USSR believed the whole range of humanitarian issues covered by the Helsinki accords should be studied in Moscow. He indicated that what the Soviet Union considered to be social rights should be discussed along with the political and civil rights stressed by the West. He referred to freedom of expression, access to culture and education, and the provision of credible information. He went on to mention right to work, housing, leisure, and medical care. He also seemed to suggest that peace issues should be on the agenda by saying that people also demanded that "their right to life be guaranteed, given the realities of today when peace has become the supreme asset common to all mankind."

Kovalev did not mention family reunification, marriage between citizens of different states, or the right to travel abroad, which the West considered, along with the free flow of information, to be the heart of the humanitarian chapter of the Helsinki accords.

Kashlev explained that the Soviet Union wanted a conference and not a meeting of experts. In the Helsinki process, a meeting of experts had usually lasted six weeks, while conferences had been longer.

Soviet officials did not propose a date for the conference, but Kovalev suggested it could begin while the Vienna conference was still in progress. This suggestion met with a frosty reception from Western delegates. The head of the US delegation, Warren Zimmermann, said it would be "unprecedented" and unacceptable to the United States.

Follow-up gatherings to a Helsinki review conference had always been held after the review conference and had had to submit a report to the next one. The West considered this system essential to ensure that follow-up gatherings remained subordinate to the review conference, which was the heart of the Helsinki process.

The key question presented to Kovalev and Kashlev at the press conference received an evasive answer each time it was pressed--i.e., would the Soviet Union grant entry permits for the proposed humanitarian conference to nongovernmental organizations and émigré groups? In the West, these groups were a part of all meetings and conferences conducted as part of the Helsinki process. Some nongovernmental organizations were given a semi-official status by Western delegations, particularly by the United States. Others operated independently, holding demonstrations and talking to citizens. Zimmermann told the press that, if such groups were banned from Moscow, no Western states would attend the conference.

Kovalev told the press that the USSR would organize the proposed conference "in keeping with international standards." He was pressed to explain whether "international standards" meant that the USSR would grant entry visas to all citizens and groups that wanted to participate, including émigrés. Kovalev merely added: "We are not afraid of critical voices."

Later an Austrian peace group that opposed nuclear energy asked whether Western groups such as his would be granted entry permits and whether they would be permitted to engage in contacts with unofficial organizations. Kashlev began his reply by noting that the mandate for a conference such as the Moscow one, never included provisions calling for the attendance of certain organizations. He then said that human rights organizations also existed in the Soviet Union. He mentioned the Soviet Committee for European Security, which, he said, monitored activities in the USSR on behalf of the Soviet public. "So we do not exclude the possibility that organizations involved in the Helsinki process could participate," Kashlev said. "But at present it is difficult to be more specific. We'll have to take the existing norms and standards in this particular area into account."

This evasive answer contrasted with Kashlev's comments in an interview carried by the Czechoslovak newspaper *Práce* on December 10. Talking about meetings held as part of the Helsinki process, Kashlev said the US delegation "brings to

the organizing country representatives of many
anti-Socialist, anti-Soviet, Zionist, and other
organizations, dissidents and the like. It rallies all
anti-Soviet bawlers around the conference." The unanswered
question for the Soviet delegation remained: Did it want
the Moscow conference so much that it would be prepared to
allow "the anti-Soviet bawlers" to attend?

Moscow Peace Forum. On February 14-16, 1987, a
Kremlin-sponsored international forum "For a Nuclear-Free
World, For the Survival of Humanity" met in Moscow. It was
an impressive media event designed to promote the USSR's
image as the world's foremost champion of peace and nuclear
disarmament, and thereby give fresh impetus to its
longstanding peace offensive. Having succeeded in
attracting over 900 foreign notables to Moscow, Gorbachev
failed, however, to use the occasion to unveil any new
initiatives in the areas of disarmament and arms control.
As a result, the gathering turned into what can only be
described as a lavish follow-up to the sweeping proposals
made by the Soviet leader on January 15, 1987, calling for
the phased elimination of all nuclear arsenals by the end
of the century.

To some extent, the peace forum was overshadowed by
events showing that, for all Gorbachev's emphasis on "new
thinking" many of the old ways remained. The manner in
which peaceful protests in Moscow by Soviet Jews calling
for the release of the imprisoned Jewish activist Iosif
Begun were brutally broken up on several consecutive days
the week before and the similar treatment on February 15 of
members of an unofficial peace group who also tried to hold
a demonstration soured the atmosphere. On February 14 there
had been a brighter note when Academician Andrei Sakharov
participated in the forum and was allowed to deliver a
brief speech to a closed session of scientists. Even then,
however, the Soviet media did not report Sakharov's renewed
call for the release of all political prisoners and freer
emigration. What is more, although TASS and Moscow Radio
and Television did acknowledge that the leading human
rights campaigner had taken part in the forum, they focused
on his opposition to SDI and failed to mention his
criticism of the Soviet negotiating position on arms
control.[5]

The authorities were clearly worried about the adverse
publicity generated by their handling of the protests by
Jews and unofficial peace activists. On February 15, after
TASS had condemned attempts by "refuseniks" to appeal to
participants in the international peace forum, calling this

action a provocation abetted by opponents of détente and nuclear disarmament,[6] and after it had emerged that members of the unofficial Group to Establish Trust Between the USA and the USSR had been prevented from holding a demonstration,[7] efforts were made to repair the damage. First, in the afternoon Dr. Evgenii Chazov, head of the Soviet Academy of Medical Sciences, informed participants in the forum that Begun had been freed.[8] Soon afterwards, senior Soviet official Georgii Arbatov declared on US television that he had just been informed of the dissident's release.[9] The fact that a day later members of Begun's family were being told by the USSR Ministry of Internal Affairs that it had received no instructions to release Begun from Chistopol Prison[10] seemed to confirm how hastily the move to limit the damage to the major public relations effort had been made.

The week had begun with the announcement of the release of numerous political prisoners and assurances that the pardoning process would continue, as well as with a demonstration in Moscow by Begun's relatives and friends that to everyone's surprise was not broken up by the police. Yet by February 13, Jewish demonstrators, and for that matter Western journalists who were watching them, had been beaten up and detained. In the meantime, Foreign Ministry spokesman Gerasimov had also indicated that the pardoning process was of a strictly limited nature and that some officials wanted to toughen, not soften, legislation.[11]

Harder Line in Vienna. Western diplomats in Vienna said that little of Gorbachev's promised "new thinking" was evident in the Soviet performance at the conference. None of the thirty-two Soviet-sponsored proposals on the table in Vienna dealt with humanitarian problems; nor were Soviet delegates in Vienna willing to discuss in any detail the reported changes in Soviet emigration policies. Most of the Soviet-sponsored proposals continued to emphasize military issues, cooperation among young people, and steps to promote peace.

The chief British delegate, Laurence O'Keeffe, told the conference that there had been widespread disappointment that most of the Soviet and Warsaw Pact ideas were carry-overs from previous conferences "when new thinking was rare if not downright unpopular." O'Keeffe called on the Soviet delegation to offer proposals that would show that the new social and economic policies were being put into effect.

Similarly, Italy said that a proposal on religion

sponsored by the Soviet Union, Bulgaria and Czechoslovakia was virtually the same as the one presented at the human rights meeting in Ottawa two years previously. Italy said the proposal stressed the restrictions on religion rather than religious freedom "and does not reflect in any way the new course of Soviet policy of which we hear so much."

Western diplomats emphasized that their criticisms should not be interpreted as disbelief that changes were really taking place. They accepted that the leadership was making important moves in a number of areas. They were genuinely surprised, however, that so little had trickled down to the Vienna conference, which could have been a showcase for the changes. Several reports from Moscow, for example, spoke of allowing more people to travel abroad for family meetings, but these statements were not matched by any Soviet-sponsored proposal in Vienna on easing regulations governing the issuance of exit visas.

The only Soviet-sponsored proposal on travel concerned entry visas. In effect, it was a repetition of a longstanding Soviet complaint about the procedures faced by trade unionists, peace groups, and members of similar organizations in gaining entry visas to Western countries. Diplomats said it was aimed particularly at the United States. There was no mention in the proposal of travel for family reasons.

A separate Hungarian proposal on entry visas that did refer to family ties was not supported by any other Warsaw Pact country. It called for entry permits for family meetings to be granted within seven days. Western diplomats speculated that the Hungarian proposal could be embarrassing for the Soviet Union and most of its allies, because it would apply to East European émigrés wanting to make a short trip home. East European countries generally banned return visits by émigrés who had gone to the West.

Soviet officials also promised a reform of the legal system, yet when Western delegates to the conference advanced a proposal stipulating that no one should be subject to arbitrary arrest, detention, or exile and no one should be kept in isolation for long periods, there was no discussion.

Western diplomats in Vienna said the Soviet delegation was unwilling to go far toward accepting humanitarian proposals, insisting that its maximum concessions were contained in the draft final document offered at the 1986 meeting on humanitarian problems in Bern, Switzerland.[12]

Diplomats at the Vienna conference said that in March

the Soviet delegation had apparently received orders from Moscow to be more aggressive. On March 30, Soviet delegates attacked Western social problems, including housing and unemployment, in unusually harsh terms. Western diplomats protested against the tone and the "exaggerations" in the Soviet speeches. They accused the Soviet Union of trying to suggest that social problems existed only in the West, despite evidence in the Soviet press of social problems. Diplomats said the Soviet delegation was also taking a very hard line in corridor discussions of the human rights and humanitarian issues that were at the heart of East-West differences at the conference.

The change came only ten days before the conference was scheduled to adjourn for a month. Some analysts believed that by taking a hard line Moscow wanted to dampen Western hopes that major concessions could be won on humanitarian issues. Some Western diplomats had said openly that the Soviet Union was eager for a new conference on military security and should be made to pay for it with concessions in the humanitarian field. Others believed that developments initiated by Gorbachev had opened opportunities for the West to obtain such concessions. Individual Soviet diplomats had always maintained, however, that the USSR would not bow to Western pressure with regard to humanitarian issues.

Diplomats said the new hard-line attitude was particularly evident in the Soviet response to Western demands that the USSR and its allies introduce easier regulations for foreign travel, especially in the case of family reunification. In the previous weeks, the United States, Canada, Britain, Holland, and West Germany had pressed the USSR to honor the obligation accepted in the UN Charter and other documents allowing citizens to leave and return to their own country. One of the boldest proposals advanced was an Austrian-Swiss initiative calling upon the Soviet Union and its allies to give travel permits to all applicants by September 30 and to promise later applicants speedy handling of their papers. The Soviet delegation reacted with anger and sarcasm. Its major tactic, however, was to suggest that the natural right of citizens to leave their own country should be matched by a right to enter a foreign country. This was rejected out of hand by the West, which said that entry visas had to be controlled for a variety of economic, social, and political reasons.

Diplomats said there was no doubt that the Soviet Union saw a new conference on military security as the major goal of the Vienna conference. There were thirteen Warsaw Pact proposals on various aspects of military security but there was not even one Soviet proposal on individual human rights. Senior Soviet diplomats told a number of Western delegates in separate conversations that there would be no agreements on any humanitarian issue until the military issue was settled.

Diplomats said there was a strong suggestion in all these conversations that the USSR was prepared to be "generous" with regard to humanitarian issues if the West would make concessions on the terms of the military conference. The Soviet Union was hinting broadly that humanitarian issues could be settled in two or three weeks. Most Western diplomats reacted skeptically, doubting whether it would be possible to obtain worthwhile texts on such major issues as religious freedom, travel for family reunification, and minority rights in such a short time.

Two military conferences were under consideration in Vienna. One was a continuation of the 1986 security conference in Stockholm on exchanges of information and other confidence-building measures. The other was to negotiate cuts in conventional forces and weapons across Europe from the Atlantic to the Urals. It would replace the MBFR conference which had unsuccessfully tried to negotiate on conventional weapons just in Central Europe since 1973. Preliminary talks on the new conference had been under way between the twenty-three members of NATO and the Warsaw Pact for several weeks. Participants said that ideas on what should be discussed at the conference converged in some areas but that there were also deep differences.

Diplomats said the Soviet half-promises regarding human rights were aimed at winning support for their ideas for the conference on conventional weapons. There was no decision as to what sort of link should exist between the conference on weapons and the Helsinki process. There were differences within NATO and in the neutral group as to what the link should be and even whether there should be one at all. The Warsaw Pact's official position was that the talks should be fully integrated into the Helsinki process with the participation of all thirty-five signatory states. Some diplomats believed that this problem alone would take months to be settled to the satisfaction of all. The Soviet Union and its allies were pushing hard, however, for a quick agreement on all issues.

FERMENT AMONG SOVIET NATIONALITIES

30
THE KAZAKHSTAN RIOTS

Bess Brown

On December 16, 1986, TASS announced that a plenum of the Central Committee of the communist party of Kazakhstan had released Dinmukhamed Kunaev from the post of first secretary in connection with his retirement. Kunaev, a Kazakh who had headed the party organization of his native republic for nearly twenty-five years, was succeeded by Gennadii Vasilevich Kolbin, formerly first secretary of the Ulianovsk Oblast Party Committee, who was not known to have any previous connection with Kazakhstan. The primary concern of the authorities in Moscow was probably to install a capable administrator who would not be influenced by personal associations that might interfere with the process of cleaning up the corruption and inefficiency that had developed in the Kazakh SSR during the Kunaev years. In addition, the choice of Kolbin to replace Kunaev served as an illustration of the vigorously espoused principle of exchange of cadres between republics.[1]

On the day following Kunaev's removal, students of higher educational institutions in Alma-Ata took to the streets in the Kazakh capital to protest the decisions of the plenum, according to TASS,[2] which reported the events with unusual promptness. The wording of the report indicated that the students' anger was primarily the result of the selection of a Russian to head the republican party organization. During the Kunaev years, Kazakhs had come to dominate the party and state apparatus of the republic and, at least in Alma-Ata, the higher education establishment as well. It was understandable, therefore, that nationally conscious members of the Kazakh population feared what the choice of a Russian to head the republican party organization could portend for the Kazakh cultural and political gains made during the Kunaev era.

Initially, unofficial Soviet estimates of the number of participants in the Alma-Ata disturbances ranged from a few hundred to 10,000.[3] The protesting students, according to an APN account, armed themselves with sticks and iron rods and rampaged in the city's central square, shouting "Kazakhstan for the Kazakhs".[4] Other accounts claimed that the students carried banners with slogans such as "We Want To Join China", "America Is with Us, The Russians against Us," "Kolbin Go Back to Russia" and demands for a separate seat for Kazakhstan at the United Nations.[5] It is unclear at what point persons other than students joined in the disturbances. TASS merely stated on December 18 that the situation was taken advantage of by "parasitic and other anti-social persons" to attack law enforcement officials, set fire to a food store and private cars, and "insult" citizens. Several of the unofficial accounts of the disturbances claimed that an attempt was made by rioters to seize the building of the republic's Party Central Committee and the central prison. If the latter was an objective, the rioters presumably sought to free Kazakh officials arrested for corruption in the first tentative steps in a clean-up campaign which, although it would be greatly accelerated by Kolbin, had in fact begun before Kunaev's removal.

On December 18, Mikhail Solomentsev, head of the CPSU's Party Control Committee, was dispatched to Kazakhstan to investigate the disturbances. In the company of Kolbin and the first secretary of the Alma-Ata Oblast Party Committee, he toured factories and a kolkhoz market, taking a conspicuous interest in the problems of ordinary people, which had been complicated by the economic decline of the later years of Kunaev's period in office. After stops at two institutions of higher education, Solomentsev lectured republican Komsomol leaders on shortcomings in internationalist upbringing. It appeared from press reports on Solomentsev's stay in Alma-Ata that the authorities in Moscow were taking advantage of the tense situation to highlight the problems that had developed in the republic under Kunaev and justify the choice of a tough manager like Kolbin to deal with them.

<u>Background to the Riots</u>. Solomentsev's criticism of the Komsomol, which was undoubtedly directed at the manifestations of Kazakh nationalism during the Alma-Ata riots, was only one indication of Moscow's impatience with the presumably excessive growth of Kazakh national consciousness during Kunaev's time. Although Kunaev himself seemed fully russified, he presided over the appointment of

Kazakhs to more high party and government posts than their share in the republic's population would justify. For a few years even the head of the republican KGB was a Kazakh. Kunaev allowed a situation to develop in which the Slavs, who made up more than half of Kazakhstan's population, perceived themselves as having become second-class citizens. Now Moscow chose to stress the multinational character of the republic and to restore ethnic balance in the staffing of official positions.

In previous years, emigrants from the Kazakh SSR had complained that the Kazakhs were "taking over" the best jobs as well as official positions in the republic.[6] Certainly, Kazakh national self-consciousness had been growing along with the educational level of the population, and the Kazakhs, particularly many members of the intelligentsia, had come to believe in their right to dominance in what they regarded as their own republic. In 1983, an outspoken proponent of Kazakh national pride, Olzhas Suleimenov,[7] was elected head of the Writers' Union of Kazakhstan. During the latter years of Kunaev's rule, the Kazakh-language press contained numerous discussions of the importance of retaining and developing the native tongue, while Kazakh historians sought to demonstrate that, although their ancestors were nomads, they did not lack a developed culture before the advent of the Russians. Kazakh national pride undoubtedly also received a boost from the knowledge that the Kazakh share of the republic's population had been steadily increasing, while the Slavic share had been declining.

While the "Kazakhization" of Kazakhstan proceeded, the republic's economic performance was declining. Both industry and agriculture made a poor showing during the Eleventh Five-Year Plan period, with the grain harvest ranging from poor to indifferent. In August 1986, the CPSU Central Commmittee sharply attacked the republican leadership for the failure of the livestock industry to meet its plan targets.[8] For most of the year the Moscow press seemed to delight in focusing on the shortcomings of the republican economy. The fact that the republic had met its grain procurement target was not considered particularly interesting. On December 4, *Izvestiia* commented that the meat industry in Kazakhstan had shown some improvement, but that the shortfalls of previous years had been too great, and that despite a large increase in meat procurement, Kazakhstan--along with its neighbor Kirgizia--had the lowest percentage of plan fulfillment among the republics. All of this was clearly a reflection on Kunaev's ability to guide the economy of one of the Soviet Union's economically most important republics.

Moscow's interest in Kazakhstan's economic development was evidenced not only by the attack in *Pravda* in August on the state of the republic's livestock industry but also by the visit of chairman of the USSR Council of Ministers, Nikolai Ryzhkov, to the oilfields of Uralsk and Gurev Oblasts in early December. At that time, Moscow let it be known that Kazakhstan was expected to play a much greater role in total Soviet oil output in the future.

The extent of official corruption in Kazakhstan under Kunaev apparently bore some resemblance to that in Uzbekistan under Rashidov. Little of this had, however, been revealed in the republican press, which had not provided much evidence of *glasnost*. Before Kunaev's fall most information on corruption in Kazakhstan came from the central press.

Aftermath of the Riots. In Kazakhstan, a seemingly unending series of "lessons" were being drawn from the events in Alma-Ata. These included the need for the moral regeneration of political and social life in the republic, and for Komsomol officials to be more responsive to the needs of young people. *Komsomolskaia pravda* complained on May 12, 1987, that the Komsomol organization of Kazakhstan seemed not to have learned the necessary lessons from the riots and amended its style of working.

A correspondent of the propagandists' weekly *Argumenty i fakty* tried to gain specific information on what took place in Alma-Ata from the head of the Kazakh Central Committee's Department of Propaganda and Agitation, A. A. Ustinov, in the course of an interview published in April.[9] Ustinov said he thought that the largest number of participants at any one time was 3,000, but stressed that the size of the crowd varied during the two days of the disturbances. Ustinov was critical of claims broadcast by foreign radios that there had been numerous casualties, claiming that only one volunteer law enforcement official had been killed.

However, in early February 1987, APN chief Valentin Falin told an interviewer from *Die Welt* that there had been no deaths among the demonstrators but that some of those responsible for keeping order had been killed.[10] A few days later, Nursultan Nazarbaev, chairman of the Council of Ministers of Kazakhstan, told foreign correspondents that two people had died in the disturbances, a public order volunteer and a student. An APN account distributed in May by the Soviet Embassy in Vienna reported that some 200 people who had been injured required medical treatment and that an employee of the Kazakh Television Center, S. Savitskii, died as a result of his injuries. Other accounts identified Savitskii as the volunteer militiaman earlier described as having died in the riots.

Unofficial accounts of the numbers of persons killed, injured, or arrested during the riots varied widely. One samizdat account, published in the Russian-language Israeli journal *Strana i mir* and purporting to have been written by an eyewitness, claimed that 280 students and 29 law enforcement officials had been killed.[11] According to *Strana i mir*, the Ministry of Internal Affairs in Kazakhstan let it be known that 280 people had been arrested in connection with the rioting, which suggests the author of the article may have been passing on rumors in which numbers and categories became confused. This account suggested that law enforcement officials had been able to obscure the number of deaths because many of the demonstrators came from outside Alma-Ata, so that those killed would have been buried away from the capital.

In January and February, three persons were sentenced for their role in the riots. Zh. A. Sabitova, a schoolteacher, was convicted of incitement for having prepared a poster and leaflets that supposedly stirred up hatred between nationalities. K. Rakhmetov, a former Komsomol secretary in the physics department of Kazakh State University, was convicted of having incited students to disturb the peace and not followed the orders of law enforcement officials.[12] M. Asylbaev, an unemployed chronic alcoholic, was convicted of having participated in the riots on December 18 and having incited others to disturb the peace and assault policemen, military personnel, and public order volunteers.[13]

Rather than publicly prosecuting low-ranking individuals involved in the riots, the establishment concentrated on seeking out the alleged organizers of the disturbances, said by Kolbin to have constituted a very narrow circle of extremists, who wanted to protect their privileged positions. References to the riots, having been made possible because of the climate created by the shortcomings of the Kunaev era, suggested that the culprits were being sought primarily among close associates of Kunaev.

31
LANGUAGE DEMANDS IN BELORUSSIA AND THE UKRAINE

Roman Solchanyk

<u>Belorussia</u>. "What is Belorussian about our urban general education schools?" Kastus Tarasau asked in the September 1986 issue of the Belorussian literary weekly *Literatura i mastatstva*. Virtually nothing, was the answer. In the entire Belorussian SSR there was, according to the republic's Ministry of Education, only one urban school where Belorussian was the language of instruction--the secondary school No. 108 in Minsk.

A problem no less important was the inclination of parents to request that their children be exempt from studying Belorussian as a subject. In Minsk, where there were more than 100,000 pupils, over 11,000 had been exempted from studying Belorussian. These were mostly the children of physicians, engineers, military officers, and other professionals. Most disconcerting was that among those who had successfully requested exemptions were teachers, university lecturers, and employees of the republic's Ministry of Education, including Belorussian-language specialists. The problem was that well-educated parents, wishing the best for their children, including a good education, saw no benefit for their children in studying the Belorussian language.

> "This kind of situation cannot be permitted to go on any longer. It has come to the point that, at meetings of the pedagogical council, individual teachers and pupils who dare to speak Belorussian in the school have been accused of--'nationalism'(!)."

The quotation is from a collective letter signed by thirteen teachers at a Minsk school and published in *Literatura i mastatstva*.[1] It is one of many that the editors said had been sent by readers in response to an earlier letter and accompanying commentary lamenting the dismal situation in the republic's schools with regard to the study of Belorussian. The proposals advanced by the readers amounted to nothing less than a return to the *korenizatsiia* [indigenization] policy of the nineteen-twenties. They included the suggestion that legislation be adopted to safeguard the Belorussian language.

The thirteen authors of the collective letter demanded that their school, the Minsk Republican Boarding School of Music and Fine Arts, be transformed from a Russian into a Belorussian institution. They argued that the school was originally founded for the express purpose of providing rural children with an opportunity to obtain a fine arts education. Yet, among the twenty-five students admitted to the fifth grade, only one was from a rural area because admission procedures discriminated against applicants from the countryside, where the Belorussian language still predominated.

A resident of Minsk thought that anyone applying for admission to institutes and technical colleges in Belorussia should be required to pass an examination in the Belorussian language and that all the humanities should be taught in Belorussian. The most forthright and emotional response came from a journalist in Gomel:

We have nothing more Belorussian than the language. If the language dies, there can be no talk of any kind of Belorussia. . . . We are talking about the future of our people, of our children.

The debate on the status of the Belorussian language continued in *Literatura i mastatstva*, with an article by P. Sadouski. The author raised the question of when pupils should begin studying the Belorussian language in schools with Russian as the language of instruction. In order to determine this, a year-long experiment was conducted in two raions of Minsk in which pupils were taught Belorussian from grade one. The results were positive. "The views of parents, teachers, and scholars," writes Sadouski, "were unanimous: Begin teaching [Belorussian] in the first grade."

However, at a session of the collegium of the Ministry of Education, which met to discuss Belorussian textbooks for beginning classes, the plan was aborted by First Deputy Minister of Education, M. M. Kruglei. Sadouski describes the scene:

All who were present knew about the results of the experiment, but M. M. Kruglei effectively put an end to the issue, saying essentially the following: "You know, comrades, the view exists that we should wait with this; we could be misunderstood in Moscow. Just now a decree has been issued about improving the teaching of Russian."

On December 15, 1986, twenty-eight Belorussian cultural figures addressed a letter to Gorbachev expressing their concern for the fate of the Belorussian language, and urging that steps be taken to preclude "the spiritual extinction" of the Belorussian nation. The letter carried the signatures of writers, artists, composers, journalists, and scholars, including well-known literary figures. Attached to it in the form of a supplement was a document entitled "Comprehensive Proposals for the Fundamental Improvement of the State of the Native Language, Culture, and Patriotic Upbringing in the Belorussian SSR."

The existence of the letter was revealed by another Belorussian writer, Ales Adamovich, in early March 1987 at a press conference in West Berlin held in connection with the international film festival there. The result, he said, had been that a commission from Moscow was dispatched to the republic.[2] The letter was subsequently made available by the Association of Byelorussians in Great Britain.[3]

The authors pointed out that between 1981 and 1984 the percentage of literary works issued in Russian by the republic's publishing houses increased from 89.9 percent to 95.3 percent. Films in the Belorussian language were practically nonexistent. Only three of the fifteen theaters staged productions in Belorussian. "The Belorussian language as a working language and the language of correspondence is virtually absent in the party, soviet, and state organs and institutions of the republic."

The letter argued that the existing situation had resulted in a growth of national consciousness that had, in turn, led to "a negative reaction from the bureaucracy." Individuals who used the native language were often automatically regarded as "nationalists," and it therefore required a certain amount of "civil courage" to consistently utilize the Belorussian language.

The following measures, said the authors, were necessary as the first order of priority:

(1) introduction of the Belorussian language as the working language in the party and state organs;

(2) introduction of compulsory examinations for graduation in Belorussian language and literature in the secondary schools and in Belorussian language in the eight-year schools irrespective of the language of instruction;

(3) introduction of compulsory entrance examinations
    in Belorussian language and literature for all
    graduates (except those coming from outside the
    Belorussian SSR and the USSR) in all
    institutions of higher education and in
    Belorussian language in secondary specialized
    education institutions (technical colleges) in
    the republic.

The Belorussian language should, the letter continued,
be protected by state legislation, and its utilization in
all spheres of public life guaranteed and promoted by a
series of measures for patriotic upbringing.

The entire system of education, according to the
proposals, should provide for language continuity. If
there was to be education in the native language, it would
have to begin in the preschool institutions and continue on
to the universities. All rural schools should be
Belorussian, and Belorussian schools should be opened in
the cities in numbers corresponding with the national
composition. Schools with Russian as the language of
instruction should teach the Belorussian language beginning
with the first grade. A journal entitled *The Belorussian
Language and Literature in the School* should be
established. All pedagogical institutes in the republic
should be reorganized into Belorussian-language
institutions.

The proposals envisaged both scholarly works on the
development of the Belorussian language and research
devoted to the history of Belorussian literature and
culture. Specific series of facsimile publications
entitled "Monuments of the Belorussian Language,"
"Monuments of Belorussian Culture," "Monuments of
Belorussian Literature," and "Monuments of Social Thought
of Belorussia" should be issued. Books by associates of
the Social Sciences Division of the Belorussian Academy of
Sciences as well as those of all other divisions dealing
with regional topics should be published in Belorussian.

In March 1987, the campaign in defense of the native
language elicited a response from the top leadership of the
Belorussian Communist party. Addressing the sixth plenum
of the party's Central Committee, First Secretary Efrem
Sokolov, while admitting that the use of Belorussian had
fallen off somewhat, categorically rejected critics'
assertions that there were any problems in this area.

Sokolov grouped his counterarguments into three
categories. First, Leninist nationalities policy guaranteed

individuals the right to decide freely for themselves what language they wished to use. In Belorussia, Sokolov said, practically the entire population understood both Belorussian and Russian, and he cited the census results for 1979 to the effect that almost 80 percent of the republic's inhabitants claimed Russian either as their native or as their second language.

> No one tells anyone what language they should use when conversing with friends or speaking from the rostrum. No one tells anyone in what language poems and novels should be written.

Second, Sokolov argued, it would be necessary to take into account the increasingly intensive processes of urbanization and internationalization and the growth of multinational collectives in the republic, where the language of discourse is Russian. Third, according to the Belorussian party leader, "all the [necessary] conditions have been created in the republic for the development of the Belorussian language and Belorussian national culture as a whole."

The Belorussian party leader made a *political* statement saying, in effect, that from the party's standpoint the discussion about the need to improve the role and status of the Belorussian language was over and that those who had raised these issues in the first place were mistaken. According to Sokolov,

> those who would like to dramatize the situation should be aware that this does not serve the cause of restructuring.

Sokolov may have acted more or less independently. Some Western observers suggested that Kremlin opinion on the most important issues of the day was far from being unanimous and that the party's political leadership remained in a state of flux. Notwithstanding the categorically negative response from the first secretary, the proponents of change were keeping the pressure on. At a plenum of the Board of the USSR Writers' Union convened in Moscow at the end of April, the well-known poet and literary critic Nil Hilevich focused primarily on the language question.[4] He explained that without language there could be no literature:

> The artistic level of a work is directly dependent on
> the linguistic skill of the writer, on the richness
> and vivacity of his vocabulary, on how natural his
> phrase sounds. Where and how can a Belorussian
> writer enrich and improve his working language? The
> national language, after all, develops under natural
> conditions--in private life, in the family, in
> people's production relations. But what if these
> conditions for its development are not there?

Hilevich informed his listeners that at a meeting of Belorussian writers, the major topic of discussion had been "one greatly distressing discovery"--namely, that neither in Minsk nor even in any small town in the republic could a single Belorussian school be found. "There are English, French, and Spanish schools but no Belorussian schools." This, then was the state of the language in Belorussia, said Hilevich, which resulted from "objective" as well as "subjective, voluntaristic reasons." In order to turn the situation around, he continued, there had to be outside help.

Ukraine. Several developments in Ukrainian literature and the arts indicated that the liberalization of Russian cultural life may have had a "fallout effect" in the Ukraine. Although by no means as all-embracing as the changes in Moscow or Leningrad, there were signs that the relaxation of controls that had led some observers to speak of a cultural renaissance in the Soviet Union, was having an impact in Kiev as well.

In November 1986, it was announced that Oles Honchar's controversial novel *Sobor* (The Cathedral) would soon be available once again to Ukrainian readers.[5] The work caused a political storm when first published in the Ukraine in 1968 because of its criticism of the destruction of Ukrainian historical and cultural monuments. Honchar focused on the issue of national identity and historical continuity as symbolized by an ancient Cossack cathedral that was threatened with destruction at the hands of an eager "cultural worker" in a small village in the industrial heartland of the Ukraine. Interwoven with this main theme were such issues as the philistinism of mindless bureaucrats and the ecological disasters that had resulted from the destructive drive for "progress" at all costs.

In October, the Ukrainian cultural weekly *Kultura i zhyttya* reported on a meeting between leading figures of Ukrainian theater with the republican minister of culture, Yu. O. Olenenko. Among the "leading figures" who attended the meeting, the newspaper named Les Tanyuk, identifying him as the chief director of the Kiev Youth Theater.[6]

In the early nineteen-sixties, Tanyuk's innovative style and inclination toward experimental techniques proved too much for the Ukrainian cultural establishment. Shunned by conservative theater directors, Tanyuk was forced to "emigrate" to Moscow.[7]

In 1987, the Ukrainian cultural press was exceptionally forthright in its criticism of the Ukrainian theater, emphasizing the urgent need for a radical overhaul. At the meeting attended by Tanyuk, the Minister of Culture explained that "the cardinal question" was the need to do everything possible with all speed to raise the ideological and artistic level of creativity. He noted that bad productions "have taken deep root in our practice. . . . One sometimes gets the impression that some of our theaters stage productions only in order to meet output figures."[8]

Ukrainian writers continued pushing for an improvement in the overall status of the native language in the Ukraine. The plenum of the Board of the Ukrainian Writers' Union convened in Kiev on November 18 discussed the problem of "literature and acceleration."[9]

The meeting opened with a speech by Yurii Mushketyk, the newly elected first secretary of the Board, who encouraged his colleagues not to gloss over longstanding sore points. Prose writer Volodymyr Drozd called for state decisions in support of the Ukrainian language:

> Appeals to respect the Ukrainian language alone are not enough. What is needed here are decisions by the state. The Ukrainian language must become fundamentally indispensable in everyday life, in the theater, in scholarship, and in institutions of higher learning; then there will be no need for appeals, and even the Philistine will draw the appropriate conclusions.

Drozd was suggesting nothing less than a return to the Ukrainization policies of the nineteen-twenties.

Writer Serhii Plachynda in the March 1987 issue of *Literaturna Ukraina* suggested that in each of the Union republics two languages should be given the status of state languages and that in the Autonomous republics three languages should be designated as state languages. The experience of Switzerland, and the constitutions of the three Transcaucasian republics Plachynda argued, showed that this was realistic.[10] Plachynda also made the following observations:

1. Russians and other national minorities residing in the Ukraine should learn Ukrainian. Plachynda quoted from a *Pravda* article by Iulian Bromlei, chairman of the USSR Academy of Sciences' Scientific Council on Nationality Problems, who argued that it was important for Russians and other nonindigenous groups to learn the language of the republic in which they resided.[11] This process could be helped along, said Plachynda, by the establishment at various enterprises, institutions and universities, of clubs for native-language enthusiasts, with sections for each of the languages spoken in the republic.

2. The provision of the draft Statute on secondary schools,[12] giving parents the right to decide whether their children would attend a school with the native language or some other language, most often Russian, as the language of instruction, should be dropped. In its place, Plachynda proposed the following alternative: "The language of instruction in the school [should be] determined by the Council of Ministers of the Union republic in accordance with the national composition of the pupils."

Statistics revealed that in the twenty-year period between 1953 and 1973 the percentage of pupils in the Ukraine receiving their education in Russian almost doubled, rising from 23.8 percent to about 40 percent.[13] According to figures cited by Mikhail Guboglo, one of the leading Soviet specialists on ethnolinguistic processes, the Ukraine and Belorussia were the only two republics where enrollments in native-language schools decreased between 1965 and 1972.[14] Given the national composition of the Ukrainian SSR--73.6 percent Ukrainian and 21.1 percent Russian--the effect of Plachynda's proposal would be the ukrainization of the school system, particularly in the urban centers, regardless of parents' wishes. Moreover, it would give Ukrainians who lived in compact groups in other republics access to Ukrainian-language schools for the first time since the early nineteen-thirties.

3. The letter "g" was arbitrarily removed from the Ukrainian alphabet during the Stalin period by linguists who feared that its continued existence would "'disunite' the fraternal [Ukrainian and Russian] languages." In effect, Plachynda was saying that a political decision had been made to impoverish the Ukrainian language in order to demonstrate the often repeated Soviet slogan of "indissoluble unity of the Ukrainian and Russian peoples."

In view of this, in my opinion the letter G should be returned to the bosom of the Ukrainian alphabet: why should the language be artificially impoverished?

At a session of the Presidium of the Board of the Ukrainian Writers' Union held on February 10, 1987, speakers cited Lenin's support for the Ukrainian language and pointed to "abnormal phenomena" said to be taking place in the schools in the Ukraine.[15]

The meeting, which was called to discuss the role of literature in an international and patriotic upbringing, was transformed into a forum for wide-ranging criticism of the second-class status of the native language. Several of the participants, like Ivan Drach, appeared ready to test the limits of *glasnost* in their remarks:

Attention [should be turned] to what is going on in some of our schools, where the Ukrainian language and Ukrainian literature have become a subject for derision and mockery, where gentrified Philistines with a chauvinist deviation, hiding behind the shield of pseudo-internationalism, frequently scoff at the roots from whence they came.

"Why", asked Drach, "do our colleagues in Moscow and Minsk raise all the acute problems of the period of restructuring more openly, more courageously, and in a more principled fashion?"

Other speakers followed suit, urging a re-evaluation of existing practices. "The unjust, condescending, and thoughtless attitude toward the Ukrainian language must be eliminated" said Dmytro Pavlychko. "Responsibility for learning the native language," he continued, "should not rest with parents, and all the more so not with pupils, but with our state."

According to *Literaturna Ukraina*, the Presidium of the Board of Writers' Union resolved to form a permanent commission responsible for maintaining ties with the schools, and decided to devote a forthcoming plenum of the board to the question of the status of the Ukrainian language in the republic.

According to the newspaper, the first session of the commission was attended by Mykhailo Fomenko, the republic's minister of education, and A. I. Tymchyk, the head of the Public Education Board of the Kiev City Executive Committee. Fomenko told the meeting that at the time there were 15,000 schools in the Ukraine using Ukrainian as the language of instruction.   This represented 75.5 percent of the total number. In addition, 2.5 percent of the schools were bilingual--that is, with parallel classes in Ukrainian and Russian.

Much more important was the proportion of pupils attending those different kinds of schools. Thus, according to Fomenko, 50.5 percent of pupils in the republic were taught in Ukrainian, and 48.7 percent in Russian. More or less the same proportion, he said, existed in the preschool institutions. "Without doubt," said Fomenko, "in the microraions of Ukrainian schools, upbringing in the kindergartens and preschool institutions should also be conducted in the Ukrainian language."[16]

Fomenko's statistics indicated that since the mid-nineteen-sixties, the proportion of pupils who received their education in Ukrainian had decreased by about twenty percentage points.[17]

In a speech to the Fifth Congress of Teachers of the Ukrainian SSR held in Kiev on May 15 and 16, Fomenko conceded that the arguments put forth regarding the need for changes in the language provisions of the Draft Statute on the Secondary General Education School "deserve attention" and requested that the Ministry of Education in Moscow "take them into consideration."[18] The proposals that were forwarded focused on Section Four of the Draft Statute, which allowed the parents or guardians of children to select the schools that the children would attend--in the overwhelming majority of cases, schools with either Russian or Ukrainian as the language of instruction--and made the study of a second Soviet language optional.

32
NATIONALITY DISCORD IN ESTONIA

Toomas Ilves

In a republic long plagued by ethnic discord between native Estonians fearful of losing their culture, and immigrant Russians resentful of the ethnic Estonians' higher living standards and hostility toward outsiders, no topic had been so assiduously avoided in the press as the daily problems between ethnic groups. The November 1986 issue of the cultural weekly *Sirp ja Vasar*,[1] however, carried an article on political culture in which Holger Pukk, an author of children's books, sharply criticized the prejudicial attitudes of local Russians toward Estonians.

A comprehensive attack on Russification appeared in *Sirp ja Vasar* five months later. Its author, Teet Kallas went beyond the problems of everyday prejudice among Russians to attack the offensive, crude, and often blatantly chauvinistic policies toward Estonians[2] that, on the one hand, isolated Russian immigrants from the native population, thereby perpetuating a lack of understanding of Estonians and, on the other hand, led Estonians to feel that their culture was being destroyed. The result, according to Kallas, was a tinderbox of social tensions.

Estonian Lessons in Russian Schools. The poor relations between Estonians and Russians in the country stemmed, according to Kallas, from the unequal language requirements placed on the two groups. Native Estonians could not cope in their own country without Russian; Russians had no need to learn Estonian. Kallas condemned the "decades-long cultural and linguistic isolation" of non-Estonians living in the republic, which began with a school curriculum that offered extremely limited opportunities to study Estonian. As a result, Russians in Estonia lagged far behind Russians in other republics with regard to learning the local language. While the study of Estonian was a required course in all Russian-language schools,[3]

> in many . . . , especially in the larger cities, Estonian has been and continues to be a subject that is above all a formality. . . . In some schools Estonian is absent altogether in certain classes.

From this state of affairs, Kallas adds, developed the "us-and-them" attitude. Contributing to this alienation was a fact that Kallas did not mention, namely, the great pressure placed on Estonians to learn Russian. Indeed, in later years, more class time was allocated in Estonian schools to studying Russian than Estonian. Kallas laid the blame for the poor relations between the two groups squarely on those Russians who, even though their families may have lived in Estonia for several generations, had never learned the language of the republic.

The Second-Class Status of Estonian. What angered Kallas more than the Russians' lack of Estonian was that Estonian had, as a result, become a second-class language and simply could not be used to carry out some tasks of

daily life. In a country where a significant portion of
the   population   remembered   when   signs were printed
exclusively in Estonian and where the language of the
Estonian majority had enjoyed some priority for most of the
previous forty years, Estonian had been steadily "reduced
to a secondary place" on signs or deleted altogether, so
"that in certain parts of Tallinn it is not at all clear
that one is in the capital of Estonia." Kallas cited a
series of cases in which Estonian was secondary or not used
at all, including signs for many official buildings (among
them an Estonian-language high school); crossroad signs and
street signs, which in some cases were no longer written in
the Latin alphabet, but in Cyrillic. Kallas found it
particularly offensive that the offices of various Estonian
cultural establishments were posted in Russian first,
Estonian second.

Nor was the problem merely a matter of signs. Kallas
suggested that it was no longer possible to solve the
simplest problems of everyday life in Estonian and that the
status of the language had so deteriorated that telephone
operators for emergency police, fire, ambulance, and
gas-leak calls could not be assumed to have an adequate
knowledge of Estonian.

Reappearance of Nonpersons and "Nonbooks". According
to the August 1986 issue of the literary journal Looming,
participants at the congress of the Estonian Writers' Union
in April 1986 had criticized the Estonian press sharply for
not even announcing the death of Uku Masing, one of the
most influential poets in Estonia, who had died in
anonymity in Tartu in 1986, and whose postwar works had
previously been published only in the West. The same August
issue of Looming published . six of his melancholy,
semireligious poems without mentioning that he had been a
nonperson for forty years.[4]

A second case of censorship raised in an article in
Looming was the "nonexistence" of the most recent book of
poetry by Hando Runnel. Having passed an apparently lax
censor, Punaste Õhtute Purpur [The Purple of Red Evenings]
was found to be anti-Soviet upon its release in 1982; and
mention of it in the Estonian press was forbidden. Several
writers at the congress protested against the book's
suppression. Later the ban on mentioning the book was
partially rescinded: a piece in the November issue of
Looming on the book's illustrations provided the first
appraisal of Punaste Õhtute Purpur.

The November 24 issue of the otherwise staid and
conservative party daily Rahva Hääl attacked the entire

censorship apparatus for not allowing a word to be printed about *Naised* [Women], a controversial and extremely popular play in Estonia, whose performances were sold out well in advance. The Komsomol daily *Noorte Hääl* also took up the theme of literary censorship on November 23, 1986. At issue this time was Mats Traat's novel of a childhood in the late Stalinist era, *Uksi Rändan* [I Wander Alone]; almost a quarter of the book was removed by the censor.

Restoration of Pre-Soviet Names. Following the announcement in August that several streets in Moscow were to have their prerevolutionary names restored, *Sirp ja Vasar* appealed for the restoration of Estonian names that had been changed by the Soviets, most notably in the case of the city of Kuresaare, whose 500 year-old name (meaning island of the storks) had been changed in 1952 to Kingissepp after a minor Estonian Communist revolutionary. Following the proposal, a longer article questioned a whole series of changed names that had been imposed during the time of the "left-wing zealotry of the cult of personality."[5]

Signs of Official Approval for the Defense of Estonian. It seemed a promising sign that even such a normally docile cultural functionary as Chairman of the Estonian Writers' Union Vladimir Beekman spoke out for Estonian language rights.[6] That Beekman should do so during the same meeting of party activists at which Gorbachev called for greater efforts to be spent on "internationalist" education in the wake of the riots in Kazakhstan, made it all the more noteworthy. Beekman, however, came down rather hard on "simple-minded recipes" to solve the nationalities question, such as "the suggestion, which sometimes is made in complete seriousness, that mixed kindergartens be set up." He portrayed nationality relations as a "battle for people's sympathies in which we have no right to lose points"; and he noted that "the incompetent handling [of nationality issues] can strike rather deep wounds." Beekman also noted in his speech that an unsophisticated approach to the nationality question as pursued under Brezhnev, which simply stated that all problems had been resolved, could no longer be followed.

A Scathing Attack on Language Policy. In May 1987, the Tartu daily *Edasi*,[7] Estonia's liveliest newspaper, published an article by Mati Hint, one of Estonia's leading linguists, which discussed the issue of language rights in as outspoken a manner as anything that had ever appeared, officially or unofficially, in Soviet Estonia. The article reportedly caused a sensation for expressing, perhaps for the first time in official Soviet Estonian press, the deep anger and resentment Estonians felt over linguistic Russification. Earlier articles dealing with the issue had been more circumspect and cautious, as if this policy were a mere bureaucratic misinterpretation of an otherwise wise and caring Leninist nationality policy.[8] Hint, however, did not mince his words, claiming that the language issue, which he called the question of "linguistic democracy," was in essence a question of the continued existence of the nation.

Hint argued that the attempts to denationalize Estonians by limiting their language rights differed little from tsarist and Nazi attempts to do the same. The latter attempts were now condemned, he said, but talking about the need to develop "bilingualism" and "internationalist" attitudes and attacking the defenders of language rights for their "nationalist tendencies" amounted to the same thing.

> Before the current gust of *glasnost*, talk started up again about the Estonians' [need for] bilingualism, naturally not with the goal of Russifying them; but for some strange reason, the apologists for bilingualism use the same arguments as the pan-Slavs and pan-Germans: Estonian does not allow access to world culture, and without a knowledge of Russian an Estonian cannot become cultured. . . . Some theorists of bilingualism have suggested that it would be very useful if, instead of publishing in the languages of little nations, more would be published in Russian; and indeed it would be good for everyone: more reading material for Russians as well as bilingual non-Russians.

Just as in the nineteenth century and under the Nazi occupation, the question remained one of existence.

Hint was especially disturbed by the fact that the language question had been turned into a political and ideological issue, in which concern for the mother tongue had at times been equated with the political crime of nationalism. Hint concluded that only legal guarantees could assure the continued existence of the Estonian language and, thus, the continued existence of the Estonians themselves.

33
PAMIAT TAKES TO THE STREETS

Julia Wishnevsky

The Soviet media reported on a number of occasions on
public disquiet about the exploitation of *glasnost* and
democratization by antidemocratic and anti-Western elements
in Soviet society.[1] A meeting between members of "Pamiat,"
an association describing itself as a historical-patriotic
association, and Boris Eltsin, the first secretary of the
Moscow City Committee of the CPSU, was apt to further
aggravate such feelings.
     On May 6, 1987, Eltsin received participants in a
demonstration of 400 Pamiat members, and talked with them
for more than two hours. According to TASS, the meeting
was spontaneous. The demonstrators had gathered on a
square in Moscow and marched to the Moscow City Soviet
carrying banners with such slogans as "We demand a meeting
with Gorbachev and Eltsin" and "Down with the saboteurs of
restructuring." The subjects of their discussion with
Eltsin were the preservation of old buildings in Moscow and
the struggle against the opponents of reform.[2] In its
report on the meeting, the newspaper *Moskovskaia pravda* did
not mention Pamiat by name, nor did it say anything about
the nature of the association.[3] *Moscow News* described the
association as being "notable for its sharp contrasts." On
the one hand, it advocated the preservation of monuments
and   environmental   protection;   on   the other, it
"disseminates absurd fictions" about a "conspiratorial
organization" operating on a worldwide scale which was said
to be seeking to Americanize Soviet society by utilizing
"bureaucracy--that monster of world masonry, Zionism, and
imperialism." According to the newspaper, the members of
Pamiat were intolerant of the opinions of others and tended
to denounce their opponents as "agents of the CIA, or even
worse."[4] The Paris-based émigré newspaper *Russkaia mysl*
claimed   that   Pamiat   was a   militant   anti-Semitic
organization, whose adherents denounced Christianity
because of its Jewish origins and advocated a return to the
old Russian pagan faith.[5]
     Pamiat gained prominence following a speech delivered
by one of its activists, the journalist and photographer
Dmitrii Vasilev, at a meeting of the society on December 8,
1985.   Vasilev read out excerpts from the notorious
anti-Semitic forgery "The Protocols of the Elders of Zion,"

claiming that they were authentic. Cassette recordings of the meeting were circulated in Moscow, and some copies reached the West. A number of Western publications printed the text of Vasilev's speech.[6] Thereafter, *Russkaia mysl* published three samizdat accounts of various Pamiat meetings, one of which took place on March 25, 1987. The author of the first of these articles described Pamiat as "an embryo of the organizational structure of national Bolshevism as a mass movement."[7] Its members blamed the destruction of ancient Russian churches on a Judeo-masonic conspiracy and regarded the main enemies of ancient Russian architecture as being elements of international Zionism entrenched in the Main Administration for Architecture and Planning in Moscow.

Apart from Vasilev, the leadership of the organization included Professor Evgenii Pashkov, a geologist; Viktor Vinogradov, an architect; Andrei Gorskii, an artist; and Vladimir Gromov, a librarian. They claimed that it was not Stalin himself, but Lazar Kaganovich--the only Jew in Stalin's Politburo--who had been responsible for the destruction of so many architectural landmarks in Moscow. Another of the culprits, in their view, had been Lev Trotskii, Lenin's Jew. The members of the association seemed to be genuine admirers of the existing leadership, in particular of Gorbachev himself, chief Politburo ideologist Egor Ligachev, and Eltsin. At the meeting of the association on February 18, 1987, however, a speaker by the name of Lemeshev went so far as to call Gorbachev a puppet of his foreign policy adviser Georgii Arbatov, who was a Jew.[8] At a later meeting, while praising the other leaders, Vinogradov was said to have attacked Aleksandr Iakovlev, a candidate member of the Politburo who had lost his post as acting head of the Propaganda Department of the CPSU Central Committee under Leonid Brezhnev because of his criticism of Russian nationalists among Soviet journalists and literary critics.[9] Vinogradov said that Iakovlev had, in an article in *Literaturnaia gazeta* in November 1972, spread the seeds of Western ideology--a disease worse than AIDS. Another accomplice of Zionism, in Vinogradov's view, was Oleg Efremov, the director of the Moscow Arts Theater, who had led the revolt of theater workers late in 1986.[10]

Pamiat and other similar organizations were criticized in the media for their preoccupation with a freemasons' conspiracy.[11] In an article in *Sovetskaia kultura*, Andrei Cherkizov wrote that members of "a certain association" in Moscow had harassed and assaulted people whom they had accused of being freemasons. According to Cherkizov, "it would seem that rumors about freemasonry are becoming an obsession in a certain sector of society."[12]

CZECHOSLOVAKIA:
THE TOUCHSTONE OF GORBACHEVISM

34
THE SPRINGS OF PRAGUE AND MOSCOW

Vladimir V. Kusin

Both Czechoslovak and Soviet officials refused to see similarities between Gorbachev and Alexander Dubček, the reformist leader of the Czechoslovak Communist Party.[1] They said that the Prague Spring of 1968 had weakened socialism and the leading role of the party, thus clearing the way for a counterrevolution, whereas the Soviet efforts underway were to do the opposite. In particular, the reformers of the past were said to stand no chance of being allowed to re-emerge from "the rubbish heap of history" and take "parasitical advantage" of Gorbachev's program.

Whether the final word on the subject had been spoken or not, it was less important for both Prague and Moscow than working out a new, reformist blueprint for the future. What was to happen in the future was of greater consequence than a revision of what had happened in the past. To an outside observer, the comparison was apt to elucidate the nature and extent of the reform proposals underway.

Typology of Change. Four different attempts to change communism occurred in Eastern Europe: through emancipation from Soviet tutelage, as in Yugoslavia since 1948; through a popular revolution, as in Hungary in 1956; through the pressure of a mass popular movement, as during the Solidarity period in Poland in 1980-1981; and through "reform from above," as in Czechoslovakia in 1968, in Hungary since 1968, and in the USSR under Gorbachev. None of these categories was exclusive. In particular, "reform from above" was present in all the other types.

Similarities and Differences. What Prague had wanted in 1968, Moscow wanted in 1987, namely, a change that would make ruling communism more responsive to the challenges of the time. This was to be attained by altering the practices of the previous regimes--Antonín Novotný's and Leonid

211

Brezhnev's, respectively--and by modifying some of the doctrine by which the previous leaderships were guided.

The basic components of Prague's course in 1968 and Moscow's in 1987 were the same: an economic reform resting on the belief that the market could exist under the control of a one-party government, and a less oppressive attitude toward the populace. The new leadership in Prague in 1968 had permitted a cultural thaw, relaxed police coercion, and allowed a freer flow of information; the same was now being done by Moscow. Another common feature was a shift toward more benign features of Marxist doctrine--young Marx's strictures for freedom and against alienation (emphasized by the Prague reformers) or the New Economic Policy Lenin instituted in 1921 (a favorite topic of Soviet reformers). As in Czechoslovakia in 1968, so the reforming party in the Soviet Union was fostering the belief that democracy and communism were not only compatible but mutually reinforcing.

However, the Prague Spring's reform program had been better thought-out than Gorbachev's and had also enjoyed greater popular support. The Czechoslovak reforms met with much less domestic opposition than the Soviet ones.

The Prague Spring had its origins in intellectual and popular dissent, not in the party leadership's recognition that a reform had to be undertaken for efficiency's sake. The reformist concept had gestated throughout the nineteen-sixties, long before personnel changes in the party leadership made its promulgation possible, whereas in the Soviet Union, reform began to take shape only after most of the old leaders had been thrown out.

Whereas the "human factor" was introduced into Soviet reforms as a means of promoting the primary objective of repairing a stalling economy, in Czechoslovakia it had been the "human factor" itself--the writers, the scholars, the Slovaks, the economists, the students, and the younger generation at large--that had pushed the leaders into reformism. There had been disaffection and desire for change in the party itself long before the Prague Spring, beginning in 1956; and party and nonparty reformers coalesced into a pressure group before the top leaders saw the light. In a sense, the Prague Spring was not a typical "reform from above," because the comrades above had to be pushed by the comrades below.

Popular Contribution. Even before 1968, the Czechoslovak public had responded favorably to the prospect of reform, and support grew rapidly once a program began to take shape. A momentum was thus created that pressured the leadership into a search for increasingly radical solutions to an ever wider variety of issues. By contrast, the Soviet program at least initially largely manifested itself inside the various bureaucracies; and, despite its gradual enlargement and acceleration, the reform was still imposed from above rather than developing as a result of interaction between the establishment and the public. It seemed that Soviet reformism had yet to fire the popular imagination.

Both approaches to reform had their advantages and disadvantages for the reformer. When popular wishes did not (and were not allowed to) have much influence on the reform program, the party was better able to keep everything under strict central control; but a reform that was eagerly embraced by the populace could proceed faster, and its proponents could use public pressure to overcome resistance and opposition inside the system.

The Nature of Reform. Because of its popularity, the Prague Spring program had soon become more profoundly reformist than the Soviet program did after two years of Gorbachev's rule. The Czechoslovak economic reform had laid greater stress on a transition to a truly market-based economy; openness in public affairs and the media was closer to a true freedom of expression than the Soviet glasnost. Democratization proceeded more swiftly: the Youth Union disintegrated, the trade unions became less centralized, while new organizations, societies, and clubs mushroomed. Religious control was also relaxed.

The democratic traditions of the Czechs and the national aspirations of the Slovaks came into play very early, being extensively debated even before any reform had begun. Many people viewed reform as a way toward the restoration of democracy, liberalism, and freedom; a society they felt was superior to communism on the basis of their past experience. The Slovaks, and also many Czechs, saw the reforms as a means of righting national injustices of the past through the establishment of a state in which Czechs and Slovaks might live a more balanced coexistence.

In comparison, Gorbachev's plans for greater democracy were utilitarian, not of value in themselves but as an instrument for helping to improve the country's performance and chances of survival as a superpower. Similarly, the objectives of the Soviet reforms could not possibly have represented any "return" to a precommunist society.

Foreign Context. The main foreign concern of the leaders of the Prague Spring had been the hostility of the

Soviet bloc, fostered by Moscow soon after the reforms had started and avidly supported by Czechoslovakia's two influential neighbors, the GDR and Poland. Relations with the West were complicated by its dilemma between sympathy for the Czechoslovak experiment and the knowledge that its outcome was ultimately to be determined by Moscow.

By contrast, while obviously not getting full support from some of its client states, Moscow's reform program was immune to outside intervention. There was no one outside the USSR to cut Gorbachev down. The GDR, Czechoslovakia, and Romania could prevaricate, but not intervene. The foreign political considerations for the Soviet reformers differed substantially from those of the reformers in 1968. There was the preservation of the USSR's status as a superpower; the shoring up of domestic progress by foreign policy successes; the retention of the bloc's cohesiveness; and the disentanglement from such damaging conflicts as the arms race and Afghanistan.

Finally, there was a difference in personalities. As Andrei Gromyko said, behind Gorbachev's benign smile there were "teeth of iron"--which Dubček did not have. The Prague Spring had been more gentle and humane than its Soviet counterpart.

<u>Popularity of Gorbachev</u>. The Soviet leader, and especially his supposed condemnation of the generally disliked Czechoslovak leadership, caught the popular fancy. The rumor mill worked overtime. It claimed that Alexander Dubček had been summoned to Moscow to act as an adviser to Gorbachev. It even assigned the same role to the exiled Professor Ota Šik.   Complaints about Czechoslovak bureaucratic behavior were allegedly being addressed to the Soviet embassy. A former enterprise manager, having been dismissed for political unreliability, was supposed to have applied for emigration to the USSR, where his talents would presumably be appreciated.   Gorbachev was consistently referred to as *Misha* in popular parlance, a term of endearment carrying a message of hope.

Some suspected that the authorities had themselves been taken aback by this show of popular enthusiasm and had countered by spreading disbelief in Gorbachev's staying power. Doubts were sown in the people's minds: Would *Misha* suffer the same fate as Khrushchev? Might terrorists not kill him? Might he suffer a heart attack?   The public would have liked to believe that none of this would happen and that Gorbachev would succeed in bringing change to Czechoslovakia.

One dissident, later a laborer, reported that her fellow workers retrieved the yellowed pages of old newspapers they had kept in their clothes lockers at the factory to explain to their younger work mates what the Prague Spring had been all about. The dissident drew an optimistic conclusion: "The seeming indifference of people to politics is merely a thin layer on the surface, like the dust on old newspapers. The moment propitious winds begin to blow, both disappear."

Dissidents' Responses. Among the dissidents, it was mainly the former communist victims of Brezhnev's invasion in 1968 who spoke and wrote about Gorbachev and his reforms; they felt vindicated. They also had a better understanding of the ins and outs of internal reformism and hence were better able to interpret the trends within the Communist party.

For some of them, personal vindication and rehabilitation seemed to be all they wanted. Dubček might have belonged to this small category of former party members. He did not say anything but was frequently rumored to have sent letters to various quarters, including the Kremlin, offering himself for political office again. He never stood up for the thousands of his persecuted colleagues or signed Charter 77. His personal standing among the majority of dissidents was not particularly high, even if they all valued him as a symbol--a role not to be dismissed in politics--of what had also been their own cause.

Many more former communist reformers looked at Gorbachev from a greater distance and with greater realism. Their illusions had been shattered after 1968; and they had learnt to appreciate the democratic values that had not figured so highly in their thinking before and during the Prague Spring. Moreover, they realized that in 1987, the future of their country was being shaped by different factors than those of twenty years ago. They accepted the importance of Gorbachev, both for the USSR and as a prime mover of change in Czechoslovakia, but also recognized that the Prague Spring was history and that any new attempt at reform could not be expected to place much emphasis on rehabilitation. The main concern now was to prepare the way for change, to find new people within the new establishment to lead the way, and to set the reform process in motion.

Ludvík Vaculík was representative of that category of former party members whose opinions had changed beyond recognition since 1968. He said forcefully that it would be indecent to submit to another Soviet *diktat* and that the Czechoslovaks did not need a Gorbachev to show them the way. Much needed as change was, it should be started and implemented by the Czechs and Slovaks themselves. All they asked was that the Soviets leave them alone.

35
THE ULTRACAUTIOUS REFORMERS

Vladimir Sobell

Of all the Soviet bloc regimes, the Czechoslovak earned the distinction of being the most conservative. While Hungary and the GDR had been experimenting with reforms, there had been no comparable search for improvements in Czechoslovakia since the late nineteen-sixties, no personnel changes comparable to those in Romania or Bulgaria, nor any upheavals such as those in Poland. Vigilant antireformism prevailed for fifteen years. In "normalized" Czechoslovakia, the Gorbachevian philosophy of "acceleration" and "restructuring" presented the sharpest contrast to the prevailing immobilism. Under these circumstances, the central issue for the Czechoslovak regime was adaptation to the new dynamism of the Kremlin.

The Presentation of Soviet Restructuring. The Czechoslovak media found the presentation of Soviet developments a relatively easy, though delicate, task. While Soviet affairs continued to receive considerable coverage, there had been a distinct tendency to cut out anything that might disrupt the still Czechoslovak waters. For example, the media presented the Eighth Congress of the Soviet Writers' Union as the usual dull affair, which it certainly was not.[1]

The main problems were how to present the new Soviet departure to the public in such a way that Brezhnev (under whose patronage the Prague regime of Gustáv Husák was formed) was not cast in an excessively unfavorable light; how to explain why reform was necessary in the USSR when everything had supposedly been all right under Brezhnev; and how to present the far-reaching personnel changes in the USSR without suggesting that Czechoslovakia should follow suit.

The regime opted for the tactics of de-emphasizing the calls for restructuring and letting the Soviets themselves explain the rationale behind the new policies. This implied that although events in the USSR were necessarily of interest, they were strictly Soviet affairs and therefore not directly relevant to Czechoslovakia. Accordingly, the key articles in the Czechoslovak press on the subject of change in the Soviet Union were translations from Soviet authors.

Attempts at Synchronization. On October 13, 1986, a large contingent of Czechoslovak ideological and media luminaries arrived in Moscow. The officials conferred with the directors of the Soviet media and Moscow party boss, Boris Eltsin, a leading supporter of Gorbachev. The delegation was headed Jan Fojtík, a leading CPCS authority on ideological matters.[2] On October 20, *Pravda* carried his article, which was the most explicit statement to date on the need for "Gorbachevism" in Czechoslovakia.

Fojtík stated that the 17th Congress of the CPCS held in March 1986 had rejected the practice that had "concealed the real state of affairs, embellished and painted it in rosy colors, and that made apologies for, and excused errors." He said that the CPCS had found inspiration in the current restructuring.

The Soviet example, however, had to be followed cautiously, Fojtík said. Account had to be taken of the different conditions in Czechoslovakia. One of the lessons the party had learned from the "crisis" of the late nineteen-sixties was that it had to mobilize the so-called "human factor" to avoid slipping into counterrevolution. Otherwise, efforts to activate society, could lead to disasters: "petty bourgeois spontaneity," "social tension," "crisis situations," and "the alienation of a not insignificant section of the working people from the socialist state and the party."

According to Fojtík, propagandists had to promote openness in the discussion of economic affairs. Propaganda should counter the attitude of satisfaction with what had been achieved, rather than trying to achieve even more. It should combat the belief that waste and "irrational behavior" were "attributes of socialism" and demonstrate that excessive egalitarianism was "one of the most pernicious deformities of socialism."

Propagandists also had to come to terms with market economics. They had to "grasp the role of the laws of value and commodity relations under the conditions of a socialist economy." Thus, being sensible instead of

hysterical about the market came to be regarded as a
precondition for the survival of socialism.
     Reluctant Restructuring. At the meeting of the
Central Committee of the CPCS, held on December 4 and 5,
1986, party and state chief Husák said:

> The present system of management and planning no
> longer corresponds to the substantially more
> complicated and demanding conditions, tasks, and
> objectives of further development of the national
> economy.[3]

     In order to bring the "present system of management
and planning" into line with these "complicated and
demanding conditions," Husák promised a "restructuring of
economic management by the party and the government." He
announced that on January 1, 1987 an experiment would begin
in selected enterprises to test the decentralization of
enterprise management.   Chairman of the State Planning
Commission Svatopluk Potáč added that outdated production
lines would be closed and that this would also affect
"well-established and even traditional production
branches."
     Husák's speech confirmed that Czechoslovakia was under
continued pressure to bring its policy into line with that
of the Kremlin.[4] He stressed the need to "bring the
Czechoslovak economic mechanism closer to measures being
adopted in the Soviet Union."
     Details of the Program. The document on restructuring
published in January 1987, contained thirty-seven
principles. Central planning bodies were to concentrate on
such strategic issues as modernization, overall economic
balance and regional development; central administrative
direction was to be reduced "drastically." The
responsibility of enterprises "for the real satisfaction of
society's needs" was to increase significantly; enterprises
were to become fully self-accounting and would receive no
subsidies. Planning bodies would set a binding range of
long-term performance indicators within which companies
would operate rather than having to meet definite targets.
Enterprises were to become the "basic economic units"
responsible for planning their own development; they would
have more say in shaping their internal structure and links
with their partners, including foreign partners.
     The process of planning was to change accordingly.
More attention was to be paid to financial aspects of the
plan, to pricing, and to material incentives. Net output

and profit were to become the main criteria of success. The existing distortion of prices, which resulted, among other reasons, from protecting loss-making branches, was to be phased out. Prices, interest rates, exchange rates, planning in terms of value, and taxation were to become more realistic. There was to be more emphasis on wage differentiation, and wages were to be linked to individual performance. These measures were expected to produce a sharper distinction between unprofitable and profitable enterprises; the identification of the former would serve as a starting point for an analysis of the causes of losses and the adoption of recovery programs. These programs might include the phasing out of certain production lines, changes in management, retraining and re-allocation of labor, or the incorporation of the loss-maker in another, larger (self-accounting) organization. The principle that no such recovery measures might be carried out "at the expense of the justified social security of workers" would have to be observed.

A Minimalist Reform. At variance with the Hungarian and Chinese type, the Czechoslovak regime opted for a minimalist approach. The former type aimed at relaxing vertical command controls and introducing genuine horizontal, market-based links in proportion to the vertical relaxation to the point at which the horizontal links would become at least as important as the vertical. By 1986, the outcome was a hybrid "market-socialist" system that combined features of market economies with those of central planning. In the less ambitious Czechoslovak alternative, a measure of central relaxation was effected and vertical command was weakened; but its importance was unlikely to be matched by the emerging horizontal linkages. Rather than initiating a process that might ultimately lead to the "withering away" of Soviet-type central planning, this approach tried merely to streamline the orthodox mechanism to ensure that the most glaring sources of waste and inefficiency were identified and controlled.[5]

The difference between the two reformist philosophies was suggestive of the difference in the political outlook of the respective regimes. The Hungarian and Chinese leaderships were more open to genuine change; willing to sacrifice ideological orthodoxy in return for economic gains. They were also willing to handle the risks of unwelcome by-products of marketization, such as inflation, greater wage income differentials, and exposure to external influences. The minimalist reformers were motivated by different objectives. Ideological orthodoxy remained sacrosanct, but the need for a modicum of change, in the face of overwhelming waste and inefficiency, was recognized.

The document on the "Principles of Restructuring" indicated no change in the political color of the regime. A reform was announced, but there were no signs of a genuine commitment to its implementation. The key ideas sounded sensible and familiar; they had been discussed in Eastern Europe since the nineteen-fifties. The document, however, betrayed a lack of will to implement them.

In particular, the document did not deal satisfactorily with the most pertinent issues, such as the restructuring of the central planning and ministerial bureaucracies. A "drastic" reduction in central direction was announced, but there was no indication of how the power of the change-resistant bureaucracies would actually be reduced; no mention was made of cutting them down to size and employing their staff elsewhere. Similarly, the "Principles" mentioned the desirability of clearly identifying loss-making enterprises and industries. They stopped short, however, of abolishing the principle of the "justified social security" of workers. Genuine industrial restructuring could not be carried out without some unemployment. An attack on these sacred cows of orthodox central planning would have required a change in the political outlook of the regime.

The political prerequisites for such a change were simply not there. Indeed, the announced program of action did suggest that no real change was imminent: the implementation was not to start until 1990.

The "Principles" were above all the regime's response to the need to assimilate Gorbachev's new ideas. Mimicking Gorbachevism without embracing its substance was the precept for survival.

A Rehabilitation of the 1968 Reforms? Top party activists, government officials, and economic managers and bureaucrats met in Prague on January 27, 1987, to discuss the country's economic problems. In his speech, Prime Minister Lubomír Štrougal admitted that "the long-standing problems of our economy are not getting any better . . . but are in some areas becoming more acute."

Štrougal announced several emergency measures to prop up the intensification effort.[6] His treatment of the sensitive issue of the 1968 reforms and the "normalization" that followed provided clues as to how the proreform section of the regime, which he himself represented, might attempt to maneuver out of the impasse into which "normalization" had led.

According to Štrougal, "restructuring" raised questions not only of the "economic base" but also the "entire superstructure" and "all other spheres of social life." Only by taking all these things into account, he said, could the economy recover its dynamism. This bore a marked resemblance to the measures advocated by the discredited Czechoslovak reformers of the nineteen-sixties.

Štrougal suggested that the notion of a reform was not erroneous in itself. What went wrong in 1968 was that reform was abused by the right-wing enemies of socialism in pursuit of their own ulterior ends. According to Štrougal, the swing to antireformism carried out in the early nineteen-seventies may have been understandable; viewed with the benefit of hindsight, however, the complete negation of reforms pursued under the banner of "normalization" was a mistake.

Štrougal drew an explicit comparison between the planned Czechoslovak reform and Gorbachev's restructuring in the Soviet Union. In the Czechoslovak context, the rehabilitation of the word "reform" in official speeches was no meager step forward.

The Metamorphosis of Husák. Although the ability to bend with the wind has always been a vital trait for any East European politician, Husák had relied on this ability more than most. First swept into prominence by the reformist currents of 1968, it was his subsequent ability to convince the Soviets that he was the right man to carry out antireformist "normalization" that secured him the top party post. Now Husák had to oversee the regime's transition into the reformist age of Gorbachev and thus undo 18 years of "normalization."

Husák's speech to the March plenum of the Central Committee suggested that the reformist cause was gaining ground: it was closer to the pragmatic, proreform position of Štrougal than to the dogmatic position articulated mainly by presidium member Vasil Biľak. In fact, neither Biľak nor any of his recognized companions in orthodoxy spoke at the plenum.

According to Husák, the reform would amount to the most "significant intervention in the economic system" since the nationalization of 1948. He implied that the draft Law on Socialist Enterprise would largely follow the Soviet example but that some elements would be shaped in accordance with Czechoslovak conditions. Husák hinted that some seemingly radical principles, such as the election of "leading employees," were under consideration. He also said that the possibility of secret ballots in party elections was being "looked into." He dwelt on the need "to activate" the social organizations under the umbrella of the National Front and hinted that the regime was contemplating an electoral reform. "We are studying the experience of fraternal countries and we are looking for optimum forms suitable for our conditions."

Husák's proposals lacked the vigor of Gorbachev's. Not only were changes hinted at rather than plainly stated, leaving any specific action a distant prospect, but his words also contained no definite commitment to greater democracy. The allegedly planned co-optation of nonparty citizens into responsible positions did not imply any erosion of the principles of *nomenklatura*, for who would decide who was "faithful to socialism" or "honest" other than the party itself? Husák made clear that "we will also proceed in the future from [the premise] that cadre policy is an area in which the leading role of the party is strictly observed."

Husák dismissed Western "fabrications" about alleged disputes between the CPCS and CPSU leaderships and about divisions within the Czechoslovak leadership.

The Pressure for Adaptation. Unlike the leaders of the GDR and Romania, the Prague "normalizers" responded relatively promptly to the need to synchronize with the USSR. Their sanctioning of the Soviet line was not just verbal. Czechoslovakia was preparing a blueprint for a Soviet-style restructuring of its economic mechanism.

The sudden reformist zeal of the most conservative regime in the bloc served to prevent unnecessary friction with the Kremlin and hence prolong its own life. The GDR, with its "exemplary" economy, and the traditionally maverick Romania had some grounds for their less than enthusiastic stance toward the Soviet reform proposals. The Prague regime's position was very weak by comparison. Being a direct product of Soviet pressure for "normalization," and having found itself in considerable economic difficulty, the regime stood and fell with Soviet support.

The need to adapt to the new conditions resulted in a certain movement within the regime. The division between the ideologically orthodox and the pragmatic, proreform tendencies, which had always existed in a latent form, became more open; and the debate between the two-- previously conducted behind closed doors--was being brought

out into the open.   It was possible to distinguish between
three different though overlapping positions.
   The Orthodox Line. Bil'ak, the living embodiment of
"normalization," had   been   most   vocal   in formulating the
response   by   the   most   conservative   and   hard-line
"normalizers."[7] Given the inevitability of accommodation to
the Soviets, Bil'ak conceded that Soviet "restructuring" had
some utility as a model for Czechoslovakia.   At the same
time, however, the acknowledgment of the need to assimilate
the "impulses" from the Soviet Union was qualified by the
necessity to account for specific Czechoslovak conditions;
in this Bil'ak did not differ from the official consensual
line   and   from the line taken elsewhere in the bloc.   His
reservations did not,   however,   end at the insistence on a
separate road to reform. If Czechoslovakia were to draw on
Soviet experience with reforms, then, according to Bil'ak,
the Soviets (and the entire bloc) would have to take into
account the lessons that the Czechoslovak model had to
offer.   Czechoslovakia, Bil'ak said, had had its own
"restructuring" in 1968; but the movement had turned into a
"counterrevolution." It was now the Czechoslovak comrades'
internationalist duty to declare not their opposition to
the new Kremlin line[8] but rather a warning that the
socialist purity of "restructuring"   would have to be
constantly guarded.
   This was being accomplished first by warning their
domestic as well as their entire bloc audience that the
"enemies of socialism," who had still not accepted their
defeat, entertained the hope that reform might usher in the
same kind of counter-revolutionary policies as those of
1968.   Secondly, the "enemies of socialism" themselves were
being told not to expect any rehabilitation.
   The Official Middle-of-the-Road Position. The official
line emanating from Husák was decidedly middle-of-the-road.
Its main purpose was to ensure that the regime was not torn
apart   prematurely   and   that   maximum   continuity   was
preserved.   It was concerned primarily with domestic issues
while delegating the "internationalist duty" to Bil'ak.
   Husák never had any difficulty in acknowledging the
relevance of Soviet experience; in contrast to Honecker or
Ceauşescu, he was not an outspoken defender of a "separate
road to reform." When meeting Soviet Foreign Minister
Eduard Shevardnadze in early February, Husák was reported
to have assured Shevardnadze that Czechoslovakia would
"apply the findings of the CC CPSU January plenum to its
own conditions."[9]

The Pragmatic Line. The pragmatic, proreform end of the spectrum was represented by Štrougal. The Prime Minister, a former member of the 1968 leadership, had always displayed a technocratic tendency matched by a disinterest in ideology; in 1980 he made an unsuccessful attempt to steer the economy in the direction of reform. After the ascent of Gorbachevism, he was quick to capitalize on the greater room for maneuver and can be credited with the relatively quick adoption of a Gorbachev-style "restructuring" program in Czechoslovakia.

The pragmatic line did not significantly differ from the official middle-of-the-road position, but its emphasis and language were more reformist. Štrougal was stressing the inevitability of reforms and the universality of the Soviet reform model; the importance of the specific Czechoslovak conditions was played down. He lashed out at the conservatives:

> Attempts became evident to limit the significance of the new experience of the CPSU . . . to the USSR alone. . . . It is interesting that such views are articulated by people who previously recognized such national specifics only when [the specifics] were in the deep shadow of universally valid principles. If they previously made absolute the universal, now for a change they are tempted to make absolute the specifics. One can ask whether this attitude does not hide . . . their reluctance to change anything fundamental in our Czechoslovak circumstances.[10]

36
THE TRIAL OF THE JAZZ FANS

Vladimir Sobell

On September 3, 1986, Western media reported the arrests of seven leading members of the Prague-based Jazz Section of the Czech Union of Musicians after searches of their homes.[1] The seven were charged with illegal commercial activity, illegal publication and distribution of printed material. The section's offices, library, and art gallery were padlocked by the police.

On September 7, the wives of five of those arrested protested the police action and questioned its legality in

a   letter   addressed   to   President   Gustáv   Husák.
Subsequently, a declaration of protest was issued by an ad
hoc "Committee of Activists of the Jazz Section."
    This   dramatic   flare-up of the long-standing   dispute
between the regime and the Jazz Section of the Musicians'
Union   raised   the   question of why   the   Czechoslovak
authorities found it necessary to come down so heavily on
this seemingly innocuous group of music enthusiasts.   The
answer can be traced   back   to   the   origins of the
"normalization" regime in Czechoslovakia.
    The saga of the Jazz Section began in 1971 when a
group of jazz enthusiasts submitted an application to the
Ministry of the Interior for permission to form a Union of
Czech Jazz Musicians. The application was turned down, but
the ministry recommended that jazz musicians join the newly
established Czech   Musicians'   Union.[2] Apparently, the
functionaries of the union misinterpreted the instructions
from the ministry; rather   than   merely allowing jazz
musicians to join the union on an individual basis,   the
Czech Musicians' Union allowed the jazz musicians to set up
their own independent section.   The section was established
before the ministry could intervene; once set up, it could
be disbanded only by the union itself.
    Another   oversight   that posed a problem was that,
although a limit of 3,000 members had been set for the
section, no provision had been made to ensure that its
chairman was appointed by the ministry.
    One of the few privileges that groups such as the Jazz
Section enjoyed in the "normalized" state was the right to
publish periodicals   and   newsletters   or   specialized
monographs for their members which, although submitted for
inspection, did not go through the rigorous censorship
procedures.   The regime permitted these publications
because the subjects they covered were judged to be
esoteric and their circulation limited.
    Leaders of the Jazz Section were quick to take full
advantage of this loophole, however. At first the section
published only one bulletin, *Jazz*, but in the mid-nineteen-
seventies it started to issue a paperback series called
Jazzpetit and a series of art monographs called *Situace*.
The publications became a haven for nonconformist authors
unable to find other   channels   for expression. These
included artists and art theorists interested in a variety
of genres and schools, and the subjects covered ranged well
beyond the confines of jazz.[3] The publications became much
sought   after.   In the nineteen-eighties, membership
of the section was reported to have increased to

7,000, and its publications were circulated widely among nonmembers, too. The young were particularly eager to lay hands on these rare specimens of unofficial culture. According to one conservative estimate, each edition of the *Jazzpetit* series had a readership of 80,000 to 100,000 people.[4]   In addition, the section held annual Prague Jazz Days and other festivals, as well as organizing lectures and seminars on a variety of art subjects.

The section had to endure constant harassment from the Ministry of the Interior; Karel Srp, the section's indomitable chairman, lost his job as an editor in a printing house, which exposed him to the charge of "parasitism." On the other hand, the section proved a very hard nut for the authorities to crack. In July 1983, the Czech Musicians' Union finally gave in to the official pressure and ordered its Jazz Section to be disbanded. Soon afterwards, however, the union, which was always supportive of the jazz musicians, permitted the section to re-enter its Prague branch. This move dissatisfied the authorities, and more pressure was exerted. In July 1984, the entire union was suspended until it purged the section from its ranks. Only then was the union allowed to renew its activities; but it continued to shelter the section which, although officially disbanded in 1983, continued to exist in practice.

In 1980 the Jazz Section took a step that subsequently proved of considerable defensive value. It applied for membership at the International Jazz Federation, which was accredited to UNESCO. This accorded the section an international status and life, despite official nonexistence in Czechoslovakia, and succeeded in bringing international attention to the section's tribulations. Persecution of the section was condemned by Western delegates at the Helsinki (CSCE) conference on cultural matters held in Budapest in the fall of 1985. Srp himself went to Budapest to publicize the section's case.

A year later, the section's ad hoc committee of activists wrote an open letter to the Vienna CSCE meeting and another to the Czechoslovak press agency CETEKA in an effort to publicize its case.[5]

The letter to the meeting in Vienna stressed that the section's activities were purely cultural and not political and told of the section's growing popularity in Czechoslovakia. It also drew attention to its good standing as an organization accredited by UNESCO. In light of these facts, the letter expressed the section's abhorrence at its persecution by the Czechoslovak authorities and asked the participants at the conference for moral and legal support.

The letter to CETEKA informed the agency that the section's committee of activists had been set up to continue the work of the arrested members of the regular committee. The letter said that the provisional committee had convened on September 30 and adopted an Action Program, the key elements of which were efforts to secure the release of the arrested members and continue the section's work.

All Western commentators, including journalists who had traveled to Prague for the trial of the Jazz Section on March 11 and 12, and had talked to local dissidents, expressed surprise that the trial took place. Not only had the Jazz Section's story received extensive international publicity, for example at such forums as the CSCE follow-up conference in Vienna, but the timing also seemed wrong. Trials of this nature were not being held at the moment elsewhere in the bloc, including the Soviet Union.

The delay of the trial suggested that differences existed among those responsible for sanctioning it. There were rumors that some leaders had wanted it while others had suggested that the case be quietly dropped or indefinitely postponed. The decision to proceed might have been related to the crystallization in the CPCS leadership of a middle-of-the-road, presumably consensual attitude to reform. According to this attitude, the cardinal difference between reforms in Czechoslovakia and the USSR was the need for Prague to take special precautions lest the adverse experience of 1968 repeat itself.

The holding of the trial was tantamount to taking such precautions. It meant saying what Vasil Bil'ak had said with a vengeance and that others in the leadership had repeated rather more elegantly: Czechoslovakia would "apply the findings of the CPSU CC January plenum to its own conditions."

The regime had found a way of pretending that the trial was not political. The leaders of the Jazz Section continued to sell printed matter (books, leaflets, bulletins) to their members after the authorities had declared the section disbanded. They also announced their wish to take the matter of disbandment, which they considered unlawful and in violation of the country's Constitution, to the Constitutional Court. The Constitutional Court, however, while provided for in the Constitution, had never been created; there could, therefore, the authorities argued, be no recourse to legal

proceedings over the legality of the disbandment. In the
meantime, the Jazz Section, which claimed that   this
situation was legally untenable and that the regime should
do something about it, continued to go about its business.
The money that changed hands during this period was the
object of the court proceedings.

The trial ended on March 12, with the sentencing of
the Jazz Section's leader, Srp, to 16 months in prison and
its secretary, Vladimír Kouřil, to 10 months. Since both
men were credited with the six months that they had already
spent in prison since their arrest, they had only ten and
four months more to serve, respectively. The other
activists on trial received suspended sentences and were
placed on probation.

Observers regarded the case of the Jazz Section as the
key test of the temper of the Czechoslovak regime and an
important pointer for the future. The fact that charges
were not dropped, despite a wave of protest in the West,
and that prison sentences were handed out, suggests that
the regime had decided (though perhaps not unanimously) to
signal a warning: economic reforms and "openness" should
not be seen as the forerunners of cultural liberalization
and a softening of the line on dissent. The Kremlin had
either decided not to intervene too obviously in the
internal affairs of Czechoslovakia, or it was persuaded by
Prague that the situation in Czechoslovakia was
significantly different as far as the limits of dissent
were concerned. The dilemma faced by Prague and Moscow
alike was whether to risk greater political dissent through
cultural relaxation or to signal "business as usual" and
risk undermining the credibility of reform. The outcome of
the case suggests that the latter course was perceived as
the less damaging.

At the same time, the authorities had clearly decided
to contain the damage by not trying two of the activists
arrested in September (Vlastimil Drda and Miloš Drda) on
health grounds and by handing down relatively lenient
sentences on two others. Moreover, the trial was conducted
in a comparatively "liberal" atmosphere, which lent it a
Kafkaesque absurdity and reflected the current ambivalence
of tightly controlled "openness" in Czechoslovak policy.
Outside the courtroom, there was a noisy throng of Jazz
Section supporters, including Charter 77 signatories; in an
unprecedented move, three Western journalists, including
the Vienna correspondent of the Voice of America, were
allowed inside the courtroom. In his summing up of

the case, the judge praised the quality of the section's work.

Despite Western protests and possible Soviet displeasure, the regime had made its point: regardless of any reforms, dissent would not be tolerated and artistic freedom not appreciably extended. The Jazz Section would remain disbanded, and the position of unorthodox artists would remain as difficult as ever. On the other hand, the representatives of Western governments protested the sentences, and the Jazz Section's activists made it clear that their campaign for the section's eventual rehabilitation would continue.

37
GORBACHEV'S DELAYED VISIT

Vladimir V. Kusin and *Kevin Devlin**

A Split in Prague? No journalists or politicians in Czechoslovakia ever publicly expressed opposition to, or doubts about, Gorbachev's policy. The bone of contention between what appeared to be two factions in the leadership lay in how far the new reforms should differ from those of the ill-fated Prague Spring of 1968.

It was rumored in Prague that Moscow had become worried and had warned that Gorbachev's visit would have to be delayed if the Czechoslovaks did not make up their minds about their approach to reform. It would not have been advisable for Gorbachev to be seen as being involved in domestic differences in a bloc state during an official visit--at least not publicly. That, according to rumor, was why CPSU Politburo members Eduard Shevardnadze and Lev Zaikov had gone to Prague in early 1987: to impress on the Czechoslovak leadership that the polemics had to cease and a choice had to be made. If the Czechoslovaks were to decide that they had reservations about reform or would only pay lip service to the idea, Gorbachev could postpone the visit. This rumored version of developments could not be confirmed but was supported by veiled references in the official Czechoslovak media.

---

* Author of the section on the Jacoviello article.

A debate among the Czechoslovak leaders allegedly
ended in unanimous support for a full-fledged program of
reform.[1]   President Gustáv Husák delivered a forceful and
unequivocally reformist speech   at the March CC plenum.
Originally, the plenum had been conceived as just another
exercise in   exhortation   relating   to scientific and
technical advancement. Husák's keynote address must have
been inserted at the last moment, because none of the
well-rehearsed speeches from the floor really referred to
it--an unheard of lack of response to the leader's remarks.
The absence of any contribution from the hard-liners
implied a message: they did not counter, but nor did they
publicly condone.
    A Split in Moscow? Gorbachev's trip to Czechoslovakia
was delayed by three days.   Explanations for the delay
ranged from the official announcement that the General
Secretary had "a slight cold", to the speculation that he
had been seeking to meet with Alexander Dubček, the 1968
reformist leader, and that the Prague regime had been
opposed to this. The Dubček story relied on a report in
the popular West German newspaper Bild, which had often
been proved wrong in the past.   This explanation was
improbable, as a rehabilitation of the Prague Spring in
this way was not on the agenda. Nor was Gorbachev likely
to be all that ill; he had spent many hours with British
Prime Minister Margaret Thatcher barely a week earlier and
had apparently chaired a Politburo meeting on April 2. It
may have been at this meeting that the decision to postpone
the Prague trip was taken.
    A contribution to speculation on the real reason for
the unprecedented last-minute postponement came from the
dissident Italian Communist journalist Alberto Jacoviello,
now Moscow correspondent of the independent Rome daily La
Repubblica. Jacoviello claimed that there had long been a
division in the CPSU leadership over policy--"two poles,"
represented by "innovators" who looked to Gorbachev and
"conservatives" led by Egor Ligachev, the party's chief
ideologist--and that there had been a dramatic sharpening
of these differences over issues raised by the visit to
Prague.[2] According to Jacoviello, Gorbachev's election as
general secretary was "certainly not unanimous."

Starting with that situation, he was obliged, in
order to maintain power and develop his policies, to
keep opening up new fronts, continually mobilizing
the country's most vital energies. This, however,
was also the cause of his weakness. By dint of

attacking the errors and inertia of the past, he
provoked fears, resentment, and resistance that
finally coalesced against him, seeking a pole of
reference. That pole--it has now become very
clear--is Ligachev.

It was not certain, however, whether the ideologist
generally reckoned to be second in the party hierarchy had
deliberately sought to assume that polar position. He,
too, after all, was one of the "team" urging renewal in the
USSR, but "with greater prudence." It was this caution,
Jacoviello suggested, that had made Ligachev the rallying
point not, indeed, for downright opposition but for "fears,
resentment, and resistance." The aim of this inchoate
alliance would perhaps have been not to reverse the new
course but rather "to brake a process that, because of its
rapidity, was dividing the party and the country." Yet
Ligachev's camp had a weakness of its own: for them, a
return to the past was out of the question.

Jacoviello suggested that Czechoslovakia was the most
sensitive link in the Soviet camp. "In Prague, unlike in
Warsaw, the reforms for which Gorbachev was fighting in the
USSR were anticipated by forces within the party, not
outside it," They were led in fact by Dubček, the former
first secretary who, though expelled from the CPCS, was
still alive in seclusion as a point of reference for
"considerable forces in Czechoslovakia, not all of them
outside the communist party." Under the circumstances, it
was not easy to assess in advance the impact of utterances
that should neither destabilize the Czechoslovak leadership
nor represent "a step backward by Gorbachev the reformer."
In a putative Politburo debate, Ligachev would not have
been alone in urging the general secretary to be cautious
and avoid anything that might compromise the stability of
the camp.

Difficult foreign policy issues were also involved.
Thus, short-range Soviet missiles in Czechoslovakia had
become relevant to East-West negotiations on the "zero
option," and there had been signs that Moscow might be
preparing to respond to Western demands on that score. To
do so, however, might also have been presented as a
response to Charter 77's call, on the eve of the Gorbachev
visit, for the withdrawal of Soviet forces from the ČSSR,
and the possible repercussions in that country had to be
weighed. The impending visit of US Secretary of State
George Shultz to Moscow was yet another piece in the
mosaic.

It is understandable why here in Moscow one has the impression of living through a very delicate moment. Everything is, in fact, linked: the persistence of the internal dialectic within the CPSU Politburo; the political destiny of Gorbachev; the stability of the empire; the international perspective. The silence of official sources and of a press that is making giant strides on the road of *glasnost* can only strengthen that impression.

Gorbachev's Arrival. The Soviet leader landed in Prague on April 9. At the banquet in his honor in Prague Castle, Husák expressed unreserved support for Soviet reforms, pledged that Czechoslovakia would proceed along the road of "restructuring," socialist democracy, popular participation in government, and greater openness, and committed his regime to promoting bilateral ties in all spheres.

Gorbachev said he had come to Czechoslovakia "at a very interesting time marked by great transformations." The Soviet Union was in the middle of "extensive and tumultuous processes of restructuring, acceleration, and democratization." He added:

We are also convinced that transformations in all spheres of Soviet life correspond to the interests of the other socialist countries, too, as well as to the interests of progress and peace. . . . We understand and regard as close to us, your endeavor to remove shortcomings and to speed up socioeconomic developments. We see that in striving to meet the set aims you are proceeding in a creative way and with perseverance, and that you are revealing the truly unlimited potential of socialism in an ever fuller manner. . . . We shall naturally be glad if our experience can be in any way useful to fraternal Czechoslovakia.

In formulating the Soviet-East European relationship in this way, Gorbachev seemed to emphasize as much as he could--without unduly embarrassing his hosts and other client states--his interest in reformism elsewhere in the bloc. His mention of the "creative way" in which the Czechoslovak comrades were pursuing the new program was his only concession to the hard-liners who had been concealing their reservations about reforms behind references to the "peculiar conditions" and "different traditions" of each country. Gorbachev appeared to regard his new course as being universally applicable and seemed to concede differentiation only insofar as it was clearly subsumed under the general thrust toward the objectives that he had mapped out.

Neither Husák nor Gorbachev chose to mention the Czechoslovak reform of 1968. This, some Czechoslovak dissidents argued, was significant, because it may have helped remove a stumbling block on the road to change. Not to mention 1968 was better than to condemn it.

<u>The Main Speeches</u>. On the second day of the visit, Husák and Gorbachev delivered speeches in the Palace of Culture in Prague. Husák gave his unqualified support to the new line pursued by Gorbachev, saying that there was a "unity of views and action" between the two parties and that they were striving to achieve "identical aims while traveling along identical roads." Husák thus cast his lot with Gorbachev. Moreover, he had evidently again succeeded in bringing about a consensus in the CPCS leadership.

Like Husák, Gorbachev extolled the two parties' "common attitudes" toward both domestic and international matters. He praised Czechoslovakia for its accomplishments, including the high standard of living, but said there were difficulties too, and stressed that it would be necessary to "think about them" jointly.

Gorbachev spoke strongly about the need to overcome old ways. While "the socialist house" rested on solid foundations and even the walls were strong, the defects were too numerous to be repaired piecemeal. A general overhaul was necessary. He referred to a "fundamental breakthrough" that had "a revolutionary character." Democracy was to be the main instrument bringing about efficiency.

On Eastern Europe, Gorbachev said that every socialist country had its own specific features and national peculiarities. That which the USSR was now attempting to achieve, others might have begun to solve or have solved already. A new stage in relations, characterized by equality and with mutual responsibility as its guiding principle, had begun, according to Gorbachev: there was no boss, and no party held a monopoly on truth; the parties were independent and responsible to their own nations; "mutual advantage and mutual assistance" guided their interaction.

Finally, Gorbachev talked at some length about the alleged Europeanism of his policies, internal and foreign. He claimed that the USSR, too, was an heir to European

civilization;   and European togetherness was   necessary   as
not only a nuclear   but also   a conventional war would make
the continent uninhabitable.
     The   visit   elicited a commitment from the CPCS   to   a
reform that would not differ substantially from Gorbachev's
precepts   for   the USSR.   Husák had already   given   such   a
commitment at the March   party   plenum; but a reaffirmation
in Gorbachev's   presence had a binding   force   of   special
significance.   The   specter   of   the   Prague Spring was not
invoked either as a means of curtailing the existing policy
or as a   weapon   that   Gorbachev   might   use   to   drive the
incumbents   out   of office.   At the same   time,   sufficient
leeway was left for   those   Czechoslovak   hard-liners who
would   drag their feet because of "national peculiarities."
No indication of any   consequence was   given that the USSR
would   want   to revive the earlier   Czechoslovak   reformist
experience.   Most   important   in   this   respect, the troops
stationed   in   Czechoslovakia since   the   1968   invasion
remained.
     Gorbachev   addressed   the   Prague   Spring and its
suppression   in   impromptu   remarks when   talking   to
bystanders.   This left room for   differing interpretations.
TASS chose to underline his remarks at a Prague factory, in
which   he   seemed   to   condemn   the   Dubcek   reforms.   He
apparently   castigated   the 1968 reformers for calling   the
workers a conservative force and for seeking to present the
intellectuals   as revolutionaries who, among other   things,
wanted to "return the economy to private hands." Elsewhere,
he emphasized that 1968 had been a difficult time for   both
the USSR and the   Czechoslovaks,   but that lessons had been
drawn   and much had been done since to make   Czechoslovakia
"a modern country."
     Gorbachev asserted   his   reformist   personality   in an
environment where change of the kind he advocated   had long
been banished from the list of   political   considerations.
This   probably   strengthened the hand   of   those   genuinely
wishing   to   imitate   him.   However,   the   visit   had   not
resolved any specific issues.
     The Leadership Must Stay.   While the need for a reform
was being explained by references   to a changing world that
required   the   injection   of   "more   socialism and   more
democracy" into the system,   the proposition that a changed
leadership should perhaps administer this reform met with a
firm rebuttal.   For the   CPCS, the policy might change, but
the leaders would have to stay.
     Jan Fojtík, a leading hardlinder, was quite   explicit
on this point; he responded, without   mentioning any names,

to the courageous speech by the Czech actor Miloš Kopecký
at the May 5-6 Congress of Film and Theater Artists.
Kopecký had said that he was disquieted by the fact that
"the same old, well-known, and mournful figures" who had
botched up so many good things in the past were now
proclaiming "new thinking" and pretending that they were up
to the new challenges. Kopecký had advised these figures
to "leave in time, that is, immediately, and you may still
receive thanks. . . . If you really have the fate of
socialism at heart, . . . leave!"[3]   Not so, according to
Fojtík. In their cadre policy the Marxists-Leninists had to
"respect revolutionary continuity," Fojtík said. The
fundamental class-based criteria had to be upheld and
confusion in "elementary concepts" prevented.   In other
words, the Husák leadership was to stay.   Furthermore,
sentiments like the ones expressed in Kopecký's speech had
to be countered, as Fojtík put it, through more intensive
political and ideological activity, "lest the party's
practical work become disoriented."

Despite the apparent consensus, there was evidently
tension inside the Czechoslovak establishment.   Fojtík
railed against the twin dangers of "dogmatism and its other
side, namely, pragmatism and technocratism." Both were, he
claimed, "deformations" as well as reflections of "an
attitude to life held by those who underestimate political
work." The dogmatists "haughtily admonish," while the
technocrats manipulated people   "with the help of
administrative methods," he said.   The consensus,
understandable as it was and advantageous to the power
holders in both Prague and Moscow, could turn out to be no
more than a passing stage on the road to a more committed
and radical brand of reform.

EAST GERMANY, HUNGARY, AND REFORM

38
GDR: COMPLACENCY OF THE UNREFORMED

Barbara Donovan

The East German leaders made it clear that they did not consider Gorbachev's attempts at domestic reform to be relevant to their own situation. A conspicuous silence about Gorbachev's calls for "openness" and "democratization" was accompanied by fulsome praise for the GDR's own "achievements and successes." As a leader who valued efficiency and performance above all else, Gorbachev was probably willing to support the GDR in its course because of its relative economic success.

The GDR's reservations about certain aspects of Gorbachev's policies were already evident in the the media's treatment of the 27th CPSU Congress in Moscow in February 1986 and at the SED's congress in April of the same year. Although Gorbachev's speech was reprinted in full in the party newspapers, East German coverage of the Soviet congress was selective, avoiding the more controversial discussions. The 11th SED Congress, in striking contrast to the self-critical congresses elsewhere in Eastern Europe, was marked by a celebration of the GDR's achievements as a "politically stable and economically efficient socialist state." There was no sign that the SED saw any reason to change its course.[1]

Nor did the SED have any second thoughts about Gorbachev's ideas between then and the CPSU CC plenum in January 1987; it continued to distance itself from reform and criticism. After the plenum, which contained Gorbachev's most dramatic appeals for change, the SED's behavior only confirmed its deep-seated aversion to applying Gorbachev's ideas in the GDR.

Departing from its custom of printing the full text of the Soviet leader's speeches, the East German press gave

237

only a summary of Gorbachev's opening speech to the plenum.[2] Moreover, while mentioning the various proposals for electoral reform, the version of the speech the SED chose to publish failed to mention the criticism made of the Brezhnev era and the severe abuses of authority by party and state officials. The personnel changes made at the plenum were given scant coverage, appearing on page five of *Neues Deutschland* in an article announcing the close of the plenum. The SED clearly took pains to avoid presenting the plenum in a way that might suggest it had inherent implications for the GDR.

The SED made no official comment on the plenum, apparently to show that a public discussion of Gorbachev's proposals was out of the question. A series of indirect commentaries did, however, appear. While the plenum in Moscow was in progress, *Neues Deutschland* published a two-page report on the SED's social policy, which supported and confirmed the correctness of the SED's most fundamental policy since the early nineteen-seventies--the "unity of economic and social policy."[3] Furthermore, in a bold comment about the superiority of the East German economy, the paper reprinted a article by a Soviet specialist praising the East German combine system and the efficiency with which it functioned.[4] These claims of economic effectiveness served to vindicate the GDR's economic path and reinforce the East German conviction that what Gorbachev was attempting in the USSR had long been the practice in the GDR.

Soviet Foreign Minister Eduard Shevardnadze's visit to East Berlin on February 3 and 4 gave little indication of Soviet dissatisfaction with the GDR's economic system. Indeed, the visit only provided the SED with another opportunity to praise itself. Erich Honecker reportedly told Shevardnadze that "the good [economic] balance of the year 1986 presents a solid starting point for the further dynamic development of the [East German] economy."[5] In return, Shevardnadze praised East German "successes," saying that [the GDR] had "inspired us."[6] The foreign minister left East Berlin having, in his own words, "thoroughly informed" East German officials about the electoral reforms proposed by Gorbachev but not, it seems, having prompted the GDR to adopt the Soviet course itself.

Only two days after Shevardnadze's departure, Honecker made a long speech at a gathering of regional party secretaries in which he avoided any mention of Gorbachev's initiatives while directly confirming his country's present policies.[7] The speech appeared intended for domestic consumption in order to dismiss any uncertainties among the rank and file of the party as to how the SED was going to react to Gorbachev, and to send a message to the population not to expect any changes. "We have no reason to be silent about our achievements . . . our successes," he said in affirmation of the policies that had brought the GDR relative prosperity, international prestige, and internal stability. Despite the admission that there were still "large tasks to be taken care of," the speech contained no appeals for "openness" or innovation and no discussion of social ills, such as those characterizing the speeches of Soviet leaders.

The leaders of the SED, however, appeared nervous that Gorbachev's criticism of past policy in the Soviet Union could undermine the legitimacy of his own regime and theirs.   The Brezhnev era, now being criticized in the Soviet Union, had been the period during which the GDR began to enjoy its first substantial economic and social achievements. As a result, Honecker had attempted to emphasize continuity; in his speech he said that the policies   followed   since   the   beginning   of the nineteen-seventies, when he came to power, were responsible for the successes the GDR now enjoyed. Moreover, the SED still felt that its legitimacy partly depended on that of the Soviet Union; according to Honecker, "regardless of how one speaks of the Soviet Union, it is clear that the October Revolution and the rise [of the USSR] to a first-class world power has been an event of truly historical significance." Nevertheless, the thrust of the speech was that the leadership of the SED was facing the future with self-confidence.

Honecker exhibited muted enthusiasm for change within the Soviet Union and its effects on foreign policy particularly in his talks with the visiting Italian Communist Party leader Alessandro Natta.   He did not, however, mention any repercussions for the GDR to Natta.[8] The Neues Deutschland account of the visit did not report Natta's impression that Honecker held the changes in Moscow's foreign policy in high esteem, nor did Natta's remark that the changes in the Soviet Union were of importance not only for the USSR but also for its allies, make its way into official print.[9] On the other hand, the readers of the party daily did learn that Natta believed that each ruling party should be autonomous and responsible for its own policies and decisions.

Thus, the GDR's economic performance seemed to save the SED from having to embark upon any course of reform.

Gorbachev himself had shown a great deal of respect for the GDR's economic accomplishments, and official Soviet statements indicated that the USSR was willing to accept independent approaches to economic development by its allies. In an interview with a West German newspaper, Valentin Falin, head of the Novosti Press Agency, said that Moscow had no "recipe" for the change that it expected the East Europeans to follow: "Our friends will decide for themselves what they find appropriate . . . . that is true for the GDR as well."[10]   Soviet Ambassador to Bonn, Iulii Kvitsinskii, speaking at a news conference suggested, however, that reform was to be a "task for all socialist countries."[11]   He assured his listeners that "how these tasks [are to be] carried out under [differing] national conditions . . . is, of course, each country's own affair" but with regard to the plenum's main objective of making socialism more attractive, "there are no two minds about this among us fraternal parties."

In the following weeks the East Germans began to be less conspicuous in ignoring events in the Soviet Union. Gorbachev's speech at the Moscow peace forum received live coverage on television and radio and was printed in full in the party paper. *Neues Deutschland* also published the full text of the speech to the media, thus informing its readers that, according to Gorbachev, "there is no alternative to a transformation" and that "openness, criticism, and self-criticism are the norms of our lifestyle." Despite the now ambiguous nature of the SED's reaction, the East Germans showed no willingness to institute any type of "reform," whether cultural or economic. Economically, there seemed to be no reason yet for change; but potentially more dangerous for the SED was a demand by Gorbachev that they loosen their cultural controls, as he had done in the USSR, to make "socialism more attractive."

On April 23, Honecker delivered a speech to the 11th Congress of the Free German Trade Union Federation,[12] in which he once again indirectly asserted that Gorbachev's domestic reform program was not necessarily suitable for the GDR. While not mentioning the reform process initiated by Gorbachev in the Soviet Union, Honecker argued that the revitalization of the East German economy was not necessary. He maintained that the GDR, unlike the Soviet Union, had already responded to the problems of economic modernization:

Life is not static. Instead, it demands that one analyze attentively all processes of internal and

external   development   and   draw   the   necessary
conclusions . . . .In the last one-and-a-half decades
we   have   instituted   deep-seated   changes   in   our
economic system.

According to Honecker, the GDR's high growth rates
were "only made possible by the process of economic
intensification introduced and implemented at the beginning
of   the   nineteen-eighties." Honecker   was   apparently
referring to a series of measures that were introduced in
the previous years to increase the financial responsibility
of the combines and to raise productivity.   As a result,
Honecker said, the GDR now possessed over an "effectively
functioning system of economic and social planning, which
allows it to react in a flexible manner to new challenges."
Furthermore, in order to dispel any uncertainty among the
public   over   the future course of economic development in
the GDR, Honecker said that the policies outlined at the
11th party congress in April 1986 had produced convincing
solutions to future problems and, thus, the planned course
would "continue to be pursued consistently."
The first direct comment by an East German leader on
the potential impact on the GDR of Gorbachev's ideas came
from CC Secretary for Ideology Kurt Hager. In an interview
with the West German magazine *Stern*, which was subsequently
published in the SED newspaper *Neues Deutschland* and other
East Berlin newspapers, Hager summarized the GDR's position
by asking, "If your neighbor chooses to repaper the walls
of his house, would you feel obliged to do the same?"[13]
On the one hand, the SED could argue--as Honecker did
in his speech--that the GDR was one step ahead of the
Soviet Union and therefore   under little pressure to
institute economic reforms. On the other hand, the scant
coverage of events in the Soviet Union and the SED's
optimism with regard to economic performance could be
traced to a perceived need   to discourage people from
expecting too much in the way of reform and to quell
uncertainty within the party. Party journals were replete
with articles about the need to persuade the party and the
public of the correctness of the GDR's policy as outlined
by   Honecker   in   his speech before regional   party
secretaries.[14] The East German authorities continued to be
anxious to avoid prompting a domestic discussion either of
Gorbachev's ideas or of political and economic problems
within the GDR.
The East Germans also seemed to be waiting to see
whether Gorbachev would succeed before they themselves

considered venturing into unknown waters. Indeed, some observers speculated that the East German leaders, wanting to maintain stability and political control, might have been hoping that more conservative forces in the Soviet Union would eventually gain the upper hand.

Above all, the GDR's reluctance to reform could be traced to Erich Honecker himself. The period that Gorbachev was criticizing as one of ineptitude, corruption, and stagnation in political life was the nineteen-seventies and eighties, the years in which Honecker's political policies were instituted and carried out. Honecker would, in fact, have been stripping his political rule of much of its legitimacy if he were to begin criticizing and dismantling the policies of that era.

39
HUNGARY: DESPONDENCY OF THE REFORMED

Ivan Volgyes

By mid-1987 in Hungary, the parallels with the summer before the revolution of 1956 seemed inescapable. Once again the state's administrative bodies and the party's local organizations were in disarray. Once again the party elite seemed to have run out of ideas and, unable to execute a genuine reform of the system and follow a consistent policy, was trying to avoid taking any action at all. Most significantly, once again the party elite blamed "personalities" and "the inadequate understanding of party leaders and cadre members" as well as "external circumstances" (world market forces) for what was clearly the failure of the system.

Economic Reform Runs Out of Steam. The disarray and enfeeblement of the state administrative system was most visible in the economic sphere. The economic reform, renewed four years previously, had attempted to change the structure by moving a mixed economy toward greater decentralization, technological progress, and heavier reliance on free-market forces. As these reform processes stalled, the repayment of Western loans at the exceedingly high rate demanded by the Seventh Five-Year Plan meant that practically all investment stopped and crippled the process of "technological restructuring." In addition, a 1986

deficit of nearly 47,000 million forint (compared with a
planned 22,900 million) and the widening disparity between
the incomes of successful participants in the second
economy and those living on regular salaries alone had
compelled the government to introduce a heavily progressive
income tax system by January 1988.

The structural change necessary for modernization was
also hindered by the simple fact that under the existing
arrangement enterprises and organizations with money to
invest were actually penalized by the tax system. As a
result, such firms loaned out their excess capital at
extortionate rates (15-25 percent) to ailing companies
instead of investing it, as originally expected, in
technological progress.

The result was economic stagnation, inflation
(officially predicted at seven percent for 1987 but by all
accounts already over twenty percent by July), a decline in
the standard of living for the sixth year in a row, and a
pervading sense of hopelessness.[1] Two devaluations of the
forint, the first in 1986 and the second in 1987, led to a
further erosion of consumer spending power, with the result
that only 5-10 percent of the population could afford
nonessential purchases. While Hungarians might still quip
that the "situation is hopeless but not yet bad," the joke
had to ring particularly hollow for the generation of young
people whose first apartment, if they were lucky enough to
find one, would cost at least 15 times their gross annual
income. Gone were the ambitious days of "state-built"
apartments "for everyone". For all the talk about the
state building some 100,000 new apartments a year, in
1986 only some 1,500 such housing units were built.[2]

In the state sector of the economy, very few
enterprises worked efficiently. Of the 273 firms that
accounted for some 79 percent of industrial production,
more than half operated with heavy subsidies; it was
impossible to know if even the "productive" factories were
operating in a truly cost-efficient manner. The hope of
eliminating inefficient factories was quashed by two
factors. First, many of these firms were producing goods
contracted for by other CMEA countries at prices that could
not be unilaterally altered, and thus heavy state subsidies
were required for the fulfillment of Hungary's
"international fraternal" obligations. Second, the closing
of bankrupt firms on a large scale was unacceptable because
of the danger of triggering massive unemployment.

Widespread Inertia. Systemic inertia crippled the
state administration's will and capability to carry out

change. Although this was perhaps preferable to an outright sabotage of reform by the bureaucracy, the signs of paralysis were unmistakable. The policies introduced by the ministries could rarely be implemented. Local interests at the county and even enterprise levels systematically foiled state plans that ran counter to them. Insofar as they operated at all, even the central bureaucracies worked under the pressure of multiple forces and lobbies.

The Party in Crisis. Signs of apathy and enfeeblement were also visible at all levels of the party. In many units perfunctory party meetings were held once or twice a year. The sight of local secretaries literally begging party members to show up was more common than the discipline and ritual found earlier in Hungary and elsewhere in Eastern Europe.

Nowhere was the disorganization and disintegration so evident as at the top of the political pile. The contest for Kádár's mantle and for implementing divergent policies was fierce. At 75, Kádár had aged tremendously; but he still refused to surrender his position. He seemed to have little comprehension of the gravity of Hungary's problems and lacked the energy and will to govern effectively. Rather, he tended at every opportunity to reminisce about the past and tearfully evoke his successes.

Kádár's refusal to acknowledge the crisis caused concern and restlessness even among his close associates. Csaba Hámori, a Politburo member and first secretary of the Communist Youth League (KISZ), observed that the option for a "decent retirement" from high office was not available or utilized.[3] Power effectively remained in the hands of Kádár and his long-time supporter György Lázár, Kádár's former long-time prime minister (1975-1987) and his current HSWP deputy general secretary. The elevation of Károly Grósz to prime minister and of János Berecz to full Politburo membership did little to alter the balance of power in the elite. An old guard that refused to accede to widely voiced demands conjured up another image from 1956. Then, the demand for Rákosi's departure had been voiced increasingly openly; but when he was finally driven out of office, he was simply replaced by his alter ego, Ernő Gerő. By the time the major personnel changes were effected in 1956, popular demands had far outrun the party's willingness to adjust.

The trouble with the personnel changes was that neither Berecz nor Grósz represented a really different policy. Grósz was regarded as a tough administrator and

centralizer. Although he accepted the necessity of some
unemployment as a stimulus for revitalizing the economy, he
sought improvement within the confines of the existing
system and was reputed to be willing to use more police
methods as well. Berecz, judging from his performance at
the Writers' Union congress in November 1986 and other
pronouncements, seems to have had no other policies than an
expressed desire to restore "order" in the political,
social, and economic spheres. Due both to their lack of
political power vis-à-vis Kádár, and to lack of viable
alternative policies, it was, therefore, very unlikely that
these two men could bring about the much-needed revival.

 <u>Pressure for Change</u>. Many Western analysts felt that
the Gorbachev era offered a chance for Hungary to continue
its reform and that the Soviet Union could use the
Hungarian model as an example and so support the reformist
forces in Hungary.[4] For their part, most astute political
observers in Hungary felt that Gorbachev wanted above all
to maintain Eastern Europe's political stability while
maximizing its economic contribution to the bloc and that
he cared little about how the local party leaderships
achieved these goals. The personnel changes in Hungary did
not suggest an acceleration of the reform.

 Domestically, there were two major forces pressing for
change. The first was society in the broadest sense. In
the course of 20 years, Hungarians managed to attain one of
the highest levels of living in the East; they grew
accustomed to certain luxuries and came to regard them as
necessities. Although the majority had suffered a decline
in their level of living during the previous eight years, a
small group of "haves" also emerged, consisting of the most
skillful, successful, and enterprising elements of the
population. As the proportion of those with an income
below the <u>official</u> subsistence level approached the forty
percent mark, the resentment of the "have-nots"--the
elderly, single-parent families, newlyweds without a hope
of getting their own apartment and young
intellectuals--began to affect the morale and morals of
society at large. One found a sullen populace with high
suicide, alcoholism, divorce, and heart-attack rates--all
indicators of a society under stress. Such a society could
not deliver the high performance needed for modernization;
it could, however, quietly undermine the regime's policies.

 A second, more positive pressure for change came from
those who still believed that the communist system could be
reformed. This reformist lobby, led by "reform economists,"
articulated its views in the programmatic "Turning-point

and Reform" statement issued by the Patriotic People's
Front.   Marketization of the economy and pluralization of
the political system were their fundamental objectives;
they drew support from dissidents and environmentalists,
from dissatisfied youth and the spreading religious "basic
communities"--in general, from all those who wanted to turn
Hungary into a more open and less paternalistic society.[5]

Finally, there were the party's own reformers, many of
whom had been actively working for the revitalization of
the party, and specifically of the KISZ. They drafted a
major reform program, "Our Future Is At Stake," which
mirrored the reform lobby in advocating temporary
unemployment and acceptable levels of inflation, the
broader legalization of the right to private property, and
a diminution in the direct managerial function of the
party.[6]   These reformers realized that if the KISZ were to
be revitalized, it would have to align itself with the
reform lobby, for it was generally recognized that in its
present state the KISZ was "practically nonexistent; where
it existed it did not work, and where it worked the
students simply hated it."[7] This remarkable initiative of
the KISZ reformers was abruptly terminated, however,
apparently both because <u>as a party initiative</u> it was
rejected by the vast majority of the Hungarian youth, and
because the Politburo viewed it as a potentially
"dangerous" intitiative of opening the road to real
political participation by the masses.

The adoption of a "restructuring" program that would
go far beyond the present reform did not appear to be
politically feasible. The system's own reformers, to use
the evocative words of Tamás Bácskai, former deputy
director-general of the Hungarian National Bank, became
"dizzy with failure." Meanwhile, defeated in successive
battles for further reform, those who wished to see real
reforms had rested their hopes in the political ascendancy
of such popular reformist figures as Imre Pozsgay, general
secretary of the PPF, and Rezső Nyers, one of the
architects of the original New Economic Mechanism. These
hopes were quashed by both the newly announced 1987 Program
of the HSWP, and the personnel shuffles of July 1987.

To avert a major crisis, the party, having learned the
lessons of 1956 and of Solidarity in Poland, took effective
steps to prevent the intellectuals and students from
coalescing into a cohesive pressure group with the workers.
Furthermore, amid the general disarray in the
administration, the security and armed forces remained
intact and represented the ultimate guarantee of the

regime's survival. Third, the shadow of 1956 inhibited not only the regime's repressive tendencies but also the reformers' readiness to take new risks.

In the words of the noted writer György Moldova, power in Hungary had during the last four decades " become just as much a fetish as was capital in capitalist states."[8] Just as in 1956, however, in 1987 society had become restless, people were grumbling about their impoverishment, a passive resistance tantamount to sabotage--and occasional acts of arson--was spreading, and the economy continued to fall further and further behind the West. Yet the regime was still able to find "partners" to collaborate with, even if "only those who are truly at its mercy can be real partners in the exercise of power."[9] Under such circumstances, economic renewal and the reforms needed to catch up with the West and to create a liberal, democratic consensus remained a distant prospect.

40
EAST GERMANY'S RESTIVE CHURCHES

B. V. Flow

By 1987, the situation of the churches in the GDR had grown extremely complex. On the one hand, many of the old problems persisted: atheistic indoctrination continued; relations between the state and the Evangelical Church and the minority Roman Catholic Church were stagnating; membership in both Churches was dwindling; only one in five of the babies born in the GDR was baptized, and the trend continued downward. The churches seemed helpless in the face of the increasing secularization of East German society. A leading Evangelical Church official spoke of a "profound resignation" within the Church's own ranks.

At the same time, a revival of interest in the church continued. The Evangelical Church spoke of a "new religious need" in the population. This was seen in the growing attendance--predominantly of young people--at Church meetings and concerts and their membership in Church-sponsored peace and ecology groups. A resurgence of interest in the Bible had also been noted. Popular demand for Bibles soared in later years and far outstripped the annual output of 44,000 copies. Similarly, interest in Church-related jobs was growing.

Yet while some of the revival of interest in the church was certainly due to the spiritual vacuum left by Marxist ideology, much of it was clearly not primarily religious. The Evangelical Church found itself rapidly changing into a forum for a wide range of social and political concerns. This nonreligious following, however, also reflected a faith in the authority of the Church. As a leading Church expert concluded in a sociological study: "Expectations in the 'Church' and in 'Christians' are . . . unbroken. . . . The Church is considered a moral authority whose definition of norms and values can do justice to contemporary problems."

A New Role for the "Church in Socialism"? The GDR alone of the Soviet-bloc countries had a predominantly Protestant tradition. The role of the Evangelical Church--which defined itself as a "Church in Socialism"-- was undergoing a profound change. Once a powerful majority Church, it was steadily turning into a minority Church, as former Chairman of the Federation of Evangelical Churches Albrecht Schönherr put it. Once officially boasting 7,700,000 members--almost half the GDR's population--the Church's membership was thought to be no more than 1,500,000 in 1987. Since some 45 percent of the members were over 65, the decline could only be expected to continue.

This "loss of quantity" (in the words of Deputy Evangelical Church Federation Chairman Manfred Stolpe) was balanced, however, by a new "astonishing circle of sympathy." This circle of mostly nonreligious sympathizers was growing steadily. It had resulted in the curious phenomenon that (as one Church paper put it) the "baptized emigrants" who left the Church in large numbers until the early nineteen-sixties were now being replaced by a wave of "unbaptized immigrants." The integration of these nonreligious groups was posing a serious challenge to the hierarchy and was at the center of a major debate within the Church's ranks. Some voices were warning of a growing "secularization" of the Church itself; others were calling on the Church to extend its role to include giving these groups a sense of purpose.

Two themes dominated in these groups: peace and ecology. The Church itself addressed both with increasing urgency and frankness. While backing the "peace policy" of SED leader Erich Honecker, the Church's pacifism went far beyond that accepted by the regime. Apart from categorically rejecting the concept of nuclear deterrence, the Church also stepped up its longstanding criticism of the militarization of East German society. Above all, it urged the regime to give young East Germans the option of doing civil "peace service" rather than military training.

The peace issue was linked to a broader advocacy of justice and human rights. Arguing that permanent peace could only be secured through justice, the Evangelical Church criticized existing "inequalities" in East German society with unprecedented frankness--official travel restrictions being the principal cause for complaint. At the same time, however, the Church began to appeal to its members to accept the division of Germany and to embrace life in the GDR as a "positive task."

Ecology had become another central concern. The GDR's deteriorating environmental situation had been the subject of special Church services and seminars, and it featured in most of the Evangelical Church's public statements. Not surprisingly, after the nuclear accident at Chernobyl the first letter of protest, addressed to the East German Council of Ministers, came from a small Church group in East Berlin. Long neglected, the nuclear issue later became a central theme in the ecological debate within the Church; and this debate focussed on a fundamental questioning of official economic growth policy.

The state watched the Church's increasingly visible role as a social platform with some discomfort. Church-state relations had been in a delicate balance ever since the two sides had achieved a kind of concordat in a meeting with Honecker in March 1978. The SED was clearly of two minds about the Church's activities: on the one hand, it gave the Church a certain leeway, depending on it to channel areas of popular discontent that would otherwise be difficult to control; on the other hand, it was only too aware that, in doing so, the Church was acting as a safety valve in articulating and organizing popular discontent.

Indeed, relations between the two sides had been stagnating. A second meeting between Honecker and the Federation of Evangelical Churches, initially planned for the fall of 1985, had not materialized by 1987. At the 11th SED party congress in April, Honecker did not even mention relations with the Church in his opening address. Although both sides repeatedly appealed for "constructive" talks, there was no doubt that Church-state relations were deadlocked for the time being.

<u>Some Movement in the Catholic Church</u>? There had always been a freeze in the state's relations with the

country's small Roman Catholic Church. This situation did not change even after Honecker's visit to the Vatican in April 1985. The Catholic Church, which had some 1,200,000 members (7.85 percent of the population), continued to observe a strict demarcation between Church and state while cultivating close links with Rome. Cardinal Joachim Meisner, head of the Bishops' Conference, never officially met Honecker.

At the same time, there were signs that the Catholic Church had quietly begun to be somewhat more assertive in East German society. In May 1985 the Church held a three-day youth congress in St. Hedwig's Cathedral in East Berlin. Addressing the 1,000 young participants, Cardinal Meisner warned that Christians were expected to be "witnesses" rather than "fellow travelers."

Conclusion. There was continued and growing interest, particularly among young people, in the Churches in the GDR. Some of this interest was not strictly religious, especially in the case of the Evangelical Church. Nevertheless, the new watchwords, such as peace, justice, and the environment, indicated a quest for universal human and ethical values that were evidently not provided by official ideology. Indeed, the view was growing among East German Church intellectuals that Marxist society was actually responsible for producing religion. As one Church official put it:

> A certain society was conceived, which was to be areligious. Other values were established, which were gradually to replace the religious ones. Suddenly it becomes clear that a side effect is being produced, a vacuum of unfulfilled needs and unattainable longings.

41
HUNGARIAN EXPERIMENTS CONTINUE

Karoly Okolicsanyi

The Bankruptcy Law. A dwindling labor pool, declining productivity, and mounting deficits by state-owned enterprises led to the promulgation of Communist Hungary's and Eastern Europe's first bankruptcy law. The new statute, which went into effect on September 1, 1986, set guidelines for abolishing or reorganizing chronically insolvent enterprises, which had become a huge drain on the state budget.[1] It meant that creditors, unpaid suppliers, and other enterprises could start bankruptcy proceedings against insolvent or delinquent companies.

There were now three possible stages in a Hungarian bankruptcy case: arbitration, reorganization attempts, and finally liquidation. Arbitration procedures were to be conducted by the local Chamber of Commerce or, in the case of agricultural enterprises, by the local Agricultural Cooperative Council; all parties with outstanding claims were to be required to participate. Thirty days were allowed for arbitration, by the end of which time at least half of the requested outstanding payments were to be made and at least two-thirds of the injured parties had to have been satisfied.

If arbitration was unsuccessful, the case was to go before the Reorganization Committee of the Finance Ministry.[2] This committee, which would have its administrative and supportive expenses provided for in the state budget, was to include representatives of the Armed Forces, the Foreign Ministry, the National Trade Union Council, the State Wage and Labor Office, the Chairman of the Chamber of Commerce, and the Chairman of the National Material and Price Control Board. The Finance Ministry officials were to take the leading role in deciding whether an appropriate state agency should help to reorganize or bail out the insolvent enterprise. The three major factors to be taken into consideration were to be the degree of unemployment likely to result from liquidation, the enterprise's international obligations, and its commitment to the defense forces. To be the sole market supplier of a commodity or service would not be enough to qualify for state help in reorganization.

If the committee were to decide that an enterprise should not be rescued, the case would go to the courts. The courts would then make a further attempt at reorganization before resorting to bankruptcy proceedings. Certification of insolvency would follow the failure of this final rescue attempt.

Marking a major departure from previous practice in bankruptcy proceedings themselves, no state agency or bank would have its claims treated differently from those of other creditors or suppliers. Only the satisfaction of workers' outstanding compensation demands would have priority.

If ten or more workers were laid off in the liquidation of an enterprise, the law prescribed twelve months of "relocation support" to be paid to them. This allowance was to be paid by the state through the Finance Ministry once the mandatory three-month notification period (during which the enterprise must continue to pay workers their full wages) had expired. During the first six months, the worker would receive a monthly allowance equal to his former salary. This payment would fall to 75 percent of that figure in the following three months, and to 60 percent during the last three. During this 12-month period and the 3-month notification period, the state was required to make every effort to find a new position for the worker. The new job would have to pay no less than 90 percent of the worker's former salary and be within one hour's commuting distance each way.

It was calculated that between 100,000 and 150,000 workers would be affected by the new bankruptcy law.[3]

The suspension by the Council of Ministers on March 16, 1987, of all trading by the Veszprém County State Construction Enterprise VAEV, marked the start of the first bankruptcy proceedings.[4] A government commissioner was appointed by the state. The enterprise had recorded chronic losses, amounting to about 500,000,000 forint ($11,000,000 at the official exchange rate) and involving debts to 400 creditors and suppliers. The enterprise had been employing about 2,500 workers and had sales of approximately 1,000 to 2,000 million forint.[5]

The Advent of Unemployment. The dismissal of hundreds of workers at fifteen enterprises reflected the authorities' greater determination to tackle the problems of low labor productivity and labor redundancy. The majority of people affected were from the Veszprém County State Construction Enterprise and the Metallurgical Works of Ózd, where past and planned dismissals ran into the thousands. According to Iván T. Berend, President of the Hungarian Academy of Sciences, the

> idea of total employment used to be an untouchable principle, but the situation [has] now changed, and the government believes that structural unemployment is inevitable . . . . Such unemployment will not exist as a permanent feature. It will exist only for a transitional period, which may last for some years but not forever.[6]

Rezső Nyers, a leading economist and the "father" of the 1968 Economic Reform, said "We must acknowledge the economic fact that structural unemployment is inevitable, even under socialism."[7]

The opening of a nationwide network of more than 400 employment offices[8]; the provision of retraining, and the granting of relocation support (actually unemployment benefits) were augmented by public works projects. The jobs included park and sewage pipe maintenance and cleaning, garbage collection, and road work. Participation was voluntary for those unskilled workers who could not find other jobs because of prison records, layoffs, or a lack of skills.[9] If they accepted such work, however, they were then given preference when other jobs opened up.

In May 1987 there were about 10,000 people officially without work, of whom 4,000 had only an elementary school education or less. They were not classified as unemployed but counted as "looking for work." At the same time, there were about 60,000 unfilled job openings listed in Hungary; a drop of 11 percent from the fourth quarter of 1986.[10]

In an article about the wave of layoffs, László Gyurkó, the official biographer of party leader János Kádár, told his readers that it had been clear from the previous two decades that this situation would arise. Everybody, he said, knew that "labor restructuring" and unemployment would come, as unfulfilled plans and broken promises mounted. Now, for the first time, the specter of an uncertain existence had materialized and had changed the country's mood from one of nervousness to one of insecurity. He knew people, he continued, who had turned in their party membership card, because they disagreed with today's policy of unemployment, which "questions everything--our ideas, 40 years of history, and socialism." The situation had become so bad, he said, that enterprise leaders talked about enterprise problems instead of women at parties. Furthermore, Hungarians were accustomed to their wages being based on the number of children in the family, drunken husbands, and parents rather than on their productivity.[11]

At a meeting of enterprise leaders and managers, one speaker suggested that an unemployment rate in Hungary of 1-2 percent (50,000 to 100,000 workers) would be beneficial to industrial production. The suggestion was received with applause. At the same assembly, Minister of Industry László Kapolyi announced that 15 percent of those employed in industry (about 219,000 people) would be affected by "structural modifications" by 1990; and about 73,000 of these positions would be completely eliminated.[12]

Reform of the Banking System. The Hungarian banking reforms that went into effect on January 1, 1987, gave the banks more freedom and responsibility.[13] It was the third time that changes had been made in the banking system since the New Economic Mechanism had been introduced in 1968, and conceptually they were the most ambitious thus far. A reform initiated in 1971-1972 led to a limited decentralization of the banks; further measures in 1982 enabled banks to issue bonds. From January 1, 1987, a two-tier banking system was to be established.

The National Bank of Hungary was chosen to act as a central and reserve bank, retaining its monopoly on foreign exchange and on the issuing of forint; it also became a central clearing bank. In addition, through the reserve ratio requirement (which stipulated that part of any deposit had to be held by the central bank for reserve purposes), it assumed general but not operational control over the five new second-tier commercial banks and the ten specialized development banks. It was to act as the banks' bank and as the bank of last resort.[14]

The amount of money that the five new commercial banks could lend was made dependent on their profits. They remained state-owned, but they and the reserve bank were to be related through some kind of stock ownership, albeit without an open market on which to trade the stocks. This was typical of the Hungarian economic reforms, which stretched existing types of state ownership to accommodate market-oriented economic elements. The five new commercial banks and ten specialized banks were housed in existing branches of the Hungarian National Bank and other existing banks and were allocated a mixture of well-run and inefficient enterprises as their customers. In a major departure from past practice, enterprises were to be free to change their bank if they wished after a six-month period of grace.[15]

The main purpose of these reforms in the banking system was to allow state enterprises to operate more efficiently by offering them diversified banking services, to increase capital and its movement, and to make banks adjust gradually to market conditions. By separating the money supply function (a state concern) from the commercial lending function (an enterprise concern), the bank reform resolved a major contradiction inherent in one-tier banking systems. Bank credit was simply planned as part of an enterprise's annual budget, distributed by the Hungarian National Bank in its capacity as a fiscal agent. This made it difficult to distinguish state interests from those of the enterprise. Banks acted as part of the state apparatus.

Although all new banks would be given a start-up fund, they would be forced to generate their own income based on their lending practices. It was also hoped that the commercial banks would become active partners in the business life of enterprises, as opposed to their previous distant and unconcerned approach.

Capital investment had declined in the previous two years because of a lack of capital. The banking reform was largely influenced by the need for capital, which it was to help generate in two ways. First, the multilayer banking system was to have a multiplying effect in creating more capital. The reserve ratio was 20 percent on long-term deposits and 10 percent on current deposits. This meant that 100,000 forint in new, long-term deposits would allow the bank to extend 80,000 forint in new loans. As this 80,000 forint was redeposited into another bank (only made possible by the new system), 20 percent was given to the central bank for reserve purposes and 64,000 forint was again available for new loans. This process then continued to multiply. The system could not produce the optimal results because of the limited number of commercial banks (15); but this number was to increase. In addition, profitable enterprises were expected to deposit their idle capital, lured by the new, attractive interest rates, and thereby increase the pool of money in circulation.

Secondly, more capital was made available as foreign banks that were both competitive and sensitive to interest rate differentials became more willing to lend to the government. The groundwork had also been laid for foreign banks to lend money to the new commercial banks in Hungary, which would free the state budget from payment obligations. The latest banking reform was probably prompted by the growing number of joint venture companies in need of complex and efficient banking services and by the insistence of the IMF and the World Bank on modernization (on which they generally made their loans conditional). In fact, the reorganization was partly financed by a World Bank loan. This sum, however, was not to be used as starting capital but was to provide electronic equipment and computerization for the new system.[16]

From January 1, 1987, the newly established State Development Institute was authorized to issue government bonds to cover the state's budgetary deficit.[17]   By November 1986, bonds had been sold (they were not available to the public) to the value of 5,000 million forint, or $111,000,000,[18] which made sounder economic sense than covering the deficit simply by printing more money, which Hungarian officials admitted had been done in the past.[19] Aside from issuing bonds, however, neither the precise functions of the State Development Institute nor its division of responsibilities with the Hungarian National Bank were clear.

The Worsening Economy. The HSWP Central Committee meeting on November 19 and 20, 1986, focused entirely on economic matters. This was not surprising, since the authorities had already indicated their alarm about the decline in the economy earlier in the year. The ensuing resolution confirmed both their anxiety and the deterioration of the economy.[20]

The CC acknowledged that there had been no economic growth in 1985 and 1986. Government expenditures, according to the resolution, had exceeded income, and the country had consumed more than it had produced. Foreign debt payments, investments, and personal incomes had grown faster than estimated. The attempt to coordinate the activities of enterprises with national economic policy had failed. The resolution alluded to external factors in explaining the dismal economic situation but also blamed planning, regulatory, and other agencies for failing to maintain equilibrium and to uncover new economic resources. The resolution also admitted the responsibility of the executive bodies of the Central Committee and government.[21]

The blame was shifted from external factors (such as the decline in the value of the dollar, the EEC's ban on Hungarian agricultural exports after the Chernobyl accident, and the deteriorating terms of trade) to domestic factors. This countered Soviet warnings about Hungary's dependence on "capitalist" markets.

Turning to specifics, the resolution emphasized the need to increase workers' interest in raising enterprise production. It also urged that the practice of consuming more than was produced be stopped. The resolution contained a number of truisms: exports must increase, an adequate range of goods for the population must be provided, overregulation was harmful, and the organization of work and the standard of management must be improved.[22]

Central to the problem of the Hungarian economy was the slowdown of investments since 1979-1980. Taking 1950 as the base year, investments in 1980 were 754; they dropped to 590 in 1985 (236,600,000 forint or $5,257 million), a decline of 21.8 percent.[23] Investments for the atomic power plant at Paks alone accounted for more than $3,900 million.[24] Aging machinery, wage ceilings, and a deteriorating infrastructure were the result of a shortage of capital. Other factors included the nonconvertibility of the forint, limits on entrepreneurial undertakings, centralized and overstaffed regulatory and bureaucratic bodies, and a long tradition of neglecting businesslike thinking. Above all, the bureaucracy's continued interference in business affairs was responsible for the lackluster performance.[25]

The beneficial effects of foreign loans, Hungarian membership in the IMF and the World Bank, and the penetration of the Hungarian economy by Western firms in the form of joint ventures and licensing and cooperation agreements were slowly being exhausted. Moreover, within the framework of Hungary's laws and regulations, Western companies were gradually reaching the limits of the possible. New and bold measures, such as the breaking up of monopolies, were needed.

Many of the peripheral areas of the economy--such as trade outlets and restaurants run privately under contract with the state; economic work cooperatives in enterprises; and small-scale, private farming--were already beyond the direct control of the state. These sectors, however, were not being encouraged by the existing accounting and tax regulations to augment their assets through further investment.

Large state enterprises suffered staggering losses. The media reported that a major government rescue operation had taken place in May 1986, when 40,000 million forint ($888,000,000) were diverted to help four large steel and iron plants.[26] The rescue package consisted of writing off debts and pumping in more capital. The 1986 state budget amounted to 706,000 million forint, *i.e.*, $15,688 million.[27] The plants had been running at a loss because of the gross inefficiency of the metallurgical industry. Only in 1986 did the steel industry stop using its last Siemens-Martin furnace, installed in the 19th century. As a result, the per unit cost of Hungarian steel was almost double that of West European steel industries, which were themselves inefficient.[28] In 1985, 157,000 million forint, or 25 percent of the state's budget, was spent on supporting inefficient enterprises.[29]

The Wage Freeze. In an attempt to appease Hungary's existing and future foreign lenders and to balance revenues and wage expenditures, the government imposed a four-month wage freeze starting on December 2, 1986.[30] The "postponement of wage increases" did not affect contractual and other previously agreed increases. Centrally prescribed increases in the judiciary, educational, and health sectors were also exempted.

Hungary's shortfall in industrial output, its trade deficit, the stagnation in productivity, the stockpile of unsold merchandise, and unexpectedly high government expenditures had forced the authorities to act. The last attempt came after two other measures in 1986: the devaluation of the currency by 12 percent and the enactment of the law on bankruptcy. It was suggestive of indecision in ruling circles; the freeze came shortly after a Central Committee meeting of November 19 and 20, which made no mention of any limitation on wages in its final resolution. The resolution had in fact recommended larger than average wage increases at profitable enterprises.[31] The freeze gave the impression of a temporary measure to gain time.

Since Hungarian labor was inexpensive by international standards, it would have been logical to assume that accounting and tax rules would benefit those enterprises using more labor and less capital; but this was not the case. A link between wage levels and profits was not established. Enterprises were allowed to pay higher wages to keep up with the 8-10 percent inflation because of complicated guidelines with many loopholes. These included the use of "manpower padding," i.e., employing people with low skills and wages in order to permit the employment of highly paid professionals. The combination of low and highly paid labor resulted in the lowering of average pay and thus lower taxes.[32]

Wages in Hungary differed from wages in a market economy. There was no personal income tax, and a myriad of social benefits were not considered part of wages. Nominal industrial wages in December 1985 were 7,458 forint a month, or about $166.[33] This meant that real wages were 95.5 percent of what they had been in 1980.[34]

Comparison of Productivity and Wages, 1981-1986

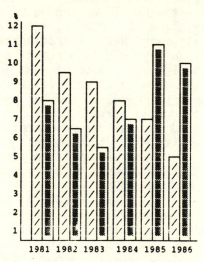

1981 1982 1983 1984 1985 1986

Jan.-Oct.
Productivity (at current Price)
Average Wage (nominal)

Source: *Figyelő*, 11 December 1986.

Monetary Policies. Minister of Finance Péter Medgyessy said at the beginning of May that inflation in Hungary in 1987 would exceed the planned seven percent and suggested that this was the result of too much money chasing too few products.[35] This situation had arisen, he said, because industrial production was lower and wages were higher than had been anticipated.

On May 3 it was announced that the Hungarian National Bank had reduced the money supply.[36] This move restricted the credit available to the newly created commercial banks and consequently also limited loans to enterprises.

Furthermore, Berend acknowledged that one-third of Hungary's Domestic Net Material Product came from private or semiprivate sources.[37] Monetary control of this large segment was in its infancy, since there was no personal income tax in Hungary. Thus, the large private and semi-private sector went largely untaxed. In an attempt to remedy this situation, a new tax system that would include personal income tax was to be instituted.

The government's latest intention was to make enterprises gear their operations more to interest rates, and it used the new commercial banks to do this. The Nat-

ional Bank, which served as a reserve bank (having shed
most of its commercial bank responsibilities), had already
turned its attention to the fine tuning of the money supply. In a clear admission that Hungary's inflation rate had
exceeded those of its major Western trading partners, Hungary devalued the forint by eight percent against Western
currencies on March 11.[38] The move was not just an adjust-
ment to inflation but also an attempt to stimulate exports.

Unpublished Report Proposes New Reform. On February
20, 1987, *East European Markets*, a supplement of the
Financial Times, told of a report compiled under the
auspices of Hungary's Patriotic People's Front on the
Hungarian economy. On March 19, the Italian CP daily
l'Unità carried an extensive summary of the report entitled
"Turning Point and Reform--1986."

According to *l'Unità*, the document was drafted in
November 1986. Written by 29 experts from the Hungarian
Ministry of Finance and the Institute of Economics at the
Academy of Sciences, its 62 pages and 160-page appendix
were reviewed by 62 other experts, among them the prominent
economists János Kornai and Rezső Nyers and the sociologist
Elemér Hankiss.

In the report, the economic results of the
nineteen-eighties, especially those for 1985 and 1986, were
shown to reflect in five ways the sorry state of the
Hungarian economy, which had seemingly lost its direction.
First, labor, energy, raw materials, and capital were being
squandered. Second, Hungary had been unable to adjust to
new trends in the world economy. Third, CMEA deliveries
were no longer secure. Fourth, tension within the economy
had been caused not by external factors but by basic
domestic problems and the postponement of further reforms;
in fact, existing practice would lead to, rather than
prevent, a crisis. Finally, waste had led the system of
allocating funds into a serious crisis.

According to the authors, the political environment
was not conducive to a realistic assessment of the
problems. The report said that the government should be
willing to criticize its policies and performance and
accept responsibility for existing ills; a comprehensive
program of political as well as economic reforms was
needed.

The report estimated that, based on the trade
performance for 1985 and 1986, Hungary's foreign debt and
interest payments would take up 92 percent of the country's
export earnings by 1989.

The report bluntly put the blame for the poor guidance of the national economy on the absence of the profit motive. All but a few small enterprises were dependent for profits (that is, fund allocations) on bureaucracies, not the market, despite the state's attempt to replicate market forces. Market simulation never successfully substituted the "invisible hands" of a self-regulating economy.

The Hungarian mixture of central regulation and would-be market forces had the following characteristics. (1) Medium-size and large enterprises depended on regulators and not on the market; bankruptcy was not a realistic danger for them. (2) Monopolies existed whose privileged status in trade and finance was guaranteed by law; there were even cases in which the state was at the mercy of these monopolies. (3) There was no capital market stimulating supply to meet demand; therefore, capacities were utilized (or, rather, underutilized) according to central regulation. (4) Enterprises and the whole economy were inherently uninterested in developing external relations. These characteristics led to the squandering of resources by enterprises, since efficiency was not a determining factor in securing supplies. Indeed, the more resources an enterprise wasted, the more central support it was assured.

The report urged a comprehensive, market-based, and decentralizing reform, as well as political changes. The first step in this direction, it said, would be for the government to take an openly critical look at its policies and to admit that they had not met expectations and that fundamental changes were needed. "Our citizens and communities deserve an open description of the present difficulties and how we got into them."

A new, comprehensive reform, the report warned, would bring social conflicts into the open, and the government would have to face dismantling certain ailing industries. Although such a reform would be in the interests of society as a whole, certain groups and individuals would lose their privileges.

The survey made the following recommendations:

1. <u>Monetary Regulations.</u> It urged that the money supply be restricted--not by imposing regulations but by making loans less readily available and increasing interest rates. Profitable enterprises should be allowed to keep the money earned; income reallocation should be avoided. The government deficit should be reduced. The bankruptcy and reorganization law should be systematically applied.

2. <u>Prices and Currency Controls.</u>   A drastic devaluation of the forint was advocated in order to promote price equilibrium and increase exports.   Currency convertibility should also be pursued, but first an interim two-tier system involving a convertible and a nonconvertible forint was recommended.

3. <u>Budgetary Policy.</u> Increases in social and welfare expenditure, which were likely to occur once conflicts surfaced over price increases, could be financed by cutbacks in the tax benefits now extended to enterprises. A tax reform based on consumption and the introduction of personal income taxes could also help. A new tax law might also lead to a better evaluation of how enterprises perform. Wage ceilings should be eliminated. Overall, such a taxation system would put the relationship between the state and the individual on a new footing and thus increase the public's say in such matters.

4. <u>Market Formation.</u>   New forms of enterprise, including stock ownership, should encourage entrepreneurial opportunities and remove existing barriers to cooperation between enterprises.   These new forms of doing business should be politically and legally guaranteed.   Interest groups should be allowed to represent their views, which would help to safeguard rights and interests. These new enterprises should automatically have unhampered access to resources and foreign trade rights.

5. <u>Managing Ailing Industries.</u>   The most surprising recommendation was for foreign stock ownership in institutions (such as banks) that might initiate bankruptcy proceedings against insolvent enterprises; taxation and controlling the money supply, however, were seen as the first line of attack against inefficient enterprises.

6. <u>Investment Policy.</u>   There should be a move away from investment in energy- and material-intensive industries toward processing and labor-intensive industries.   Such projects as the Gabcikovo-Nagymaros hydroelectric power complex and the Yamburg pipeline as well as the planned expansion of the coal-mining sector were criticized; their long-term viability was questioned as was their cost, which would inevitably run over budget. The government was urged to withdraw from these projects and free the resources tied up in them.

7. <u>Foreign   Trade.</u>   The   report   recommended a reassessment   of   the   CMEA   countries'   external   trade. Although it   acknowledged   that   the   new Soviet leadership might   create   favorable conditions for change, the   report did not   foresee   a   transformation   in   Soviet economic management in the short run.   Greater trade was urged with such countries as China,   Poland, and Yugoslavia which, the report   said,   were   pursuing   similar   reforms.   Currency convertibility should be offered to these countries.

Openness,   popular   participation,   and   the representation of interest groups were seen as the means by which society could exercise greater control over the government's economic and welfare programs. The party was urged to support the report's recommendations for reform, but the separation of the party from the state was also urged on every level.   The division would ensure that economic failure for the government would not mean a political crisis.   Elected and representative bodies within the party, the report said, should act to reduce the decision-making power of the party apparatus.   The individual's rights also had to be protected under law in accordance with the constitution and the country's international commitments. The report went on to say that no party or government body should be above the law, and that the genuine independence of the judiciary should also be pursued.

The report presented three possibilities for the country's future: a continuation of the existing malaise, recentralization, or a new and consolidating reform.   The third scenario was said to be the only realistic choice. By following its proposals, the report said, economic collapse could be averted; the gap between Hungary and the world market could be closed; and high productivity, self-motivation, and nonadministrative regulation could become the order of the day.

PROGRESS IN POLAND?

42
AMNESTY AT LAST

Louisa Vinton, *Roman Stefanowski*, and *Anna Swidlicka**

    <u>The Initial Conditions</u>. On July 23, 1986, a first group of 369 prisoners was released under the "Law on Special Procedure toward Perpetrators of Certain Legal Offenses" approved by the Sejm on July 17. As had become traditional, the Patriotic Movement for National Rebirth formally proposed the law as a gesture of official beneficence to mark the July 22 anniversary of the founding of People's Poland. Government officials announced that this act would allow the release of approximately 20,000 people by the end of 1986.[1] While publicly admitting a total of only 189 persons incarcerated for "noncriminal offenses," the Polish authorities let it be known that they expected between 220 and 250 political prisoners to be released.
    The act required that political prisoners both acknowledge their guilt, and pledge to refrain from oppositional activity as a condition of their release. The bill offered pardons only to those who "give grounds for the expectation that they will actively join public life in Poland and will not return to crime." It was not clear what this would entail for individual prisoners. At a press conference following the Sejm's approval of the bill, Prosecutor General Józef Żyta was reported to have said that "the court or the prosecutor can amnesty a prisoner if he makes a statement in writing pledging not to resume his activities."[2] Deputy Minister of Justice Tadeusz Skóra commented subsequently that a declaration of

*Louisa Vinton is the author of the first section, Roman Stefanowski that of the second, and Anna Swidlicka that of the third.

loyalty was not "a compulsory precondition", but that "attempts to evade it would cast into doubt the good will of the person offered a chance to leave." Without a declaration, he said, "the court would have no grounds to assume with justification that the perpetrator will abide by the legal order."[3]

The law empowered the authorities to weigh the fate of every political prisoner individually. The amnesty explicitly excluded several crimes: treason, espionage, conspiring to overthrow the political system, membership in a secret or criminal organization, major economic crimes, and sabotage; this automatically ruled out pardons for Poland's most prominent political prisoners. The Solidarity leaders and advisers Władysław Frasyniuk, Bogdan Lis, and Adam Michnik had been convicted in 1985 of "participating in the activities of an illegal union," while the leaders of underground Solidarity, Zbigniew Bujak, Tadeusz Jedynak, and Bogdan Borusewicz, as well as the independent publisher Czesław Bielecki, were awaiting trial on charges of preparing "to overthrow the constitutional order of People's Poland by force." The leaders of the Confederation for an Independent Poland (KPN) convicted earlier in 1986, and the founders of the Movement for Freedom and Peace (RWP) were also excluded. But in what the law called "exceptionally justified" circumstances, even those charged with these offenses might be set free on application to the Supreme Court. Andrzej Gwiazda, Solidarity's former deputy chairman, called this "a very clever move, because [the authorities] have total freedom in assessing each case."[4]

By the end of August, according to available official information, 6,927 people had been released from prison, including 59 political prisoners and 31 people who had turned themselves in to the police.[5] Of some forty most prominent jailed opposition activists and leaders, only Lis and Michnik had been released.

Prominent prisoners still being held under Article 278 of the Penal Code for leading an illegal organization included Frasyniuk, Leszek Moczulski, Krzysztof Król, Adam Słomka, and Dariusz Wójcik of the Confederation of Independent Poland, convicted in April 1986 to prison terms of up to four years, as well as those still awaiting trial on the same charge.

The Law on Special Procedure also provided for the discontinuation or noninstitution of proceedings against political offenders who voluntarily surrendered to the police before December 31, 1986, on the condition that they sign a pledge to cease their activities, reveal details of what they were doing, and turn over any equipment used in connection with these activities. The authorities were very keen to get as many underground activists as possible to turn themselves in. For long they had not been able to produce any spectacular successes in this respect. None of the well-known Solidarity leaders who might have been expected to influence other activists' decisions had come forward. The credibility of the two who had come forward and had been presented on television was doubtful. There was a hint of blackmail in the way the authorities seemed to be waiting for some prominent underground leaders to surface before they themselves moved to release any of the prominent people they were holding.

The discretionary powers the authorities granted themselves in the Law on Special Procedure enabled them to take their time and keep people in Poland and the West guessing. They could release as few or as many of the more prominent political prisoners as they wished; they could do so in a slow trickle, raising the price of their clemency and making propaganda capital out of each individual case. They had until September 15 to empty the prisons.

A Genuine Amnesty. All political prisoners, with the exception of those sentenced for acts of terrorism, spying, sabotage, and for betraying state secrets, were released by September 15, the last day that the Law on Special Procedure was valid. This action, which came as a surprise, turned the conditional clemency law into a full amnesty.

The authorities' decision had been preceded by interviews with some 3,000 underground Solidarity activists, who had been shown the "error of their ways." The interviews were obviously designed not only to show the authorities' generosity in not making arrests for their known illegal activities but also to impress on those involved the insignificance and futility of their efforts and to discourage other or potential underground Solidarity activists, thus ending opposition for good. The official announcement said that these interviews had "reinforced the political results of the prisoners' release initiative."

The release of prisoners[6] was accompanied by a propaganda campaign inviting positive reactions from the Catholic Church hierarchy, those activists who had been "misled" into oppositional activity, and Western governments; the campaign also suggested how these three groups should react and placed much value on their anticipated responses. Indeed, the interview given to

PAP by Minister of Internal Affairs Czesław Kiszczak on September 11 indicated that any humanitarian considerations that might have prompted the authorities of People's Poland to release the prisoners took second place to the expectation of political capital to be made from such a move. The timing and dramatic staging of the announcement on September 11 did, indeed, generate an atmosphere of excitement and anticipation that lasted for several days amid speculation about what concrete moves both the authorities and Solidarity might now take toward a national reconciliation.

Reactions to the Release of the Political Prisoners. The Church hierarchy delayed its official statement pending the actual releases. Only on September 15, after 225 prisoners had indeed been released, did the Press Office of the Polish Episcopate issue a statement expressing the bishops' satisfaction with the "bold" decision that had created "a chance for the closure of a painful period of our history" and their hope "that new conditions would arise to enable the elaboration of a real national agreement without which there was no hope of pulling our country from its deepest crisis since the end of the war." Looking ahead, the bishops pointed to the steps that should follow this "political, social, and humanitarian" decision. Stressing that no one's "contribution of suffering and sacrifice in shaping the Poland of today" should be underestimated, they appealed for a future in which people of different political outlooks could make better use of their minds, knowledge, and energies for the good of their country. Such a perspective of solving Poland's crisis, the bishops said, assumed not only the production of more material goods but also the strengthening of human dignity, brotherly communion, and freedom.

Speaking to Polish pilgrims at Castel Gandolfo on the same day, Pope John Paul II also expressed his satisfaction at the release of the prisoners and his hopes that this would signal the start of an authentic dialogue that would help Poland overcome its internal crisis and ensure cooperation with all the peoples of Europe and the world.

Among the opposition, there was no feeling of gratitude toward the authorities. Instead, the gratitude of those released was reserved for the people at home and in the West who had not forgotten them and had continually called for their release, as well as for those who had continued the struggle after they themselves had been arrested. Father Henryk Jankowski, speaking at St. Brygida's Church in Gdańsk summed up such feelings when he said that the decision to release the prisoners was not an act of mercy but "simply represented honest justice and opened the path to a national understanding."[7]

Most of the early, impromptu statements made by oppositon leaders indicated that the releases were seen as a positive gesture and a step toward an improvement in relations between the rulers and those ruled. Lech Wałęsa said that the authorities' decision had cleared the ground for talks with the government. The Solidarity adviser and historian Bronisław Geremek assessed the release of the political prisoners as conducive to breaking the deadlock:

> The Polish leadership now has the possibility of carrying out a positive policy for the first time since December 13, 1981. But it demands a political decision to introduce dialogue between society and the government.[8]

All the opposition activists stressed that further concessions were necessary. The leader of the Confederation of Independent Poland, Leszek Moczulski, also welcomed the releases and expressed the hope that the authorities had finally understood that the time had come for "a more frank dialogue." "It is good that we are free, but it is high time that Poland herself was free," he said.[9]

Western reaction tended more to skeptical optimism. The British Foreign Office said that Britain was concerned about the need for national reconciliation in Poland and welcomed the release of political prisoners as a step in the right direction. The office of Italy's Prime Minister, Bettino Craxi, greeted the news "with approval and satisfaction pending an in-depth assessment of the information coming from Warsaw," and it intimated the likelihood of Craxi's meeting with the Polish Ambassador to Italy. Such a meeting did, indeed, take place the following day.[10] In France, a spokesman for the Socialist party expressed hope but cautioned that it was too early to draw conclusions.

The US administration also reacted promptly. The White House spokesman, Larry Speakes, was quoted as saying: "We hope that this is a genuine and complete amnesty. We will be monitoring the release closely to see that the government of Poland keeps its commitments." He also foreshadowed "significant and concrete steps" if the government of the PPR took "meaningful liberalizing measures." One day later, State Department spokesman

Charles Redman confirmed and elaborated upon this position, expressing satisfaction at what he called a step on the road to dialogue with the people. He added that once all the political prisoners had been freed, discussion on the lifting of sanctions could begin. The attitude of the West was thus one of consistent encouragement tempered by caution and unwillingness to be rushed into the crucial political and economic decisions that Kiszczak had presented as "a test of the Western partners' political realism and good will."

The importance of the response of Western governments to the amnesty was emphasized by Zbigniew Bujak shortly after his release. If the West insisted on internal liberalization and reform in Poland as a condition of providing the economic aid demanded by the PPR, "this, combined with the internal pressure we would be able to create, would force the regime to consult and agree with us on some kind of economic policy."[11]

The Polish authorities themselves apparently believed that the releases had closed the book on Solidarity and its underground leadership. In a speech to a party conference in Zielona Góra on September 16, Jaruzelski made it clear that the rulers were not prepared to enter into a dialogue with those they had rejected on December 13, 1981:

Today Poland is a different country from the one it was five years ago. Today the strength of the authorities is not measured by the number of overpowered opponents but the number of supporters won over.

43
NEW CONSULTATIVE COUNCIL

Jan B. de Weydenthal

On December 6, 1986, General Wojciech Jaruzelski established a "social consultative council," intended to act as an institutional instrument "in the process of consulting and planning as well as management and government, in a manner that would conform to the conditions of the socialist system and strengthen the rationality and effectiveness of the government." The council was attached to the Council of State, presided over by Jaruzelski himself.

The council consisted of 56 individuals, all of them appointed by Jaruzelski. Most of them were members of the institutional establishment, such as educational officials, former politicians, artists, and social activists. Among the very few potential critics of the government was a former Chairman of Warsaw's Catholic Intelligentsia Club (an autonomous group of lay Catholics supported by the Church) and a former legal advisor to Solidarity.

The establishment of the council was a politically significant event. It was heralded by the authorities as a development "without precedent in the history of Poland or the other socialist states." It created the impression of movement in the country's politics, although its meaning remained obscure and its future uncertain.

The emergence of the council was not a breakthrough in the long-lasting chasm in relations between the authorities and their critics, nor a major step toward a true process of "national reconciliation." Opposition activists were critical of the body, regarding it as having little potential significance. The Church remained silent, while most lay Catholics refused to be drawn into it. Indeed, the authorities themselves appeared to regard the new body with a mixture of apprehension and hope, which suggested that the council provided no more than "a new possibility" and "a new beginning." At the same time, it was clear that the council was created on the government's initiative. This confirmed the authorities' willingness to make new departures in politics, suggesting both determination and resourcefulness.

By the same token, the government's decision to set up the council implied its recognition that all other attempts to reach the people and to channel their energies through available institutions had failed, and that these institutions had proven inadequate. This point was reiterated by several critics of the council. Some of them, such as Solidarity's adviser and political analyst Jacek Kuroń, wondered whether the council would have sufficient autonomy to take authoritative positions on economic and social issues. Others, including a former member of the Sejm, Edmund Osmanczyk, were puzzled by the basic ambiguities behind the very concept of the council itself, inquiring "if the council is to debate government policies," and speculating whether it would assume the role of a political institution with defined prerogatives and responsibilities. Lech Wałęsa was reported to have expressed "few expectations about the council," although he did add that he "could be wrong."

A few Church officials might privately have been willing to support the establishment of the council, seeing in it a vehicle that would facilitate some accommodation between the authorities and various groups in the population (particularly from among the intelligentsia) and thus contribute to the maintenance of social peace. On the other hand, other Church leaders as well as the great majority of lay Catholic activists were strongly opposed to any form of direct participation in, and support for, the council. The immediate consequence of the council's establishment was an increase of the already prevalent political uncertainty.

44
SOLIDARITY ATTEMPTS TO REGROUP

Anna Swidlicka

Provisional Council. In an attempt to reinstate Solidarity as an openly active and officially recognized public movement that might help overcome Poland's political and economic crisis, Lech Wałęsa appointed a Provisional Council composed of seven prominent union leaders, all former members of the underground Provisional Coordinating Committee (TKK). These were Bogdan Borusewicz, who had been a dissident since 1969, a member of KOR, a founder of the Free Trade Unions of the Baltic Coast, and active in the Gdańsk shipyard strike in August 1980 and in Solidarity; Zbigniew Bujak, Chairman of the Mazowsze Region of Solidarity and a member of the Presidium of Solidarity's National Commission (NC); Władysław Frasyniuk, Chairman of the Lower Silesia Region and a member of the NC's Presidium; Tadeusz Jedynak, a member of the Silesia-Dąbrowa Regional Board and of the NC; Bogdan Lis, Deputy Chairman of the Gdańsk Interfactory Strike Committee in August 1980 and a member of the NC; Janusz Pałubicki, Secretary of the Wielkopolska Regional Board; and Józef Pinior, Treasurer of the Lower Silesia Regional Board.

The task of the Provisional Council was to "elaborate upon and agree on a new model of open and legal activity" that would enable the officially disbanded union to end its underground activities and thereby remove "the most painful and one of the most difficult social and political problems at the present time."[1] The decision was taken in response to the authorities' release of the vast majority of political prisoners, which had been seen by the council as "creating a chance for a change in the social climate."[2]

Solidarity's offer to abandon clandestine activity was accompanied by the demand that each Pole should have the opportunity to contribute to "the future of the country, the durability of the state, and the identity of the nation," and be convinced that he really could influence events. The council, discerning in the authorities' moves an "awareness that the current situation gives large social groups no voice, that the organization of public life does not reflect the pluralism of Polish society, and that civil rights need to be defended," emphasized that the creation of new "façade institutions" would not solve any of the problems. These could be eased only if people were allowed to voice their own opinions and create independent, representative social institutions. Wałęsa hoped for confidential talks with officials at an expert level as an initial step toward some kind of new social agreement.[3]

The Provisional Council was in effect an ad hoc interim body supposed to initiate and supervise Solidarity's transition from clandestine to overt activity. The independent union activists did not abandon underground operations, however, preferring to keep the TKK in place for the time being, both as a coordinating center for the remaining underground groups and as a recourse in case of new arrests of Solidarity activists. This was decided at a meeting between the TKK and Wałęsa on October 12.[4]

On October 4, Wałęsa and the seven Provisional Council members were summoned by the Social and Administrative Department of the Gdańsk *voivodship* Office and warned not to break the law. On October 9 they were served with an order banning the existence and operation of the Provisional Council on the grounds that it "presented a threat to peace and public order in the country."[5] Solidarity leaders claimed, however, that the council was not a new organization but an internal body in a labor union that had been operating in accordance with ILO Conventions and that it did not require formal approval. Nonetheless, several members of the regional Solidarity bodies were subsequently warned and some of them even detained and questioned.

Campaign for Trade Union Pluralism. Since the release of the majority of political prisoners in September 1986, the Solidarity leaders had been searching for a way of implementing trade union pluralism, which they saw as the cornerstone of any agreement that would enable the people to work together with the authorities toward economic recovery. Speaking at a party conference in Zielona Góra on September 16, however, General Wojciech Jaruzelski rejected pluralism, which he said was understood by "the opponents of our system . . . as a transfer onto a legal plane of activities that are in essence illegal, antisocialist, and destructive."[6] He offered, instead, a vision of "unity within diversity, that is, within the opulence of forms and substances that [constitute] socialist democracy."

Solidarity members from the Tarnów *voivodship* did not wait for a lead from above. More than 940 workers from the Stalowa Wola steelworks, the Communications Equipment Factory in Gorzyce, and other local enterprises petitioned the Sejm for the restoration of "our justified right" to create trade unions according to the workers' own choice, drawing attention to the fact that the 1982 trade union law had provided only for a temporary suspension of labor pluralism.[7] The signatories received no acknowledgment that their letter, sent on 20 October 1986, had been received by the Sejm; instead, secret police officials arrived at the steelworks and factories and began questioning the signatories and threatening them with loss of bonuses or promotion, disciplinary transfers, or dismissal. The reaction of many of the signatories was to write a second letter to Sejm Chairman Roman Malinowski protesting such treatment.[8]

Workers from the Baltic port of Swinoujście tried a different approach. After a meeting at the Catholic workers' chaplaincy on November 4, a group of workers from the Repairs Shipyard and another from the Port Authority decided to set up founding committees of new Solidarity union locals and apply for their registration through the normal, official channels. The Repairs Shipyard Workers' Trade Union "Solidarity" submitted its application to the Szczecin *voivodship* court on November 6, while the Port Workers' Trade Union "Solidarity" applied on November 12.

The security police were the first to react. Between November 5 and 12, they questioned 140 workers, some of whom were threatened with dismissal or criminal proceedings.[9] Acting unusually quickly, the Szczecin *voivodship* court met in closed sessions on November 14 and 15. It rejected both applications on the grounds that the 1982 trade union law provided for the existence of only one union organization in any enterprise and that such an organization was already in existence in both the repairs shipyard and the port.

On November 28, a group of seven respected lawyers formally asked the Chairman of the Constitutional Tribunal to institute proceedings to determine the incompatibility of Article 60, Paragraph 3 of the 1982 trade union law with Article 84 of the Constitution which guaranteed freedom of association, as well as with provisions of the International Covenant on Civil and Political Rights and ILO [International Labor Organization] Convention no. 87 on labor freedoms. The lawyers were the professors Jan Rosner, Krzysztof Skubiszewski, Andrzej Stelmachowski, and Tadeusz Zieliński; the defense lawyers Andrzej Rozmarynowicz and Władysław Siła-Nowicki; and the retired Supreme Court judge and Minister of Justice from April 1956 to February 1957 Zofia Wasilkowska.[10] Skubiszewski and Siła-Nowicki were also members of the newly constituted Social Consultative Council attached to the Council of State.

The motion gathered widespread support in union circles. Many people added their signatures to a letter of support addressed to the Chairman of the Constitutional Tribunal and signed originally by Wałęsa and some 80 other Solidarity leaders from twelve regions. At a press conference on December 16, government spokesman Jerzy Urban told correspondents that the government would first have to be certain that union pluralism would not be exploited against the interests of the socialist state before considering whether to allow more union organizations in any enterprise.

<u>Combating Official Lawlessness</u>. In a statement dated December 10, 1986, Wałęsa entrusted the democratic opposition veteran Zbigniew Romaszewski with organizing a Commission for Intervention and the Rule of Law. Wałęsa said that legislative practice concerned matters of fundamental importance to the union as well as civil rights and that it was imperative for Solidarity to tackle the problem of the rule of law on a national scale. He indicated that the commission should be concerned with research and analysis as well as offering legal advice and intervening on behalf of repressed union activists and supporters.[11]

The creation of the commission was an attempt to go beyond the strict trade union formula in Solidarity's search for new forms of overt activity. Many opposition activists believed that Solidarity should accept patronage over the diverse social initiatives that had developed autonomously as part of the "underground society" in the previous five years. Wałęsa's decision was also prompted by his concern to re-establish a direct link between the union's leadership and its rank-and-file supporters at a time when internal differences over the strategy to be adopted after the amnesty of September 1986 had not only placed the union on the defensive but also threatened to alienate the majority from the increasingly élitist groups of activists. Romaszewski was known to have advocated practical action that would answer immediate social needs and relate to positive goals. He had placed particular emphasis on the need to provide at least partial protection of the worker in his place of work and to intervene in specific cases.[12]

In a founding statement released on December 22, 1986, and entitled "The Union's Tasks in the Defense of the Rule of the Law," the commission's 14 members reiterated one of the fundamental principles of democratic law: whatever the law did not forbid was ipso facto permitted. The reverse, that only what the law specifically allowed was permitted, was an unacceptable restriction on civic freedom. Arbitrary decisions made by the authorities in this sphere had led to the erosion of the legal system. While the signatories left open the question of the authorities' intentions in releasing the majority of political prisoners, they said that any broadening of the people's participation in public life would have to involve liberalization both in the legislative sphere and in judicial practice.[13]

The commission set itself three tasks: to analyze the existing legislation in the light of inalienable human and civil rights and to demand the necessary changes, to exercise public control over the way that state agencies applied the law and justice was administered, and to provide legal support for victims of official repression or bureaucratic insensitivity. The commission declared its readiness to cooperate with charitable initiatives organized under the aegis of the Catholic Church and appealed to the legal profession for support.

A New Strategy. The abuse of the law by the authorities dated back to the very foundation of the communist state. As the political situation evolved, however, so did the ways in which the law was being officially broken or manipulated. It became increasingly difficult for the police to break the law flagrantly and with impunity, as people came to know their rights and made use of them. Accordingly, official policy shifted from penal to administrative repression, with increasing emphasis on legislative amendments that would disguise unjust and unlawful practices with an appearance of legality.

In this situation the opposition adopted a new strategy aimed at ensuring the rule of law. Romaszewski's commission was prepared to exert pressure on the Constitutional Tribunal, the newly formed Social Council, and the

proposed civil rights spokesmen, making sure that they had
their hands full of authentic social problems and making it
difficult for them to remain façade institutions.

45
DIPLOMATIC ISOLATION BROKEN

Anna Swidlicka and *Roman Stefanowski**

    <u>Jaruzelski in Italy</u>. General Wojciech Jaruzelski paid
an official visit to Italy from January 12 to 14, 1987. It
was the first official visit to a Western democratic
country by Poland's head of state since the imposition of
martial law in December 1981.
    Jaruzelski's visit was presented by the Polish
authorities as an exercise in public relations, aimed at
demonstrating to the public at home and abroad that the
"normalized" Polish People's Republic (PPR) had reclaimed
its rightful place among the nations of the world and was
ready to play a more significant role in international
affairs. Even before the visit took place, official
spokesmen had hailed it as evidence that Poland had finally
come out of its isolation and gained international approval
for its domestic policies. Euphoric reports on
Jaruzelski's successes in Italy were carried by the
official media during the visit.
    The Italian government, on the other hand, emphasized
that the visit had been made possible only by the release
in September of the majority of political prisoners in
Poland. The decision to invite Jaruzelski had been dictated
by a desire to encourage democratization in Poland by
direct contacts on the official level and to expand the
East-West dialogue in general, rather than to indicate
approval for Jaruzelski's normalization policies.[1] In the
course of formal meetings with Jaruzelski, Italian Prime
Minister Bettino Craxi twice stressed the paramount
importance of human rights. A communiqué released by
Craxi's office after a 30-minute talk between the two
politicians spoke of human rights as being "a priority area
for intervention in order to promote a climate of greater

---

*Anna Swidlicka is the author of the first section,
and Roman Stefanowski that of the second.

collaboration among the European peoples and countries." It quoted Craxi as having admitted that some progress had been made in human rights but expressed Italy's continued "hope for a more punctual and generous application of the commitments assumed by the signatory states" to the Helsinki Final Act.[2]

The high point of Jaruzelski's three days in Italy was his visit to the Vatican.   While the honors accorded Jaruzelski and his entourage in the Vatican were not those reserved for visiting heads of state--the PPR had no formal diplomatic relations with the Holy See--he was nonetheless treated with great courtesy and attention. Pope John Paul II granted Jaruzelski a private audience of 70 minutes and then greeted his entourage, which included Jaruzelski's 22-year-old daughter. The Pope was said to have remarked that he hoped that "this visit will have the desired results for the benefit of Poland and Europe." After exchanging gifts, Jaruzelski met the Vatican's Secretary of State, Agostino Cardinal Casaroli, and concluded the visit with an extended tour of the Vatican.

The Vatican visit, which lasted an unprecedented three hours and forty minutes, was hailed by the official Polish press as "the recognition of transformations that have already taken place and of efforts aimed at further stabilization."[3]   The Vatican, in a departure from its traditional silence on private audiences, issued a brief statement that gave no hint of such recognition: "The conversation was serious, clear, and profound and permitted an analysis of the problems of Polish society, the relations between Church and State in Poland, and questions regarding international peace."[4]

Summing up his visit at a press conference shortly before his departure, Jaruzelski said that it had been very successful and that it would bear significant fruit in the long term, but declined to give any details.   The visit also once again brought the Polish predicament to the West's attention.   Despite Jaruzelski's earlier gestures and conciliatory behavior in Italy, Poland was still linked with issues that the West felt must be emphasized; issues such as human rights and freedoms, and a dialogue between government and society.

Sanctions Removed.   On February 19, 1987, President Ronald Reagan removed all but one of the remaining US sanctions against Poland[5],which had been imposed by his administration in the wake of the declaration of martial law in December 1981. In a White House ceremony attended by Polish-American leaders, the President signed an order restoring the status of "most-favored-nation" to Poland, and canceling the ban on government credits and credit guarantees. One other sanction, on government-level meetings, was in practice removed by the Warsaw visit of US Deputy of State John Whitehead.

(No mention was made in the President's statement about transfers of high technology, the banning of which the Polish authorities regarded as a sanction. Strictly speaking, even though the ban on the export of high technology had been mentioned in Reagan's sanctions speech of December 23, 1981, it was not a sanction imposed in the wake of the declaration of martial law. Reagan had said at the time that he was proposing "to our allies a further limitation of exports of high technology to Poland." Restrictions on high technology to bloc countries were a standard practice and were tightened up or relaxed depending on the state of East-West relations. The Soviet invasion of Afghanistan and the declaration of martial law in Poland were among the reasons for the stricter observation of this ban.)

The list of the original sanctions, imposed in 1981 and 1982, was much longer. Reagan had announced on December 23, 1981, that exports of American agricultural products (grain and dairy products), civil aviation traffic, and fishing rights in American territorial waters would be suspended. Additional sanctions, introduced later, had amounted to an effective blocking of the debt rescheduling negotiations with the Paris Club (Poland's government creditors), Poland's entry to the International Monetary Fund and to the World Bank, and the suspension of scientific and technical cooperation and exchanges.

The Polish authorities' response to the imposition of the American sanctions had been equivocal. While they argued that the sanctions amounted to political interference and were designed to destabilize the country's economy, they were initially also inclined to play down their impact, maintaining that the sanctions merely served to demonstrate Poland's ability to make economic adjustments. The Polish authorities had also not been slow to use the issue for propagandistic purposes. They contrasted the Americans' behavior with the Soviet Union's friendship toward Poland, stressing that Moscow had not only continued to provide aid but had considerably increased it in order to help Poland overcome the damage inflicted by the West generally and the US specifically. The granting of fishing privileges in Soviet waters was often cited as an example of such aid, as was the extension of Soviet credits (including one in hard currency) and the USSR's continuing tolerance of Poland's negative trade balance.

While there can be no doubt that the US sanctions had indeed been damaging to the Polish economy, Poland's claims that it had lost up to $15,000 million as a result appeared to be grossly exaggerated. This was particularly true in view of the rather modest trade between the US and Poland prior to the imposition of sanctions. In 1980, for example, Polish-US trade had amounted to only 3.3 percent of Poland's total foreign trade turnover. As far as the US was concerned, Polish-US trade had been so small as to be practically unrecordable as a percentage of the US total trade. Because of Poland's increasingly poor credit-worthiness, trade between the two countries would have suffered in any case, with or without sanctions.

From the political point of view, both the imposition and the lifting of the sanctions had a more complicated dimension. While the US imposed them on political grounds and their gradual removal had generally been seen as a response to positive developments in Poland, the Polish authorities had all along tried to avoid the impression that any changes made in domestic politics--for example, the release of political prisoners--could be related in any way to the US attitude.

They had been even more vehement in distancing themselves from opposition leaders' demands for the lifting of sanctions. The opposition had originally supported sanctions, believing that they were useful and justified. They soon were no longer popular among ordinary Poles, however; as long ago as 1983, at a time when their lifting would not have been supported either by ordinary Poles or by the West, Lech Wałęsa opposed sanctions. His argument was that their removal would deprive the Polish authorities of their only excuse for the economic debacle in the country and would leave the Poles with no one else to blame for the state of affairs but the communist leadership.[6]

Since then, demands for the removal of the remaining sanctions had become common in Poland, as Congressman Stephen J. Solarz reported after his visit to Warsaw in September 1986.[7] Solarz talked both with influential establishment figures (including Politburo member and CC Secretary Józef Czyrek) and with Polish Primate Józef Cardinal Glemp and Wałęsa, who all urged the lifting of sanctions. Another element in the decision to remove the sanctions was said to have been the fact that Reagan received messages from Pope John Paul II, Cardinal Glemp and from Wałęsa, asking him to restore trade with Poland.[8]

The lifting of the sanctions completed the process of bringing the country out of its political isolation and indicated that Poland now merited recognition, if not yet full acceptance, and was respectable enough, even if not adequately stable, to resume fuller economic cooperation with the world outside.

Reagan's decision to remove the sanctions was received by the Polish government "with satisfaction," even though the government spokesman, Jerzy Urban, described their imposition as being lawless and said that he hoped that their removal would be "a starting point toward a further improvement in Polish-American relations, the development of which must be without [American] attempts to interfere in our internal affairs."[9]

Radio Warsaw was more specific about the kind of interference implied: attempts to make Poland accept solutions "made in America"; the continuance of an anti-Polish radio propaganda campaign financed and inspired by the US administration; and the US support for the Polish opposition.[10] The general tenor of the broadcast[11] was that the sanctions had been removed because the US found itself isolated on the issue. While praising the American administration's "realism and rationalism" as the main reason for the lifting of the remaining sanctions, *Trybuna Ludu*[12] criticized all those "who used the opinion of the Polish opposition as a supplementary source of information about Poland." According to Radio Warsaw's commentator, it was only "to save face" that Reagan had given as one of the reasons for the removal of the sanctions "the urging of the leaders of Solidarity and of the Church to encourage further steps toward national reconciliation in Poland."

46
SPECIAL RELATIONSHIP WITH MOSCOW

Roman Solchanyk and *Anna Swidlicka**

<u>Poland To Open Consulate in Lvov</u>. Polish government spokesman Jerzy Urban announced at his weekly press

---

*Roman Solchanyk is the author of the first section, Anna Swidlicka of the second section.

conference on March 10, 1987, that Warsaw would soon open a consulate in the West Ukrainian city of Lvov. Responding to a question from the floor, Urban said that the new consulate would serve as a branch of the Polish Consulate General in Kiev, the Ukrainian capital, and that this reflected the broadening of Polish-Soviet contacts in all areas.[1]

The strengthening of bilateral relations, particularly in the economic sphere, could be traced directly to two documents--an agreement on coordination of economic planning covering the period 1986-1990 and the "Long-Term Program for the Development of Economic, Scientific, and Technical Cooperation between the Union of Soviet Socialist Republics and the Polish People's Republic for the Period up to the Year 2000"--both of which were signed in 1984. The latter agreement, formalized during a visit to Moscow by Polish leader General Wojtiech Jaruzelski in May of that year, called specifically for the establishment of direct links between Polish and Soviet enterprises and planning agencies.[2]

This innovative twist, which bypassed the state foreign trade bodies normally controlling economic transactions, may have played a large part in the decision to establish a Polish diplomatic presence in the regional "capital" of Western Ukraine, where three oblasts (Lvov, Volyn, and the Transcarpathian) bordered on Poland. Not surprisingly, it was precisely in this region that the first local cross-border ties had been established more than thirty years previously, and it was here, too, that such contacts had been most intensive and wide-ranging.[3]

According to the Polish ambassador to Moscow, Włodzimierz Natorf, "direct cooperation of enterprises was inspired and intensively propagated for several years by Comrade Jaruzelski, and it is now becoming a visible reality."[4] Indeed, on virtually every occasion when the issue of Polish-Soviet ties had been raised, there had been an accompanying emphasis on the need to develop and expand direct links between the participating institutions. This was the case during the talks between Polish Prime Minister Zbigniew Messner and his Soviet counterpart Nikolai Ryzhkov in February 1986 and again in October of the same year[5]; in Gorbachev's speech to the Tenth Congress of the Polish United Workers' Party in June 1986; and in the appraisal of Polish-Soviet ties by the Politburo of the PUWP the following October.[6] In January 1987, the concept of direct links was embodied in a long-term program of ideological

cooperation between the two countries that was negotiated
by a Soviet delegation headed by Soviet Central Committee
Secretaries Aleksandr Iakovlev, Anatolii Dobrynin, and
Vadim Medvedev. As described by Pravda, the program
foresaw

> broadening the geography of cooperation of republics
> and oblasts of the Soviet Union with the linked
> *voivodships* of Poland. In this connection, paramount
> importance is attached to increasing the
> effectiveness of local ties, which serve the
> spiritual drawing together of the peoples of both
> countries.[7]

An article in a Kiev newspaper provided a detailed
description of how such direct contacts functioned, as
exemplified by various joint undertakings between Volyn
Oblast and neighboring *voivodships* across the Polish
border.[8]

Another factor in the decision to open a consulate was
Moscow's apparent willingness to loosen controls previously
imposed on ties between the Warsaw government and the
Soviet Union's Polish minority (1.1 million, according to
the 1979 census). This was reflected in the official visit
of a Polish delegation headed by Jaruzelski to Vilnius at
the end of February 1986, where the Polish leader met with
representatives of the Polish community. The gesture was
repeated in January 1987, when the Polish minister of
culture, Aleksander Krawczuk, stopped off in the Lithuanian
capital while in the Soviet Union at the invitation of his
Soviet counterpart, Vasilii Zakharov. One outcome of that
trip, according to Krawczuk, could be a separate cultural
agreement between Poland and Lithuania.[9] Vilnius, like
Lvov, had a centuries-old history of ties to Poland, was
part of the prewar Polish Republic, and continued to hold
special significance for many Poles.

These moves fitted into the broader context of an
overall improvement in Polish-Soviet relations,
attributable to the ostensibly warm personal relations
between Jaruzelski and Gorbachev. The fact that
Literaturnaia gazeta, one of the most widely read
newspapers in the Soviet Union, published an interview with
the Polish primate, Cardinal Józef Glemp, certainly
indicated a changed atmosphere.[10] Shortly before the
publication of that interview, Glemp revealed that he had
received (but turned down) an invitation from the Russian

Orthodox Church to participate in a church symposium in Moscow scheduled for mid-February.[11]

Support for Gorbachev in Poland. Ever since Gorbachev came to power as General Secretary of the CPSU, Western analysts had been seeking evidence of his approval for Jaruzelski. The progress of "normalization" in Poland was seen as a barometer of Polish-Soviet relations and Jaruzelski's praise for the USSR's "inspiring and innovatory solutions" in June 1985 was regarded by many as being mere lip service. By 1987, the situation seemed to have changed; Gorbachev was now adopting some of the solutions already tried by Jaruzelski and the Polish comrades were hastening to voice their support for the Soviet leader.

In an explicit statement of support for Gorbachev, Jaruzelski told Warsaw party activists on February 21, 1987, that the party had been following developments in the USSR "with bated breath" and that Gorbachev himself, with "his energy, boldness, and far-sightedness," deserved "deep respect and the sincere, sympathy of us Poles." Gorbachev's policies would not weaken socialism but prevent its "mummification." He said that Poland and the Soviet Union were in the same "historic current of change" and that "Poland has not experienced such a happy convergence for the whole of the past millenium."

Jaruzelski's comments were echoed by two of his close associates who were in the West at the time. Mieczysław Rakowski, Deputy Prime Minister when martial law was declared and later Deputy Speaker of the Sejm, told journalists in Bonn that he was "almost enthusiastic" about the "revolutionary" developments in the Soviet Union. "We support [Gorbachev's] concepts with our whole hearts," he was quoted as saying. He claimed that the Soviets had observed the Polish experiment with great interest and he described developments in Poland and the USSR as a process of "mutual influencing." Reporting on Rakowski's remarks, Radio Warsaw's Bonn correspondent noted that the Western press "stressed that Poland supported the policies of Mikhail Gorbachev and that Poland was, next to the USSR, the driving force behind reforms that opened up new possibilities for cooperation . . . in Europe."

The effect of all these obviously orchestrated declarations was to emphasize Poland's special relationship with the Soviet Union. The fact that Jaruzelski's speech was carried simultaneously by PAP, TASS, *Trybuna Ludu*, and *Pravda* reaffirmed the Poland's position as the Soviet

Union's principal ally; a position that had been lost with the birth of Solidarity and not regained until the 10th PUWP Congress in June 1986. This high point in bilateral relations suggested that a period of stability may have been setting in, which could have been exploited by the PUWP leadership for internal reforms.

In contrast to some of the East bloc states, the PPR's official media always reported fairly comprehensively on important developments in the Soviet Union. Gorbachev's major speeches and CPSU resolutions were being published in full by the PUWP daily *Trybuna Ludu*. The release of the dissident physicist Andrei Sakharov from internal exile and the decision to "pardon" other important dissidents--Anatolii Koriagin and Iosif Begun, for example--were reported promptly, if somewhat baldly, as if there were no need to explain who they were. The disturbances in Alma Ata and the subsequent personnel changes in Kazakhstan were reported, quoted from the Soviet media.[12]

Nonetheless, only in 1986 did the official media begin to comment upon these developments; moreover, while the tone was almost enthusiastic, the substance remained more modest. The so-called Peace Forum in Moscow attracted the most interest.[13] A Radio Warsaw commentator, claiming to be discussing unidentified agency reports, praised Gorbachev's openness and courage in addressing difficult, controversial, and taboo subjects. He mentioned the removal of "blank spaces in history" as one of the characteristics of the "process of great renewal that has engulfed the USSR and that is embracing all spheres of life, despite understandable difficulties of a psychological and formal nature."

The official Polish press also started publishing interviews with Soviet reformers. The weekly *Polityka* carried an interview with the playwright Mikhail Shatrov, who discussed the aberrations of Stalinism, analyzed the problems facing Gorbachev, and was openly critical of the middle levels of the apparat. The lawyers' biweekly *Gazeta Prawnicza* interviewed a leading Soviet specialist on the prison system, N.A. Struchkov, on changes in Soviet penitentiary policy.

At the same time, contacts between Polish and Soviet institutions and organizations greatly increased, with the traffic passing increasingly from the USSR to Poland. A Polish-Soviet academic and ideological conference held in Warsaw included a group of Polish graduates of Moscow's

Lomonosov University and a delegation from the university, including its deputy rector.

The opposition's attitude to Gorbachev and his policies had been evolving from disillusioned pessimism to interest and cautious, if still skeptical, optimism.   This optimism was engendered more by the implications for Poland of a cultural and political "thaw" in the USSR than by any real hopes of true democracy in the Soviet Union. "The Soviets will remain Soviets and will always try to confuse everybody; but, whether we like it or not, we should watch these changes, because our future might always depend on them," wrote an underground Soviet-watcher in November 1986.

The release of some of the USSR's political prisoners was, however, seen by some analysts as a move conferring a degree of credibility on reform-oriented declarations that were hitherto dismissed as propaganda or, at best, as involving only cosmetic changes. The underground press reported on developments in the Soviet cultural, economic, and political spheres with an impressive knowledge of detail, gleaned also from Radio Liberty broadcasts. The official Solidarity weekly for the Warsaw region, *Tygodnik Mazowsze*, said that something had stirred in Soviet social life and that "signs of change and a forecast of evolution" were evident. It said that although criticism had named the evils, it had not reached their roots and it spoke of a "spectacular, albeit undeclared collapse of ideology." It concluded that if the Soviet evolution continued, it could not but be advantageous in the long run to all the countries in the bloc. The underground publication *Wola* said that Gorbachev was proceding with new policies without reference to ideological argumentation. It described his economic measures as insignificant and meager, but said that his policies in general were advantageous to the Polish opposition in as far as they put pressure on the Polish authorities to keep up with Gorbachev's reformist image.

Several of the opposition's spokesmen voiced similar opinions. Jacek Kuroń expressed hope that the effects of Soviet developments would be felt throughout the bloc. "If Gorbachev survives," he predicted, "no one will be able to stop the process of reform." Janusz Onyszkiewicz spoke of "a promising trend" and speculated whether the PPR's authorities would be prepared to put to good purpose any room for maneuver that Gorbachev might allow them.

This was the most important question facing the Poles. Poland had outstripped the Soviet Union in experimenting with reform and had long enjoyed some of the rights now being tentatively offered to Soviet society. The Poles realized that any liberalization in the Soviet Union extended the limits of the possible in Poland; Jaruzelski seemed to have seized the initiative. Conscious of the constant pressure for economic reform, social justice, and civil rights "from below," he took advantage of Gorbachev's opening and what one Polish party official described as "the historical verification of our party's ideas", to launch an offensive within the party to mobilize grass-roots activists in support of a controlled reform steered "from above." Whether he would succeed in this, remained to be seen.

47
THE POPE'S VISIT

Jan B. de Weydenthal

Pope John Paul II went to Poland on June 8 for his third visit since being elected Pontiff. Many observers had expected the eight-day visit to contribute to a breakthrough.

Expectations. The expectations were linked to a widespread feeling that some impulse from outside the country was needed to affect the existing stalemate, since neither the authorities nor their critics appeared capable of resolving Poland's multifaceted problems by themselves.

The government's activities concentrated on two elements: first, an effort to associate official policies, particularly those dealing with peace and disarmament, with positions taken by the Vatican; and second, an attempt to present the Pope and General Wojciech Jaruzelski as compatriots who, while heading separate states, dealt directly with each other in the interest of international cooperation. Those claims were accompanied by repeated official and semi-official suggestions that this apparent affinity between the two men might eventually contribute to new political developments related either to the situation in Poland (there were official hints that Poland would soon establish diplomatic relations with the Vatican)[1] or to international political issues (it was rumored that Jaruzelski might somehow make it easier for the Pope to obtain an invitation to visit the Soviet Union).

The government made a major and well publicized effort to be cooperative about preparations for the visit during the preceding months. Considerable funds were made available to organize various aspects of the visit, special government committees were set up to facilitate the work, and elaborate steps were taken to ensure public order as well as the Pope's safety during the trip.

Man and Social Solidarity. The Pope described his trip as a pastoral pilgrimage and selected two major themes for it. One was the central importance of the individual in all aspects of public activity and the corresponding need to respect and defend his human and civil rights; the other was the need for solidarity within society and between societies as a means of overcoming social problems. Both themes conformed to traditional Christian teaching about the primacy of man. They acquired a particular poignancy in the Polish context.

The Pope introduced the theme of the individual's special quality in an address to Poland's political leaders on June 8 in Warsaw in response to a formal greeting by Jaruzelski in which the Polish party secretary told the Pope that the public's agitation for autonomy had "subsided," that the government's policies and methods were "irreversible," that the "socialist" system had provided Poland with "social justice" and cultural development, that Poland needed a "theology of work," that the Church should cooperate with the government in persuading people to work harder, and that it was "particularly important for us to see that the Polish Pope has become so deeply involved in the search for peace" between nations.[2]

The Pope neither rejected nor questioned Jaruzelski's arguments; he simply disregarded them. Instead, he noted that "if one searches for peace, [one] has to remember the human individual"; and he told his listeners to "remember also man's right to religious freedom, his right to free association [and] to free expression, and to remember his dignity, which brings into focus the activities of all communities and all societies." Then, remarking that "any violation of or disrespect for human rights endangers peace," he said that success in ensuring peace in Poland also depended on the authorities' recognition of human and civil rights there.

The theme of "the primacy of the individual" in all aspects of social and public activity was repeated by the

Pope in all his subsequent announcements: in his addresses to representative groups of scholars (Lublin, June 9) and intellectuals and artists (Warsaw, June 13) as well as in sermons during religious services and in occasional speeches at public meetings.[3]

The Pope's emphasis on the need for social solidarity apparently reflected his conviction that in the prevailing atmosphere of disillusionment and apathy, only a common effort could provide the momentum for tackling difficulties. This approach was close to the ideals and goals of the Solidarity movement which, led by the labor union of that name but also comprising numerous other independent public organizations, symbolized in the eyes of many Poles the general longing for participation to ensure fair and effective management of public affairs.

The Pope repeatedly defended the achievements of the movement while prudently stopping short of demanding the resurrection of its organizational form. He emphasized specific aspects of the issue in separate sermons. In Tarnów (on July 10) he denounced "the economic and moral crisis" affecting the "rural world" and called for the "full realization" of the 1981 agreements between the government and representatives of several independent farmers' groups. The agreements had paved the way for the establishment of Rural Solidarity, an autonomous farmers' union. In Szczecin (on June 11) the Pope recalled that the 1980 agreement reached in that city between the government and the workers had contributed to "the enhancement of the dignity of work" and said that this principle should remain the guiding light for all aspects of private and public activity in Poland.

The Pope was even more specific in his sermon in Gdynia (on June 11). He focused on the new meaning given to the word "solidarity" as a result of the 1980 strikes and the subsequent emergence of the Solidarity labor movement and the new understanding that "one cannot live according to the rule 'all against all' but only according to the rule 'all with all' as well as 'all for all.'" Otherwise, the Pope said, noting that these principles conformed to traditional Christian teachings and had universal applicability, "how could we cope with the growing differences between the West and the East, between the North and the South--differences within the world as a whole."

That new meaning of solidarity had been established in Poland during the years 1980-1981, said the Pope, adding that "the world must not forget that." He went on to note

that this feeling of solidarity should motivate all social
and human activity: "We [mankind] will never move if pushed
by the imperatives of arms production and the perspective
of self-destruction. . . . We will never progress so long
as we fail to respect human rights in the name of
solidarity between societies." "Solidarity must take
precedence over struggle," he said, noting that solidarity
made another form of struggle possible, "the struggle for
man, for his rights, for his true advancement, and for the
fullness of his life."

The Pope continued this theme during a sermon in
Gdańsk (June 12), focusing on the importance of "work" as a
means of reaching "human and social fulfillment." Arguing
that the process of work centered on man, the Pontiff said
that through work man also defined himself as a member of a
larger social community. In this context, the Pope said
that workers everywhere had the right to self-determination
in professional matters (the right to set up unions
independent of employers' control); that since work
contributed to the "welfare of society as a whole," workers
had the right to take part in decisions affecting that
society; and that the 1980 Gdańsk Agreement between the
strikers and the authorities had been "the expression of a
growing consciousness of the working people's
responsibility for social and moral order," a
responsibility that remained "the task to be fulfilled."

<u>Church-State Relations</u>. The Pope emphasized the
urgent need for the institutional establishment to reach
some sort of accommodation with society in order to
overcome current problems. He consistently insisted that
for such an accommodation to succeed, it would have to
include an official recognition of the human and civil
rights of all individuals and groups as well as the
principle of solidarity within society as the foundation
for all public activities.

The Pontiff specifically insisted that the Church had
an "obligation" to become involved in shaping the character
of public life. He told the Polish bishops during a special
meeting on June 14 that the thrust of that involvement was
to be in expanding pastoral work and explaining "the truth
about man and his rights, about social life, and about the
rights of nations."[4] Moreover, the Pope told the bishops
that "the Church has a duty" to defend the principle of
public "participation in deciding about matters that
concern one's own society, including those in the political
sphere, without any discrimination" as well as the
principle of public self-determination.

The Pope made these remarks while setting conditions for the establishment of diplomatic relations between the Vatican and Poland, a statement that the Polish authorities had been eagerly seeking for more than a year. The Pope noted that the establishment of full diplomatic relations would require approval by the episcopate (the bishops had already expressed their support provided that the government legalized the status of the Church as a public institution); recognition by the authorities of the special role fulfilled by the Holy See with regard to the Polish episcopate (the strengthening of the "bond between the Holy See and the episcopate"); and recognition by the authorities of the "close bond" between the Holy See, the episcopate, and the overwhelmingly Catholic nation as a whole. The Pope's reference to the "international community" lent the issue significance far beyond the purely Polish context. The establishment of such ties with Poland would set a precedent for other communist countries.

The Lithuanian Issue. The Vatican had long maintained the objective of securing a place for the Church in every communist state, but was hampered by obstacles and problems. The Pope drew forceful attention to this fact when he told a congregation in the Cracow cathedral on June 10 that he still could not fulfill his wish of visiting Lithuania to participate in the commemoration of the 600th anniversary of that country's conversion to Christianity.[5]

The Pope repeatedly made public his desire to visit Lithuania, a traditionally Catholic country whose 2,500,000 Catholics constituted 80 percent of the population. The Vatican never recognized the Soviet annexation in 1940, a position that inevitably complicated the Pope's efforts to secure Moscow's acceptance of his visit.

It was not clear whether the Pope's statement in Cracow was prompted by a new refusal by the Soviet authorities to permit him to visit Lithuania or merely meant that there had been no change in their attitude. More important was the fact that the statement had been made publicly and during a visit that had been presented by the Polish authorities as a demonstration of rapprochement between the communist world and the Vatican--a visit possibly paving the way for a future papal visit to the Soviet Union. There had been persistent rumors that the Pope might be invited by the Soviet authorities to attend the 1988 celebrations of the Christian millenium organized by the Russian Orthodox Church.

Aftermath of the Visit. Poland's Catholic bishops

issued a public statement on June 21 expressing their conviction that the teachings imparted by the Pope during his visit to Poland would "trigger new collective efforts to tackle the problems the country is now facing, including the problems of social reconciliation and peace."[6] They added, however, that progress in this direction

> requires the invigoration and expansion of pastoral work and the creation of proper social and professional bodies so that everyone, without discrimination, might have the necessary room in which to carry out their tasks and duties, both in private life and in public, through participating in deciding on matters that concern their own society, including the political sphere.

The statement defined the main directions of the Church's activity and presented them in broadly social, rather than narrowly religious, terms. The essence of the bishops' position was the assertion of the public's right to self-determination within a national community. That right was regarded by the bishops as fundamental to maintaining a "proper" social order in which the state played merely a political role that derived its legitimacy from society as a whole. That view was forcefully expounded by the Pope when he told the bishops on June 14 in Warsaw that "the state's sovereignty responds to a need of the ethical kind only when it is the expression of the sovereignty of the nation in the state[7]; that is to say, the government is legitimate when it expresses the public's free will."

The Pope directed the local Church hierarchies and clergy to make major efforts to expand their involvement in shaping the character of public life in their societies. The thrust of that involvement would be in expanding pastoral work, the Pope said, on explaining "the truth about man and his rights, about social life, and about the rights of nations." The Pope told the bishops that "the Church has a duty to emphasize the key importance of society and the related issue of protecting the rights of the human being" and that the Church would have to defend the public's right to "participate in deciding about matters that concern one's own society" as well as the principle of public self-determination. The Pope emphasized that such a duty resulted from the Church's "social teachings" expressed in religious traditions as well as in numerous documents and statements. The bishops'

statement was a public pledge to follow the Pope's
instruction.

THE BALKAN WAYS

48
REFORM ALBANIAN STYLE

Louis Zanga

Limited Openings to Foreign Countries. Party chief
Ramiz Alia's statement on foreign policy at the Ninth
Congress of the Albanian Workers' Party in November 1986
was in the best tradition of his maker and mentor, the late
Enver Hoxha. He said that an improvement in all manner of
relations with foreign countries would be pursued without
the slightest compromise on ideological principles.
Foremost among these was his total rejection of any form of
relationship with the two superpowers. On the other hand,
Alia was relatively pragmatic when speaking about Tirana's
desire to improve relations with the rest of the world, in
particular with neighboring and other European countries.
Alia began with a positive assessment of
Greek-Albanian relations. Greece retained first place among
those countries with which Albania was developing friendly
relations. Even when speaking of the normalization of
Greek-Albanian relations, however, he seemed to be somewhat
apprehensive about their future course, saying that
"efforts are being made to overcome those difficulties that
remain." Here, he seemed to be referring to the continued
existence of the formal state of war between the two
countries and the claims and counterclaims about the rights
of the Greek minority in Albania.
Of greater interest was the mention of Italy in second
place. The improvement of relations between Rome and
Tirana had come to an abrupt halt when a group of Albanians
sought refuge in the Italian Embassy in Tirana in December
1985. Alia's remarks on the state of Italo-Albanian
relations suggested that there was serious interest in a
thaw. Having mentioned the development of relations in

295

various fields, Alia said that it had been and was Tirana's "aim and desire that these relations should advance in the future too."

More space was given to the state of Turkish-Albanian relations. Alia's closing remarks mentioned the "traditional bonds" between the two countries. He said that the relations had been improving steadily, mentioned the contribution that the Albanians in Turkey had made to the development and progress of that country, and proposed that the manifold contacts and exchanges between the two countries should be promoted even more.[1]

The 500 years of Ottoman rule had left a lasting imprint on Albania. The Albanian diaspora remained particularly strong in Turkey; moreover, many ethnic Albanians also returned from Yugoslavia in the nineteen-fifties. In the multinational Ottoman Empire, Albanians had made up a significant percentage of the multi-ethnic Moslem ruling elite; in the 15th and 16th centuries, 11 out of 49 Grand Viziers were Albanian. This was due to the fact that Albanians were considered one of the ruling rather than the ruled peoples. In 1986, Istanbul was the only foreign city in which Tirana maintained a consulate.

After Alia made his remarks, a number of interesting events took place. In late December, a Turkish-Albanian trade agreement was signed in Tirana, and a Turkish Minister of State, Mustapha Tinaz Titiz, was received by Albanian Prime Minister Adil Carcani.[2] In late January 1987 a protocol on tourism was signed between the two countries in Tirana.

In mid-March a delegation of the Turkish Grand National Assembly headed by its speaker, Necmettin Karaduman, paid an official visit to Albania. Alia said that the relations of friendship and cooperation between Albania and Turkey, despite the two countries' different political systems, were good and were constantly improving, but that there were still possibilities for expanding them.

In late March an agreement was signed in Ankara on cooperation for the 1987-1988 period between the Enver Hoxha University of Tirana and the University of Ankara.[3] Details were given in an interview with the Rector of Tirana University, Professor Osman Kraja, head of the Albanian delegation.[4] Publications and scientific documentation were to be exchanged and the University of Tirana was to send teachers and academics to Ankara to lecture on developments in education in Albania, and scientists and geologists to exchange experiences with the Turks about geological exploration and research into chromium, magnesite, and bauxite; Albanians were to use archives in Ankara to study the history of the Ottoman period.

In his speech at the party congress in November 1986, Alia devoted considerable time to the need for normal friendly relations with Yugoslavia, but added the usual anti-Yugoslav diatribes. He was harsh about the treatment of the Albanians in Yugoslavia. Yugoslav commentators said that Alia's remarks confirmed that there had been no change in Tirana's policy toward Belgrade and that this was "surely" no way to normalize Yugoslav-Albanian relations.

Among the West European countries mentioned, with which Albania was developing relations in "positive directions and through whose joint efforts ways can be found to carry our concrete collaboration further," were France, Austria, Switzerland, Sweden, and other Nordic countries. Alia again said that "with good will and joint efforts," relations with the Federal Republic of Germany could be normalized.

What was new was Alia's mention of East European countries and of China, with all of which, he said, Tirana wanted to develop normal state relations. Tirana began to mend official fences with the GDR.

In June 1986, a major trade agreement was signed in Tirana between the two countries.[5] The high-level delegation headed by East German Minister of Foreign Trade Gerhard Beil was unusual, as was the amount of money involved. Even more unusual was the announcement that Albanian Prime Minister Adil Carcani had received the East German delegation--the first time that a high Albanian government official had met with a top-level, Soviet-bloc delegation since 1961. The long-term agreement provided for the export of complete East German plants and technology for the foodstuffs and metalprocessing industries as well as combine harvesters, tractors, and chaff cutters for "speeding up" the mechanization of Albanian agriculture. The agreement also called for the continuation of the traditional East German supplies of trucks, motors, scientific equipment, medical and laboratory technology, and chemical and metallurgical products. Chromium ore for the supply of the metallurgical industry was among the main Albanian exports to the GDR.

The Unanimous Elections. The only surprise of the Albanian national elections, which were held on February 1, 1987, was that they allegedly drew an even higher turnout than the previous elections in 1982. The 250 parliamentary deputies were elected unanimously with only one invalid ballot, in contrast to the results in 1982, when 99.99 percent voted for the "candidates" and 1 person against, with eight invalid votes. This time, the Albanian ATA news agency claimed[6] that 1,830,652 of the 1,830,653 registered electors voted for the Democratic Front candidates, with one ballot declared invalid.

The absurdity of the results notwithstanding, the elections for the 11th legislature are worth examining not only because they were considered a "great" political event in the country but also because the deputies' backgrounds and the numerous articles and speeches delivered during the election campaign period can help elucidate Albanian politics and priorities of the time. Of the 250 deputies, 97 were new, a large turnover in the composition of the new parliament. References to the new deputies suggested that they were young, competent professionals, mostly with economic backgrounds. Although most of the deputies were communist party members, the ideologists were not as heavily represented as in the past. Also, 66 of the deputies (one-fourth of the entire parliament) were women. While no statistics on age were available, it seems that there were more young people in the new legislature, which was in line with the general trend of bringing new blood into the country's administration. All the top party leaders were members of the new parliament, while a number of high government and other officials were not.

Among the more interesting themes of the election campaign were extending socialist "democracy" and the perennial subject of "party-people" unity. In a campaign speech, Ramiz Alia stressed the need to develop socialist "democracy" even further, saying that the interests of the state and the rights of the citizen were inseparably connected:

> A special distinguishing characteristic of our socialist system is [the fact] that the higher the level of the rights that emanate from socialist democracy, the greater the responsibilities of social groups and individuals. Unless the work of the state functions properly, there cannot be prosperity for anyone. Without progress in the economy as a whole, there can be no improvement in the well-being of [either] the masses or special individuals. State property, the land, factories, schools, [and] hospitals [all] belong to the people. Therefore, every worker has, and must constantly strengthen, a feeling of responsibility toward the state, which

will contribute to its consolidation and its proper administration.[7]

This was something new in Albania; it is significant that such emphasis was being put on improving living standards, on the condition, however, that everyone contribute to developing the country's economy. Ideological exhortations did not seem to play the role they did in the past.

In discussing "unity," Alia said that the class struggle would continue to be waged without any respite, but then concluded with an economic message:

Nowadays, under the actual conditions of building up the country, true socialist patriotism demands that everyone make his selfless contribution toward fulfilling the tasks of economic and social development, assimilating and developing culture, and affirming and deepening the norms of socialist life.

The unanimous turnout and approval by voters might have made Albania appear to be Europe's last bastion of Orthodox Stalinism, but the background of the new deputies to parliament and Alia's address during the campaign seemed to belie this. Alia seemed to be more sincere in his political pronouncements and less inclined to engage in ideological rhetorics than his predecessor. His determination to proceed on a more pragmatic economic course was unmistakable.

A More Rational Economic Policy. The aim of economic measures introduced in 1987 was to boost the stagnant economy by increasing material incentives. They sought to ease the country's highly centralized economic management and improve economic expertise. Although by no means comparable to the reforms in the Soviet bloc, which were criticized by Tirana, the new economic regulations showed that the Albanian leadership had also decided to remodel some of its outdated and constraining economic practices.

The question of how to improve efficiency was dealt with at CC plenums as well as in numerous major speeches and press articles. A particularly telling article appeared in the party's theoretical monthly *Rruga e Partise*, which examined the question of improving relations in production:

The ways that have been opened and the tasks assigned require revolutionary thinking and action and concrete solutions in the revolutionary practice of the masses as well as struggle against indolence, against the toleration of backwardness, and against expecting others (such as the district authorities, the ministry, or the state) to solve problems . . . The clear-cut and correct Marxist-Leninist stand of our party on these issue leaves no room for ambivalence, for fear that we "might slide into revisionism," or for metaphysical concepts that treat economic relations as static.[8]

The article's unprecedented reference to the specter of "revisionism" is of particular interest. Any past attempts to introduce changes in economic management had been swiftly put down by Alia's predecessor Enver Hoxha. The clearest example of the late leader's hard-line economic policy had been the major purge in the mid-nineteen-seventies of reform-minded officials--such as Politburo members Abdyl Këllezi and Koco Theodosi--for their alleged attempts to introduce "revisionist self-management" methods. It was, therefore, not surprising that some people in the country were now apprehensive about expressing new ideas. The party monthly seemed to be suggesting that there was no reason for economists to entertain such fears; they should be more daring and innovative in their suggestions.

In his economic report to the parliament, Niko Gjyzari, Chairman of the State Planning Commission, disclosed that a number of measures aimed at improving relations between the various branches of the economy would come into effect during 1987. The press had already been discussing some of these measures. The party organ *Zeri i Popullit*, for example, carried an editorial entitled "The Better Harmonization of the Moral and Material Incentives and of the Interests of Society with Those of the Individual."[9] In the past, emphasis had been placed on moral incentives and the interests of society, now it appeared that the importance of material incentives and the role of the individual were being given greater consideration.

The editorial mentioned three new laws entitled "The Stimulation of the Growth of Production Through Salaries," "For a More Correct Use of the Supplementary Material Incentives and of the Special Fund," and "About the Criteria for the Evaluation of the Financial-Economic Activity of Socialist Enterprises." According to the editorial, copper miners and coalminers, provided they "are not absent from work without justification," now received bonuses of up to 2 percent of their salaries if they exceeded their production targets.   In an effort to raise dairy production, agricultural workers had been offered incentives amounting to between 15 and 30 percent of their regular salaries.

Alia's speech in mid-February to the party's second plenum triggered a new campaign against excessive centralization.   There was a considerable difference in emphasis between what Hoxha had said about the principle of "democratic centralism" and what Alia was saying. Alia was clearly recommending less rigid centralism and greater democracy in terms of "initiative" and "self-motivation." He took a similar line when speaking about the rights and responsibilities of the various state and economic bodies and about the relationship between centralized management and the masses, between the central authorities and the workplace. He saw that a distinction had to be made between what was primary, "which must be preserved and developed," and what was secondary, "which undergoes change and constant refinement." Regarding those in central authority, he demanded that they perform their duties not

mechanically but creatively, not as officials who pass on instructions, but as cadre members and working people with fertile minds who manage and organize with imagination and communist responsibility.

He also spoke of pursuing "productive" work methods, encouraging grassroots initiative, and spurring progress:

The central bodies must examine, create, and support advanced thinking. Administrative bodies must increase their demands on themselves and on their dependent enterprises, especially as regards improving the quality of production. Every sector, every plant and factory, must consider how to be creative, how to improve quality, how to improve production, and how to satisfy the people.

Experiments increasing the decision-making power at the managerial level in state-run farms in several agricultural regions had already been set up in accordance with government decisions taken earlier in 1987.   These farms could draw up their own production plans and distribute incomes following state quotas, while farmers were encouraged to plant vegetables in private plots to increase supplies.   Also, a complete indexing system, including a comprehensive means of evaluating technical, economic, and social progress, was introduced to assess the performances of these enterprises.

In a speech to the third CC plenum on April 23, 1987, Alia dealt in an unprecedentedly open manner with the state and future prospects of the country's food supply. He indicated that a crisis had been reached. The Albanian population's sustained, relatively high growth rate; worsening shortages of meat and dairy products; rising expectations of a predominantly young populace for more and better consumer goods, expectations that had been frustrated by the leadership's insistence on living within the country's means and strictly adhering to Albania's constitutional ban on foreign credits ("no imports without exports")--these were some of the reasons for the urgency with which Alia set about tackling problems in the agricultural sector. Alia's speech took up three pages of the standard four-page issues of the country's main dailies. For maximum publicity and impact, the unusual measure was taken of broadcasting his speech on television and radio.[10]

Alia began by listing the advances made in the sector and in promoting the well-being of the people. For over a decade, he said, Albania had been meeting the people's needs for bread from its domestic resources; now the country produced enough food for a population that had tripled and increased its demands. Life expectancy in Albania was over 71 years, he said, and the mortality rate (deaths per 1,000 population) was the lowest in Europe. Also, the Albanian citizen's daily diet contained almost as many calories as the average diet in a number of other European countries; this dietary base, according to medical specialists, was sufficient to assure a high level of physical and mental welfare.

Alia then changed his tone, speaking openly about shortcomings:

There has been a squeeze in many areas, as well as some limitations. If this has become more apparent today, it is because the growth in production per capita, especially for dairy products, has been slightly slower and the demands of the people have been higher. This has been brought about by a certain discrepancy between production levels and the buying power of the people, a discrepancy that has been widening annually. From an assessment of the present supply situation, it emerges that our fundamental task must be to ensure as soon as possible, at least by the end of the five-year plan, that the value [*sic*] of food products on the market respond to the basic demands of the workers and correspond to their buying power throughout the country.

Alia went on to say that the state of the food market could be deemed healthy only when enough milk and eggs, enough fruits and vegetables, and enough meat and fish could be found to meet the basic needs and satisfy the buying power of the people. Discussing the possibilities for reducing shortfalls in supply, he cited the expected increase in egg production, at the same time disclosing that eggs had until recently been frequently unavailable in some cities. He said that the planned increases in milk production would be modest; "let us be realists," he said, "for the time being these are our capacities."

In 1987, the growth rate of the Albanian population was among the highest in Europe (although some experts maintained that the growth rate among ethnic Albanians in Yugoslavia was even higher). The decline in arable land was basically due to the expansion of urban areas and of industry on the plains that made up less than one-fourth of the country's predominantly mountainous territory. In a study made for the Joint Economic Committee of the United States Congress, the British expert Michael Kaser estimated that Albania's 600,000 hectares of arable land would have to support 6.5 people per hectare by the turn of the century--quite inconceivable given the yields available at the time.[11] Faced with such forecasts, it was no wonder that the Albanian leaders were greatly concerned by the problems of feeding the population.

Poor management, organization, and distribution were also criticized by Alia, who said that increasing the supply of food was not merely a question of raising production but of improving organization as well: for example, although the output of food products in the intensive cooperative sector had increased, deliveries to the state had dropped. No satisfactory food supply could be provided for urban areas without first satisfying the farmers' own food requirements. To achieve this, Alia recommended that, among other things, the role of the private plot be strengthened.

Alia reiterated that the produce from private plots served the needs of the cooperative farmers' families and was not a means of private enterprise. He also argued that food production was not merely an agricultural issue but also a problem of industry, collection, distribution, trade, and transport. As for pricing, it was the executive committees (local government) and the finance departments that needed to act quickly and flexibly "in order to achieve a proper and steady balance between supply and demand for each commodity."

A key problem was apparently the very poor organization of the collection and marketing of agricultural produce. Alia disclosed that trade organizations frequently failed to collect farm produce from the cooperatives when plan targets were exceeded; this created waste and caused losses. If the cooperative farmer "sets out for the city with a basket of figs, parsley, or ten eggs in hand," Alia said, "time and effort is lost in production"; when individuals went to the market or sold the produce of their plots privately, "the farmers' valuable time is wasted and private enterprise is promoted."

Alia's speech confirmed the new policy of giving top priority to the consumer sector. However, his concluding remarks made it clear that the road ahead would not be an easy one: "Life in the future will present new problems that are no less difficult."

A Less Rigid Society. In August 1986, an article in the party organ Zeri i Popullit by Zenel Hysa, an official in the Central Committee apparatus, examined the social services sector in the country. First pointing to the many shortcomings in this sector, an area receiving growing attention as the government sought to raise the standard of living in Albania, Hysa came to the conclusion that inefficiency tended to promote private initiative.[12] Officialdom in Albania not only frowned upon any form of private enterprise but also never missed a chance to draw critical attention to the allegedly extensive use of private enterprise in "revisionist" countries. It seemed from this article, however, that private enterprise could be found in the service sector in Albania, too.

Manifestations of private work are encountered in almost all areas of the communal services sector, whatever their size. Enterprises must, therefore, take preventive measures. Above all, work must be carried out to expand those services, in which quantity, quality, and promptness do not meet the required standards, such as in home repairs, home appliances, painting, and tailoring--areas in which demands are greater and in which private activity is

fostered by the failure to meet these demands.
Greater cooperation among various mass organizations
is required in order to check on those who engage in
private work or on those who rely on private work.

This was the first time that the press had dealt in
such detail with the growth of private activities in the
service sector. It seemed that as the sector expanded and
the demand for various services rose, so private activities
came to shoulder more and more of the burden, despite the
party's continued opposition.

Also in August 1986, *Zeri i Popullit*[13] carried an
article entitled: "No Compromise with Foreign Tastes and
Manifestations." The article was prompted by the busy
summer vacation season and the authorities' evidently
growing concern at displays of "uncivilized" behavior as up
to 70,000 vacationers congregated on some weekends along
the Durres beach, the largest of its kind in the country.
The daily pointed out that despite the fact that Radio
Tirana was broadcasting a special program of musical
entertainment, some vacationers played "screaming jazz" and
other foreign music programs on their radios.

There is also no shortage of interest in vulgar
television programs. One evening in the Iliria
section [of the Durres resort] a person was watching
a foreign, tasteless, distorted, and totally
worthless program on his portable television in front
of his cabin. When the citizen's attention was drawn
to this fact, his reply was: "Why don't you leave me
alone, I'm minding my own business, aren't I?

Zeri i Popullit then noted that some people had been
asking: "Is it illegal to listen to foreign radio stations
or to watch foreign television?"

The Albanian press continued to publish articles on
the authorities' problem of how to deal with an
increasingly unruly and undisciplined younger generation,
which was allegedly exposed to strong foreign influences.
The problem was compounded by the fact that the younger
generation constituted the largest social group in Albania,
where the average age was only 26, the youngest in Europe.

Pessimism among older Albanians regarding the younger
generation was expressed in a lengthy article by Hamit
Beqeja for the party daily entitled "Intellectual Culture
and Moral Culture."[14] Beqeja, a professor at Tirana
University, was known as the country's leading psychologist

and a prolific writer on youth affairs. His writings were frank and up-to-date by Albanian standards. Foreign journalists had even been able to question him on such sensitive issues as the status of religion in Albania. Beqeja answered that while "institutional religion does not exist now, religious consciousness does. We can never stop that through legal means."[15]

A "negative phenomenon" noted by Bejeqa was a tendency for young people, despite all the talk about revolutionary motivation and ideals, to look for an easy way through life and for comfortable jobs that avoided challenging work. The motivation among young people to work and study was shallow, he said, lacking in ideals, and with only short-term intellectual benefits, which in the final analysis bred a kind of "parasitism" in the young generation.

While it was generally parents and the older generation who seemed alarmed by the signs of degeneration among young people, there was also the impression of a conflict within the leadership over how to handle young people. Those who would have liked to take a harder line on youth affairs were now in the minority.

49
CEAUŞESCU AND GORBACHEV

Anneli Ute Gabanyi

Romanian-Style Restructuring. Romanian propaganda claimed that the country had long been embarked on modernization and structural reorganization, and portrayed Ceauşescu as the dynamic, innovative proponent of a thorough restructuring and democratization process encompassing all spheres of Romanian society. As long ago as the 1986 27th CPSU Congress, Ceauşescu had adopted this pose, even saying that the workers of a Moscow factory whom he had met during his stay in the Soviet capital had praised Romanian self-management and workers' participation as a worthwhile model.[1]

Ceauşescu's pretended "Gorbachevization" of the Romanian system while putting his stakes on the Kremlin conservatives had a tradition in postwar Romanian policy. Ceauşescu's predecessor, Gheorghe Gheorghiu-Dej, adopted a similar stance toward Khrushchev's pressure for de-Stalinization in Eastern Europe, pretending that his purging of the Stalinists associated with Ana Pauker in 1952 had made him the first de-Stalinizer in the bloc. Dej had, in fact, backed the Kremlin diehards, who had succeeded in reversing the de-Stalinization process following the outbreak of the 1956 Hungarian revolution.

Ever since, the RCP leader and the Romanian media went out of their way to claim that Romania had initiated its own brand of a "new economic-financial mechanism" as far back as 1978; that a well-devised system of workers' self-management and enterprise self-financing had been set up and was to be implemented; that the "socialist principle of remuneration" according to performance was being applied; and that the role of science in the process of modernization and the importance of expertise had long been acknowledged. Moreover, Ceauşescu repeatedly presented himself as the staunchest promoter of this restructuring drive against alleged inertia and opposition from the party and state apparatus.

Ceauşescu as Defender of Ideological Purity. In a speech on January 26, 1987[2]--his birthday--Ceauşescu compared his policies favorably with unnamed models of "socialist construction" on the grounds of their ideological purity. Indirectly admitting to criticism of the Romanian model of "multilaterally developed socialism" from other countries of the bloc, particularly the Soviet Union, Ceauşescu typically used an offensive posture as a defense. He admitted that "mistakes" had been made in implementing socialism; he made it clear, however, that this had happened before he had assumed office in 1965. He also admitted "shortcomings"--although he said that their "decisive" cause was to be sought in the even more distant past, in the so-called "exploitation" of Romania by "foreign empires" as well as "monopolies" and "imperialist states." He made a special point, however, of saying that the socialist system was basically just (although periodically in need of strengthening and improvement) and that the RCP's overall political strategy was entirely in keeping with the fundamental guidelines of "scientific socialism," such as the maintenance of socialist property and the leading role of the party.

Ceauşescu criticized unspecified attempts at "socialist renewal" and "perfecting socialism," which, he said, although presented by their proponents as being in accordance with the "objective laws" of the building of a communist society, violated basic ideological precepts:

> Speaking about the need to improve and develop
> socialism, in my opinion our basis should be the
> lessons, the experience, and the practice of
> socialist construction as well as the invincible
> principles of scientific socialism, of communism.
> One cannot speak about socialist renewal, about
> perfecting socialism, unless one starts from these
> principles. . . .   There is no way of speaking about
> socialist perfection and [at the same time] about
> so-called market socialism and free competition--and
> all this in the name of objective laws.

Ceauşescu was equally categorical in rejecting enterprise autonomy on the grounds that this endangered the guiding role of the party over the economy.

Opposition to Foreign Models. On February 24 ,1987, the Romanian leader touched on the subject of Soviet reforms at a minor meeting of party activists and managers. He discussed whether the Soviet reforms were meant to be confined to the Soviet Union or were intended to spill over into the rest of the "socialist community" in order to pave the way for closer and more efficient integration within the CMEA.

In contrast to his birthday speech on January 26,[3] this time Ceauşescu depicted himself less as a defender of pure Marxism, than as a national Marxist leader defending Romania's social and political patterns against outside interference:

> We are in favor of broad exchanges of experience with
> socialist countries and other states. But, I repeat,
> we are against a mechanical, dogmatic imitation of
> the example and practice of any one place or
> another--and we will work consistently to adopt the
> best solutions arising from general laws and world
> experience, taking account of our circumstances and
> the ways of our people.

In a subsequent speech at a gathering of representatives of the Hungarian and German minorities, Ceauşescu voiced satisfaction that Romania's alleged, earlier start at reform and liberalization, which had previously met with criticism in the bloc, had now been vindicated:

> I believe it is not wrong of me to mention that over
> all this period of more than twenty years, during

which we have improved our forms of management in all
domains, starting with the party, [and] the
democratization of our general life, more than once
have we been openly or indirectly criticized for this
so-called straying from the general experience and
norms. . . . Now we have a feeling of satisfaction
that what we have done has been proved right.[4]

Ceauşescu professed to be particularly pleased with
the trend toward greater "socialist democracy" and public
participation.

Reluctant Coverage. The initial coverage of
Gorbachev's CPSU plenum speech of January 27, 1987 in the
Romanian daily press was a 50-word item buried in the back
pages.[5] Several days later a 2,000-word report on the
speech was published in all the major dailies and in the
foreign policy weekly Lumea.[6] Yet nothing was said about
the Soviet leader's criticism of the social malaise
prevailing in the Soviet Union as a result of corruption,
servility, and excessive praise--characteristic of not a
few communist regimes, including Brezhnev's as well as
Ceauşescu's. Neither shortcomings in the supply of goods
nor in the transportation and health systems, nor
Gorbachev's references to cultural stagnation were
mentioned. The Romanian reports also ignored the list of
remedies that Gorbachev proposed for the Soviet (and
perhaps not only the Soviet) malaise: glasnost, greater
autonomy for enterprises, the rejuvenation of the cadre,
and criticism of leading party figures. Romanian readers
were spared both Gorbachev's proposal for multiple
candidacy in elections for party bodies and his comments on
the national question.

No commentary on the CPSU plenum appeared in the
Romanian press. As if to compensate, the Romanian service
of Radio Moscow devoted great attention to the speech and
commentaries on it. In interviews with Romanians at the
February 1987 Moscow Peace Forum, Soviet broadcasters tried
to convey the impression that the Romanian intelligentsia
and artistic community supported "the great political
figure"[7] of Gorbachev and his "free and open style."[8]

The Issue Behind Reform: CMEA Integration. The RCP
Political Executive Committee neither expressed support for
the Soviet policy nor explicitly backed Ceauşescu's stand.
At its meeting on February 20, 1987, the committee did,
however, adopt a common stand on the issue of joint
ventures with the Soviet Union and other communist
countries--a long-standing controversy between Romania and

the Soviet Union. Romania had been the only CMEA country
that had still not concluded a governmental agreement with
the Soviet Union on the establishment of direct links
between enterprises.   In his speech to the Political
Executive Council (PEC), Ceauşescu said that no "new
special legal provisions" were needed for joint venture
agreements concluded between members of the CMEA.[9]

The main reason for Romania's opposition to greater
integration within the CMEA was its fear of losing sole
control over the Romanian economy. Soviet reform was not
the leadership's primary concern; what did bother them was
the perceived Soviet strategy of restructuring the CMEA to
force greater integration.

Semi-official Romanian commentaries showed that the
RCP was under considerable pressure to follow the lead of
communist countries whose economies had been faring better,
which probably also meant that there had been criticism of
Romania's dismal economic performance from within the bloc.
Bucharest refused to accept criticism from abroad, which,
it was claimed, was based on "criteria and principles
borrowed from the barely 'renovated' old-type society," a
reference to the USSR. "Socialism," the official Romanian
reasoning went, embraced "a society that is always open to
improvement along its own economic, political, and
ideological lines."[10]

Romanian commentators protested against the fact that
"different concrete experiences of socialist construction"
were being placed in a certain "hierarchical setting" and
that "certain 'pilot' experiences" were becoming
"fetishes."[11] Among communist parties there were no
"universally valid recipes," and nobody had the right

to impose on other parties the road they should
choose in their struggle for socialism . . . .The
continuation of an historical process in one country
or another weakens the possibility of a 'transplant,'
or the importing or exporting of a revolutionary or
counterrevolutionary process.[12]

Unnamed "adepts of suprastate and supranational
integration" were charged with viewing "nations and nation
states, with their sovereign attributions" as "artificial
constructs that can be 'demolished' or manipulated at will
by certain theorists or politicians."[13]

Rightly or wrongly, the Romanian leadership perceived
itself as being confronted with the same CMEA strategy of

country specialization that it had successfully fended off 25 years earlier.

Soviet Policy in Perspective. In its dealings with crisis-ridden Romania, the Soviet leadership had devised a sophisticated policy. While not wanting to be seen as supporting Ceauşescu's domestic and foreign policies, the Soviet leadership did not appear interested in destabilizing him to a degree that would threaten the stability of the communist system in Romania. The Soviets were avoiding giving him a pretext to fan national or even anti-Soviet feelings among the population.

However, Soviet propaganda was clearly trying to show the Romanian public--as well as the political, technical, and cultural elite--that the Soviet Union had turned into a locomotive of progress within the bloc and that increased economic cooperation with Moscow would be beneficial. Soviet propagandists pointed out that the increase in bilateral Romanian-Soviet trade in previous years had been a direct result of Romania's greater readiness to make investments on Soviet soil and boost production cooperation and specialization with its neighbor to the East. Even greater relief was promised in exchange for Romania's willingness to establish direct links among enterprises and joint ventures along the lines desired by the Soviet Union. Such arguments, even if not fully applicable under the existing Romanian leadership, might have found more support from a future generation of Romanian leaders as well as among the Romanian people, who had been deeply disappointed with Ceauşescu's specific brand of "socialism" even if it was clad in the national colors.

Gorbachev in Romania. Romania was the last East European country for Gorbachev to visit; Ceauşescu had been the last party leader from the bloc to go to the Soviet Union.

Gorbachev and his wife Raisa were greeted at Bucharest's Otopeni airport on May 25, 1987, with all the honors Romanian protocol reserved for state visits. Although observers noted an "unusual coolness" in the way the two leaders greeted each other, the Romanian media emphasized the warm and enthusiastic welcome extended to the Gorbachevs by a traditionally hospitable people.

Romanian radio and television broadcast the welcoming ceremony live, while Soviet stations played down the importance of the event by giving it a more restrained and casual treatment. The Soviets did, however, show a considerable and perhaps not entirely spontaneous amount of *glasnost* in their detailed reports of Gorbachev's stroll around Victory Square. The Soviet "Vremia" television newscast at 7:00 P.M. registered in detail Gorbachev's vain attempt to converse (it was, in fact, a monologue) with Romanian women dumbfounded with fear, yet unable to conceal their worries and misery.

At one point, he turned to the women in the crowd and asked them why they were silent. He told them that if they claimed that everything was in order, he would not believe them. There were problems in every country, he said, and these problems and their solution could be discussed among socialist countries.

Ceauşescu's Dinner Speech. Although nothing substantial emerged about the content of the two leaders' first official talks, which lasted for about three-and-a-half hours, the speeches delivered at the official dinner that night gave an unusually clear picture of the differences between them.

Ceauşescu's speech was a paean to Romania's allegedly long "experience" in increasing efficiency, modernization, self-administration, self-financing, and democratization. He then turned to "the Soviet people's concern about fulfilling the decisions of the 27th CPSU Congress and the recent party plenary meetings to reorganize Soviet society and develop democracy and all economic and social areas." Romania followed these efforts "with interest" and, "as a neighbor and a friend," wished the "dear" Soviet comrades "ever bigger successes on that road." Unlike Jaruzelski, Zhivkov, and Kádár, however, he did not say that the Soviet experience was as relevant to Romania as it was to the rest of the bloc, or that his country would heed and follow it.

Ceauşescu then turned to bilateral and multilateral cooperation, which he said had been discussed at the official talks; but he did not pretend that any agreement or identity of views had been reached. Ceauşescu took the standard Romanian position, expressing keen interest in cooperation in fields of "mutual interest" while turning a deaf ear to pressure for closer CMEA integration. He even went so far as to express disappointment about "a certain lag in economic exchanges, production cooperation, and specialization" and urged that action be taken to solve problems "in all CMEA countries" by joint efforts.

Although expressing Romanian support for Gorbachev's nuclear disarmament initiatives, his ideas differed somewhat on such issues as conventional disarmament, rules of international conduct, and Romanian-Soviet foreign policy cooperation. With regard to conventional disarmament, Ceauşescu called for "a firmer passage [sic] to conventional arms reduction," pointing to Romania's unilateral actions in this field, which reflected his country's "firm determination" to act in consonance with "all the forces of disarmament, détente, and peace." In his habitually ambivalent manner, which did not explicitly exempt the USSR, Ceauşescu expressed the opinion that "firmer action" was also needed to "rule out the threat and use of force from international relations," thereby allowing each country to "develop in freedom and independence."

Gorbachev's Dinner Speech. In contrast to Ceauşescu's polite and flattering welcome to Gorbachev, the Soviet leader was brisk and matter-of-fact, avoiding even a hint of effusiveness. Going straight to the matter of greatest importance, Gorbachev gave a brilliant diplomatic performance in replying to the points set forth by Ceauşescu. He did not refer directly to the issue of reform, but the failure of the "Romanian model" and the negative effects of Romania's reluctance to become involved in further CMEA integration were clearly implied. In keeping with Soviet policy toward the other communist countries, Gorbachev pointed to the need for a "qualitative change" in Romanian-Soviet relations. The "mechanism of cooperation" needed "improvement" and had to be "brought into line" with requirements. He clearly rejected Ceauşescu's policy of pursuing cooperation pegged to Romanian interests while turning a deaf ear to the Soviet Union's overall program. Although "considerable headway" had been achieved in a number of areas, he said that "there are other areas where progress has been, so to speak, average or even poor." "Today it is difficult to hope for considerable success through breakthroughs along separate directions [sic]. This can be achieved only by broadening ties along the entire front."

He outlined specific areas in which greater Romanian cooperation was required: "a fuller study and comparison of each other's experience" (an unmistakable reminder to follow the Soviet model in socialist construction); and greater cooperation among party organizations and labor collectives as well as in science and ideology.

Gorbachev made it clear that expanded cooperation in trade and production was possible only if Romanian goods met Soviet quality requirements and that higher quality and technological standards could be achieved only by "pooling the material and intellectual resources" in pursuit of a "sharp acceleration" in economic improvement and by "deepening the whole integration process" within the CMEA.

He said that the first steps toward "improving the effectiveness of Soviet-Romanian cooperation" had been made; the establishment of direct production ties between a number of industrial units had been agreed, and joint venture projects were also under discussion. He felt that the "political will" to go along these lines existed in both countries.

Gorbachev's rhetoric on foreign policy sounded almost identical to Ceauşescu's standard phrases on foreign policy and disarmament issues. By giving credit to the common Soviet and Romanian approaches and efforts in this field, Gorbachev seemed to pull the rug from under Ceauşescu's aspirations to foreign policy autonomy.

"Restructuring," Democratization, and "Openness" Explained. On May 26, a friendship rally took place in Bucharest at the Palace of the Socialist Republic of Romania. Although the audience of about 3,000 hand-picked officials had obviously been instructed when to applaud during Gorbachev's speech and when to remain silent (that is, during the passages praising "restructuring"), the Soviet leader must have been aware that his address, broadcast live by Romanian radio and television, was perhaps the only direct means of conveying his reformist message to the Romanian people.

The concept of reorganization in the Soviet Union, Gorbachev said, was not confined to face-lifting but was geared to "fundamental, radical reforms." It was absolutely necessary, he said, to

> give full play to the initiative of the people . . .
> remove bureaucratic barriers . . . [and give] . . .
> every member of society real guarantees for the
> defense of his legitimate rights and interests.

In order to develop democracy, "wide-ranging and open information" was "an obligatory precondition." It was precisely with "openness," Gorbachev told an audience used to perhaps the most tightly controlled information system in Eastern Europe, that the "renewal of socialism" in the Soviet Union had started. Any information withheld from the people or repressed, he said, eventually made the situation worse: "A half-told truth is worse than a lie." "Honesty and sincerity in politics" was the key to the solution of difficult problems.

In his remarks about the importance of changing the method and style of party work, Gorbachev was clearly implying a comparison with Ceauşescu's tightly centralized and personalized style of leadership and the absence of discussion and collective input into decision making. His implicit criticism of the aging Romanian leadership was even more evident in his reference to the new Soviet practice of dismissing party cadre "who are not up to their jobs, who cannot keep up the pace," and particularly those who had compromised themselves by, among other things, nepotism. He was clearly appealing to the new generation of leaders in Romania.

Gorbachev made it unequivocally clear that the Soviet Union viewed the relationship between the economy and social policy differently from the Romanians, who gave priority to industrial development over consumption. People worked the way they lived, he said, and if living conditions were ignored, then both the standard of living and production would suffer.

Gorbachev Raises the Minority Question. Perhaps the most striking aspect of Gorbachev's speech was his implied criticism of Romania's handling of the minority question. Speaking about the need to strengthen "internationalist" education and friendship among peoples, Gorbachev said:

> It is known what great importance it [relations between the minorities] has for us and what great importance Lenin accorded to all aspects of national relations, asking that delicacy and special attention be given to solving these problems. I think that the Leninist precepts in this respect are still topical today. We intend to follow them.

Despite high-level official Soviet and Hungarian claims to the contrary, there were indications that on the eve of Gorbachev's visit to Romania and the forthcoming Warsaw Pact summit meeting, Hungary may have tried to raise its concerns about ethnic Magyars in Transylvania with the Soviets. The Sunday Times reported on May 24, on the basis of unidentified "senior Soviet sources," that the Hungarian government had sought to persuade Gorbachev to call off his visit to Bucharest, because it might be seen as a tacit endorsement of the maltreatment of the Hungarian minority. The deputy director and party secretary of the Hungarian Academy's Institute of History, Ferenc Glatz,[14] had said in 1986 that Hungary was pressing for the establishment of an institution that would control minority policies in the bloc or at least for the issuing of a declaration of principles and a joint policy on minorities in Eastern Europe.

Gorbachev's remarks indicated that he was not unaware of the problem. In his speech at the Bucharest rally, Ceauşescu, obviously rejecting Gorbachev's insinuation, claimed that all Romanian citizens, "notwithstanding their nationality," enjoyed "ideal working and living conditions" in Romania.

Romanians Urged To Consider the Soviet Model. Clearly in response to recurrent Romanian claims (reiterated in Ceauşescu's rally speech) about the right and the need of each communist party to pursue its own line and model, and of each country to devise its own development strategy in accordance with its national interests, Gorbachev defined the Soviet double-track policy on this issue in the way he had done in Prague. The socialist countries, he said, enjoyed "independence in establishing their political line"; and the Soviet "restructuring" model was patterned specifically on Soviet conditions. He also made it clear, however, that communist countries had a "collective responsibility for the fate of world socialism" and that the Soviet Union would be "glad if the fraternal countries found something useful for their own activity" in the Soviet experience.

As if to show that Soviet-style "openness" applied to foreign policy, too, Gorbachev suggested that the Soviet Union might have committed some mistakes in its relations with communist countries in the early postwar years and even that not all Soviet bloc arms control initiatives had been "well thought out and have always been successful." Praising joint independent actions and proposals by the smaller Warsaw Pact countries, among them Romania, Gorbachev suggested that if an agreement were reached on setting up a nuclear-free zone in the Balkans, the Soviet Union might consider giving these countries the necessary guarantees that it would not place or use nuclear and chemical weapons there.

Visiting "Potemkin City". On the third and last day of his visit, Gorbachev took a three hour ride through Bucharest's boulevards. He was driven to the sites of the Dimboviţa river regulation project, the subway, and Ceauşescu's grandiose "civic center" built on the ruins of a bulldozed residential area of old Bucharest. A Pravda report of May 25 published Gorbachev's remarks to Bucharest dwellers. After asking them whether they were pleased with their "beautiful city" in which he saw "major reconstruction" underway, Gorbachev, clearly alluding to the massive destruction that had accompanied Ceauşescu's "urban *perestroika*," expressed the "hope that historical architecture will be preserved." He said that "we failed to do this in some places in Moscow, and now we are regretting it."

The Romanian media reported Gorbachev's ride around Bucharest as a success story. Western correspondents, however, noted that immediately after the official motorcade had left one of the unusually well-supplied markets, thousands of people finished chanting the obligatory "Ceauşescu-Gorbachev" slogans and stormed the market stands, despite police efforts to stop them.

The Communiqué. The joint Romanian-Soviet communiqué issued at the end of the visit almost ostentatiously avoided mentioning the names of those accompanying the CPSU Secretary on his visit. No names were given for the Romanian delegation either. Could it be that Gorbachev objected to accepting Elena Ceauşescu as a participant at the summit? It is not difficult to divine what Gorbachev's attitude toward the putative succession scheme prepared for Elena was; his condemnation of "nepotism" in his rally speech made this clear.

The visit was described as having been held in an atmosphere of "friendship, cordiality, and mutual understanding" without any reference to identity or closeness of views. According to the communiqué, the two leaders briefed each other on "topical problems of socialist construction." Contrary to standard practice, the communique did not pretend that Ceauşescu and Gorbachev had congratulated each other on successes attained in this field.

The communiqué juxtaposed the Soviet and Romanian "models," saying merely that "the importance of mutually studying the experience of socialist construction was noted."

The section in the communiqué devoted to Ceauşescu's depiction of Romania lacked any new features, while Gorbachev's presentation of "restructuring" contained barely disguised, albeit indirect, criticism of Romania's economic and social policies as well as Ceauşescu's style of leadership. Gorbachev emphasized, for example, "individual labor activity," an anathema to Ceauşescu. He also said that production should not be overemphasized at the expense of the standard of living.

While apparently resisting the notion that he should reform his antiquated system along Gorbachevian lines, Ceauşescu seemed to give in to Soviet pressure for extended cooperation and production specialization. Whereas increasing mutual trade and energy and raw material deliveries on terms favorable to Romania was only called a "mutual desire" that the two sides reaffirmed,

> it was decided to . . . establish direct links in particular in the leading branches of industry, both to satisfy one's own requirements and for export to third countries by means of setting up mixed enterprises and scientific organizations in different spheres of mutual interest.

This was an important decision, which contrasted with Romania's previous refusal to enter into joint ventures with the Soviet Union.

It was ironic that Ceauşescu, known for two decades as a proponent of an autonomous foreign policy, should now have been seen as showing a higher degree of overlapping and consonance with Gorbachev on foreign policy issues than on domestic and ideological ones. The communiqué made no mention of Ceauşescu's constant pressure for unilateral Warsaw Pact reductions of troops and costs; nor, however, did it reproduce the biting criticism of the American and NATO stands on disarmament that Gorbachev made in his friendship rally speech on May 26.

The two sides appeared to have found a way of coexisting with each other. This *modus vivendi* permitted a fairly open expression of differences about the nature of the respective "models" of a communist regime, while concentrating on bilateral economic relations, an area in which both parties could and wanted to cooperate.

50
GREEK-BULGARIAN FRIENDSHIP TREATY

Stephen Ashley

On September 11, 1986, a "Declaration on Friendship, Good Neighborliness, and Cooperation" was signed by the Bulgarian leader, Todor Zhivkov, and the Greek Prime Minister, Andreas Papandreou, during the latter's two-day visit to Sofia. Papandreou went to Sofia immediately after a state visit to Bucharest, where on September 10 he had signed a "Declaration on the Issues of Disarmament, Peace, and Cooperation in Europe and Worldwide," with the Romanian leader Nicolae Ceauşescu.[1]

On the surface, the declaration appeared to consolidate the process of Greek-Bulgarian rapprochement that had begun even before the fall of the military junta in 1974 and had gathered pace since the first election victory of PASOK (the Panhellenic Socialist Movement) in 1981. The declaration had been some time in the preparation and was discussed during the visit to Sofia in December 1985 by Karolas Papoulias, the Greek foreign minister.[2] The Bulgarian media were quick to extol it; *Rabotnichesko Delo* wrote on September 14 that the declaration was "an historic achievement, a model of good neighborliness." Zhivkov stated that Greek-Bulgarian "relations serve as an example of what two countries of different social orders can achieve if their foreign policy is based on the desire for peace, trust, and understanding."[3] Speaking at the state dinner in the Boyana Residence in Sofia on September 11--an occasion attended by the entire Bulgarian Politburo--Papandreou adopted a similar tone, saying that relations between Bulgaria and Greece had "surpassed the conventional borders of good neighborliness."[4] On his return to Greece he praised the declaration as "historic" and as a contribution toward the renewal of East-West détente.

International Comment. In other countries, however, comment was less favorable. A number of Western reports misjudged the scope of the declaration, describing it as an alliance or a nonaggression pact, and questioned Bulgaria's good faith in signing such a document with a NATO country. Other reports focused on the vagueness and contradictions in the declaration. Both *Die Welt* and *Stuttgarter Zeitung* stressed that it would make no difference to either Greek membership in NATO or Bulgarian membership in the Warsaw Pact; both newspapers concluded that the clause calling for bilateral consultations in the event of a local emergency would be overridden in an East-West confrontation.[5]

Neue Zürcher Zeitung, *Frankfurter Allgemeine Zeitung*, and *Le Monde* interpreted the declaration as a statement of solidarity between the two countries in their quarrels with Turkey.[6] These same three newspapers saw the declaration as also serving to resist pressure from Macedonian nationalism emanating from Yugoslavia. Both Greece and Bulgaria had been denying that they had Macedonian minorities and had even refused to recognize Macedonian as a language. Both had remained impervious to protests from Belgrade that interstate relations in the Balkans should be founded on respect for the rights of national minorities. Indeed, the Greek-Bulgarian declaration purposely made no mention of minorities but rather affirmed that the signatories would, if necessary, collaborate to prevent the use of their territories for agitation or action that might imperil the integrity of the other state. This clause could, in theory, be invoked for mutual defense against minority claims.[7]

Yugoslav and Turkish Reactions. The Yugoslav and Turkish governments were swift to respond to the Greek-Bulgarian summit. On the eve of Papandreou's arrival in Sofia, TANJUG reported that Stane Dolanc, a member of the Yugoslav Presidium, had said that Greece had pledged that it would grant official recognition to Macedonian as a minority language.[8] Although this was quickly denied by Papandreou, this Yugoslav intervention had the effect of raising the Macedonian issue and causing international embarrassment to both Greece and Bulgaria. After the conclusion of the Greek-Bulgarian summit, Ankara announced that the Turkish President, Kenan Evren, would visit Belgrade within weeks.

One of the strongest critics of the Greek-Bulgarian declaration was *Nova Makedonija*, a daily published in Skopje. On October 10, in an article entitled "An Unserious Declaration," *Nova Makedonija* expressed its support for the arguments of the conservative New Democracy opposition in Greece. It contended that by concluding a bilateral agreement open to interpretation as a hostile move against Turkey and Yugoslavia, the Bulgarian and Greek governments had in reality exacerbated interstate tension in the Balkans and reduced the possibility of the peninsula becoming an "area of peace and cooperation." Far from providing "an example to other states," the newspaper concluded, the two signatories had engaged in an exercise in hypocrisy.

Spokesmen for both the Greek and Bulgarian governments, however, denied that the declaration was aimed against a third party. In Athens, Antonis Kourtis said that it was nothing more than a statement of principles regarding cooperation between the two signatories.[9] Radio Sofia affirmed on September 13 that Bulgaria wanted to restore good relations with Turkey by conducting "an active dialogue on all questions of common concern." The radio quoted Zhivkov as deploring the deterioration in relations between the two states and as saying that "reason and good neighborliness require that holdovers from the past be shed as soon as possible." However, on previous occasions when Sofia had appealed for dialogue with Ankara, it had refused to place the oppression of the Turkish minority in Bulgaria on the agenda on the grounds that it was a purely internal matter.

Assessment of the Declaration. The tenth clause of the declaration contained an avowal that the agreement "is not directed against a third party"; and, indeed, on examination the published text seems so vacuous and contradictory that it is hard not to believe this avowal. Seven of the ten clauses either reiterated support for existing international agreements, such as the UN Charter and the Final Act of the Helsinki Conference, or recapitulated, in extremely general terms, the principles that had already governed bilateral relations for many years: periodic consultations between leaders; nonaggression; economic, scientific, and cultural exchanges; and the reciprocal promotion of tourism. The sixth clause restated the well-known commitment of the two leaders to establishing a nuclear- and chemical weapon-free zone in the Balkans, as a step toward establishing "stability, peace, and détente" in the region. The ninth clause voiced support for the essential elements of Soviet "peace" politics: a halt to the arms race and to nuclear testing, and the abandonment of the Strategic Defense Initiative (SDI).

Perhaps the most crucial part of the whole document was, however, the final part of the 10th and last clause: "The two sides declare that this declaration . . . does not affect the rights and obligations ensuing from valid international treaties and agreements signed by them." This statement proved that the declaration fell far short of being an alliance. It allowed Bulgaria to maintain its obligations to the Warsaw Pact and the CMEA, and Greece its commitment to NATO and the EEC. It made clear that, should there be any clash of interests, the bloc loyalties of the states would override any commitment to "Balkan détente." In fact, so provisional did this last ideal become, that it is hard to disagree with the New Democracy argument that the declaration was a "chimera." It seems therefore difficult to explain why Zhivkov and Papandreou, both usually shrewd and realistic in their approach to diplomacy, should have set so much store by the declaration.

No Nuclear-Free Zone in the Balkans. Part of the explanation lies in the two leaders' failure to make progress with their project for a nuclear- and chemical weapons-free zone (NCWFZ) in the Balkans. The proposal to establish it had been first made in the nineteen-fifties, and had been revived by Zhivkov on October 20, 1981, immediately after the PASOK election victory, undoubtedly in a preliminary attempt to win support from the new, left-of-center Greek government for Soviet-inspired "peace" politics. Observers said that Papandreou had been initially cautious but that, as the project became fraught with difficulties, he began to speak increasingly in its favor. The explanation for this apparent policy change was that the NCWFZ issue had begun to prove a useful counter to left-wing criticism of his failure to withdraw Greece from NATO.[10]

In January 1984, a meeting of Balkan nuclear experts was held in Athens (without the participation of either Albania or Cyprus), but because of Turkish opposition to the project it proved impossible to convene a second meeting. The issue lay dormant, until late 1985 when Bulgaria, Romania, and Greece began to explore the feasibility of establishing a NCWFZ without Turkey, Albania, or Cyprus. The great obstacle to the establishment of a four-country NCWFZ was, however, the reluctance of Yugoslavia to proceed without the participation of Turkey, which reportedly had by far the largest stocks of nuclear weapons of any Balkan country.

Greece and the NCWFZ Project. Greece's determination to go through with the NCWFZ project must be questioned. Since the introduction in January 1985, of a new Greek defense policy that focused on Turkey as the greatest threat to Greek security, the Athens government had shown particular concern that the military imbalance between the two countries should not increase. The inclusion of Greece and the exclusion of Turkey from a Balkan nuclear disarmament treaty was likely to prompt NATO to increase its military investment in Turkey, something viewed in Athens as seriously detrimental to Greek interests. Another consideration was the weak state of the Greek economy, which obliged Athens to turn to its Western allies for more aid.

The introduction in 1985 of a severe austerity program after a first four-year term in which PASOK had allowed the Greek foreign debt to rise to $14,000 million and the current account deficit to $2,800 million, came as a severe shock to the party. In November 1985 a leading radical, Kostas Laliotis, who had been in charge of government propaganda, resigned and George Raftopoulos, a loyal supporter of Papandreou, was unseated as president of the

General Confederation of Greek Workers. A general protest strike by public sector workers, also in November, demonstrated the depth of popular aversion to the austerity program. A further consequence of PASOK's change of course was a loss of the tacit support of the pro-Moscow communist party.

Papandreou's diplomatic moves partly served to appease the Greek Communist Party (KKE) by expressing support for détente in the Balkans. Indeed, Papandreou had often used the "peace" tactic to preserve the unity of PASOK which, as a young party that did not adhere to the European group of socialist parties, remained unsure of its precise political orientation and was hence prone to internal splits.

The Greek appeasement of the Warsaw Pact alarmed the USA and its West European allies, especially since the policy was being pursued with demagogic flourish, featuring the denunciation of such bulwarks of Western stability as NATO and the EEC. To an extent, such rhetoric was little more than calculated electioneering, but this was not always understood, largely because of the contrast in styles between Papandreou and the convinced politicians of the right, such as Reagan and Thatcher.

Bulgarian Motives. The Bulgarian motives for signing the declaration were altogether different from the Greek. To some extent, by promoting Moscow's causes of disarmament and détente in Greece, a Western democracy, Bulgaria was playing its usual role as a Soviet surrogate. It cannot be entirely ruled out that Zhivkov, by then 75, genuinely desired to be seen in Europe as a peacemaker and pragmatic politician. Bulgaria also had good reason for seeking rapprochement with Greece to counter the drastic deterioration of relations with Turkey; significantly, Greece refrained from outright condemnation of the assimilation of the Bulgarian Turkish minority in international forums. Moreover, if Sofia's avowed aim of good neighborliness in the Balkans was to seem a plausible goal (even to the Bulgarian public) then, after so many years of sloganeering, a tangible result had to be offered. If all that proved feasible was a vague and contradictory bilateral declaration, so be it. At least the signing of a document could be cited as proof that there had been a local attempt to revive something of the spirit of East-West détente.

However, the significance of Papandreou's "peace" politics could easily be exaggerated. An accord had been signed (on May 31, 1973)[11] between Sofia and the Greek military junta; in many ways PASOK's "opening to the North" continued the diplomatic initiatives made by previous Greek governments. In 1974-1981, the New Democracy administration led by Konstantin Karamanlis negotiated several joint enterprises with Bulgaria and first committed Greece to the controversial project to construct a Soviet-designed alumina sorting plant in the vicinity of Mount Parnassus in Central Greece. Trade with Bulgaria was consistently higher in real terms under New Democracy than it was since PASOK assumed power.

Problems in the Relationship. There were several reasons for the decline in Greek-Bulgarian trade. Perhaps the most important was that Greece's 1981 entry into the EEC had obliged it to restructure its external trade and increase its purchases of raw material, foodstuffs, and manufactured goods from its community partners. In April 1984, moreover, Greece had suspended all purchases of Bulgarian electricity after rejecting a 10 percent price increase.[12]

Another element was Greece's refusal to tolerate the huge imbalances in bilateral trade that had built up by 1980. In October 1984, during the visit of Deputy Economics Minister Kostas Vaitsos to Sofia, Bulgaria pledged to increase its purchases from Greece to $150,000,000 per annum by 1987. An essential part of the transaction was that Bulgaria signed a 5-year contract worth $40,000,000 for the repair of its commercial vessels at the Elefsis shipyards near Athens.[13] Figures for 1985 show that although Greek exports to Bulgaria did increase, they totaled only $61,600,000, thus falling short of the PASOK government's expectations.[14]

The basic problem was the incompatibility of the two economies. Both countries sought to export and import the same types of goods, exporting foodstuffs, chemicals, raw material, and low-technology manufactures and importing energy, consumer goods, and advanced technology.

Three problematical projects proved to be permanent causes of difficulty. For many years the two countries had been unsuccessfully attempting to finalize an agreement for the joint exploitation of the River Mesta (Nestos in Greek); they were unable to reach a compromise over the amount of water that each side might take.

A second cause of difficulties was the project to build an alumina plant at Agia Efthymia near Mount Parnassus with Soviet technical aid. In March 1984, it had been agreed that the plant would begin production in 1988 or 1989, and that Bulgaria would purchase a third of its output (200,000 tons of alumina per annum). In December

1985, Bulgaria asked to pay entirely in goods. When the Greek government refused to accept this modification of the original agreement, Sofia threatened to withdraw entirely from the project. In June 1986, Vassa Papandreou, a Deputy Industry Minister, stated that it was considered unlikely in Athens that Bulgaria would go through with the transaction as it had suspended the construction of its planned aluminum plant. She said that the Greek government had asked the USSR to absorb Bulgaria's share.[15]

There were also disagreements between Bulgaria and Greece over the improvement of road links between the two countries and over Bulgarian access to the ports of the North Aegean. In 1984, the Greek government refused to agree to the construction of a new road from Bulgaria to the port of Alexandropoulos and objected to the opening of a border crossing point to the south of Svilengrad on the River Maritsa (Evros).[16] Both refusals were justified on the grounds of national security.

The PASOK government paid surprising attention to security questions and, despite rhetoric, did not allow its "opening to the north" to dammage its commitment to NATO. Indeed, after 1985 the Papandreou government undertook a major improvement and modernization of the Greek armed forces primarily as part of its new defense doctrine against Turkey. It contracted to buy 40 French Mirage 2000 fighter aircraft and 40 American F-16s; it also announced that it would build 4 frigates and 5 landing craft and renovate 5 destroyers. It is revealing that these plans were strongly opposed by the KKE on the grounds that they would further consolidate Greece's membership in NATO and would limit the amount of money that could be spent on welfare programs and education.[17]

In any case, the relations between Greece and Bulgaria remained more complicated than Zhivkov and Papandreou liked to pretend. Problems in coordinating policies and clashes of interest were inevitable between members of different economic orders and different defense alliances. Greek-Bulgarian relations were no exception to this rule, and in many ways the two countries did not really move closer at all in 1985-1986.

51
GENOCIDE IN KOSOVO?

Milan Andrejevich

On November 3, 1986, nearly 200 Serbs and Montenegrins from the Kosovo district of Priština, primarily from the village of Plementine, appeared before four high-ranking officials at the Federal Assembly in Belgrade to protest against the worsening situation in Kosovo. The villagers told the officials that "we will fight for justice even if it means bloodshed."

This was the third time in 1986 that Serbs and Montenegrins from Kosovo had gone to Belgrade to vent their frustrations. On February 26 about 100 farmers told officials in Belgrade: "Either we live united in Kosovo, or we will move out." On April 7 nearly 500 farmers and young people from Plementine expressed their concern over the "lack of freedom and equal rights" in Kosovo. They also declared that if the situation were "not corrected," they too, would be forced to leave.

On June 20 police in Kosovo forcibly halted a massive migration effort by Serbs and Montenegrins in the town of Kosovo Polje. The growing exodus of the non-Albanian minority forced officials in Belgrade to take a more serious view of the situation in Kosovo. At numerous party meetings, it was said that Kosovo's status had to be reassessed and practical steps taken to avert any further worsening of the situation.

Kosovo was one of two autonomous provinces within the Socialist Republic of Serbia, covering an area of 10,877 square kilometers in the southeastern part of Serbia. According to the 1981 census, the 1,226,736 Albanians made up an overwhelming majority of the population; in addition, there were 209,498 Serbs, 34,125 Gypsies, 27,028 Montenegrins, and 12,513 Turks. In Yugoslavia as a whole there were about 1,730,000 Albanians.[1] Kosovo was the least developed province in Yugoslavia and had the highest unemployment rate (54.5 percent compared with the national average of 16.7 percent)[2] and birth rate (in 1951-81 there were 37.5 live births per 1,000--2.5 times greater than the national average[3] and since 1981 around 27 per 1,000, two or three times more than the national average, and reportedly the highest in Europe). Average personal income was among the lowest in the country for the first nine months of 1986 (54,493 dinars--about $132 per month).[4] All government and public affairs were conducted in Albanian and Serbo-Croatian, and in those districts where there was a Turkish minority, in Turkish as well. Kosovo had been the center of tension between Yugoslavia and Albania for years. During the nineteen-eighties, demonstrations, riots, "antistate activities," the destruction of personal property, and the desecration of Orthodox churches and gravestones became commonplace.

The Issues Involved. The Kosovo issue had been threatening to erupt for some time and occasionally incidents occurred that sent tremors throughout the entire country. After the rape of an 11-year-old Serbian girl by a 17-year-old Albanian boy at a wedding reception on October 19 in Plementine, the villagers went to Belgrade to protest against their local officials, who did not formally charge the boy with the rape. An attempt to meet with party officials in Priština had been rejected by the authorities as well. One week after the November meeting in Belgrade, the boy was sentenced by a Priština court to 10 years in prison, the maximum penalty for sexual assault in Yugoslavia.

The broad national coverage of the case focused attention once again on the discontent of Kosovo's minorities.[5] A delegate from Plementine summed up the feelings of the minorities in Kosovo when he told the Federal Assembly, "[we] have come [to Belgrade] to win our freedom, because as it now stands we can't take it any longer." Blame for the deterioration of the situation was placed solely on the federal, republican, and provincial leadership.

The Migration of Minorities. Another issue discussed in the assembly was the growing exodus of Kosovo's minorities. According to a report by the Provincial Commission for the Prevention of Emigration, 20,416 Serbs and Montenegrins emigrated from Kosovo between 1982 and the end of June 1986. During the same period 2,714 returned to the province.[6] Official figures show, however, that 22,307 Serbs and Montenegrans left Kososvo between 1981-86;[7] since 1971 some 68,505 Serbs and Montenegrans emigrated and from 1971-1981 2,037 Gypsies (Romanies), 1,640 Croats and 1,263 Moslems (mostly ethnic Turks) left Kosovo.[8] From 1981 through September 1986, 9,587 Serbs and Montenegrins emigrated from Priština alone to somewhere outside of Kosovo and only 299 returned.[9] Between 1945 and 1961 an insignificant number of Serbs and Montenegrans emigrated from the province.[10]

The pressure applied by the Albanian majority on the minorities was cited as the main reason for emigration as well as the lack of governmental measures to resolve differences within the province and guarantee the safety of all minorities. Momčilo Trajković, Executive Secretary of the Priština Presidium, said that the only way of halting future migration was by establishing "conditions for the return of those have have left."[11] On November 11, the Municipal Assembly of Priština went some way to taking such measures by guaranteeing 400 new jobs for those Serbs and Montenegrins who had moved out of Priština and wished to return.[12]

The Plementine delegation to Belgrade no longer viewed emigration as a solution to their problems. There were indications that Kosovo's minorities were prepared to resort to other means. The Belgrade weekly *NIN* pointed out that most of the 30 speakers had declared at some point in their presentations that "if Yugoslavia cannot defend us, then we will defend ourselves."[13] The last delegate to speak, Zagorka Mitrović, said:

> Let us say that you [the Yugoslav government] cannot guarantee our safety and civil rights. If you do not help us then you will be to blame for our actions, and don't be too surprised if you hear that we have resorted to killing one another. . . . I am sorry that our Albanian comrades are not present; in fact, I am surprised to find that no member of the Kosovo leadership is here in order that it can be said "let us come to a solution". . . . Raping is not sexually motivated but is an act of nationalistic hatred. Brotherhood and unity cannot be built in this way.

Mounting Tension. In March 1986 a group of 212 Serbian intellectuals, including members of the Serbian Academy of Arts and Sciences and retired army generals, used the term "genocide" in a petition submitted to the Yugoslav and Serbian National Assemblies. They demanded immediate measures to end "the lengthy process of genocide" allegedly practiced by the Albanians against their neighbors.[14]

Dušan Dragosavač, a Serbian communist leader from Croatia and member of the Yugoslav party's Central Committee, stated at the 7th CC plenum in late April that Yugoslavia had to rid itself of "the elements of genocide"; and a Belgrade weekly posthumously published an interview conducted six years previously with Kadri Reufi--a leader of the ethnic Turks until he had been purged about fifteen years before, but since rehabilitated--in which he claimed to have been "a victim of genocide" at the hands of the Albanians.[15]

The United Nations Convention on the Prevention and Punishment of the Crime of Genocide defines genocide as

> any of the following acts committed with intent to destroy, in whole or in part, a national, ethnic, racial, or religious group, such as (a) killing members of the group; (b) causing serious bodily or mental harm to members of the group; (c) deliberately inflicting on the group conditions of life calculated to bring about its physical destruction in whole or in part; (d) imposing measures intended to prevent births within the group; (e) forcibly transferring children of the group to another group.[16]

The charge of "genocide" was a dangerous addition to an already potent and volatile brew. As the core of the medieval Serbian state and the site of its ultimate conquest by the Ottomans, Kosovo was of immense emotional importance to patriotic Serbs and to Montenegrins. The Albanians' claim was based on the principle of majority rule. Although most of their spokesmen denied that they sought anything more than the status of a republic within the Yugoslav federation, the Serbs and Montenegrins suspected that such an arrangement would be but the first step toward detaching the province from Yugoslavia and joining it to Albania. The problem was compounded by poverty, unemployment, and high birth rate. Matters came to a head with massive Albanian demonstrations and riots in the spring of 1981, and Kosovo was rarely far from the Yugoslav political limelight thereafter.

Dragosavać Discusses Genocide. Dragosavać said that the party would have to clarify whether the charge of genocide was justified, if necessary "through an urgently convened extraordinary Congress of the LCY [with] free elections and multicandidate lists." Should the charge be proved, the party should "let those people come to the top who are capable of dealing with the genocide." He did not, however, cite the definition given by the United Nations Convention on Genocide but only noted that Belgrade had signed the 1948 pact and that it had to be enforced.[17]

While ethnically-motivated murder seemed hardly commonplace, there was a strong feeling among the Serbs and

Montenegrins both inside and outside the province that various forms of "bodily or mental harm" occurred regularly in a general campaign by "Albanian chauvinists" to create "an ethnically pure Kosovo" by intimidating the Slavs and other non-Albanians. According to the party weekly *Komunist*, nearly 650 of the 1450 settlements in Kosovo were ethnically pure, usually Albanian. In 1981 this figure was 606 out of a total of 445.[18]

A Problem for the Whole of Yugoslavia. There appeared to be a consensus among Serbian party members that Kosovo had to be treated not just as a Serbian problem, but as one affecting the entire country. Serbian CC Presidium President Slobodan Milošević told a large gathering in Kosovo Polje that the Serbian authorities were committed to changing and improving the situation. He argued that the citizens of Kosovo "must work together with progressively minded people throughout Yugoslavia," pledging that matters "will be changed" through the efforts of all Yugoslavs.[17]

New measures were required precisely from the central authorities, not from the provincial or republican ones. The Serbs were likely to find ample sympathy from the Montenegrin and Macedonian Slavs, who felt they had an "Albanian problem" of their own; but the Croats, Slovenes, and (Slavic) Moslems (mainly of Bosnia-Herzegovina) would think at least twice before lending support to what could appear to be an attempt to restore Serbian minority rule, even if only in one remote part of the country. (The Albanians denounced any hint of a return to minority rule in Kosovo as "Yugoslav apartheid.") Some sort of compromise between the Serbs and Albanians was the ideal solution; but emotions were running high in and over Kosovo, and even the wisest and most far-sighted statesmen were certain to find this an extremely difficult problem to solve.

The Party Plenum on Kosovo. On the eve of the League of Communists of Yugoslavia ninth plenum (June 26 and 27), which was called to deal exclusively with the situation in Kosovo, two leading Serbian intellectuals, Dobrica Cosić and Vladimir Dedijer, openly placed most of the blame for the critical state of affairs there on Serbia's communist leaders. In addition, the state-run media and various political circles throughout the country paid more attention to Kosovo in the weeks leading up to the plenum, adding to an atmosphere of tension. In an unprecedented move, moreover, leaders outside the Socialist Republic of Serbia officially acknowledged that the problem of Kosovo was of crucial importance to the entire federation rather than to Serbia alone, as had previously been maintained. There appeared to be agreement that the problem could not be allowed to go on indefinitely.

Cosić reprimanded Serbia's top communist leaders for having neglected the situation in Kosovo for the last 30 years. He argued that they did not defend the constitutional rights of all nationalities in the province to personal safety and security, thus leaving the non-Albanians to live in fear.

In his speech, which was entitled "Are We To Blame?" Cosić identified the Kosovo question as the most critical problem to confront Serbia since 1941, when Yugoslavia was thrust into the Second World War. He said that finding a solution to the Kosovo problem would be "a crucial test for the Serbian people . . . that will show Europe and the world [Serbia's] historical maturity, level of civilization, democratic potential, and political vision." Cosić warned, however, that urgent solutions were necessary because "time is running out, time may [even] have expired." He added, "our greatest enemy lies among us [Serbs]" and went on to say, "Kosovo is not our final test, but rather Kosovo is the final warning."

For Cosić, the most difficult question was how to solve the Kosovo problem peacefully, given that "the Albanian side only employs powerful antidemocratic and barbaric methods." Cosić also asked why the Yugoslav government seemed more concerned about freedom and human rights in Arab and African countries than about the rights and freedom of Yugoslavs, namely, the non-Albanians of Kosovo. He warned, however, that "we must be very careful not to infringe upon the democratic freedom and citizens' rights of the Albanian people or of any other nationality with whom we live."

While Cosić did not single out any specific leader, Vladimir Dedijer openly attacked one of Serbia's foremost leaders, Petar Stambolić (Yugoslav state president from 1982 to 1983, prime minister from 1963 to 1967 and head of the Serbian CC from 1948 to 1957), for taking part "in the horrible liquidation of Serbian 'princes' [communist leaders] in 1972," when Tito purged the Serbian leadership, including several officials who were known defenders of Serbian interests in Kosovo. A member of the Serbian National Assembly, Stambolić was also described as one who "decides [everything down to] even the most trivial issues," implying that he had been involved in the Kosovo problem as well. Dedijer asked whether Stambolić was "bored" and remarked that "you should finally remove your dead hand from the throats of the younger comrades in Serbia."

The plenum's opening speech was delivered by Marko Orlandić, a Montenegrin member of the CC Presidium. He said that the situation in Kosovo had been worsening since the Albanian nationalist riots in the spring of 1981 and as a result posed a "serious threat to the stability of Yugoslavia." He stressed the need for eliminating the "pronounced differences between the leadership of the Republic of Serbia and the leadership of Kosovo."

Orlandić attacked the "illegal activities of counterrevolutionary forces" in the region, a phrase generally used to denote Albanian nationalists. Such activities had been critical in bringing about the general deterioration in Kosovo, he said. "Instead of [simply] staging public demonstrations," Orlandić added, these forces had resorted to various forms of illegal action throughout the country and even within the Yugoslav People's Army.

Orlandić blamed the increase in "illegal counter-revolutionary activities" on interference by Albania in Yugoslav affairs. By responding to Albanian party and state leader Ramiz Alia's statement on the alleged mistreatment of Yugoslavia's ethnic Albanians, Orlandić underscored that the LCY "will resolutely prevent Albania or anyone else from interfering in Yugoslavia's internal affairs . . . under the pretext of concern over the allegedly endangered position of the Albanian nationality in Yugoslavia."

In view of the escalation of Albanian nationalism and the depressed state of Kosovo's economy, Orlandić said that the LCY would ask the Kosovo Provincial Committee (Central Committee) to determine the political accountability of the officials in Kosovo responsible for the policies that had led to the riots of April 1981 and the state of affairs thereafter. This statement came in response to allegations that the former head of the Kosovo party and former member of the Yugoslav State Presidency, Fadil Hoxha, had been personally responsible for directing Kosovo's political and social policies in the nineteen-seventies and early nineteen-eighties. These policies were regarded as having laid the foundations for subsequent nationalist activities. Hoxha had also been accused of harboring former Albanian Fascists. In spite of the stand made by Sinan Hasani (the former head of the State Presidency) against any special investigation of Kosovo's officials, past and present, the plenum decided to set up a special commission to investigate the allegations against Hoxha.

The plenum approved twenty-two proposals for tackling the imbroglio in Kosovo. The document suggested a general willingness among CC members to view the Kosovo "drama" as a matter of "grave concern" for the Yugoslav federation as a whole and not as a problem solely for the Republic of Serbia. It was the first time that the importance of being politically united on the issue had been stressed in this way.

The. very fact that a consensus was reached at the plenum clearly dealt a severe blow to "Albanian separatists," who in the past had exploited the divisions among the Slavic nations in the federation.   It was concluded that "the counterrevolutionary activities in Kosovo" and the deterioration of relations between the various nationalities in Yugoslavia amounted to "the gravest and deepest political problem of both Kosovo and the whole of Yugoslavia."

The plenum also made clear that for some time the Kosovo issue had been manipulated by several interest groups, that is, the government and party on the local, republican, and central levels as well as Albanian or Serbian groups. They competed against one another and, at times, within their own ranks, making any decision on how to tackle the problem all the more difficult.   This difficulty illustrated a deeper truth; the Kosovo problem might well be simply insoluble, and the less than bold course adopted by Yugoslavia's top party organization might prove what the internationally recognized Dobrica Cosić had suggested: "Time may have already expired."

DISSENSION AMONG DISSIDENTS

52
YUGOSLAVIA'S DIVIDED OPPOSITION

Slobodan Stanković

Five Types of Dissent.   Being   a   multinational country   with   a   more   or   less   "liberal"   communist system,   Yugoslavia   witnessed   at   least   five   types of   dissent: 1) dissent   resulting   from   nationality quarrels;   2) dissent   in   response   to   the   economic crisis;   3) dissent   brought   on   by   political issues; 4) dissent over religious issues; and 5) dissent within the state apparatus, that is, the struggle   between federal and regional authorities.

All   five   were   interconnected   and   influenced   one another. The conflict between the Serbs and the Croats, for instance,   had   ethnic, economic,   and   religious   aspects, which influenced both   ideological   issues and the conflict between   the   federal and regional   authorities.   Strikes, too, had not only an economic but also an ideological basis insofar   as   they also expressed   workers'   dissatisfaction with the central government.

Regardless of how displeased the regime was with these various   types of dissent,   their disunity   actually   helped the   communist   party   survive,   despite   its   tremendous failures and inability to govern.

Four   Yugoslav republics--Serbia,   Croatia,   Slovenia, and Bosnia-Herzegovina--accounted for the largest number of dissidents.   Macedonians   and   Montenegrins were   no   less dissatisfied, but their   political   energies   were directed mainly   against "Greater Bulgarian" and "Greater Albanian" aspirations,   the   former in Macedonia and   the   latter   in Montenegro.

All five types of dissent manifested themselves   daily in Serbia,   which   was   divided   into   three   parts: Serbia proper,   and   the   Autonomous   Provinces   of   Kosovo   and Vojvodina.   A memorandum   drafted by the Serbian Academy of

Arts and Sciences in September 1986 exacerbated strife in Serbia by claiming that both the Serbian Communists and non-Communists had violently opposed the "Albanian counterrevolutionaries" in Kosovo, while fighting among themselves over other ideological, economic and religious issues.

In Croatia, dissent took the form of what the regime called "greater Croatian chauvinism," and it was mostly young people who were sent to jail for "antistate activities" that were usually linked to Roman Catholic "militancy." Cardinal Franjo Kuharič, the Primate of the Catholic Church in Yugoslavia, was attacked by the Yugoslav media for his "stubborn defense" of one of his predecessors, Cardinal Alojzije Stepinac, who had been denounced as a "war criminal" after World War II and had died in internal exile in 1960.

In Bosnia-Herzegovina, "Moslem fundamentalists" had been sentenced to lengthy prison terms for alleged "antistate activities" linked with various Arab countries and Iran. A group of young Serbian, Croatian, and Moslem students in Sarajevo was said to have organized a "meeting of mayonnaise fascists,"[1] at which they allegedly carried Nazi regalia while demanding "democratic freedom." The authorities later admitted that "the fascist birthday party" in Sarajevo had had no fascist leanings, but was "ideologically disoriented."[2]

The most liberal groups in Yugoslavia, even among the Communists, were to be found in Slovenia, the country's westernmost republic, bordering on Austria and Italy, which had been part of Austria for more than 800 years. The Slovenian party leaders had, moreover, more or less tolerated dissent. Slovenian youth organizations, for example, had refused to take part in the formal annual celebration of Tito's birthday (May 25), had demanded that military service be done in civilian dress, and had called for a new system they called "the civic socialist society" as a pluralistic alternative to communism.[3] They even proposed an "Alternative Movement" as competition to the communist party and stronger ties between Slovenia and Western Europe.

Slovenia Leads Dissidence. In January 1986, a young Slovene sociologist, the 32-year-old Tomas Mastnak publicly expressed his doubts about Branko Mikulič's suitability as Prime Minister, a post for which he had already been nominated and to which he was subsequently "elected" in May. Mastnak wrote an article expressing these doubts for the outspoken weekly of the Slovenian communist youth organization, *Mladina*; but the weekly's editorial board withdrew the item at the very last moment under pressure from party officials. In protest at this censorship, the editorial board left several columns of its publication blank.

If the editorial board of *Mladina* shied away from publishing Mastnak's article, Radio Student had no such qualms and broadcast the piece under the title "Another Step Toward Democratization." In a key paragraph Mastnak had commented that "Mikulić's contribution to repression, which is seen in the repression of intellectuals, should be given particular emphasis."[4] Mastnak then refered to various trials that had taken place in Bosnia-Herzegovina.

This list of incidents in which Mikulić was said to have been involved prompted the Ljubljana public prosecutor to act. He submitted a proposal to indict Mastnak under Article 112 of Slovenia's Penal Code, which provided for a sentence of three years imprisonment to be given to anyone "offending another constituent republic," in this case, the Socialist Republic of Bosnia-Herzgovina, whose representative in the State Presidency Mikulić was until May 15, 1986.

On July 10, however, after very strong protest throughout Slovenia and elsewhere in Yugoslavia, the Ljubljana State Prosecutor, Franc Mazi, dropped the charges against Mastnak, giving the following explanation:

> Despite all elements of a criminal act, I cannot but employ the term "insignificant social danger," as required under Section 2 of Article 8 of Yugoslavia's Criminal Code, and have therefore dropped all charges.[5]

Mazi's statement was greeted with tremendous applause in the courtroom, where Mastnak had been defending his position for an hour.

Slovenes differed from the rest of their compatriots in two major ways: they had a much higher living standard and were more Westernized. By travelling frequently to neighboring Austria and Italy (very seldom to Hungary), the Slovenes maintained their traditional Western orientation to such an extent that not only was the communist propoganda emanating from the eastern parts of Yugoslavia regarded as an anomaly, it was also firmly rejected.

An example was the controversy over how to mark the Day of Youth, celebrated every year on May 25, Tito's birthday. From 1945 on, it had culminated in a Soviet-type spectacle in the People's Army Stadium in Belgrade, during which Tito was extolled, and young people presented a torch that had been carried throughout Yugoslavia. After Tito's death in May 1980, some of his successors took part in the ceremony; but they lacked his stature, and the event became an empty ritual. It was Slovene youth leaders who were the first to suggest that "this unworthy spectacle" be stopped.

On December 11, 1986, Ljubljana University students set up a stand and solicited signatures to four petitions. One appealed for the abolition of the "antique rituals" surrounding Tito's birthday; another demanded the abolition of Article 133 of the Penal Code in order to give so-called political criminals special status, better treatment, and facilities separate from common criminals; a third demanded that young people be allowed to perform social work as an alternative to military service; and the fourth asked that the further construction of nuclear plants be put to a referendum.

Almost anywhere else in Yugoslavia such an open expression of dissent would have brought sharp and swift repression. Not in Slovenia. Moreover, when on November 23 a special referendum was organized in Ljubljana asking people whether they would be willing to pay a special tax that would be devoted to solving ecological problems, the majority of voters rejected it.   Of the 171,115 voters (72 percent of the potential electorate), 96,103 (or 56.16 percent) voted against;   70,738 (or 41.33 percent) voted in favor; and 4,274 (or 2.51 percent) votes were invalid.[6] The Ecological Group in the Ljubljana youth organization distributed leaflets criticizing the referendum in which they said: "Those who pollute nature should pay; if not, they will continue to pollute it." A leader of the Socialist Alliance in Ljubljana, Tone Florijančič, said that people were opposed to the new tax, because the old taxes were being   used   improperly."   Another Socialist Alliance   member, Vlado Plamberger, implied that   the referendum had nevertheless been successful as an exercise in democracy, since more than half of the electorate had voted.[7]

The Serbian Academy's Memorandum.   In September 1986, the Serbian Academy of Arts and Sciences drafted   a controversial memorandum consisting of two parts: the first dealt with the economic and political crisis in Yugoslavia in general; the second discussed the "serious situation" of the Serbian people in Yugoslavia.   Non-Serbian leaders, such as the Croats Tito and Bakarić and the Slovene Kardelj, were criticized; and it was argued that the

Serbian nation must be given complete equality in Yugoslavia, which, it said, it now lacked. The 74-page draft provoked a strong reaction from the Yugoslav party and was finally banned, but continued circulating throughout the country and abroad.

The Serbs generally believed that Yugoslavia existed primarily as a result of the Serbian blood shed in both world wars. They also felt entitled to primacy as they were the most numerous people in the Yugoslav federation and possessed a long tradition of independent statehood. They particularly resented what they regarded as the unfairly powerful position of Croatia, Slovenia, and Kosovo's Albanians.

The Communists had promised to solve the national question on the basis of equality, and they instituted a de facto federal arrangement during World War II. Although their prewar policies had often been critical of Serbian "hegemony" in Yugoslavia, the Communists had needed the Serbs, who predominated in the ranks of the partisans. They maintained much of their power until July 1966, when Aleksandar Ranković, the Serbian party leader who was slated to become Tito's successor, was purged, and he and his followers, mostly Serbs, were again accused of "Greater-Serbian nationalism and hegemony." This was also the beginning of the strengthening of the Kosovo Albanians, who until 1966 were said to have been "oppressed by Ranković and his Greater-Serbian followers."

The Serbian Communists began defending the interests of their nationality more actively only after Tito's death and after the Albanians in Kosovo had started their "counterrevolution" in March 1981. They were particularly incensed by the "White Book" distributed in Zagreb by Croatian Communists, in which the Serbian communist leaders were accused of "anarcholiberalism" and even anti-Titoism.

The original title of the draft memorandum was "The Crisis of the Yugoslav Economy and Society." In a short introduction the authors of the memorandum said that "a serious crisis has affected not only the country's political and economic system but also the whole of public life." They said that "the current crisis might end in social upheavals with unforeseeable consequences, even including the disruption of the Yugoslav state."

The authors of the memorandum cited many examples to show how "incapable" Yugoslavia's political and economic leaders had been not only since Tito's death but even during his lifetime. Foreign credits had been taken irresponsibly, especially from Western countries, and had then either been used for general consumption or had been badly invested.

The government, the memorandum went on, had ordered a general tightening of belts, which had inevitably caused public dissatisfaction and had forced the country's leaders to admit that the crisis was not only an economic one but had also become a political one. They had been forced "to make their admission about the crisis by stages, even denying it; and in this way they have lost precious time." Instead of making a determined effort to resolve the problems, the leadership had used "political propaganda" to create the impression that "serious attempts have been made to find a way out." As a result, the regional authorities in the republics and the autonomous provinces had been strengthened, while the central government had become weaker. The slogan, "We must separate in order to unite" had won the day, together "with a persistent campaign against exaggerated and overvalued unitarism," a phrase that usually had the connotation of control by a Serbian-dominated center.

In the opinion of the authors of the memorandum, it was Yugoslavia's constitution, adopted in February 1974, that had turned the country's federal system into a "loose confederation." The idea that everything must be agreed upon "through consensus" among the individual republics and provinces had resulted in a situation in which one constituent republic or province could veto a decision agreed on by all the others. The constitutional provision whereby "all federal laws must in principle be implemented by the republics and provinces frequently leads to the nonimplementation of any law." Moreover, "The current political system in Yugoslavia has to a great extent become contradictory, unfunctional, and very expensive."

The most sensitive part of the memorandum dealt with Serbian grievances against the Yugoslav communist party, against Stalin and the Comintern, and against non-Serbian party leaders, such as Tito and Vladimir Bakarić (both Croats) and Kardelj (a Slovene). The authors of the memorandum believed that "thanks to the political position of their leaders," Croatia and Slovenia had become obstacles to Yugoslavia's unity:

> The prevailing ideologies in these two republics have obliged their leaders not to defend the interests of the country as a whole, and not even the economic interests of their own two republics, if it means curtailing their political autonomy.

According to the memorandum, "the only way out of this deep crisis is [through] democratization." Yugoslavia, it was said, did "not need a proclaimed democracy that does not change anything but rather a democratization of consciousness and social relationships." Different opinions were to be respected "without pronouncing them as factionalism"; and, "as a token of civilization, all repression must cease." The memorandum said that Tito's policies should be judged in the same critical way "as had been attempted in the Soviet Union and China after Stalin's and Mao's deaths," respectively. The memorandum also demanded a new constitution, "which, like the constitutions of all other countries, must be short and [must] clearly reflect the basic principles of our social order," something that was not true of the existing constitution.

Turning to the "serious situation" of the Serbs in Yugoslavia, the memorandum complained that "the Serbian nation, for instance, has not been given the right to create its own state." Large numbers of Serbs lived in other republics; unlike the various national minorities in Yugoslavia, they had no right to use their own language and alphabet. The Albanians in Kosovo were criticized for having "discriminated against the Serbs, Montenegrins, Turks, and Gypsies" in the province. Respect for human rights in Yugoslavia was demanded, together with a final halt to "the genocide in Kosovo."[8] According to the memorandum, "the economic subjugation of Serbia can be understood only if one understands its political inferiority." The "anti-Serbian coalition" in Yugoslavia had to stop regarding the Serbs "as hegemonists, centralizers, and policemen."

At an extraordinary general meeting in Belgrade on December 18,1986, a great majority of the academy members gave full support to its leaders and denied that it had incited "Greater-Serbian nationalism." Of the 115 full members taking part in the December 18 meeting, 101 voted to express full confidence in Dušan Kanazir, the president of the academy, while 8 voted against him and 6 votes were declared invalid. His deputy, Antonije Isaković, who had led the group that prepared the memorandum, received 88 votes of support, with 18 against him and 9 invalid votes.[9]

53
SOVIET DISSIDENTS ON *GLASNOST*

Nancy A. Beatty

In a taped US television interview broadcast from Moscow on June 14, 1987,[1] Academician Andrei Sakharov reiterated his petition to Gorbachev for a full and unconditional amnesty for all political prisoners and prisoners of conscience in the Soviet Union. While Sakharov acknowledged that Gorbachev's moves toward a more open society in the Soviet Union were welcome, he added that "what has been done so far is just the beginning and has scarcely affected the monolith of Soviet society."

Sakharov returned to Moscow from his exile in Gorkii in December 1986. This release aroused great hopes of renewed activism in the dissident community. In interviews with Western correspondents after his return to Moscow, however, Sakharov spoke in favor of Gorbachev's policies, including economic reform, "liberalization" in the cultural sphere, and arms negotiations with the United States. He said the Soviet leader deserved the support of the Soviet people as well as world attention for the important policies he was trying to implement. Sakharov also took part in the official International Peace Forum held in Moscow in February, 1987.

Sakharov's statements disappointed many of his former associates who suspected him of having a "soft spot" for Gorbachev and his policies. Human rights activists Malva Landa and Valeriia Novodvorskaia,[2] for example, charged that there had been a transformation in Sakharov after Gorbachev announced the decision to allow him to return to Moscow. In fact, neither Sakharov nor his wife, Elena Bonner, made any definitive pronouncements on Gorbachev's policies. They continued to call for the release of all political prisoners, especially since it seemed that this process had all but stopped. Criticized for having allegedly compromised his principles and accused of having made a deal with Gorbachev, Sakharov replied that he was merely doing what he always had done: saying what he thought.[3]

The skepticism about *glasnost* and *perestroika* grew stronger in the statements of émigrés who had been prominent members of the human rights and democratic movements while in the Soviet Union. At a forum called "Commission of Inquiry" held in Washington on January 23,

1987,[4] Iurii Orlov, who emigrated to the United States in October 1986, and Natan Shcharanskii, who emigrated to Israel in February, 1986, expressed frustration with the misguided eagerness of many in the West to see liberalization where there was merely "cosmetic change."

Orlov said that change was impossible, and emphasized that the steps taken by Gorbachev thus far did not reveal a dedication to establishing greater democracy: "The attitude toward dissidents has not changed in essence."[5]

In an interview in May 1987,[6] Shcharanskii said that Gorbachev was concerned primarily with economic issues, not human rights. Citing the West's insistence on improvements in the area of human rights as a prerequisite to granting access to technology and trade credits, Shcharanskii said he considered the release of political prisoners in early 1987 to be a demonstration aimed at the West rather than the first stage of true liberalization in the Soviet Union.

The point that the selective pardons granted to political prisoners by Gorbachev were designed to influence the West was also made by psychiatrist Anatolii Koriagin in a speaking engagement at Munich University on June 2, 1987.[7] After serving six years in prison for having condemned the abuse of psychiatry in the Soviet Union, Koriagin was released from prison in February and left the country in April, 1987. The abuses continued, Koriagin said, urging that announcements of *glasnost* not be accepted as proof of change. He warned Westerners not to be confused by illusions of democratization and liberalization. In an appeal to the heads of Western governments written after his release from prison, Koriagin stated that despite articles describing democratization, almost nothing had changed in the lives of ordinary Soviet citizens.

Describing the lack of sincerity behind the alleged changes, Koriagin noted that *glasnost* had no legal basis, *i.e.*, there existed no legislation to support or protect those who might seek to take advantage of the new policy. Furthermore, said Koriagin, Articles 70 and 190-1 of the Criminal Code of the RSFSR, which outlawed (but did not define) anti-Soviet agitation and propaganda, were still on the books and freely applied.[8]

A negative assessment of Gorbachev's release of political prisoners was given in a samizdat statement made by Georgian Helsinki Group member and leader of the unofficial rock group "Fantom," Eduard Gudava.[9] In a lengthy statement entitled "On Differences Between the Current Release of Political Prisoners and Genuine

Political Amnesty," dated February 11, 1987,[10] Gudava noted that prior to release, the majority of dissidents had been forced to sign an appeal for pardon.

In an open letter addressed to Gorbachev, Aleksei Miasnikov, sociologist and former political prisoner who had been released in February 1987, noted that official calls for "openness" and other changes were the same as those made by dissidents in the nineteen-seventies. In a hopeful spirit, Miasnikov pointed out that many newly freed dissidents would like to participate in the restructuring in the USSR. Despite the fact that these dissidents, as Miasnikov put it, "suffered for *perestroika*," they were, for the most part, not allowed to participate in it:

> People came out of exile, prisons and labor camps with hope, ready for public activity. The majority of them can make a useful contribution to *perestroika*. But unlike the mass of time-servers, climbing around posts and feeding troughs, we, as before, are ready to work not from fear, but from conscience.[11]

Miasnikov concluded that the policy of *glasnost* was sanctioned from above with very little genuine initiative from below. He also pointed out that dissidents not as well-known as Sakharov, for example, were treated as criminals by local officials and bureaucrats.

While the dissidents' views on *glasnost* and *perestroika* differed in particulars, there seemed to be a general consensus that, despite certain positive developments, Gorbachev's policies had fallen far short of the goals advanced by the human rights movement.

54
CZECHOSLOVAK OPPOSITION PONDERS REFORM

Vladimir V. Kusin

Charter 77 Debates Its Philosophy. Václav Havel, the playwright, posed a question that people in Czechoslovakia and elsewhere had been asking about Charter 77:

If the Charter is right-wing, why is it not fully
right-wing and openly so, taking all the
consequences? If the Charter is left-wing, why is it
not fully left-wing and openly so, taking all the
consequences?

In his view, Charter 77 was neither left- nor
right-wing, nor for that matter was it middle-of-the-road.
The Charter was "above all this," or, more modestly, "apart
from it all." According to Havel, Charter 77 was solely
concerned with seeking the truth.

Havel's remarks were made in a debate about Charter 77
conducted by four dissidents in Prague under the moderation
of their fellow dissident Petr Uhl. They were, in addition
to Havel, Ladislav Hejdánek (a philosopher with Protestant
leanings), Václav Benda (a philosopher and mathematician
with Catholic leanings), and Jiří Hájek (the Czechoslovak
Foreign Minister of the Dubček period).

All the discussants agreed that the individual
signatories of Charter 77 were fully entitled to hold their
own political views, right-wing or left. Benda spoke of
the art required for Charter to survive, to keep being
innovative, and to remain relevant. This would depend to a
large extent on "a kind of art of compromise," that is, a
coexistence of what the signatories were determined to
respect severally and collectively, on the one hand, and
the practical steps that individuals or groups within the
Charter could take beyond a set framework, on the other.

Hájek defended the Charter's exchanges with West
European peace groups. He defined the Western peace
movement as "a reflection of the attempt to defend man
against being manipulated by military-political machines."
According to him, the peace movement "is becoming yet
another driving force in the collective conscience of the
continent's nations."

Havel went some way toward supporting Hájek's
position. Referring to foreign critics of the Charter who
thought it was veering too far to the left, he said:

If someone thinks that the devil of communism must be
swept away, and that it can only be done under
Reagan's leadership, and that by the same token every
sign of disobedience toward this leadership means
support for the devil, then this opinion is his own,
and it is not incumbent on me today to explain to him
that he sees no further than the end of his
democratic nose.

Benda mildly objected by saying that Havel should have simply recognized the right of every person to hold his own views about President Reagan, but should not have castigated such views as shortsighted.

A Dissident's Thoughts on Reform.

In the Europe of today, the political systems are buttressed and guarded by the superpowers to such an extent that it precludes my fantasizing about some kind of fundamental plowing-over of the entrenched fields.

This is what Czechoslovak dissident Milan Šimečka, a signatory of Charter 77 had to say to another dissident author, Eva Kantůrková, in a samizdat interview. Šimečka concluded his argument on the usefulness of gradual change as opposed to revolution by saying:

I'll tell you frankly that I am not very keen on witnessing the destruction of a system for the second time in my life. Such a thing has its own, rather messy, logic.

He preferred to talk about a system "becoming more civil." The more time elapsed after the initial cruelty of wars and revolutions, the greater the system's opportunity for "becoming more civil, free, and tolerant."

Šimečka thought that Gorbachev's leadership was indeed a dramatic watershed but that the Czechs and Slovaks were not really excited about him, showing only "cautious interest." According to Šimečka, the new Soviet leadership was not very interested in the dramatic effect of change ("the experience is bad with that kind of thing"), but rather in a quick and undramatic economic stabilization.

Šimečka agreed that "in our specific situation," political pluralism should not be regarded as the cardinal issue. Referring to Austria in particular, but also to "what is at the root of the European lifestyle," Šimečka said that there was one type of pluralism that had impressed him, namely, that of public opinion, the media, the words that people speak, the thoughts and beliefs they hold, the arts and crafts they practice, and also the pluralism of travel bureaus, restaurants, and publishing houses, and, above all, the diversity of personalities. As for the Czechoslovaks, "we would be happy to have the crumbs that fall from that table in order to feel better, freer, and merrier."

The Tenth Anniversary of Charter 77. To mark ten years of its existence, Charter 77 appealed to the Czechoslovak public to stand up for democratization, reform, and civil rights. While nowhere referring to Mikhail Gorbachev's reformist designs, the document obviously noted them and the pressure that they exerted on the Czechoslovak establishment.

Everyone, according to the appeal, should take trade union membership seriously and press for the election of "those who unflinchingly champion the true wishes of the workers" rather than of imposed bureaucrats. Furthermore, the Charter boldly suggested that "we should all create . . . informal political forums for open discussion," in which no taboos should exist, not even the "unlimited power of party secretariats."

People should "demand truthful information from the media, tell them [their] truthful opinions, and perhaps found new forums and vehicles for a free exchange of views." One way of going about this, the Charter said, was for every enterprise to start publishing a factory newspaper "in which the writing could be free if only the workers seriously insisted on it."

Teachers should educate children "in accordance with their conscience" and find enough civil courage to resist "problematic instructions" from above. Religious believers, the Charter said, should not be afraid to go to church and should not conceal their faith. The clergy, for their part, ought to defend themselves when the state's "secretaries" unlawfully interfere in their pastoral duties.

Charter 77 believed that "the entire social and political climate" would change substantially if society began to make better and more inventive use of the existing possibilities. The appeal suggested a measure of trust that the influence of "Gorbachevism" would not allow the diehards to clamp down too hard on those suggesting the creation of independent political forums, speak of strikes, and denounce leadership privileges. According to Charter 77, Czechoslovakia had a chance to begin shedding the legacy of "normalization." By mapping out a road not to efficient communism but to democracy, Charter 77's concept went far beyond Gorbachev's. It concerned man, his freedom and rights, and truth rather than just discipline, technology, performance, and the survival of a one-party system.

The Impact of Gorbachev's Visit. After Gorbachev's visit to Prague early in April 1987, Czechoslovak dissidents produced several evaluations of the event as well as at least one round-up of unofficial views.[1] The tenor of most of them could be summarized as follows: a small number of former Communists as well as the general public had had high hopes and were now disappointed by what they saw as the Soviet leader's endorsement of the existing Czechoslovak rulers, while the skeptics among the dissidents now regarded their early pessimism as having been vindicated.

A number of letters from Czechoslovak dissidents were apparently sent to Gorbachev prior to the visit.[2] A group of former Communists (including Jiří Hájek, Vladimír Kadlec, and Ludmila Jankovcová) did send a letter in their own behalf, expressing support for his reforms and suggesting their own willingness to rejoin the effort from which they had been unceremoniously excluded by the rulers in Prague. A number of other former Communists and virtually all the non-Communists in the dissident community criticized this letter sharply; they said that it was an undignified supplication that curried Gorbachev's favor in a way that was too submissive.

In comparison, Charter 77's letter was much more forthright. It reminded Gorbachev of the invasion of August 1968 and asked him to renounce this hostile act by withdrawing Soviet troops and missiles. The Charter spoke up not just for reform but for "freedom, democracy, and human values," which were indivisible; if Gorbachev really wanted to attain these things in the Soviet Union, he should not block them in other countries.

Some samizdat writers used the term "romanticism" when describing the high expectations as reflected both in the letters from some former Communists and in the popular mood. It seems that none of the romantics publicly conceded disappointment after the visit, but those dissidents who had been skeptical all along made it clear that Gorbachev did less than many had hoped. Milan Hübl suggested that Gorbachev had to show solidarity with Husák because he could not be seen to be acting as the letters from former Communist "romantics" had urged him to. It was, according to Hübl, a case of a negative self-fulfilling prophecy. Gorbachev was being told to rehabilitate the Prague Spring, and so he could not do it.

55
THE FAD OF ORIENTAL RELIGIONS

Saulius Girnius

In the Lithuanian samizdat journal *Aušra*,[1] an article written under the pseudonym of P. Mastys expressed concern about the growing popularity of Eastern religions and cults. Mastys said that beneath the monolithic facade of official ideology and conformity, an increasing number of Lithuanians were trying to find their own answers to some of the most pressing problems of life. More and more people were reading unofficial publications, listening eagerly to Western radio stations, and forming informal study groups. Mastys was ambivalent about the growing interest in Eastern religions and their most important guiding principles. While welcoming the spiritual unrest, he regretted that some were turning away from Catholicism, that "authentic source, from which flows the pure truth."

Mastys suggested some reasons for the growth in popularity of Eastern religions at the expense of Catholicism. The exotic and mysterious were often attractive, while the message of the Church was no longer new.

Both Catholics and the government had previously expressed concern about the growing popularity of Eastern religions and fundamentalist Protestant sects. In a samizdat article, "Catholicism and the Intelligentsia in Contemporary Lithuania," Juozas Bočys (a pseudonym) noted a broadly-based religious reawakening in Lithuania in reaction to the spiritual vacuum caused by the sterility of official ideology. Interest was growing in mysticism, extrasensory perception, and Eastern religions, he said, and many young intellectuals were left cold by some of the traditional teachings and rituals of the Church.

The authorities were also worried by the sudden surge of popularity of Eastern religions. In 1985 the popular (official) journal *Švyturys* published a two-part article by Juozas Jurevičius about Lithuanians traveling to visit the guru Mirza in the Karakalpak ASSR in Uzbekistan. Mirza and his translator demanded and often received sex and money for promises to teach the initiates the road to spiritual contentment. In 1985 Mirza and his interpreter-assistant traveled to Vilnius to extort more money, and had one of their followers, the karate champion of Uzbekistan, movie actor and director Talgat Nigmatulin, beaten to death because he had stood idly by during a violent confrontation in Vilnius.[2] In another article, in March 1986, Jurevičius wrote about lectures and camps in Lithuania organized by self-proclaimed gurus who had visited Mirza and taught similar methods of personal liberation.[3]

The Nigmatulin murder received considerable attention in the press.[4] The trial of the murderers, which lasted a month and a half, was completed only in September 1986; and like the murder itself, received disproportionate press coverage. A variety of reasons most likely contributed to the decision to publicize the murder, but the involvement of the Central Asian guru may have been the deciding factor.

Mirza Kymbatbaev was born in 1935. A former collective farm worker who had not had legal employment since 1972, he set himself up as a teacher of "mysticism." His chief assistant was Abai Borubaev (born in 1952), a graduate of the University of Frunze. Mirza held camps in the Karakalpak ASSR, which were attended by individuals wanting to learn how to be truly independent. In many respects, Mirza's success was like that of the "self-realization groups" in the United States in the nineteen-sixties. Most of those who attended the camps seemed to be genuinely convinced of Mirza's unique spiritual powers and obeyed his instructions without question. Mirza endeavored to convince his pupils that only he could show them the true road to spiritual self-fulfillment and enable them to overcome shyness depression, stupidity, inferiority complexes, and any other weaknesses.

Mirza thought that people should not concern themselves with material possessions but should share everything with him and the other pupils. To overcome his followers' inhibitions Mirza used a method of "moral shock," by telling them, for example, to go to the local market and take off their clothes or ordering a woman to buy and drink alcohol. Mirza's teachings and method of operation seem to have been quite similar to those of a hippie guru able to convince his pupils that he had attained emancipation from the cares of the world and could teach them to do the same. Mirza's idea of sharing everything was not limited to money and other physical possessions; women, married or single, were expected to have sexual relations with him.

In 1985 Mirza and Abai went to Lithuania accompanied by several karate experts who served as bodyguards and extortionists, demanding money and sex from Mirza's

devotees and assaulting those who refused to comply. After
successfully   extorting   several   times,   the   group was
confronted by a pupil who got the karate experts and Abai
drunk   and   invited several   friends to beat them up.
Nigmatulin was present at the scene but did not use his
expertise to help his associates.   When Mirza learned of
Nigmatulin's failure to intervene in the fight, he ordered
his minions to beat Nigmatulin, who died from the blows.
Mirza's control over Nigmatulin was clearly shown by the
fact that he did not try to defend himself, although the
autopsy showed that he had received 119 blows.
     Mirza,   Abai,   and   the   three   karate   experts were
arrested for murder; but Mirza and Abai were released after
a   psychiatric   examination   ruled   that   they   were
schizophrenic and not accountable for their actions.
Experts from the V. Serbskii Institute in Moscow challenged
the decision, and the   court postponed judgment until
further testing. The court-appointed committee ruled that
the defendants could be held accountable for their actions,
except for one of the karate experts who was judged to be
unable to stand trial at the time.   Abai was sentenced to
fifteen years imprisonment. Mirza received a sentence of
twelve years.
     The primary purpose of the wide publicity given to the
case was to ridicule the growing number of educated
Lithuanians who were turning to Eastern religions and
mysticism for spiritual consolation.
     The Lithuanian press published further articles about
the malign influence of Eastern cults and the gullibility
of Lithuanian intellectuals who fell victim to charlatans
like Mirza. A   three-part   article   on   the trial in
Sovetskaia Litva focused attention on the perils of
religions such as Islam and Zen Buddhism and showed how
Nigmatulin's promising career had been ruined when he fell
under Mirza's influence.[5]   In April *Švyturys* published an
article   criticizing   the Hare Krishna sect[6]; it   was
subsequently learned that some of the more important Hare
Krishna writings had been translated into Lithuanian and
were circulating in samizdat form.

IN SEARCH OF A NEW EUROPE

56
THE EUROPEANS OF THE EAST

Kevin Devlin

For Adriano Guerra, director of the Italian Communist Party's research center for East European Studies, the countries of the region, without exception though in somewhat different ways, were undergoing a profound systemic crisis. In the second of three articles (published on 18 April 1987) written for the party weekly *Rinascita* on the impact of the Soviet reform movement on these countries, he suggested that at the core of the regional crisis lay a new contradiction between socioeconomic development and the consequent need for "greater freedom and autonomy," on the one hand, and, on the other, the persistence of "old, centralized structures of bureaucracy and authoritarianism."

Emphasis on "consumerism," in Guerra's view, had both highlighted the range of differences among the East European countries and the USSR and at the same time helped to obscure the elements of the regional crisis. This emphasis might bring with it the idea of a new relationship between socialism and well-being; but it might also produce a "moral void:"

> There is in the societies of the East . . . a profound malaise, the sign of a true crisis, one of identity and of prospects: one feels the lack of original and valid answers to the problems of the world that are based on these experiences, on what is said and thought here.

When speaking of the moral void and of the political apathy of the populations in general, Guerra noted that it was in the first place the men of the regimes themselves that had rejected politics, its values, and its instruments. Instead, they "often promoted the 'Westernization' of the shop windows--that is, a distorted policy of consumer supplies--in order to hold back the demand for reforms and participation." Yet the appearance could be deceptive:

> The societies of Eastern Europe are being affected increasingly obviously by movements of ideas and even new forms of social organization: one thinks not only of the various organizations of dissent and opposition--such as Charter 77 in Czechoslovakia or underground Solidarity, still so significant in Poland--but also of the dense network of cultural, religious, pacifist, ecological, and other groups. One should therefore not be misled by what is said about the indifference and apathy said to prevail in these societies, now that there is the new factor of Gorbachev's words and deeds and the effect they may have in various countries.

The news coming from the various East European capitals, he continued, emphasized the nature and the gravity, as well as the unifying character, of the crisis that had been affecting the countries of the bloc as a whole since the late nineteen-seventies.

Guerra ended his second article with a challenging statement and an echoing question:

> [Recent developments show that] in each case the limitations of "state socialism" are not just a matter of the management of factories and of the economy. In order to find a solution to the problem, it is necessary that Gorbachev's "revolution from above" and that from below, potentially present in the Eastern countries, should come together.

Guerra began his third article by discussing the thorny question of the "limits of tolerability" in Soviet relations with East European countries. Crises affecting those relations that had occurred in various countries between 1953 and 1956, in 1968, and again in the nineteen-eighties, he suggested, gave weight to the thesis that

> what the USSR is not disposed to tolerate . . . are acts violating principles that it regards as fundamental, because they affect, in foreign policy,

international alliances (that is, the security of the USSR) and, on the domestic level, the recognition [sic] of pluralism and the question of the leading role of the party.

This picture of bloc discipline, however, had replaced an earlier emphasis on "national ways" in the new "people's democracies" of Eastern Europe with the onset of the Cold War. It was inevitable that the growth of détente in Europe should produce the emergence of "new needs" and also "increased areas of autonomy" in those countries, as manifested in Romania's independent foreign policies, the GDR's initiatives for a special relationship between the two German states, or Hungary's stress on the role of minor states in maintaining interbloc dialogue at times of crisis between the superpowers.

Significant changes within the Warsaw Pact and Comecon have thus taken place. They should be seen, however, as the result not of a new Soviet attitude but of a relative loss of control by the USSR over its allies because of the presence of increasingly strong centrifugal forces. These are changes not encouraged but undergone by the USSR, which . . . has had to take account of the fact that there is now neither a compact socialist camp nor an international communist movement directed by the Soviet Union.

The advent of Gorbachev and his reform movement had brought further change. It was very probable that, "precisely because this time it is the Soviet Union itself that proposes to introduce such radical changes, a substantial modification of the relations between the USSR and its allies has become hard to avoid." He went on to elaborate on this prospect:

Conditions are evidently becoming ripe for a basic change in Soviet policy. They concern both the conceptions of socialism (with a consequent widening of the area of experiments and "paths" considered legitimate) and the question of the function assigned to Eastern Europe in the security policies of the Soviet state.

On this last point, Guerra suggested that the "prenuclear" limitations of previous Soviet security policies had become obvious now that Eastern Europe could no longer be viewed, in the Stalinist perspective, as "a fortress occupied and controlled by the USSR."

> Is there, however--and this is the point--awareness in Soviet policy of the implications that such a significant change, on such a decisive issue, will bring with it for the countries of Eastern Europe? The question . . . is legitimate, because it refers in the first place to an extraordinarily complex problem: that of the recognition of the European identity of these countries.

It would be difficult, Guerra went on, to speak of Eastern Europe as having a regional identity in the terms that one could apply to the West. For one thing, there was a total absence not only of unifying institutions such as the Western European Union, the European Economic Community, or the European Parliament but also of "laws that would guarantee the free passage of men and goods across frontiers." Yet the countries of East-Central Europe did have in common "the same historical formation that requires one to view this area as a specific reality of our time," one that--having stood both the test of the "liberation strategy" of former US Secretary of State John Foster Dulles and that of "forced unification based on the Soviet-Russian model and culture"--had demonstrably put down real roots. This was, however, in no small measure due to those East European intellectuals, at home and in exile, who had continued to feel themselves "Europeans of the East." If this "idea of Europe" was to advance, there was an urgent need for substantial changes in Soviet policies, and also in West European attitudes to Eastern Europe.

57
A COMECON-COMMON MARKET RAPPROCHEMENT

Jan Zoubek*

In May 1985, Gorbachev told the visiting Italian Prime Minister and President of the EEC Council of Ministers, Bettino Craxi, that the USSR was ready to change its

---

*This paper covers the period up to March 1987.

approach to the EEC and recognize it as both an economic and a political partner. At that time, hopes rose that after years during which the two bodies had first ignored one another and then attempted discussions that failed due to insurmountable differences, something positive could be achieved.

After May 1985, two official discussions took place between the EEC (Common Market) and the CMEA (Comecon) in Geneva. The first was in late September 1986 and the second from March 18 to 20, 1987. At each meeting the EEC Commission delegation was headed by John Maslen (head of the department dealing with communist countries) and the CMEA delegation by CMEA Deputy Secretary Z. Kurowski. Both sides claimed that some progress had been made on both occasions and there had been a "good and businesslike atmosphere." Differences on the key issue of the CMEA countries' formal recognition of West Berlin as an integral part of the EEC on both occasions prevented the adoption of a "joint declaration" and resulted only in an agreement to hold another meeting to complete the work already begun.

The change that took place in 1985 in the Soviet approach to the EEC marked the beginning of a new period in relations between the EEC and the East European countries. The Soviets now no longer objected to the conclusion of bilateral agreements between the EEC and individual member countries of the CMEA. Yet the two institutions proved unable to agree on the arrangements for such agreements.

History of Relations. For political reasons the East European countries and the USSR had long ignored the existence of the EEC, despite the fact that it was their most important commercial partner, the main outlet for East European goods, and the main source of technology and badly-needed finance.

The situation started to change in the early nineteen-seventies. The EEC was bound by the Treaty of Rome to institute a common commercial policy as of 1970. From that year on, negotiations and the conclusion of bilateral or multilateral agreements on commercial relations with third countries fell fully within the exclusive power of the EEC; trade agreements had to be negotiated and concluded by the EEC alone and no longer by member states.

In a speech on March 20, 1972, Brezhnev said: "We are in favor of economic relations established on the basis of equality, free of all discrimination."[1] This was the beginning of the bloc-to-bloc policy. The Soviet leadership sought to promote itself as an advocate of

change toward the EEC.   The USSR was not motivated by a
desire to help other East European countries in their
export difficulties. A bloc-to-bloc policy between the EEC
and the CMEA would require strong cohesion within the CMEA
itself and the endowment of its central bodies with new
supranational powers. Precisely this had been the Soviet
aim for many years.

In mid-1973, Nikolai Fadeev, the then Secretary
General of the CMEA, unofficially proposed in Copenhagen
that the CMEA and the EEC appoint delegations to discuss
the establishment of closer relations. This marked the
beginning of the first phase of discussions between the two
alignments.   During the first half of 1974 the EEC
formulated its *Ostpolitik*. The EEC Commission published an
"opinion" confirming that the CMEA was not a body able to
negotiate on behalf of its member countries.   It invite
the CMEA countries to negotiate trade agreements on an
individual basis with the EEC represented by the
commission.   The EEC Council then declared that it was
prepared to negotiate with any East European country
wishing to do so.

In November 1974 the EEC sent a general outline of a
trade agreement to every East European country. This draft
outline, to which the communist countries initially failed
to respond, later became the basis for the bilateral
agreement on trade in industrial goods signed with Romania
in 1980 and the setting up of a joint EEC-Romanian
Committee.

In early February 1975, the first talks between the
delegations of the EEC Commission and the CMEA Secretariat
were held in Moscow. One year later, in February 1976, the
East German deputy prime minister, then also president of
the CMEA Executive Committee, G. Weiss, handed over a
draft proposal for the conclusion of a framework
cooperation agreement between the EEC and the CMEA.

The draft was completely unacceptable to the EEC, both
politically and economically.   It required important,
unilaterally favorable trade provisions, including
most-favored-nation treatment, without offering any
reciprocal advantages.   It required EEC credit to help
finance the East European deficits.

In November 1976, the EEC proposed the establishment
of working relations between the two bodies in fields in
which the CMEA was capable of acting: in the exchange of
information on general subjects such as economic prospects,
production and trade statistics, the environment, and
standardization. The EEC reiterated that all trade aspects

of relations should be regulated only by bilateral agreements between the EEC and individual CMEA countries. Negotiations lasted from 1977 to October 1980; there was no follow-up.

Behind the scenes, however, officials from individual East European countries indicated a willingness to conclude bilateral agreements with the EEC. They urged the commission to conclude at least a minimum framework agreement with the CMEA. This agreement, they said, would give the Soviets a chance of saving face by claiming a major political victory and would, at the same time, allow individual members to negotiate without direct Soviet supervision.

Discussions were discontinued in 1980, not only because of totally divergent views but mainly because of the Soviet invasion of Afghanistan and the general deterioration in East-West relations. The increase in East European net debt from some $6,000 million in 1971 to about $70,000 million in 1980 was not encouraging for East-West trade. The oil crisis fundamentally increased CMEA members' dependence on the Soviet Union's willingness to supply them with energy carriers. It forced them to reorientate their economies even more to Soviet domestic needs and to invest in major and costly projects in the USSR.

In late May 1985 Gorbachev told Craxi: "To the extent that the EEC countries form a 'political unit,' we are prepared to consult [with] the EEC on practical and international issues." In June 1985 the CMEA's new General Secretary, Viacheslav Sychev, in a letter to the President of the EEC Commission, M. Jacques Delors proposed talks at the highest level, which were to result in a "joint declaration" on relations between the EEC and the CMEA. The EEC wanted answers to two specific practical questions. The first was a request for a copy of the draft joint declaration. The second was:

> Does the CMEA agree with the commission that any framework agreement between the community and the CMEA should under no circumstances be allowed to prejudice bilateral relations, either existing or envisaged, between the community and the individual CMEA countries?

A satisfactory answer from the CMEA resulted in the first round of discussions after a six-year break, held in Geneva in September 1986. The joint declaration was to bring about mutual recognition of the two institutions and would refer to the eventual conclusion of a restricted agreement between the two institutions to cooperate in such matters as the exchange of information and statistics and environmental issues. This would be followed by the opening of an EEC office in Moscow and a CMEA office in Brussels. More important, bilateral negotiations between the EEC and individual CMEA member countries on trade and economic cooperation could begin.

Individual East European countries quickly replied favorably to the invitation to start bilateral trade negotiations. The review of principles confirmed that the scope and quality of bilateral agreements favored those East European countries that were members of the General Agreement on Tariffs and Trade and had started to reform their economic systems.

The EEC Council approved a mandate for the commission to negotiate a new cooperation agreement with Romania that would extend mutual relations considerably beyond the scope of the original 1980 agreement. The council also approved a mandate to negotiate a bilateral trade agreement with Czechoslovakia, which would allow the Czechoslovaks to expand the scope of their exports of sensitive and semisensitive products to the EEC. These exports were of vital importance for Czechoslovak hard currency earnings. The main stumbling block to a trade agreement with Hungary was its desire to be treated as a "market economy" country and its refusal to grant some reciprocity in order to balance, at least partly, the major benefits it would obtain from the improved access for its products to the markets of the 12 EEC member countries.

Despite the claim of progress in drafting the joint declaration, the EEC-CMEA meeting in Geneva from March 18-20, 1987 failed because of the territorial application clause. The Romanians, who were already supposed to start new negotiations, requested a postponement because of "other urgent problems." Czechoslovakia appeared to be in no hurry to begin negotiations. It was believed in Brussels that this was due to delays in the approval of the mandate to negotiate with Hungary. This more favorable mandate might have set a precedent for other East European countries asking for the same privileged treatment. Apparently it was decided in Moscow at the CMEA Executive Committee meeting held in January 1987 that member countries should slow down in their approaches to the EEC and wait for progress in CMEA-EEC bloc-to-bloc negotiations.

58
EAST BERLIN CULTIVATES EUROPEAN IDENTITY

Barbara Donovan

From June 3 to 5, 1987, Erich Honecker, the East German state and party leader, paid an official visit to the Netherlands at the invitation of Prime Minister Ruud Lubbers. The visit was his third trip to a NATO country, and another step in the GDR's persistent efforts to increase its diplomatic presence in Western Europe--efforts marked by references to "common European interests." Coming at a time when Honecker was reacting to Gorbachev's reform program by stating that while the GDR had "learned" from the Soviet Union in the past, the Soviet Union was now "learning from us in various spheres,"[1] these "pan-European" tendencies could indicate that East Berlin was distancing itself from Soviet policy. However, a more active foreign policy role for East Berlin seemed to have Gorbachev's full blessing.

Honecker appeared interested in boosting trade between the two countries, which had fallen from its high point in 1984; an agreement on scientific, technological, and industrial cooperation for 1987 and 1988 was reached. The main topic of the talks, however, was arms control; and the East German leader briefed his host on the results of the Warsaw Pact summit meeting in East Berlin the week before. He conceded a "certain imbalance" in NATO and Warsaw Pact conventional forces and agreed that this was an important problem. He remained vague, however, about how to redress this imbalance, only repeating a Warsaw Pact proposal that both sides reduce forces by 25 percent. In a speech on 4 June 1987, the East German leader praised the efforts to eliminate medium-range missiles from Europe and called for further disarmament: "We are absolutely not opposed to pursuing further zero options in the field of nuclear, chemical, and conventional weapons."[2]

The Dutch raised the issue of human rights and travel restrictions in the GDR. In a dinner speech, Lubbers spoke frankly of the importance the Dutch government accorded to human rights:

The division of Europe remains unnatural. It is in the interest of all of us to make these borders a bit more transparent . . . . We therefore place value on freedom of information, on direct human contact, on

the right to freedom of expression, and on the right
to travel freely from one country to another.[3]

In an interview with Dutch newspapers, Honecker
responded to a question about human rights by remarking
that the possibilities for travel were increasing.
According to the East German leader, the travel problem
could be traced to the shortage of hard currency: thus, he
said, "better relations and more trade will result in more
travel [to the West]."[4]

The "Political Dialogue" with the West. The East
German pursuit of relations with both neutral governments
in the West and NATO members marked a conscious shift of
focus from the FRG to its allies. The goal was apparently
to use the growing acceptance of the GDR's role as a
sovereign state by other Western European states,
especially those in NATO, as a means of exerting pressure
on Bonn. At the same time, the Honecker leadership
recognized additional political and economic gains that
could be won from continued contacts with the West. First,
the SED hoped to enhance its legitimacy and stability at
home.

Second, the GDR had a keen interest in increased trade
and economic cooperation, which could only come through an
improved political standing in the West. The GDR's
incipient program of technological innovation was directly
dependent upon the exchange of scientific expertise and
material with the West.

Finally, East Berlin's interest in reducing
international tension should not be overlooked. The
political and economic advantages of contacts with the
West, especially the FRG, prompted Honecker in 1984 to
resist Moscow's policy of punishing Bonn and freezing
East-West contacts and to adopt his subsequent policy of
"damage limitation." Later the leadership's interest in
having short-range nuclear weapons removed from the GDR
played an important role in its "dialogue" with the West.
Honecker asked the Belgian, British, and Dutch heads of
state to lend their full support to the zero-solution.
Moreover, the GDR turned to the West German Social
Democratic Party, which had very similar views on security
and deterrence, as a key partner in what the GDR called a
"coalition of reason."[5]

A New Type of Thinking? Its new stature and
self-confidence prompted the SED leadership to expand upon
the concept behind their political overtures to the West.
Since the earlier discussion of "the special role of small

and medium-sized countries" appeared to have been successfully silenced by Moscow, the GDR attempted to formulate a foreign policy based on the idea of "common European interests." In a speech at the opening of the CSCE conference in Vienna in November 1986, Foreign Minister Oskar Fischer argued that common security interests made cooperation in all areas imperative. A "European identity," according to Fischer,

> is the common recognition that the European states, as different as their social and political systems may be, can face a future in peace only when they see one another not as rivals but as partners . . . who follow policies of mutual cooperation that bring benefits to all.[6]

The idea of Europe's unique security problems leading to a sense of common identity was also the subject of a speech made to the European Parliament by Max Schmidt, the Director of the Institute for International Politics and Economics.[7] More important, however, was Schmidt's outline of the GDR's stand on cooperation with the EEC and more specifically on institutionalizing the relationship.[8] His analysis reflected a recognition of the EEC's growing regional and worldwide influence and the fact that despite its heterogenity it was coming closer together. He welcomed the establishment of relations between the CMEA and the EEC as part of the necessary and general "European process of cooperation":

> The efforts of the CMEA states foresee a Europe free of trade barriers, economic discrimination, and sanctions, where . . . cooperative projects are undertaken in areas of energy, raw materials, transportation, and finances.

The willingness to recognize the EEC as an eventual partner and, perhaps more important, the emphasis on common European interests that transcended the bloc division reflected a new East German perception of relations with the West.[9] In contrast to Moscow's disapproval of East German policy toward the West in 1984, the Soviet leadership under Gorbachev appeared to support an active role for the GDR. Not only were there parallels between the GDR's concept and Soviet writings on the subject, but the GDR also assumed a leading role in encouraging West Europeans to accept Soviet arms proposals and to contribute to détente.   Perhaps the clearest sign that Honecker's policy of "dialogue with all forces of reason and realism" coincided with Moscow's policy toward Western Europe was the East German leader's remark in an interview before he left for the Netherlands that his long-awaited visit to Bonn might be possible in 1987.

59
THREE FACES OF CENTRAL EUROPE

Patricia Howard

Despite critics who insisted that Central Europe was buried for good in the ashes of World War II, the creature continued to surface in the East and West.   In January 1987, a symposium in West Berlin confirmed that although there was still little agreement on what Central Europe was or should be, the subject was by no means dead and would remain alive as long as there was dissatisfaction with the postwar division of Europe.   More important, it showed how Central Europe was apt to assume different faces, depending on whether an East European, a West German, or a Frenchman was describing it.
    The East European version of Central Europe current in the West, perhaps best articulated by Milan Kundera, was largely a spiritual claim to Western identity and a protest against Sovietization, often not without a hint of wistfulness about lost Kakania.   Yet, as Timothy Garton Ash pointed out, the East European vision of a pure Central European past was a myth, although an "understandable exaggeration to challenge a prevailing orthodoxy."[1]   The German discussion, on the other hand, was highly charged by the memory of the destruction left in the wake of German rumblings about *Mitteleuropa*.   Related to a larger debate on the political role of German history, the issue of Central Europe led West German conservatives and liberals to square off in the press about the Atlantic alliance and contacts with the East.   For the French (as well as most British and Americans for that matter) Central Europe conjured up the familiar German monster and was seen as a threat to Western resolve against the Soviet Union.
    Resurrecting Central Europe.   Only one East European, a Pole, sat on the dais at the Reichstag gathering sponsored by the Friedrich-Ebert-Stiftung at the beginning

of January. Filling in for the ailing Vice President of the Polish Parliament, Michal Kołodziejczyk stressed that he was there as an observer only, not a participant. Despite the absence of East European speakers, though, it was clear that the others were familiar with what voices from the East had been saying about Central Europe; references to Kundera and György Konrad were frequent.

Kundera and Konrad had perhaps the greatest influence on the Central European debate in the West. Protesting against the postwar order in Europe and seeking to salvage Eastern Europe from the Soviet monolith, they both worked to revive the notion of Central Europe, stressing the Western traditions and attachments this part of the world had cultivated before the border between Europe and the East was moved several hundred kilometers to the west. In his book *Anti-Politics*, Konrad offered an idealistic vision of a united Europe free of American and Soviet troops and ideologies, an idea that gained considerable support from Western peace groups. For Kundera, the cultural separation from the West was far more painful than the political or ideological division. In a 1984 essay on "The Tragedy of Central Europe" he mourned that since 1945 the West had turned its back on everything east of the Oder-Neisse border. "Does Central Europe still exist?" he asked:

> If to live means to exist in the eyes of those we love, then Central Europe no longer exists. More precisely: in the eyes of its beloved Europe, Central Europe is just a part of the Soviet empire and nothing more, nothing more.

Kundera's lament reverberated throughout the West, resonating particularly strongly in West Germany, where the East-West divide was felt most acutely. But if Kundera's Central Europe appealed to what was good and noble in the European tradition, the German version called to mind tanks rolling through Poland and cattle cars carrying millions to their deaths. Karl Schlögel, a Russian specialist who had written a book on Central Europe and was the youngest participant at the Berlin symposium, spoke frankly about Germany's Central European legacy: "It was the tanks from the 'nation of culture' and the German death factories that decimated Central Europe, devastating it beyond recognition." Since the Nazi madness, Schlögel said, the capital of *Mitteleuropa* was no longer Berlin, Vienna, or Prague but Auschwitz. For him, coming to terms with the annihilation of Central Europe--particularly the murder of the Jews, the soul of Central Europe according to Kundera--was inseparable from coming to terms with German history, a process that intensified in West Germany after Reagan's visit to Bitburg and Richard von Weiszäcker's World War II anniversary speech.

Indeed German history was looking over every speaker's shoulder: the significance of the symposium's venue was not lost on anyone. Joseph Rovan, a French Jew teaching at the Sorbonne, who had suffered at the hands of the Nazis in concentration camps and in occupied France, said the specter of German history overshadowed any discussion of Central Europe as a political model. In this he summed up the feelings of many other Frenchmen (as well as British and Americans) who shuddered at the thought of a reunited German power in the heart of Europe. This and the threat of Soviet aggression made an autonomous Central European confederation encompassing both Germanies unthinkable. For Rovan, Central Europe as a political concept belonged "to those demons of German history that should stay where we left them in 1945."

Almost every speaker agreed that Central Europe as a political model was impossible. This had also been the rallying cry of West German conservatives concerned about sentimental appeals to Central Europe at home. Conservative academic Michael Stürmer warned on the front page of the *Frankfurter Allgemeine Zeitung* that flirting with *Mitteleuropa* was a dangerous game played by West German intellectuals dissatisfied with the status quo in Europe but forgetful of the political roots of their freedom and prosperity. As far as he was concerned: "Where does Central Europe lie? In terms of reminiscences about the culture, everywhere; but nowhere on the political map."

The panel having said what Central Europe could not be, the search was on for a role it might fill. Journalist Peter Bender suggested looking upon Central Europe as a community of common interests, made up of those countries that had suffered most from the division of Europe and were most affected by the arms build-up. When it came to preserving peace in Europe, he said, West Germans had more in common with Belgrade, Stockholm, Warsaw, and East Berlin than with Paris or London.

He proposed setting up a network of economic and cultural ties that would gradually bring Eastern Europe closer to the rest of Europe. Admitting the suspicion such contacts sometimes aroused within NATO or the EEC, Bender said the Federal Republic had to make clear to these groups that "there are allies to be found not only within the

[Atlantic] alliance." He added that his suggestion might not produce much but could perhaps avoid disasters.

Whether Bender's informal community of cooperation in the center of Europe would work or not, Schlögel agreed that contacts with Eastern Europe were important to reduce the bloc mentality left over from the Cold War. The Central European revival, he said, reminded West Germans that there was more in the East than an ideological system hostile to the West. Echoing Kundera, he condemned the term Eastern bloc as a "simplistic collective concept that dismissed a complicated history and reduced the variety and individuality of peoples and states as well as their rich and colorful cultures to one abstract notion." Like Bender he spoke of the need to overcome "the wall in one's mind," a double-entendre referring to a closed-minded attitude that regarded the Berlin Wall as sealing off the East for good. He saw no improvement in the gulf between East and West until the black-and-white mentality changed.

If most of the speakers tried to give amorphous Central Europe some form, political or otherwise, the Austrian participant was the one speaker comfortable with its shimmering surface. As someone from a country that had never stopped thinking in terms of Central Europe, Paul Lendvai, a prominent Hungarian-born Austrian journalist, said it was important not to force the issue of Central Europe or use grand slogans to revive it. To speak of a new Central European consciousness was beside the point; more important were the "small steps" toward easing human contacts, making borders permeable rather than tearing them down altogether. This was taken up by Bender who suggested Austria's relations with Hungary as a model for Central European contacts: "not starting something spectacular, but always trying to do what is possible and perhaps sometimes trying what seems impossible."

The Berlin gathering did not pretend to have the final say on Central Europe but hoped only, as Schlögel said, to spur further discussion about the East-West divide. As Garton Ash pointed out in his essay on Central Europe, "even if it merely reminds an American or British newspaper reader that Siberia does not begin at Checkpoint Charlie, [the discussion] serves a good purpose." East Europeans, West Germans, and Frenchmen alike could at least agree on that.

WHITHER THE USSR?

60
POPULAR DISSATISFACTION WITH GORBACHEV

Elizabeth Teague

During a visit to the city of Krasnodar in September 1986, Gorbachev complained about those allegedly resisting the restructuring. The main concern of such people, Gorbachev said, was "to preserve old, obsolete ways and to keep their own privileges intact." Such people, he continued, were to be found "among workers, and peasants, and managers, and workers in the party apparatus. . . . They are also to be found among our intelligentsia."[1] He thus suggested that dissatisfaction was present at almost every level of Soviet society.

Noting the frequency with which Gorbachev complained about resistance to his policies, some Western observers suggested that he might be deliberately exaggerating its strength. According to this interpretation, the new leader was trying to portray himself as an embattled reformer surrounded by "hardliners," a good guy desperately in need of help both at home and abroad, in order to win the support he needed to implement his policies. That way, he would be able to lay the blame elsewhere if his policies were to fail and, in the meantime, he could use charges of "resistance" as a pretext to rid himself of rivals and opponents.[2] Reports of resistance came from so many sources and took so many forms, however, that it seems likely that real dissatisfaction was also present in Soviet society.

It did not automatically follow, however, that Gorbachev faced opposition in the form of factional groupings within the elite. While differences of opinion doubtlessly existed between various individuals and interest groupings within the leadership, there was no evidence to suggest these had resulted in the formation of rival political coalitions.

On the other hand, there was quite considerable evidence that many of the changes introduced by the Gorbachev leadership were unpopular with the general public. A leading Soviet playwright made reference to the Soviet Union's "newly discontented."[3] Elite groups aside, the following sections of the population seemed to qualify for that description.

--Bureaucrats in the central planning agency, Gosplan, were uneasy about imminent changes in the nature of their work, while many officials in the Moscow ministries were fearful of losing their prestige and authority, being relocated to outlying areas, or even put temporarily out of work when the promised devolution of day-to-day decision-making from the center to local enterprises occurred. Gorbachev complained in June 1986 that this plan was meeting not only resistance, but pure incomprehension. Rather than allow enterprises more autonomy, he said, the authorities in some republics were trying to create new bodies to oversee them in the way the central ministries had done previously.[4]

--Some enterprise managers feared the increased responsibility that greater financial independence would entail. "The reason is simple," according to a leading economist. "If something goes wrong, who is responsible now? The same people who made the decisions. Previously it was possible to write letters of protest to the top, but to whom should one write now if one has not worked properly?"[5]

--If plans were realized to widen wage differentials and tailor bonuses to match effort and quality of work, a substantial number of shopfloor workers would be out of pocket. An article published in September 1986 warned that rank-and-file workers would not willingly give up a system whereby they received an adequate salary merely by pretending to work in exchange for a system that offered good wages only in return for hard work.[6]

--A foretaste of worker dissatisfaction with higher demands came in early December 1986, when "stormy protests" were reported from the giant KamAZ truck factory. Workers there were upset by the introduction of a new system of quality control which made higher demands on them. Nor was this an isolated incident. The new system was being introduced throughout the industrial sector and the process could not, according to *Izvestiia*, "be said to be taking place smoothly."[7]

--Many ordinary citizens were infuriated that, as a result of Gorbachev's campaign against alcoholism, they now had to spend hours standing in line to buy a bottle of wine or vodka. One report even spoke of the windows of liquor stores being smashed by angry customers when stocks ran out, and said that in some places police had been put on duty outside the stores to keep the peace.[8] So strong was public resentment of the campaign that in Moscow the authorities eventually compromised by lengthening liquor store opening hours and reintroducing Sunday sales.[9]

--Other members of the public appeared distressed that *glasnost* meant the press now wrote about a great many unpleasant topics previously kept under wraps, such as drug abuse and prostitution. "Okay, so it's the truth," one such person was quoted as complaining, "but not every kind of truth is useful to us."[10]

--*Glasnost* was of course unpopular among the local officials at whom it was so often aimed. They responded by warning that the spotlight Moscow was trying turn on the misdeeds of party members would bring the CPSU into disrepute.[11] The central press complained repeatedly that regional party officials were muffling the local press, but even Gorbachev's own speeches were sometimes censored before appearing in print. The televised version of his speech in Khabarovsk in July 1986, for example, was far more outspoken than that published a day and a half later in *Pravda* and other central newspapers.

--Finally, there was a vocal band of ideological purists who, in Gorbachev's words, viewed any change in the economic mechanism as a retreat from Socialist principles.[12] The chief editor of *Pravda*, for example, said he was receiving "a lot" of letters opposing any increase in the role of commodity-money relations (that is, market relations).[13] An article in *Literaturnaia gazeta* revealed that decisions on the role of commodity-money relations had been adopted at the party congress earlier in 1986 only after "a sharp ideological struggle." The newspaper ridiculed "benighted people" (*temnye liudi*) who were afraid that allowing peasants to build greenhouses on their private plots would "hand our Soviet power over to the kulaks."[14]

--In the same vein, a leading Central Committee official said "some comrades" were expressing doubts about other theoretical propositions adopted at the party congress. In particular, letter writers were said to be asking whether Gorbachev's call for joint East-West efforts to solve "global problems" was not "a deviation from class positions."[15] Other members of the public seemed to have reservations about some of Gorbachev's arms control proposals. "Aren't we too soft in talking to foreign countries?" a voice asked from the crowd during Gorbachev's visit to Krasnodar in September.[16] And Western observers interpreted the fact that Gorbachev made three television appearances in ten days[17] to explain what happened during his summit meeting with Reagan at Reykjavik as an indication that his message was not getting across to Soviet audiences.

Gorbachev himself warned of the difficulty of identifying the sources of resistance to his policies, charging that some officials disguised their true feelings. "We see them," he told his audience in Krasnodar, "shouting about restructuring from every platform and louder than anyone else. But in reality they're the ones slamming the brakes on its implementation!"[18]

61
LIBERALIZATION AND SOVIET JEWRY

Julia Wishnevsky

Besides an increase in Jewish emigration from the Soviet Union during 1986 and early 1987, there appeared to have been some improvement in the situation of Jews still living in the USSR. Regular readers of Soviet newspapers and periodicals could notice a considerable increase in the number of Jewish names among the authors of material in the Soviet media (previously, Jewish writers were often urged to use Russian-sounding pseudonyms). Western observers also remarked upon "the apparent diminution in the volume of Soviet anti-Zionist and anti-Semitic propaganda and the curbing of some of its worst excesses."[1] In addition, there were signs of greater freedom for Jewish culture in the Soviet Union.

New Respect for Jewish Culture. On March 13, 1987, a Moldavian newspaper announced the forthcoming publication of a "teach-yourself" book of Yiddish. According to the newspaper, this "mass-circulation, fundamental" work was to be published in 1987 by the Russkii iazyk publishing house in Moscow."[2] On the same day, *Literaturnaia Rossiia* reviewed a collection of Jewish folklore published in 1986 by the prestigious Sovetskii pisatel publishing house. *The Songs of the Past* were translated from Yiddish into Russian by Naum Grebnev. According to the poet Mark Lisianskii, who reviewed the book, Grebnev was a very productive Soviet translator of Jewish descent who had translated collections of folklore of many Soviet nationalities and usually published several volumes of translations annually. This was the first time in some thirty years, however, that Grebnev had been allowed to publish the folklore of his own people.[3]

Two days earlier, *Literaturnaia gazeta* published an article by Nina Velekhova on the Jewish Studio Theater in Moscow.[4] This was not the first time that Soviet mass-circulation newspapers had written about this theater and its director Iakov Gubenko. At the end of January 1987, *Nedelia*, the supplement to the government daily *Izvestiia*, even reproduced a photograph showing a scene from one of its productions.[5] What made Velekhova's article rather unusual was her vague attempt to link the work of the theater with the Russian Jewish culture of the past. She mentioned Marc Chagall who was normally identified in Soviet encyclopedias as a French painter.[6] Velekhova also briefly summarized the history of the famous Jewish State Theater (GOSET), which was closed down soon after the assassination in 1948 of its director, the great Jewish actor Solomon Mikhoels, at the height of Stalin's anti-Semitic drive. Press items about the Jewish Musical Chamber Theater, which came into existence in Birobidzhan in 1978, had not, as a rule, provided any historical background.[7]

Press Treatment of Jews. Still more unusual was Velekhova's assertion that Soviet citizens "should not be isolated from one another" by the section in their internal passports specifying ethnic origin. In the past, the official media had always vigorously denied the existence of such a problem in the Soviet Union and had claimed that all Soviet peoples were equal.

Since the latter part of 1986, a number of articles appeared expressing the view that Jews were people like everybody else and should therefore not be singled out by reason of the ethnic entry in their passports.[8] Previously, the existence of anti-Semitism in the USSR--even at the everyday level--had been categorically denied. Now, anti-Semitism became a target for criticism in the press. *Izvestiia* published an article by Vladimir Lakshin criticizing the anti-Semitic slant of Vasilii Belov's novel *Vse vperedi*,[9] and *Komsomolskaia pravda* printed an article by Elena Losoto about the activities of the anti-Semitic Pamiat society.[10]

There were many signs that the new Soviet leadership had decided to change its policy toward Jews, but the--by Soviet standards--considerable liberalization of cultural life and the greater freedom simultaneously accorded the press suggested that the diminution of state anti-Semitism involved not only political but also ideological factors.

One aspect of the campaign against the falsification of history was the appearance of criticism of the theory of a conspiracy by Jews and freemasons to seize power all over the world.[11] The idea of a masonic conspiracy had gained wide currency in the nineteen-seventies thanks to the journal *Molodaia gvardiia*, its publishing house, and a number of other publishing houses in the provinces. Previously, the idea had been rebuffed only in specialist journals with a small circulation.[12]

62
THE GROWTH OF "INFORMAL GROUPS"

Vera Tolz

In the course of the campaign for *glasnost*, the Soviet press started to discuss in some detail the problem of informal (*neformalnye*) groups in the USSR. The term "informal" was used to describe groups or organizations whose establishment was not officially sanctioned. Soviet newspapers admitted that such groups started to appear as early as twenty years earlier; they now numbered in the thousands.[1] At first, the authorities applied two main tactics in dealing with these groups: they either ignored them, or they criticized and harassed their members. Later, the Soviet authorities adopted a more sophisticated approach toward informal groups, devoting more attention to their problems and attempting to incorporate their members into the social life.

Description of the Groups. Active in the nineteen-seventies, by the early nineteen-eighties the groups were already well established. By 1986, their numbers were, as the youth daily *Komsomolskaia pravda* put it, growing as fast as mushrooms in the rain.[2] The Soviet press carried letters from young people mentioning the existence of informal groups in almost every city and even village.

The most common kind of informal group consisted of young people interested in music--mostly rock and pop--who formed amateur music ensembles. An attempt was made in the early nineteen-eighties to register these ensembles. According to the Soviet press, by 1987 they numbered more than a hundred thousand.[3] Another very common type of informal group in the USSR was the group of sports (usually soccer) fans. They attended all the games of their favorite team and often got into fights with the supporters of rival teams.[4] Besides punks and hippies, there were Liubery (the name is derived from the Moscow suburb of Liubertsy), notorious for beating them up.[5] There were also many unofficial literary groups, the majority of these in Leningrad, as well as pacifist groups.[6]

Komsomolskaia pravda reported on self-styled vigilante groups in Pskov and Novosibirsk that fought against corruption and other forms of injustice. In 1986, the newspaper published a letter from a youth in Novosibirsk who claimed to belong to an unofficial group called "Zakon i poriadok" (Law and Order).[7] The newspaper quoted the youth as saying that the group had already solved fifty-three cases of corruption on its own, without help from the investigative organs, and that fifteen more cases were in the works. According to the youth, the group consisted of thirty-five people. It seems that similar vigilante groups were set up by veterans of the war in Afghanistan, who, after coming back from military service, found it difficult to adjust to the corruption of Soviet life. In the course of the *glasnost* campaign, the existence of Nazi-style organizations was revealed in the press.[8]

In 1987, the press started to pay special attention to groups devoted to the preservation of historic monuments and the environment. Such groups emerged not only in Leningrad and Moscow, but also in many other cities.[9] The growing interest in computers resulted in the appearance of unofficial (*Pravda* even called them "underground") computer clubs.[10]

Many of the sports groups were merely circles of close friends who playfully called themselves a group. The groups of environmentalists and monument preservers in Leningrad and Moscow seemed to have a well-defined structure and were organizations in the true sense of the word. Moreover, they had a clear program of social activities and political goals.

Why Do Such Groups Appear? The most common explanations in the Soviet press cited the tendency of young people to try to distinguish themselves from others (hence punks and hippies) and the dearth of leisure-time facilities, which forced young people to find their own amusements (hence unofficial rock groups).[11] A frequent target of criticism was the Komsomol, the main official youth organization, which, it was said, had become too bureaucratic to respond effectively to the demands of youth or channel their enthusiasm for social activities. *Pravda* reported that students from an institution of higher education in Moscow had created an informal group "for the vitalization of Komsomol work."[12]

After the advent of *glasnost*, some journalists started to suggest that the appearance of informal organizations might have something to do with societal shortcomings. In March 1987, for example, *Pravda* said that the establishment of informal groups reflected a desire on the part of young people to isolate themselves from real life. While it duly criticized this trend, the newspaper blamed it not on young people themselves, but rather on the social conditions that compelled them to behave in such a way. The gap between words and deeds that, according to the Soviet press, became noticeable in the USSR during the Brezhnev years, soured many young people on officially sanctioned public activities, which they found hypocritical.[13] Other articles in the Soviet press characterized punks, hippies, and rock music fans as the result of pernicious Western influences.[14]

Attitudes of the Authorities Compared. Many informal groups were less engaged politically, less critical of the Soviet Union, and usually less well organized than clearly dissident ones. Sometimes, however, hostile treatment at the hands of the authorities turned apolitical informal groups into openly dissident ones. This happened to the Georgian rock group "Phantom." Formed in 1984, it seemed not very different from other unofficial rock groups. Some of its members, however, also belonged to the Georgian Helsinki group. This fact was upsetting to the Georgian authorities, who started taking repressive measures against the group. The result was that "Phantom" became a dissident organization.[15]

Komsomolskoe znamia printed a neutral article about an informal group in the Crimean resort of Gursuf.[16] A member of the group was quoted as saying that it was pacifist, and the newspaper confirmed this; the group did not arouse the concern of the authorities. By contrast, members of the Moscow Group for the Establishment of Trust Between the USSR and the United States, an unofficial peace group, were constantly harassed by the authorities, who regarded them as dissidents.[17] Of course, the Moscow Group was more active politically and better organized, and therefore more obnoxious to the authorities.

Many informal groups were simply ignored by the authorities. Viktor Mironenko, the head of the Komsomol, complained at the trade-union congress early in 1987 that rock-music fans as well as members of unofficial rock groups had been ostracized by official cultural centers and clubs in the USSR.[18] In 1986, *Komsomolskaia pravda* carried several articles criticizing school teachers as well as Komsomol officials for ignoring the problems of informal groups.[19]

The police occasionally adopted a negative attitude toward members of informal groups. Punks and hippies received especially rough treatment, as did fans of heavy metal music, who set themselves apart by wearing unusual clothes. In March 1987, the Soviet press published a number of articles about "Liubery," who claimed that their goal was to rid Moscow of hippies, rock-music enthusiasts, and punks. The press noted that the victims of the Liubery usually failed to get any protection from the police, who often repressed punks and hippies for being an alien element in Soviet society.[20]

Soviet newspapers disclosed that members of other informal groups, whose activities would have evoked praise from the authorities had they been officially sanctioned, had also been mistreated by the Ministry of Internal Affairs (MVD). In March, *Pravda* reported that members of an informal group in the Far East that fought against illegal hunting had been severely beaten by poachers. For a long time the MVD refrained from initiating a case against the poachers because the group fighting against illegal hunting was informal. In the police's view, that was apparently reason enough not to extend protection to its members.[21]

Activation of Informal Groups. In June 1987, a great deal of press attention was given to the informal Moscow group Pamiat, which was composed of Russian nationalists who advocated the preservation of historic monuments and the protection of the environment.[22] Several Soviet newspapers criticized Pamiat for anti-Semitism and extreme Russian nationalism.[23] No serious steps, however, were taken by the authorities to suppress the society.

Informal groups calling for the preservation of monuments and the protection of the environment also appeared in Leningrad and were quite active. In contrast with Pamiat, however, the Leningrad groups refrained from expressing extreme Russian nationalistic and anti-semitic sentiments; thus they received very positive coverage in *Izvestiia* and *Literaturnaia gazeta*.[24] In early 1987, members of several informal Leningrad groups, including "Spasenie" [Salvation], "Mir" [Peace], "Sovet ekologii kultury" [Council of Cultural Ecology], and the literary group "Klub 81" [Club 81] staged a demonstration in Leningrad protesting the decision of local authorities to demolish the hotel Angleterre, where the Russian poet Sergei Esenin had committed suicide in 1925. Members of the group received an audience with officials of the Leningrad executive and oblast committees. Architect Aleksei Kovalev, the best known activist of the Leningrad movement and head of "Spasenie," signed an article protesting the demolition of the Angleterre, together with such leading Leningrad cultural figures and scholars as Academician Dmitrii Likhachev. The protest was printed in the newspaper *Stroitelnaia gazeta*, which officially identified Kovalev as a member of the Council of Cultural Ecology.[25] In May, Western correspondents reported that Kovalev had applied to be considered as a candidate in the elections to the Leningrad executive commitee.[26]

Evidently, the authorities regarded the groups as a problem in need of a solution. The earlier tactics of ignoring or harassing them seemed no longer effective and appropriate. Despite press criticism, however, the authorities did not intend to suppress them and punish their members.

Izvestiia and *Literaturnaia gazeta* reported that some participants in the Angleterre demonstration were briefly detained but then released; *Izvestiia* warned officials in Leningrad not to take any further repressive action.[27] Evidently, some actions approved by the Moscow leadership were to be expected only against the most radical leaders of Pamiat, including journalist Dmitrii Vasilev and former lecturer at the Znanie society Valerii Emelianov, who both spent a certain time in mental hospitals.

The main goal of the officials was apparently not to get rid of the groups but to bring them under control. Thus, the press printed a proposal to establish special departments in every raion or oblast Komsomol committee to oversee the activities of informal groups.[28] It was also suggested that a special sociological center to study informal groups be established; this center would conduct opinion polls among members of informal groups to discover their concerns.[29] Finally, it was suggested that the newly

established   Soviet Cultural Foundation try to make use of
the activities and   enthusiasm of the members of informal
cultural groups.[30]

In December 1986, a new state organization for war
veterans was founded; one of its goals was to oversee and
control informal groups of Afghan veterans.[31] Another step
was the creation of a new environmental group attached to
the   Soviet   Peace Committee. Called   "Zelenyi   mir"
(Greenpeace), the new association   seemed intended to
utilize   the   energy   and   enthusiasm   of   unofficial
environmentalists for its own purposes.[32]

The central press, apparently reflecting the opinion
of the top leadership, warned local officials against
suppressing informal groups, no matter how unorthodox they
may appear. This might have been regarded as a sign of
relative liberalization. It was clear, however, that the
leadership intended to keep all new trends in the country
under close scrutiny and control.

63
THE JUNE PLENUM: TOO FAR OR NOT FAR ENOUGH?

Philip Hanson and *Elizabeth Teague**

Preparations for the Plenum.   A high-level conference
was held in the Kremlin on June 8 and 9, 1987, to discuss
"the radical restructuring of economic management."[1]
Substantial excerpts from the proceedings were published in
the Soviet press four days later.[2] The conference was
opened by Gorbachev, who also delivered a closing address.
The main speech was delivered by Nikolai Sliunkov, Central
Committee secretary with responsibility for the economy.

Those who addressed the conference were primarily
industrial   enterprise   managers   and   directors--people
involved in the day-to-day management of the economy--and
they came primarily from the USSR's most successful
industrial enterprises.

The impression was created that the Gorbachev
leadership was taking counsel among those leaders whose

*The first section was written by Hanson and Teague
jointly, the second and fifth were written by Teague, the
third and fourth by Hanson.

support it needed to implement its declared policy of devolution of decision-making to the level of the local enterprise.

The delay in publishing details of the meeting strengthened the impression that the issues at stake were contentious. In his closing remarks Gorbachev indicated that there was considerable disagreement even among the specially selected participants. The party leader insisted that everyone had supported *perestroika* but he admitted that the discussion was not just "open and honest" but "perhaps polemical at times." He added that "different approaches and view points" had been expressed on both the economy and "other issues."

Gorbachev's remarks had a defensive ring to them. It was hopeless to expect, he said in his closing remarks, "that on the first try the country will have an ideal Law on the State Enterprise." His words suggested that the draft law had come in for a good deal of criticism, both by those who thought it went too far toward decentralization and by those who did not think it went far enough. Gorbachev also said that the law should be put into effect in order "to find out its strong and weak points." Where necessary, he said, it could then be improved.

In his speech, Gorbachev employed the words "radical reform"--a formulation that he had first used at the 1986 party congress but which he seemed subsequently to have abandoned. He denied that his reform plans would weaken socialism but he went on to say that "those who wish to propose anti-Socialist alternatives should be repulsed." He appeared to be replying both to criticism from conservatives who argued that his calls for greater "democratization" of Soviet society would lead to "anarchy," and to reformist writers at the other end of the spectrum who were beginning to raise questions about Socialist ownership itself. "There are no proposals from the people," Gorbachev said, "to alter the system." But he stressed that decentralization of economic decision-making from the Moscow ministries to the level of the enterprise was essential; otherwise the new legislation would simply be unworkable.

Personnel Changes in the Politburo. A number of important personnel changes were made at the the plenary meeting of the Central Committee held on June 25-26.[3] Three new full members of the Politburo were appointed.

Dmitrii Iazov, who had recently been appointed minister of defense, was named to candidate membership in the Politburo in place of Sergei Sokolov. Sokolov had lost his ministerial post to Iazov in the wake of the Matthias Rust affair. Iazov's upgrading to the Politburo had been widely predicted, and the military as a whole neither gained nor lost from it, for it placed him in the same position as his predecessor.

Two of the new members of the Politburo were closely associated with Gorbachev. One was Aleksandr Iakovlev who, as party secretary with responsibility for propaganda, was believed to be the moving force behind the cultural liberalization. Iakovlev had fallen into disgrace in the early nineteen-seventies after launching a public attack against Russian nationalism, and spent ten years as Soviet ambassador to Canada. He returned to Moscow only after Brezhnev's death. He had since been active not only in the cultural sphere; he was also one of Gorbachev's key foreign policy advisers.

Iakovlev's promotion to full membership in the Politburo could not have been good news for Egor Ligachev, the Kremlin's "chief ideologist". Until then, Iakovlev had been subordinate to Ligachev; now the two men were to be equal in rank, for both were "senior secretaries"--that is, full members of the Politburo and members of the Secretariat. In effect, the party now had two potential "chief ideologists." There were clear differences between the two men in their approaches to such vital matters as the treatment of Stalin and the lengths to which cultural liberalization should be allowed to go. Ligachev had warned that *glasnost* must not be allowed to go too far or too fast; Iakovlev had said that "dogmatism" was the chief danger facing the Soviet Union at the present stage. At a moment when the enemies of *glasnost* had moved from defense to open attack, the balance of power between these two ideological overlords promised to provide a key to the shifting alignments within society itself.

Also likely to prove bad news for Ligachev was the promotion to full Politburo membership of another close Gorbachev associate, Viktor Nikonov, who held responsibility within the Secretariat for agriculture. Over the previous two years, Ligachev had assumed increasing responsibility for this troubled sector of the economy. Ligachev's influence seemed to be reduced now that Nikonov also enjoyed the powers and privileges of a "senior secretary."

The third man appointed to the rank of "senior secretary" was Nikolai Sliunkov, who assumed party oversight of the economy (excluding the defense sector, which remained in the hands of "senior secretary" Lev

Zaikov).   Sliunkov was an associate not of Gorbachev   but
of prime minister Nikolai Ryzhkov. His background was that
of a technocrat and economic administrator, and his field
of expertise was the machine-building industry.

The changes made were extremely significant. First,
they bolstered Gorbachev's position within the leadership.
To a lesser extent, they enhanced the position of Prime
Minister Ryzhkov. Most important of all, perhaps, they led
to a further concentration of power within the party
apparatus and, specifically, within the Secretariat of the
Central Committee, which Gorbachev seemed bent on making
his personal, inner cabinet.

Plenum on the Economy. Gorbachev's speech at the
plenum made his ideas of reform clearer than they had been
before.[4] He seemed to be aiming at a rather awkward
mixture--a system in which part of the output would be
determined by centrally set guidelines and   "state
contracts," and part by market relations between
enterprises and their customers. The resistance even to
this "moderate" reform was severe, and Gorbachev was
apparently not able to push through a package of measures
that would cover more than part of the proposed system. He
asked the Central Committee to do two things: first, to
endorse the draft law on the enterprise; second, to approve
a set of guidelines for complementary changes in prices,
central planning, and the management of industrial
branches.

On the latter, he was apparently unable to secure
agreement on a detailed set of reforms. To get round this,
he asked the plenum to approve a document entitled "Basic
Propositions on the Fundamental Restructuring of the
Economy." This incorporated eleven documents outlining
proposed changes in the functions and staffing of the
central planning agencies, in the price system, and
probably in the management of whole branches and sectors of
the economy.

On June 26 the Central Committee duly gave the
approvals requested by Gorbachev.[5]   The resolution at the
end of the plenum stated, however, that the drafts had been
approved "in the main" (*v osnovnom*). The Central Committee
resolution entrusted the drafts to the Politburo and the
USSR Council of Ministers for implementation, "taking into
account the discussion at the plenum." This suggested
something more than trivial disagreements over points of
detail; indeed, the economist Abel Aganbegian told the
Western press that some differences had been expressed.[6]

Gorbachev's dissatisfaction with the measures taken so far was evident. Despite some improvement in economic performance, he said, the organizational barriers to faster growth had not been removed: "The deceleration mechanism has not been overcome and has not been replaced by an acceleration mechanism." Echoing views enunciated by some of the more radical economists,[7] Gorbachev spoke of the need to find incentive systems that were more powerful than those operating under capitalism.   This, he said, required a rethinking of notions of Socialist property so as to introduce competition into the economy.

Almost a quarter of Gorbachev's speech was devoted to the consumer sector. He was particularly eloquent on the advantages of small contract teams, including family groups, working on a semi-independent basis within the state and collective farms and also on the merits of the (private) household plots that produced over a quarter of Soviet farm-sector food output. He spoke approvingly of a small work-team whose average monthly earnings were 534 rubles, or nearly three times the average state farm wage. He also called for some 0.8 million vacant household plots in the countryside to be made available to city-dwellers to be used for food production. The idea of encouraging the development of small cooperatives or family concerns was presented as an important element of *perestroika*.

Another characteristic of the reform package that was made clear in the general secretary's speech was a kind of "dual economy" approach to the industrial sector. Gorbachev said that the 37,000 industrial enterprises directed from ministries in Moscow should be regrouped into "a few thousand" large, vertically integrated trusts or associations, incorporating all stages of product development from research to series production.

Gorbachev said that he did not expect the enterprises' increased powers to achieve much unless there were changes at the levels of branch ministries and central planning as well.   About these changes, however, Gorbachev was apparently unable to be specific. He spoke of the need for a radical reform of the price system; he said that more prices should be fixed between buying and selling enterprises rather than centrally set. It appeared, however, that the details of price changes remained contentious: Gorbachev called for further public discussion of the issue. Evidently, the removal, or at least reduction, of food price subsidies was on his agenda, and this was almost certainly an idea that had encountered powerful resistance.

The contentious issue of reform of the branch ministries seemed also to be unresolved. So far as the central planning agencies were concerned, Gorbachev said that Gosplan, the State Planning Committee, was to be reshaped and, apparently, to lose much of its detailed branch-planning function. The struggle over these further changes was yet to be resolved.

One indication of the nature of the resistance to Gorbachev's ideas was the list of senior officials who were criticized by name in the Soviet leader's speech. There were thirteen of them at the level of branch minister or above. They included the Gosplan chairman, Nikolai Talyzin, a nonvoting member of the Politburo, and two deputy prime ministers--Lev Voronin, the chairman of the State Supply Committee, and Ivan Silaev, the head of the Machine-Building Bureau, one of the new "superministries."

Of the thirteen, eight had been appointed since Gorbachev became general secretary. The proportion of "Gorbachev appointees" among those censured was close to the proportion of Gorbachev appointees among all branch ministers and higher-level state economic administrators. The people concerned were not necessarily opposed to Gorbachev's ideas for reform, but they were failing to achieve what Gorbachev wanted from them. This seemed to be more a matter of the departmental interests over which they presided than of their being "holdovers from the Brezhnev era."

The early indications were that a moderate, limited reform was being pushed through with considerable determination, against strong resistance.

<u>Centerpiece of Economic Reform</u>. The law on the state enterprise, approved by the Supreme Soviet on June 30,[8] was a central element in Gorbachev's economic reorganization package. As the Soviet leader himself made clear before the Supreme Soviet meeting, however, the enterprise law on its own did not constitute the reorganization.[9] There were complementary changes that he was seeking in the laws, statutes, and decrees that were supposed to govern the behavior of other players in the Soviet economic game--notably, the branch ministries and the central planning agencies. Those changes were still to come. The highest hurdle was the implementation of these well-intentioned laws and decrees. The road to the present "precrisis state"[10] of the Soviet economy was paved with good decrees.

Two new ideas were embodied in the law. One was that the labor force should have an active role in decision-making in the enterprise. The other was that the enterprise should set its own annual and five-year plans, free of directives from above, and that these should be based in part on contracts freely negotiated with customers and suppliers.

The powers of the work force and its council remained limited: the choice of top management had to be approved by the "superior organ" of the enterprise, and the law declared that the enterprise party organization was to "direct" or "guide" the work of the collective.   The work-force assembly acquired the potential, however, to be more than merely decorative. It could choose to elect its council by secret ballot, and management could not provide more than one in four of the council membership.   Neither of these provisions was in the original draft of the law published in February,[11] so the subsequent amendment had favored "democratization."

Throughout the text of the law there were references to the enterprise's "superior organ." Nowhere was the idea of subordination repudiated, and there were frequent references to the branch ministry as a body supervising the enterprise. The enterprise was to set its own annual and five-year plans, but it was to be guided by branch objectives, control figures, and state orders. The role of the ministry in confirming these orders had not been mentioned in the original draft.

Some of the other provisions of the law were clearly reformist in intention. All in all, the enterprise law contained provisions that would be compatible with a market reform.   It also contained provisions that would be compatible with a continuation of centrally administered resource allocation. In part this probably reflected the curious, semimarket schema outlined in Gorbachev's plenum speech.   In addition, however, it seemed that the law was more conservative in its general implications than Gorbachev's speech had been; and it contained both stronger provisions on labor participation in decisions and weaker provisions on the enterprise's emancipation from control by the ministry than the draft version of the law had contained in February. In other words, the law had every appearance of being a compromise document.   That did not necessarily make it ineffective, but the compromises in this case were on the critical issue of enterprise autonomy.

The reorganization scheme was closer to the "moderate" or "rationalizing" brand of Soviet reform than to the more radical market reform that some Soviet economists had espoused. Gorbachev's reform package had one advantage and one disadvantage over a "pure" or academic version of the rationalizers' scheme. The advantage was that an important part of the economy--chiefly in the farm sector and in nonfood consumer goods and services--was supposed to be converted to the market mechanism and that private enterprise and small, unplanned cooperatives were to be encouraged in that sector. The disadvantage was that the branch-ministry system seemed to have been left in place. A crucial identification mark for a real market reformer was that he or she advocated the abolition of branch ministries in general, with just a general ministry for industry left to perform functions similar to those performed by such ministries in Western countries. The fate of the ministries emerged as a key issue in the politics of the reform process.

Why was the economic reform process under Gorbachev taking such a tortuous course? To what extent did the measures taken represent the leader's own view of what was desirable? When the measures being introduced changed somewhat in character, as they had done in the preceding months, what caused them to change? Was it that the leader and his close advisers were managing to set out a larger part of an agenda they had had all along? In other words, had they changed because Gorbachev's personal authority had increased? Or had Gorbachev simply been learning on the job and changing his ideas about what was needed? The developments suggested that the acquisition of more authority was at least part of the answer.

The resort to more private (and cooperative) initiative, especially in agriculture, was particularly slow in coming. Two prominent economists, Oleg Bogomolov and Nikolai Shmelev, made the point that in agriculture a large and rapid payoff for reform was most likely. Perhaps a clue to the politics of reform was precisely that they were only now making this point--as though debate followed decisions rather than the other way around.[12] The radical reformers' view of all these unclear and often anomalous developments in the reform process was summed up by Shmelev: "Today what alarms us most of all is precisely the lack of decisiveness in moving toward common sense."

Gorbachev Answers His Critics. On July 10, Gorbachev held a six-hour meeting with senior officials of the press and the creative unions. That the meeting had taken place was not officially announced until July 14, when the text of his address was read on the main Soviet television news program, "Vremia."[13]

The meeting's ostensible purpose was to brief representatives of the Soviet press on the June plenum. Gorbachev used the opportunity to defend his policies, presumably against criticism voiced at the plenum.

Gorbachev began with a frank admission that disagreements existed over his policies and that they had "sharpened and intensified" since the January 1987 plenum. Some people, he stated, thought that *perestroika* was proceeding too slowly; others thought it was going ahead too rapidly. He made his own view clear: things were not, he said, changing "as quickly and as fully as we would have wished."

Gorbachev defended his political reforms. They were, he said, an essential precondition of economic reform. "The processes of restructuring in the economy will not work," he said, "unless they are implemented in coordination with all the other spheres of life of our society--above all, the spiritual and political, the sphere of democracy, and many others." He argued, too, as he had before, that there was no alternative to the policies he proposed. Society, he said, was "a mass of unsolved problems;" the economic situation, in particular, was "very strained."

Gorbachev stressed that his policies were aimed at shaking the Soviet population out of their state of apathy. "The most important thing, the main point of everything we are doing," he told his listeners, "is to rouse people,...to develop the process of democratization in order to involve people's energy and interest." He spoke repeatedly of the need to bear in mind the interests of the individual as well as those of the state. Society, he said, "cannot be made dynamic and viable if one does not take interests into account and if, through feedback, these interests do not have an influence on the policy of society." This could be achieved, Gorbachev asserted, through "democratization" but, to be effective, the process must be placed in a legal framework. "Now that the atmosphere of openness [and] the processes of democratization are beginning to get under way in the country," he stated, "we . . . must underpin them with an appropriate juridical foundation."

Gorbachev acknowledged that many people were unhappy with his policies and that these concerns had been raised the June plenum. He summed up the misgivings of his critics as follows:

Will not the new phase turn into a negation of all
that has gone before? Have we not forgotten our
history? Does the present policy not amount to
devaluing what was achieved by previous generations?

Gorbachev encouraged the media to speak out. Certain
comrades, he said, were already poised to demand an end to
criticism, but this position was not correct. In response
to those who accused the press of "sensationalism," he said
that, although there had been some "extremes," nonetheless
"I have no reason for any great political reproaches
[since] they took place within the framework of socialism."
He continued:

We are . . . as it were, going through the school of
democracy. We are learning. Our political culture
is still inadequate. Our standard of debate is
inadequate, our ability to respect the point of view
even of our friend and comrade--even that is
inadequate.

Gorbachev went so far as to speak of the desirability
of "socialist pluralism,"[14] calling on his listeners to
remember that "even in the most extreme point of view there
is something valuable, something rational, because a person
who defends his point of view honestly shows concern for
the common cause." At the same time, the general secretary
made it clear that there were limits beyond which the press
should not go.

Gorbachev's speech served as a reminder that the basic
objective of *glasnost* and *perestroika* was not to dismantle
the one-party Soviet state, but to improve it, to render it
stronger, more effective and more credible in the eyes of a
population no longer willing to tolerate--as Gorbachev
himself put it--"contradictions between the word and the
deed."

The Soviet leader appeared to have become convinced
during his first two years in power that popular apathy and
alienation were so great that the economy could not be
restored to health without some relaxation of political and
social controls. In September 1986, Gorbachev spoke for
the first time of the "democratization" of Soviet society
as his main priority.

After his call for electoral reform at the plenary
meeting of the Central Committee of the CPSU in January
1987, resistance to Gorbachev's policies became

increasingly outspoken, and appeared to enjoy support at quite high levels of the hierarchy.

That Gorbachev's attitude to political reform had undergone a gradual evolution could not be conclusively demonstrated.   Some Western observers   suggested   the opposite, arguing that his growing insistence on the need for political reform reflected his increasing confidence and security within the leadership.   The development that seemed to take place in Gorbachev's approach to the Stalin question lent support to the first interpretation.

Two months after his election as party leader, Gorbachev paid tribute to Stalin's wartime leadership.[15] He subsequently dismissed Stalinism as "a concept thought up by the enemies of communism."[16] In June 1986, he explained that digging up the past would "dissipate our energy and set people at odds with one another."[17]

Six months later, Gorbachev was himself making thinly veiled references to Stalin's baleful legacy.[18] On July 10, 1987, he spoke more openly than ever before about Stalin's crimes.   At the same time, his failure to acknowledge their full scope seemed likely to prompt courageous members of the intelligentsia to try to push the subject further. This in turn threatened to spur those who feared that *glasnost* had already escaped control to make a further counterattack.

NOTES

1.   Gorbachev's Changing Priorities

1 "A conversation between members of the USSR Writers' Union and Gorbachev," a samizdat account published by Radio Liberty's Samizdat Archive as AS 5785.
2 *Pravda*, February 12, 1986.
3 *Ibid.*, January 14, 1987.
4 RL Supplement 1/86, "Turnover in the Soviet Elite under Gorbachev," July 8, 1986; Michel Tatu, "Domestic Policy," paper presented at the Workshop on National Security Issues after the 27th Party Congress of the USSR, Brussels, November 6-7, 1986.
5 *Pravda*, February 8, 1987.
6 For example, Moscow Television, September 18, 1986.
7 For further information on popular reaction to Gorbachev's campaign, see paper 60, "Popular Dissatisfaction with Gorbachev" in this volume.
8 See paper 6, "The Tool of Restructuring" in this volume.
9 As reported in the US State Department's annual report on human rights observance worldwide; RFE/RL Special, Washington, February 19, 1987.
10 *Krasnaia zvezda*, September 19, 1986.
11 See *Soviet/East European Survey 1985-1986* (Durham, NC: Duke University Press, 1987), pp. 371-89
12 AS 5785
13 Moscow Television, September 18, 1986.
14 See paper 8, "Rediscovering Soviet History" in this volume.

2.   Conflict of Interests and Ideas: The January Plenum

1 Moscow Television, September 18, 1986. See also paper 60 in this volume.
2 Aleksandr Gelman, "Chto snachala, chto potom...," *Literaturnaia gazeta* September 10, 1986.
3 Valentin Tolstykh, "Sutdela," *Sovetskaia kultura*, September 16, 1986.
4 See *Soviet/East European Survey, 1983-1984*, (Durham, NC: Duke University Press, 1985), pp. 22-24
5 V. Davidovich, "Sovetskoe obshchestvo: edinstvo v mnogoobrazii," *Pravda*, September 12, 1986.

6 See Ernst Kux, "Contradictions in Soviet Socialism," *Problems of Communism*, November-December 1984, pp. 1-27.
7 M. S. Gorbachev, *Zhivoe tvorchestvo naroda*, (Moscow: Politizdat, 1984).
8 Soviet Television, October 1, 1986.
9 TASS (in Russian), October 1, 1986.
10 Radio Moscow, October 1, 1986.
11 *Pravda*, November 23, 1982.
12 Gorbachev, *Zhivoe tvorchestvo naroda*, p.11.
13 *Pravda*, October 1, 1986.
14 Quoted by Reuters, January 16, 1987.
15 *Izvestiia*, January 17, 1987.
16 *Pravda*, January 20 and 21, 1987.
17 Anatolii Butenko, "Perestroika i sotsialnaia borba v obshchestve," *Moscow News*, No. 1, January 4, 1987.
18 *Voprosy filosofii*, No. 10, 1982, pp. 16-29, and No. 2, 1984, pp. 124-29. See also Ernst Kux, "Contradictions in Soviet Socialism," *Problems of Communism*, November-December, 1984, pp. 1-27.
19 See papers 1 and 60 in this volume.
20 See Giulietto Chiesa's interview with Iakovlev published in *l'Unità*, December 9, 1986.
21 TASS, January 27, 1987.

3. Curbs on Arbitrary Behavior

1 Radio Moscow-2, October 2, 1986.
2 *Literaturnaia gazeta*, no. 39, 1986, p. 13.
3 The Russian word *prigovor* connotes both verdict and sentence, which are pronounced in a Soviet court by the judge (theoretically after consultation with the people's assessors).
4 *Literaturnaia gazeta*, no. 39, 1986, p. 13. On October 4, 1986, *Izvestiia* published an interview with Academician Vladimir Kudriavtsev, the director of the Institute of State and Law, who reiterated Iakovlev's proposals.
5 *Sotsialisticheskaia zakonnost*, no. 8, 1986, pp. 1-3; see also RL 297/86, "Former Premier of Uzbekistan Expelled from the CPSU," August 6,
6 *Bakinskii rabochii*, June 29, 1986.
7 See RL 224/86.
8 *Literaturnaia gazeta*, no. 40, 1986, p. 10.
9 *Izvestiia*, October 17, 1986.
10 See RL 394/86 "Changes in Regulations Governing

Administration of Labor Camps and Prisons," October 16, 1986.

11 *Khronika tekushchikh sobytii*, no. 28, p. 16.
12 See RL 197/86, "Some of the Formalities Soviet Citizens Face in Exercising Their Right to Go Abroad," May 20, 1986.
13 AS 5024.
14 *Vedomosti Verkhovnogo Soveta SSSR*, no. 37, 1986, Article 782.
15 See, for example, Christian Schmidt-Häuer, "Die geheime Stütze des Umbaus," *Die Zeit*, January 16, 1987; "Alles ist erlaubt," *Der Spiegel*, January 19, 1987, pp. 112-13; and "Glasnost Arrives at the KGB" *Newsweek*, January 19, 1987, p. 20.
16 "U TsK Kompartii Ukrain," *Radianska Ukraina*, January 8, 1987.
17 *Pravda*, January 8, 1987.
18 Dmitrii Kazutin, "People Who Don't Like the Truth," *Moscow News*, January 18, 1987.
19 *Pravda*, February 15, 1987.

4.   Burlatskii on Democratization

1 Moscow Television, September 18, 1986. An incomplete version of Gorbachev's speech appeared in *Pravda*, September 19, 1986.
2 *Literaturnaia gazeta*, June 11, 1986.
3 *Ibid.*, October 1, 1986.
4 October 7, 1986. See also *La Repubblica* of the same date. Gorbachev's meeting with a group of Soviet writers took place on June 9, 1986, but the full text of his address did not appear in the official Soviet media. See *Pravda*, June 21, 1986 .

5.   Experiment with Contested Elections

1 TASS (in English), January 27, 1987.
2 AP, January 29, 1987.
3 See the revealing round-table discussion on party personnel policy in *Sovetskaia Rossiia*, October 29, 1986.
4 Murray Yanowitch, *Work in the Soviet Union* (Armonk, New York: M. E. Sharpe, 1985), p. 118.

5 *Komsomolskaia   pravda*, January 6 and 21,   1987;   TASS,
  January 21, 1987; Radio Moscow, January 31, 1987.
  Opposition to the election of managerial staff seemed to
  be expressed by the   newspaper   *Sotsialisticheskaia
  industriia*, which called in its issue of February 17,
  1987, for caution in introducing the new method on the
  grounds that the USSR lacked adequate experience of such
  elections.
6 Victor Zaslavsky and Robert J. Brym,   "The Functions of
  Elections in the USSR," *Soviet Studies*, July, 1978, pp.
  362-71, at p. 363.
7 Rasma Karklins, "Soviet Elections Revisited: Voter
  Abstention in Noncompetitive Voting," *American Political
  Science Review*, June 1986, pp. 449-469, at p. 465.
8 *Komsomolskaia pravda*, November 16, 19, and 26, 1986; and
  December 20, 1986.
9 See   RL 230/86,   "Soviet Press   Treatment   of   the
  Proceedings of the Congress of Cinema Workers," June 16,
  1986;   RL 9/87, "The Congress of Theater Workers of the
  USSR," December 23, 1986.
10 *Trud*, March 6, 1987.
11 *Pravda*, *Sovetskaia Rossiia*, February 10, 1987.
12 *Sovetskaia Rossiia*, February 10, 1987.
13 *Moskovskie novosti*, February 8, 1987, p. 12.
14 *Izvestiia*, July 18, 1987.

6.   The Tool of Restructuring

1 See   RL 102/86, "Gorbachev's Speech to the Twenty-seventh
  Party Congress: Reaffirmation of *Glasnost*," February 26,
  1986.
2 *El País*, April 3, 1986.
3 For discussions of   drug   abuse   see, for example,
  Sovetskaia Latviia, September 13, 1986; *Sovetskaia
  molodezh*, September 16, 1986; and *Moskovskaia pravda*,
  September 27, 1986. Commentaries on moral decay in the
  USSR are discussed in RL 354/86, "The Morality Crisis in
  Soviet Society: Its Treatment in Samizdat and in the
  Official Press," September 12, 1986. The debate about
  Soviet health care is explored in RL 289/86, "Quality of
  Soviet Health Care under Attack," July 28, 1986.
  Criticism of censorship in the USSR is examined in RL
  366/86, "Overcautious Editors and Publishers Attacked by
  Soviet Literary Critic," September 24, 1986, and RL
  168/86, "System of Press   Control under Discussion,"

April 22, 1986.

4 *Literaturnaia gazeta*, September 17, 1986.

5 *Izvestiia*, October 2, 1986. (A reference to the dismissal of the director of MGIMO was made in a speech by Egor Ligachev at the national conference of heads of social sciences departments of Soviet higher educational institutes held in Moscow at the end of September.)

6 The interview was carried by Radio Moscow-1, September 11, 1986.

7 The report on the Politburo meeting that both shelved the river diversion projects, and rejected the design for the World War II victory monument, was published in *Pravda*, August 16, 1986.

8 At the eighth congress of Soviet writers both the design for the victory monument and the river diversion projects were discussed, and the speeches at the congress were reported in *Literaturnaia gazeta*, July 2, 1986.

9 For the text of Ligachev's speech at the party congress, see *Pravda*, February 28, 1986.

10 *Komsomolskaia pravda*, September 7, 1986.

11 RL 378/86, "Shcherbitsky Files a Report in *Pravda*," October 1, 1986.

12 AS 5761, Oleg Volkov: "Notes on *Glasnost*." See also RL 354/86.

13 Radio Moscow-1, September 11, 1986. See also RL 354/86.

14 See RL 290/86, "Soviet TV Airs Relatively Frank Discussion of East-West Relations," July 25, 1986.

15 *Pravda*, May 19, 1986.

16 See RL 177/86, "Chernobyl--'Openness' in Action," May 2, 1986, and *Soviet/East European Survey*, *1985-86*, (Durham, NC: Duke University Press, 1987), pp. 371-376.

17 See RL 187/86, "USSR Grudgingly Discloses More Facts about Chernobyl," May 12, 1986.

18 For reports on the earthquakes in Moldavia, see TASS, September 1 and 4, 1986, and *Izvestiia*, September 4, 1986. The sinking of the *Admiral Nakhimov* was reported on in *Sovetskaia Rossiia*, September 6, 1986, and *Literaturnaia gazeta*, September 10, 1986, and that of the nuclear submarine in TASS , October 4 and 6, 1986.

19 See Reuters, October 5, 1986.

20 See RL 72/86, "Little '*Glasnost*' in the Local Press," February 12, 1986.

21 For the text of Gorbachev's speech at the party congress, see *Pravda*, February 26, 1986.

22 See, for instance, *Pravda*, June 13 and 14, 1986.

23 *Literaturnaia gazeta*, October 8, 1986.

24 The program was shown on Moscow Television, 19:35 P.M. , July 17, 1986. See also paper 10 in this volume.
25 See, for instance, *Pravda*, October 1, 1986.
26 See, for instance, *ibid.*, June 8, 1986.
27 AS 5770. Excerpts from a letter to an unspecified address about some aspects of life in the Ukraine after the Chernobyl accident.
28 Radio Moscow-1, February 13, 1987, 7:00 P.M.
29 See RL 399/86, "Gorbachev Meets Soviet Writers: A Samizdat Account," October 23, 1986.
30 *Teatr*, No. 8, 1986, pp. 2-7; RL 358/86, "The Chief Kremlin Ideologist on Theater Repertoires," September 22, 1986.
31 Such statements were made many times in Gorbachev's speeches; see, for instance, the text of his speech in Khabarovsk, *Pravda*, August 1, 1986.
32 See RS 160/86; "SSSR: Novaia informatsionnaia politika (NIP), "September 30, 1986.
33 *Pravda*, March 25, 1986.
34 See RL 266/86, "Manifestations of a 'Thaw' in Soviet Cultural Policy," July 15, 1986, and RL 38/86, "The Soviet Press under Gorbachev," January 21, 1986.

7. Return of Forbidden Literature

1 *Literaturnaia gazeta*, no. 27, 1986.
2 Reuter, UPI, AP, June 30, 1986.
3 See RS 81/86, "Teatr epokhi Gorbacheva," May 5, 1986.
4 See RL 239/86, "A Disputes Commission for Soviet Cinema," June 23, 1986.
5 See RL 361/85, "Soviet Academician Defends Avant-Garde Artists," October 17, 1985; *Literaturnaia gazeta*, no. 7, 1986, p. 4.
6 See RL 357/85, "Gorbachev's New Propaganda Chief a Critic of Russian Nationalists," October 31, 1985.
7 *Politicheskii dnevnik* (Amsterdam: The Alexander Herzen Foundation, 1972), Vol. 1, p. 187.
8 For the text of the speech, see *The New York Times*, December 18, 1985.
9 See RL 48/86, "New Tone In Soviet Media's Treatment of Émigrés," January 30, 1986; RL 237/86, "Through the Looking Glass of Culture: Sketches for a Portrait of Petr Nilovich Demichev," June 20, 1986.
10 *The Washington Post*, June 24, 1986.

11 From Konstantin Chernenko's speech on the occasion of the fiftieth anniversary of the First Congress of Soviet Writers, *Izvestiia*, September 26, 1984.
12 See RL 314/85, "Classics of Twentieth-Century Russian Literature: A Reappraisal by Soviet Critics?," September 19, 1985; RL 185/86, "Reappraisal of Twentieth-Century Russian Writers Continues," May 9, 1986.
13 Aleksandr Solzhenitsyn, *Sobranie sochinenii* (Paris: YMCA, 1973), Vol. 6, pp. 39-52 and 126-28.
14 *Literaturnaia gazeta*, no. 25, 1986, p. 12.
15 *Literaturnaia Rossiia*, no. 19, 1986, p. 16.
16 See RL 239/86, "A Disputes Commission for Soviet Cinema," June 23, 1986; RS 109/86 "VIII sezd pisatelei SSSR: ego perspektivy," June 23, 1986.
17 See RL 200/86, "Former Outcast Elected Head of Cinema Workers' Union," May 21, 1986.
18 See RS 113/86 "VIII sezd pisatelei SSSR: ego itogi," June 30, 1986.
19 On these writers, see RL 353/85, "Early Twentieth-Century Writers Not Published in the USSR," September 25, 1985.
20 See RL 115/86, "The Twenty-Seventh Party Congress: Old Guard of Soviet Arts Has Its Say," March 10, 1986.
21 *The Washington Post*, July 1, 1986.
22 See RL 276/83, "Twenty-Five Years since the Death of Mikhail Zoshchenko: A Retrospective," July 21, 1983.
23 *Nedelia*, no. 46, 1986, pp. 8-9; *Literaturnaia gazeta*, December 3, 1986, p. 8.
24 See RL 9/87, "The Congress of Theater Workers of the USSR," December 23, 1986.
25 *Sovetskaia kultura*, November 22, 1986.
26 *Ibid*.
27 *Sovetskaia kultura*, October 4, 1986.
28 *Teatr*, no. 8, 1986, p. 4.
29 *Nedelia*, no. 46, 1986; *Sovetskaia kultura*, December 9, 1986.
30 *Nedelia*, no. 46, 1986.
31. For a review, see *Teatr*, no. 12, 1985, pp. 80-92.
32 *Sovetskaia kultura*, November 29, 1986.
33 See RL 9/87.
34 *Sovetskaia kultura*, September 9, 1986.
35 AP, August 26; Reuter, August 28, 1986.
36 *Sovetskaia Belorussiia*, March 24, 1964;
37 *Literaturnaia Rossiia*, no. 15, 1986, p. 18.
38 *Ogonek*, no. 17, 1986, pp. 26-28.
39 *Novyi mir*, no. 9, 1986, pp. 196-227.
40 *Ogonek*, no. 36, 1986, pp. 18-24.

41 See George Orwell's letter to Gleb Struve in *The Collected Essays, Journalism, and Letters of George Orwell,* (London: Penguin, 1968), Vol. 3, p. 118.
42 See M. Shane's introductory article to Evgenii Zamiatin, *Ogni Sviatogo Dominika: Obshchestvo pochetnykh zvonarei* (Würzburg: Jal-reprint, 1973), p. v.
43 *Literaturnaia Rossiia,* December 26, 1986, pp. 18-19.
44 *Literaturnaia gazeta,* January 26, 1983, p. 9.
45 *Literaturnaia gazeta,* no. 4 1987, pp. 1 and 12.
46 See RL 9/87, "The Congress of Theater Workers of the USSR," December 23, 1986.
47 *Nedelia,* no. 46, 1986, pp. 8-9.
48 RL 43/87, "The Unofficial Rehabilitation of Nikolai Bukharin," January 29, 1987; RL 96/87, "Russian Political Figures in the Soviet Press," March 5, 1987.
49 RL 454/86, "Lakshin's Article on Abuladze's Film *Repentance,*" December 8, 1986.
50 RL 102/87, "A Dissident Is Vindicated," March 17, 1987.
51 *Ogonek,* no. 9, 1987, p. 29.
52 *Ibid.,* p. 28.
53 *Literaturnaia gazeta,* no. 12, 1987, p. 13.
54 *Pravda,* October 12, 1986.
55 *Komsomolskaia pravda,* December 10, 1986.
56 *Sovetskii ekran,* no. 6, 1987, pp. 4-5.
57 *Literaturnaia gazeta,* no. 19, 1987, pp. 2-11.
58 *Sovetskaia kultura,* May 17, 1987; *Pravda,* May 19, 1987.
59 *Golos Rodiny,* no. 2, 1987, p. 8.
60 *Literaturnaia gazeta,* no. 1, 1987, p. 7.
61 *Sovetskaia kultura,* March 21, 1987.
62 *Literaturnaia Rossiia,* March 27, 1987, pp. 2-4.
63 *Ibid.,* pp. 6-7.
64 Mikhalkov may have had in mind the film director Sergei Bondarchuk, a favorite of Khrushchev and Brezhnev, who lost his influence in Soviet cinema during the Congress of Soviet Cinema Workers in May, 1986. See RL 211/86, "Whirlwind of Change in Soviet Cinema," May 30, 1986.
65 See RL 54/87, "*Moscow News*--The Cutting Edge of *Glasnost,*"
66 *Sovetskaia Rossiia,* March 25, 1987.

8.   Rediscovering Soviet History

1 See, for instance, the interview with historian Stanislav Tiutiukin in *Izvestiia,* May 3, 1987.
2 See Stephen F. Cohen in *The Nation,* January 31, 1987.

3 See RL 70/86, "Treatment of Stalin in Soviet Propaganda Thirty Years after the Twentieth Congress," February 13, 1986; and RL 399/86, "Gorbachev Meets Soviet Writers: A Samizdat Account," October 23, 1986.
4 *Pravda*, January 28, 1987.
5 *Ibid.*, February 14, 1987.
6 *Ibid.*, March 24, 1987.
7 *Kommunist*, No. 14, 1985, pp. 105-116.
8 *Moscow News*, No. 2, 1987; and *Sovetskaia kultura*, March 21, 1987.
9 Afanasev's institute organized lectures for Moscow youth on Stalinism. See *Frankfurter Rundschau*, March 31, 1987.
10 The issue of Stalin's unpreparedness for World War II had already been touched upon in the USSR. See RL 12/86, "More About Stalin in Mikoyan's Memoirs," December 17, 1985.
11 TASS , March 4, 1987. See also RL 93/87, "Soviet Historian Calls for Rehabilitation of Old Bolsheviks," March 6, 1987.
12 *Izvestiia*, April 3, 1987.
13 Vsevolod Meierkhold was a famous Soviet theater producer. From 1920 until 1938 he was director of a theater in Moscow, which since 1923 bore his name. Meierkhold was arrested in 1939.
14 Boris Rodos was mentioned by Nikita Khrushchev in his secret speech to the Twentieth Party Congress in 1956 as "an empty person with the brains of a chicken, a complete moral degenerate." It seems that Rodos was shot soon afterwards.
15 Vyshinskii was state prosecutor at the show trials of the nineteen-thirties.
16 *Novyi mir*, No. 4, 1987; and *Sobesednik*, No.4, 1987.
17 *Sovetskaia kultura*, February 26, 1987.
18 Issue No. 21 of *Moscow News* continued the discussion over Afanasev's views, with some Soviet historians criticizing Afanasev.

9.   Criticism of the Afghanistan War

1 RL 9/85, "Ukrainian Samizdat Journal Gives Details of Casualties in Afghanistan," January 10, 1985. See also the statement addressed to USSR Defense Minister Marshal Ustinov in June 1984, by three leading Ukrainian Catholic activists. AS 5410, pp. 8-9.
2 *Moscow News*, no. 5, 1987, p. 3.

3 UPI , January 15, 1987; *Toronto Globe and Mail*, January 22, 1987.

10. Telebridges with the West

1 *Radio*, no. 18, 1985, p. 13.
2 For more details on the new information policy, see "The Limits of Gorbachev's Openness," *Soviet Analyst*, October 9, 1986, and RS 160/86, "SSSR: Novaia informatsionnaia politika (NIP)," September 30, 1986.
3 "Ostankino-87," *Izvestiia*, January 27, 1987.
4 *Pravda*, October 22, 1986.
5 *Govorit i pokazyvaet Moskva*, no. 16, 1985, p. 19.
6 Moscow Television, January 31, 1987.
7 Soviet television selected one and a half hours out of five hours of video material. *Sovetskaia kultura*, January 22, 1987.
8 First deputy of the chief of *Gosteleradio*, L. Kravchenko, at speech to a congress of journalists, reported in *Sovetskaia kultura*, April 17, 1987.
9 "Uchit nenavisti," *Izvestiia*, March 14, 1987, p. 7.
10 The letter was addressed to the newspaper with copies to the KGB and *Gosteleradio*. Appealing to the KGB on the pages of the Soviet press is in itself unusual. It was clear in this instance that the author of the letter was looking to the KGB for support, since the KGB formally had nothing to do with television broadcasts.
11 Central Television (11:20 P.M. Moscow time), March 31, 1987.
12 Vladimir Simonov served as a *Novosti* correspondent in the United States and, before that, in Great Britain.
13 Central Television, April 4, 1987.
14 "Before and after Midnight" (*Do i posle polnochi*) was modeled on Western talk shows and was the first attempt by Soviet television to combine entertainment and current events in a single program. A similar program was planned for morning showing.
15 *Izvestiia*, November 4, 1985.
16 Vladimir Molchanov was a rising star of Soviet television. He appeared as a commentator on the news show "Vremia," where he was known for his inventive anti-Americanism.
17 See Walter R. Roberts and Harold E. Engle "The Global Information Revolution and the Communist World", *Washington Quarterly*, spring 1986, pp. 145-146.

11.   Prostitution in the USSR

1 *Literaturnaia gazeta*, no. 47, 1985, p. 13.
2 *Sobesednik*, no. 3 (January), 1986, p. 13.
3 *Sovetskaia Belorussiia*, July 18, 1986, p. 3.
4 *Sovetskaia molodezh*, August 30, 1986, p. 4.
5 *Ibid.*

12.   Drug Abuse

1 *Argumenty i fakty*, no. 5, 1983, p. 14.
2 *Novoe vremia*, no. 20, 1980, p. 30.
3 *Sovetskaia kultura*, May 20, 1986.
4 *Moskovskaia pravda*, April 20, 1986.
5 *Zhurnalist*, no. 5, 1986, p. 31.
6 *Komsomolskaia pravda*, June 8, 1986.
7 *Izvestiia*, June 27, 1986.
8 *Novyi mir*, no. 6, 1986, p. 54.
9 RL 70/85 "Novosti Press Agency Disputes Claims about Alcoholism in USSR", March 4, 1985
10 *Komsomolskaia pravda*, June 8, 1986.
11 *Pravda Ukrainy*, June 22, 1986.
12 *Moskovskaia pravda*, June 14, 1986.
13 *Ibid.*, June 12, 1986.
14 *Uchitelskaia gazeta*, January 15, 1987.
15 *Pravda*, January 6, 1987.
16 *Sotsialisticheskaia industriia*, January 13, 1987.
17 *Pravda*, January 6, 1987.
18 *Literaturnaia gazeta*, no. 34, 1986, p. 11.
19 *Time*, January 19, 1987.

13.   Faltering Health Services

1 Nicholas Eberstadt, *Wall Street Journal*, April 30, 1986.
2 *World Health Statistics Annual* (Geneva: WHO , 1985), p. 467.
3 *Ibid.*
4 Eberstadt, *loc. cit.*
5 *Ibid.*
6 Polish Situation Report/13, *Radio Free Europe Research*, August 29, 1986, item 6.

15.   Little *Glasnost* on Economic Accomplishment

1 *Pravda*, January 18, 1987.
2 The 1981-85 data can be found in *Narkhoz 85*, p. 40. The growth rates of investment and of farm output were measured between 1980 and 1985 and not (as they were often presented) between five-year periods.
3 For most products, figures accurate to one decimal place can be calculated from the *Narkhoz* data for 1985, though this cannot usually be done from the plan fulfillment report on its own.
4 See RL 439/86, "Puzzles in the 1985 Statistics," November 20, 1986.
5 *Pravda*, November 18, 1986.
6 *Ibid.*, November 27, 1985.
7 *Narkhoz 85*, p. 409.
8 *Ibid.*, pp. 411 and 469.
9 *Ibid.*, pp. 240-241.

16.   Social Justice and Economic Progress

1 V. Z. Rogovin, "Sotsialnaia spravedlivost i sotsialis-ticheskoe raspredelenie zhiznennykh blag," *Voprosy filosofii*, no. 9, 1986, pp. 3-20; T. Zaslavskaia, "Chelovecheskii faktor razvitiia ekonomiki i sotsialnaia spravedlivost," *Kommunist*, no. 13, September 1986, pp. 61-73.
2 Rogovin, pp. 4-5.
3 Zaslavskaia, p. 66.
4 *Ibid.*, p. 61.
5 Rogovin, p. 7.
6 The practice of "leveling" was first attacked by Stalin, in his six-point speech of June 25, 1931.
7 Zaslavskaia, p. 66.
8 *Ibid.*
9 V. I. Lenin, *Polnoe sobranie sochinenii*, 5th edition, (Moscow: Gosudarstvennoe izdatelstvo politicheskoi literatury, 1962), Vol. 33, p. 93. Emphasis in the original.
10 *Los Angeles Times*, September 23, 1986. See also RL 172/86, "'Nonlabor Incomes' in the USSR," April 24, 1986; and RL 229/86, "Housing and 'Nonlabor Incomes' in the USSR," June 11, 1986.
11 Rogovin, pp. 17-18.
12 *Ibid.*, p. 17.

13 Zaslavskaia, p. 69.
14 Rogovin, p. 12. Rogovin may have worked on this study ("Netrudovoi dokhod," *Izvestiia*, July 7, 1985). In any case, he likes to cite it (*e.g.*, "Lichnaia sobstvennost," *Komsomolskaia pravda*, November 12, 1985).
15 Zaslavskaia, p. 67.
16 "Nasledstvo," *Komsomolskaia pravda*, June 7, 1985.
17 "Taktika peremen," *Izvestiia*, April 18, 1986.
18 Rogovin, p. 15. It seems that a tax on royalties already existed (RL 452/83, "Rates of Income Tax in the Soviet Union," December 1, 1983, p. 3). Perhaps Rogovin meant a larger tax on royalties.
19 Housing subsidy from "Zhilishchnaia problema: kak ona reshaetsia v stranakh SEV," *Argumenty i fakty*, no. 44 (October 29), 1985; meat and dairy products subsidy from Zaslavskaia, p. 71.
20 Zaslavskaia, p. 72.
21 Zaslavskaia, pp. 72-3; Rogovin, pp. 10-11.
22 Rogovin, p. 9.
23 *Ibid*. Eltsin's speech was printed in *Pravda*, February 27, 1986.
24 Zaslavskaia, p. 70.
25 "Odin, kak semero," *Sovetskaia kultura*, January 4, 1986.
26 She notes with satisfaction that "the change in the conditions of employment" will affect "the least valuable workers" most strongly and says that "such a situation will help to raise the social value of places in public production, strengthen labor discipline, and increase the quality of work" (p. 70).
27 Moscow Television, February 25, 1986.
28 See RL 289/86, "Quality of Soviet Health Care under Attack," July 28, 1986.
29 There were indications that the campaign against "non-labor incomes" may have been hitting the wrong people, however. For example, *Pravda* reported in July that the crackdown was hurting farmers' markets in several large cities ("Vinovat li ogurets?," *Pravda*, July 14, 1986). Later, *Literaturnaia gazeta* published a letter from a mother of five who was charged with "speculation" for trying to make ends meet by selling handwork at a local market ("V seme rodilos piatero detei. Kak byt?"), *Literaturnaia gazeta*, October 1, 1986, p. 13).
30 Rogovin, p. 16.
31 "Blagotvoritelnost iz chuzhogo karmana," *Literaturnaia gazeta*, February 19, 1986.
32 In a speech of December 5, 1908, M. P. Bok, *Vospominaniia o moem ottse P. A. Stolypine*, (New York:

Chekhov Press, 1953, pp. 290-1).

33 *Bolshevik*, no. 9-10, 1925, pp. 4-5. Cited in Stephen F. Cohen, *Bukharin and the Bolshevik Revolution: A Political Biography, 1888-1938*, (New York: Oxford University Press, 1980), pp. 176-7.
34 Rogovin, pp. 13, 19.
35 Alexander Zinoviev, *The Reality of Communism*, (London: Paladin Books, 1985), p. 151.
36 Rogovin, p. 19.

17.   Expansion of the Cooperative Sector

1 *Pravda*, February 26, 1986.
2 *Ibid.*, March 7, 1986.
3 Radio Moscow, July 31, 1986.
4 *Ibid.*, August 15, 1986.
5 *Pravda*, February 26, 1986.
6 This account draws on the excellent study by Alfred B. Evans, Jr., "Developed Socialism in Soviet Ideology," *Soviet Studies*, July, 1977, pp. 409-428.
7 See James P. Scanlan, *Marxism in the USSR*, (Ithaca, N.Y.: Cornell University Press, 1985), p. 229.
8 *Programma Kommunisticheskoi partii Sovetskogo Soiuza*, (Moscow: Politizdat, 1961).
9 V. I. Lenin, *Polnoe sobranie sochinenii*, 5th edition, Moscow: Politizdat, 1958-65), Vol. 36, p.139; Vol. 40, pp. 104 and 260.
10 Pyotr Demichev, "Developed Socialism--Stage on the Way to Communism," *World Marxist Review*, no. 1, 1973, pp. 10-22.
11 Brezhnev's speech to the USSR Supreme Soviet on October 4, 1977, reprinted in *Konstitutsiia obshchenarodnogo gosudarstva*, (Moscow: Politizdat, 1978), pp. 81-98 at p. 87.
12 Vadim Pechenev in *Pravda*, May 8, 1981.
13 R. I. Kosolapov, *Sotsializm. K voprosam teorii*, 2nd edition, Moscow, 1979, pp. 523-24, cited in Scanlan, op. cit., p. 238.
14 Richard Kosolapov, "Metodologicheskie problemy teorii razvitogo sotsializma," *Problemy mira i sotsializma*, no. 9, 1974. As the source of this quotation, Kosolapov cited Karl Marx and Friedrich Engels, *Sochineniia*, 2nd edition, (Moscow: Politizdat, 1968), Vol. 46, Part I, p. 229.
15 The term "integral socialism" appears in P. Fedoseev,

"Dialektika obshchestvennoi zhizni," *Problemy mira i sotsializma*, no. 9, 1981, pp. 25-30 at p. 27; and in R. Kosolapov, "Vklad XXIV, XXV i XXVI sezdov KPSS v razrabotku teoreticheskikh i politicheskikh problem razvitogo sotsializma i perekhoda k kommunizmu," *Kommunist*, no. 5, 1982, pp. 54-67 at p. 64. Both sources cite V. I. Lenin, *Polnoe sobranie sochinenii*, 5th edition, (Moscow: Politizdat, 1958-65), Vol. 36, p. 306.

16 *Pravda*, July 31, 1981.

17 The so-called "Novosibirsk Document" was published by Radio Liberty's Samizdat Archive as AS 5042.

18 *Pravda*, March 4, 1983.

19 *Literaturnaia gazeta*, February 1, 1984.

20 *Pravda*, July 20, 1984. "Unfortunately," Kosolapov wrote, "certain people . . . depict the desired state of affairs as similar to Dühring's 'economic communes,' which are independent of one another and which compete among themselves in the marketplace."

21 R. I. Kosolapov, "Dialektika nashei zhizni," *Oktiabr*, no. 5, 1984, pp. 167-75.

22 See A. P. Butenko, "Razvitoe sotsialisticheskoe obshchestvo: sushchnost i problemy," *Voprosy filosofii*, no. 6, 1976, pp. 25-41; *ibid.*, "Kontseptsiia razvitogo sotsializma," *Obshchestvennye nauki*, no. 1, 1981, pp. 5-17; *ibid.*, "Socialism: Forms and Deformations," *New Times*, no. 6, 1982, pp. 5-7.

23 Radio Moscow, April 22, 1982.

24 TASS, June 15, 1983.

25 R. Kosolapov, "Vklad XXIV, XXV i XXVI sezdov KPSS v razrabotku teoreticheskikh i politicheskikh problem razvitogo sotsializma i perekhoda k kommunizmu," *Kommunist*, no. 5, 1982, pp. 54-67.

26 *Ibid.*, p. 63.

27 *Voprosy filosofii*, no. 6, 1984, pp. 23-39.

28 *Ibid.*, no. 8, 1984, p. 6.

29 *Pravda*, July 20, 1984.

30 *Ibid.*, October 26, 1985.

31 Mikhail Rutkevich in *Sovetskaia Rossiia*, December 13, 1985.

32 Radio Moscow, July 24, 1986.

33 "Doklad Generalnogo sekretaria TsK KPSS M. S. Gorbacheva na Plenume TsK KPSS 15 oktiabria 1985 goda," *Kommunist*, no. 15, 1985, pp. 4-11; see also RL 314/86, "The Decline and Fall of Developed Socialism'," August 19, 1986.

18.   Approaching the Ecological Barrier

1 Ulrich Weissenburger, *Environmental Problems and Protection in the Soviet Union* (Part 1), West German Federal Institute for East European and International Studies, no. 52, 1984, p. III.

2 Karl Schlögel, *The Ecological Discussion in the Soviet Union*, West German Federal Institute for East European and International Studies, no. 49, 1984, p. 3 (summary).

3 See for example B. V. Flow, "The Environmental Crisis in the GDR," RAD Background Report/164 (GDR), *RFER*, September 3, 1984; Czechoslovak Situation Report/8, *RFER*, May 13, 1985, item 2; Czechoslovak SR/2, February 6, 1986, item 9; and Charter 77, Document No. 36, December 1983. Also *Soviet/East European Survey 1983-1984*, (Durham, NC: Duke University Press, 1985), pp.304-13.

4 See for example E. M. Snell, "Economic Efficiency in Eastern Europe," in *Economic Developments in Countries of Eastern Europe* (Washington D.C.: US Congress Joint Economic Committee, 1970).

5 For a succinct comparison of the treatment of the environment, see Horst Mendershausen, "Political Economy and the Environmental Imperative," *The Rand Paper Series, P-7174*, (Santa Monica, CA: The Rand Corporation, January 1986).

6 B. V. Flow, *loc. cit.*; R. T. S., "East Germany: New Developments in Environmental Protection", RAD BR/81 (GDR), *RFER*, August 16, 1985; and Czechoslovak SR/9, *RFER*, June 18, 1986, item 5. For the situation in Bulgaria, see Wolf Oschlies, "Combines Robbing the Soil's Fertility," *Rheinischer Merkur*, 20 June 1986.

19.   Low Targets and Low Growth

1 *Ekonomicheskaia gazeta*, no. 21, 1987, p. 2; UPI, June 13, 1987.

2 *Pravda*, December 18, 1986, and January 18, 1987, respectively.

20.   Sources of Security Reconsidered

1 M. S. Gorbachev, "Politicheskii doklad Tsentralnogo Komiteta KPSS XXVII sezdu Kommunisticheskoi Partii

Sovetskogo Soiuza," *Kommunist*, no. 4, 1986, pp. 5-80, at
p. 6.

2 *Ibid.*, p. 19.

3 Gorbachev's speech to the Central Committee plenum of
April 1985, almost entirely concerned domestic affairs.
It yielded no evidence that a set of such
"considerations" was drawn up. See M. S. Gorbachev,
"O sozyve ocherednogo XXVII sezda KPSS i zadachakh,
sviazannykh s ego podgotovkoi i provedeniem," *Kommunist*,
no. 7, 1985, pp. 4-20.

4 Gorbachev, "Politicheskii doklad . . . ," *Kommunist*, no.
4, 1986, pp. 54-55.

5 *Ibid.*, p. 55.

6 *Ibid.*, pp. 55-56. At variance with Gorbachev's attack
on "peace offensives," former Foreign Minister Gromyko
remarked that the USSR was not afraid to have its
foreign initiatives recognized as such. *Pravda* (Second
Edition), February 27, 1986, pp. 5-6 at p. 6.

7 The phrase "equality and equal security" had been a
sacrosanct Soviet principle at talks on arms reduction
with the US. In practical terms, "equal security" meant
that the USSR demanded that all bilateral arms
reductions make allowance for the other military threats
faced (from China, and from the independent nuclear
forces of Britain and France, for example). In its most
extreme form, this principle made security for the USSR
mean insecurity for everyone else--that is, the Soviet
Union could claim the right to possess armed forces
equal to the total forces of all its opponents.
Although Soviet negotiators never pursued the principle
of "equal security" to this extreme, it nonetheless
severely hindered bilateral efforts at arms control. In
his report to the party congress, Gorbachev failed to
mention the principle and referred, instead, to a need
to lower military potentials "to the limits of
reasonable sufficiency" (see Gorbachev, "Politicheskii
doklad . . . ," *Kommunist*, no. 4, 1986, pp. 56 and
62). In the first instance, he stated explicitly that
"the nature and level of these limits" was determined by
the US and its "bloc partners." After the party congress
Gorbachev continued to slight the phrase "equality and
equal security," mentioning instead the criterion of
"reasonable sufficiency." See, for example, his speech
in Vladivostok on July 28, 1986. Two important speeches
by USSR Foreign Minister Shevardnadze--at the party
congress and on the occasion of Lenin's birthday--also
failed to include the phrase "equality and equal

security" (see *Pravda* [Second Edition], for March 2, 1986, pp. 3-4, and April 23, 1986, pp. 1-2). The principle was, however, cited by Dobrynin.

8 A. Dobrynin, "Za beziadernyi mir, navstrechu XXI veka," *Kommunist*, no. 9, 1986, pp. 18-31, at pp. 24-5. See the commentary by Michel Tatu in *Le Monde*, August 7, 1986, pp. 1 and 4.

9 *Ibid.*, pp. 26 and 27-8.

10 *Ibid.*, p. 28.

11 These academic discussions may well have taken place in the years prior to 1981; the present analysis, however, limits itself to the period since 1981.

12 See, respectively, L. I. Brezhnev, *op. cit.*, pp. 4-25, and Gorbachev, "Politicheskii doklad . . . ," *Kommunist*, no. 4, 1986, pp. 53-64.

13 See L. I. Brezhnev, *op. cit.*, p. 18.

14 *Ibid.*, p. 21.

15 *Ibid.*, p. 24.

16 While the evidence adduced above demonstrates a clear discontinuity between the views of Gorbachev and Brezhnev on several important foreign-policy and security issues, it is for further research to determine whether any of Gorbachev's "new political thinking" was foreshadowed in Chernenko's or--more likely--in Andropov's speeches and writings.

17 Anatolii Gromyko and Vladimir Lomeiko, *Novoe myshlenie v iadernyi vek*, (Moscow: Mezhdunarodnye otnosheniia,1984.) Anatolii Gromyko had been director of the USSR Academy of Sciences' Africa Institute since 1976. Lomeiko, a well-known journalist, headed the foreign ministry's Press Department until June 1986. According to *The Washington Post* correspondent Dusko Doder, the book was so popular that its press run of 100,000 copies sold out in one week. See "Soviet Public Debates Arms," *The Washington Post*, January 5, 1986, pp. Al and All.

18 G. Kh. Shakhnazarov, "Logika politicheskogo myshleniia v iadernuyu eru," *Voprosy filosofii*, no. 5, 1984, pp. 63-74.

19 Archie Brown, "The Future in His Hands," *Times Literary Supplement*, July 18, 1986, pp. 781-2 at p. 781.

20 A span of three months--with Shakhnazarov's article appearing first--separated the dates when Shakhnazarov's analysis and the Gromyko/Lomeiko book were signed to press.

21 Shakhnazarov, *op.cit.*, p. 66.

22 *Ibid.*, p. 74.

23 See L. Graham, "Ivan Timofeevich Frolov: New Editor of

Kommunist," *Soviet News*, Vol. II, no. 2a, May 15, 1986.

24 G. L. Smirnov, "Za reshitelnyi povorot filosofskikh is-sledovanii k sotsialnoi praktike," *Voprosy filosofii*, no. 9, 1983, pp. 3-19, at p. 17.

25 F. Burlatskii, "Filosofiia mira," *Obshchestvennye nauki*, no. 1, 1986, pp. 56-70, at p. 57 and following.

26 V. V. Zagladin, "Programmnye tseli KPSS i globalnye problemy," *Voprosy filosofii*, no. 2, 1986, pp. 3-15.

27 *Ibid.*, p. 5.

28 P. N. Fedoseev, "Dialektika v sovremennom mire," *Voprosy filosofii*, no. 5, 1986, pp. 4-22, at p. 7.

29 See Gorbachev, "Politicheskii doklad...", *Kommunist*, no. 4, 1986, at pp. 17-8. Gorbachev lists only environmental pollution and the exhaustion of natural resources as global problems.

30 V. V. Zagladin, *op. cit.*, p. 9.

31 For information on the changes in the foreign ministry, see Alexander Rahr, RL 274/86, "Winds of Change Hit Foreign Ministry," July 16, 1986.

32 For a reference to this new directorate, see *Novoe vremia*, no. 28, 1986, p. 4.

33 See Gary Thatcher, "Moscow Shifts Arms-Control Team," *The Christian Science Monitor*, July 30, 1986.

34 Starodubov was head of the Soviet delegation to the Standing Consultative Commission from 1979 to 1986, and served as a military adviser to Soviet delegations at several US-Soviet nuclear arms talks.

35 See *Pravda* (Second Edition), May 30, 1986, p. 6, for the announcement of Petrovskii's promotion.

36 A partial listing of his activities from June to September included: participation in a press conference in Moscow on June 5; membership in the delegation to Budapest with Gorbachev on June 9; speech at Geneva Disarmament Conference on June 24; participation in a press conference in Moscow on July 1; visit to the Netherlands to deliver a message to Dutch government from Gorbachev concerning arms-control matters on July 15; participation in Soviet-US consultations on nonproliferation matters from July 28 to August 1.

37 See his articles in *SShA*, no. 7, 1984; *MEMO*, nos. 6, 1985, and 6, 1986. All the articles were the lead ones in the respective issues of the journal.

38 See Charles Glickham, RL 269/85, "The Nonproliferation Treaty: A Rarity in Soviet-American Efforts at Nuclear Arms Control," August 19, 1985, p. 13, and *Soviet/East European Survey 1985 - 1986* (Durham, NC: Duke University Press, 1987), pp. 99-104.

39 Radio Moscow first identified him as head of IMEMO on December 1, 1985. *Pravda* (Second Edition), p. 4, similarly identified Primakov on December 28, 1985.

40 See, for example, Gary Lee, "Soviets Court World Press in Geneva," *The Washington Post*, November 16, 1985, p. A12.

41 See, respectively, E. Primakov, "Put v budushchee," *Pravda* (Second Edition), January 22, 1986, p. 4.; and E. Primakov, "Filosofiia bezopasnosti," *ibid.*, (Second Edition), March 17, 1986, p. 6.

42 See Charles Glickham, RL 261/86, "Signs of Change in Soviet Attitudes towards Arms Control Verification," July 14, 1986, p. 3.

43 See Leonid Brezhnev's comments in an interview with *Der Spiegel*, reprinted in *Pravda* of November 3, 1981, p. 1.

44 RL 261/86, p. 3.

45 See the comments by Major General Viktor Tatarnikov, the Soviet military representative at the Conference on Disarmament in Europe, in an interview with Novosti Press Agency on August 15, 1986.

46 The phrase was that of Roland Timerbaev, a deputy chief of the Soviet foreign ministry's International Organizations Department and a past member of several arms-control negotiating teams. See R. Timerbaev, *Kontrol za ogranicheniem vooruzhenii i razoruzheniem*, (Moscow: Mezhdunarodnye otnosheniia, 1983), p. 98.

47 See Gorbachev's remarks in *Pravda* (Second Edition), March 14, 1986, p. 1.

48 V. Shabanov, "Vazhneishii element protsessa razoruzheniia," *Izvestiia*, March 24, 1986, p. 5.

49 Michael Gordon, "Moscow Said to Signal Willingness to Work on Arms Pact Verification," *The New York Times*, June 22, 1986, p. 14.

50 For two weak analyses of the relationship between the Soviet military and the civilian leadership, see Gary Lee, "Gorbachev's Rein on Military," *The Washington Post*, July 29, 1986, p. A10, and Martin Sieff, in *The Washington Times*, July 2, 1986.

51 See L. I. Brezhnev, "Otchetnyi doklad . . . ," at p. 6; also see the article by Chief of the General Staff Akhromeev commemorating Armed Forces Day in *Krasnaia zvezda* (Second Edition), February 23, 1986, p. 2.

52 Stephen Meyer of the Massachusetts Institute of Technology was one of the first to note this change. See his comments in the article by Walter Pincus, "Soviet Ability to Accelerate Arms Debated," *The Washington Post*, June 23, 1986, pp. A1 and A18. For

the phrase, see "Programma Kommunisticheskoi Partii
Sovetskogo Soiuza: Novaia redaktsiia," *Kommunist*, no. 4,
1986, p. 131.
53 For the text of Sokolov's speech, see *Pravda* (Second
Edition), March 2, 1986, p. 6; V. Shabanov,
"Materialnaia osnova oboronnoi moshchi," *Krasnaia zvezda*
(Second Edition), August 15, 1986, pp. 2-3, at p. 2.
54 "Soveshchanie vneshnepoliticheskikh rabotnikov," *Pravda*
(Second Edition), May 24, 1986, p. 1.

21.   The Reykjavik Watershed

1 TASS, October 22, 1986.
2 *Ibid.*, October 14, 1986.
3 *Ibid.*
4 *Ibid.*, October 22, 1986.
5 *Ibid.*, October 14, 1986.
6 See RL 391/85, "Moscow and the Geneva Summit: New
Realism or an Orderly Retreat," November 26, 1985.
7 TASS, October 22, 1986.
8 Reuters, October 22, 1986.
9 TASS, October 14, 1986.
10 *Ibid.*, October 22, 1986.
11 *Ibid.*
12 *Ibid.*
13 *Literaturnaia gazeta*, October 22, 1986.

22.   Wisdom of Soviet Missiles Questioned

1 *Moscow News*, No. 10, 1987, p. 3.
2 *Ibid.*, No. 11, 1987, p. 3.
3 *Rudé právo*, March 17, 1987.

23.   Red Square Landing Shakes up Top Military

1 *Krasnaia zvezda*, May 29, 1987.
2 AP, May 28, 1987.
3 Reuters, May 30, 1987.
4 Gary Lee in *The Washington Post*, May 31, 1987.
5 See the biography in *Krasnaia zvezda*, April 13, 1985;
also *Voennyi entsiklopedicheskii slovar*, (Moscow:
Voennoe izdatelstvo 1986, p. 844.

6   Philip Taubman in *The New York Times*, June 1, 1987.
7   *Krasnaia zvezda*, July 9, 1983.
8   *Ibid.*, January 16, 1987.

24.   Toward an INF Treaty and Beyond

1 Reuters (Paris), March 6, 1987; *The New York Times*
   (Paris), March 7, 1987.
2 AP (Moscow), February 27, 1987.
3 UPI, Reuters (Washington), March 12, 1987.
4 TASS (Moscow), April 14, 1987.
5 Quoted in the *Los Angeles Times*, April 19, 1987.
6 TASS (Moscow), April 23, 1987.
7 AP (Geneva), March 23, 1987.
8 UPI (Geneva), April 28, 1987.
9 Reuters (Bonn), May 15, 1987.
10 RFE Correspondent's Report (Bonn), May 18, 1987.
11 Reuters (Stavanger), May 15, 1987.
12 *Ibid.*, (Washington), May 15, 1987.
13 TASS (Moscow), May 19, 1987.
14 Reuters (Washington), May 21, 1987.
15 *Ibid.*, (East Berlin), May 29, 1987.
16 Radio Moscow, May 26, 1987, as monitored by FBIS.
17 TASS (East Berlin), May 29, 1987.
18 Reuters and AP (Geneva), June 16, 1987; Reuter and AP
   (Washington), June 20 and 23, 1987; Xinhua (in English),
   June 17 and 18, 1987; Kyodo (in English), June 19, 1987.
19 TASS (in English), May 16, 19, and 20 and June 22, 1987;
   The Washington Post, May 20, 1987; Reuters (Washington),
   May 20, 1987.
20 *Pravda*, July 6, 1987; ČTK (Warsaw), July 2, 1987; AP
   (Budapest), June 18, 1987; *The Washington Post*, June 17,
   1987.
21 *The New York Times*, April 29, 1987; *The Times*, June 17,
   1987; *The Washington Post*, June 17, 25 and 26 and July
   3, 1987; TASS (in English), July 9, 1987.

25.   The Vladivostok Speech

1 TASS, Reuters, and AP, August 6, 1986.
2 AFP, July 30, 1986.
3 Reuters, August 5, 1986, and AP, August 6, 1986.
4 UPI and Xinhua, August 6, 1986.

5 UPI, August 6, 1986, and *The New York Times*, August 7, 1986.
6 AP , August 7, 1986; UPI, August 9, 1986; and Xinhua, August 10, 1986.
7 S. Ginzberg, "How Negotiations Stalled on Cambodia," *l'Unità*, 15 October 1986.

26.   Into Southeast Asia and the Pacific

1 *Izvestiia*, February 5, 1986.
2 Reuters, March 17, 1986.
3 *Izvestiia*, June 29, 1986.
4 AP September 5, 1986.
5 Reuters, August 27, 1985.
6 *The Wall Street Journal*, December 30, 1985.
7 TANJUG (in English), June 4, 1986.
8 *The Daily Telegraph*, March 27, 1985.
9 *The Washington Post*, June 13, 1986.
10 *The Christian Science Monitor*, June 4, 1986.
11 UPI, October 16, 1986, and Reuters, October 15, 1986.
12 *The Washington Post*, February 3, 1987, and *The Wall Street Journal*, February 2, 1987.
13 *The Washington Post*, February 3, 1987, and AP January 1987, and December 16, 1986.
14 *The Washington Post*, June 13, 1986, and Reuters, June 25, 1986.
15 Moscow Television and TASS , July 28, 1986. On the speech, see RL 294/86, "Gorbachev Takes a Closer Look at Asia and the Pacific from Vladivostok," July 28, 1986.
16 *Vedomosti Verkhovnogo Soveta SSSR*, No. 27, July 2, 1986.
17 *Neue Zürcher Zeitung*, July 6/7, 1986.
18 *Ibid*.
19 *The Journal of Commerce*, July 9, 1986.
20 Sheldon M. Simon, "The Great Powers and Southeast Asia: Cautious Minuet of Dangerous Tango?", *Asian Survey*, Vol. 25, September 9, 1985.
21 Leszek Buszynski, "Vietnam's ASEAN Diplomacy: Assertion of a *Fait Accompli, The World Today*, April 1986.
22 TASS, August 6, 1986.
23 *Izvestiia*, June 7, 1986.

27.   Iran and the Gulf War

1 See RL 61/86, "Kornienko's Visit to Teheran and the Limited Prospects for a Soviet-Iranian Reconciliation," February 4, 1986.

2 AP and UPI, August 10, 1986

3 IRNA, August 26 and 27, 1986.

4 Radio Moscow (in Persian), August 28, 1986.

5 AP, December 12, 1986.

6 *Christian Science Monitor*, December 17, 1986.

7 See, for example, Radio Moscow (in Persian), May 8; *Novosti*, May 9; Radio Moscow (in Persian), June 24; *Izvestiia*, August 29; Radio Moscow, September 16; TASS, September 18; and *Novosti*, October 29 1986.

8 TANJUG, December 15, 1986.

9 On these developments, see RL 61/86, "Kornienko's Visit to Teheran and the Limited Prospects for a Soviet-Iranian Reconciliation," February 4, 1986; RL 47/87, "Moscow and Teheran: Cultivating Mutual Interests Without Budging on Political Differences," February 3, 1987.

10 See, for instance, TASS, UPI, and Reuters, February 13, 1987.

11 See RL 61/86.
Reuters, April 8; TASS, April 16, 19, and 20, and UPI April 20, 1987.

13 G. H. Hansen, "Soviets, Saudis Make Syrians Pay the Piper," *The Los Angeles Times*, May 10, 1987; "Soviets, Saudis Aim to Unite Arab World in Bid for Mideast Meeting," *Christian Science Monitor*, May 11, 1987.

14 UPI, May 1, 1987.

15 Norman Kempster, "Gulf--U.S. Reiterates Offer To Protect Gulf Shipping," *The Los Angeles Times*, April 16, 1987; Richard Halloran, "Both Superpowers Have Warships in the Gulf," *The New York Times*, May 3, 1987.

16 Reuters, April 15, 1987.

17 IRNA and AP, April 15.

18 TANJUG, May 7, 1987.

19 *The New York Times* and *The Washington Post*, May 9, 1987.

20 *The Washington Post*, May 9, 1987.

21 AP, May 9, 1987.

22 KUNA, May 11, 1987.

23 *Al-Rai al-A'am*, Kuwait, June 17, 1987; Reuters, June 17, 1987.

24 *Ibid.*

25 AP, UPI, June 17, 1987.

26 TASS, July 17, 1987.

27 TASS, August 7, 1987; AP, August 7, 1987.
28 TASS, July 21, 1987
29 AP, July 18, 1987.
30 *The New York Times*, June 30, 1987.
31 RFE/RL Special, August 10, 1987.
32 TASS, June 29, 1987.
33 *Literaturnaia gazeta*, August 5, 1987.
34 TASS, July 21, 1987.
35 *Ibid.*
36 The Soviet Union first stationed warships in the Gulf in the autumn of 1986, after Iranian gunboats started halting Soviet cargo ships carrying arms for Iraq via the Kuwaiti port of Shwaiba. The Soviet Navy sent three minesweepers, a destroyer, and a supply ship from its base at Aden in South Yemen (*The Los Angeles Times*, August 7, 1987).
37 AP, July 17, 1987.

29.   Human Rights and Foreign Policy

1 TASS, November 5, 1986.
2 At a news conference the same day in Vienna, Soviet Foreign Ministry spokesman Gennadii Gerasimov announced new legal measures to speed up emigration procedures as part of what he called "a far-reaching process toward serious reforms that will introduce more democracy to our country." AP, November 5, 1986.
3 AP , October 29, 1986. See also RL 412/86, "Yurii Kashlev To Head Soviet Delegation to Helsinki Follow-Up Conference in Vienna," October 30, 1986.
4 AP, October 29, 1986.
5 TASS, February 14, 15, 16,1987; Radio Moscow, February 15, 1987; Moscow Television, February 16, 1987.
6 See TASS and AP, February 15, 1987.
7 Reuters, February 15, 1987.
8 *The Guardian*, February 16, 1987.
9 AP and Reuters, February 15, 1987.
10 *The New York Times* and *The Washington Post*, Febuary 17, 1987.
11 *The New York Times*, February 11, 1987; and RFE/RL Special (Brown), February 12, 1987.

30.   The Kazakhstan Riots

1 See E. Ligachev's speech at Twenty-seventh CPSU Congress, *Pravda*, February 28, 1986.
2 December 18, 1986.
3 AP, December 19, 1986, quoting Deputy Foreign Minister V. F. Petrovskii; higher figure quoted in *The Guardian*, December 22, 1986.
4 TASS (in English), December 19, 1986.
5 *The Guardian*, December 30, 1986.
6 *Soviet Area Audience and Opinion Research*, Background Reports 12/80 and 4/82.
7 RL 114/84, "Olzhas Suleimenov Elected First Secretary of Writers' Union of Kazakhstan," March 20, 1984.
8 *Pravda*, August 28, 1986.
9 *Argumenty i fakty*, No. 16, 1987.
10 February 10, 1987.
11 No. 1, 1987.
12 *Kazakhstanskaia pravda*, January 7 and 11, 1987.
13 *Ibid.*, February 4, 1987.

31.   Language Demands in Belorussia and the Ukraine

1 *Literatura i mastatstva*, October 24, 1986.
2 RL 100/87, "Soviet Cultural Figures at the Berlin Academy of Arts," March 12, 1987.
3 Letters to Gorbachev: New Documents from Soviet Byelorussia, London, The Association of Byelorussians in Great Britain, 1987, 18 pp.
4 *Literaturnaia gazeta*, May 6, 1987
5 *Literaturna Ukraina*, November 13, 1986. See also the interview with the director of the Dnipro publishing house in *Silski visti*, November 24, 1986.
6 *Kultura i zhyttya*, October 19, 1986.
7 See Roman Szporluk, "The Ukraine and the Ukrainians," in Zev Katz, Rosemarie Rogers, and Frederic Harned (ed.), *Handbook of Major Soviet Nationalities*, (New York and London: The Free Press, 1975), pp. 28-29.
8 *Kultura i zhyttya*, October 19, 1986.
9 *Literaturna Ukraina*, November 27, 1986.
10 *Ibid.*, March 5, 1987.
11 See *Pravda*, February 13, 1987. See also RL 242/86, "Academician Bromlei Writes About Nationality Relations," June 26, 1986.
12 For the Ukrainian text, see *Radyanska osvita*, February

6, 1987.

13 See Roman Solchanyk, "Language Politics in the Ukraine," in Isabelle Kreindler (ed.), *Sociolinguistic Perspectives on Soviet National Languages: Their Past, Present and Future* (Berlin-New York-Amsterdam: Mouton de Gruyter, 1985), pp. 76-78.

14 M. N. Guboglo, *Sovremennye etnoiazykovye protsessy v SSSR. Osnovnye faktory i tendentsii razvitiia natsionalnorusskogo dvuiazychia*, (Moscow: Nauka, 1984), p. 140.

15 "Dukhovna misiya slova," [The Spiritual Mission of Words] *Literaturna Ukraina*, March 12, 1987.

16 See Roman Solchanyk, "Russian Language and Soviet Politics," *Soviet Studies*, Vol. 34, No. 1 (January), 1982, pp. 23-42.

17 See Solchanyk, "Language Politics in the Ukraine," *opus cit.*, p 77.

18 Fomenko's speech is published in *Radianska osvita*, May 19, 1987.

32.   Nationality Discord in Estonia

1 *Sirp ja Vasar*, November 28, 1986, p. 4.

2 See Baltic Area Situation Report 1/87, *RFER*, January 28, 1987, item 1.

3 Russian schools required two hours of Estonian instruction a week in grades 4 through 7; three hours a week in grades 8 and 10, and four hours a week in grade 9. Four-year elementary schools also offered two hours in grades 1 and 2. Estonians, on the other hand, began Russian with either 3 hours a week in Russian beginning in first grade or four hours a week in second grade. All Estonians had to take four hours a week of Russian from grades 4 to 11, with the exception of three hours in grade 8. See *Nõukogude Õpetaja*, March 21, 1987, for the curricula of Estonian and Russian language schools.

4 *Udu Toonela Jõelt* [Fog off the River of the Land of the Dead], (Rome: Maarjamaa, 1974).

5 The initial proposal appeared in *Sirp ja Vasar*. The more substantial article appeared in the October 10, 1986 issue of the weekly.

6 *Sirp ja Vasar*, February 27, 1987.

7 May 29, 1987.

8 For a discussion of earlier treatments of these issues in the Estonian press, see Baltic Area Situation

Reports/1 and 3, *RFER*, January 28, and May 8, 1987.

33.   Pamiat takes to the Streets

1 *Sovetskaia kultura*, April 14, 1987; *Literaturnaia gazeta*, No. 17, 1987, p. 10.
2 TASS May 13, 1987.
3 *Moskovskaia pravda*, May 7, 1987.
4 *Moskovskie novosti*, No. 20, 1987, p. 4.
5 *Russkaia mysl*, March 27, 1987, p. 7.
6 For an English translation, see *Jews and Jewish Topics in Soviet and East European Publications*, No. 4, The Hebrew University of Jerusalem, Winter 1986-87, pp. 46-53.
7 *Russkaia mysl*, November 21, 1986.   The author sees in national Bolshevism a Soviet analogue of German National Socialism.
8 *Ibid.*, March 27, 1987, p. 7.
9 See RL 357/85, "Gorbachev's New Propaganda Chief a Critic of Russian Nationalists," October 31, 1985.
10 *Russkaia mysl*, May 15, 1987, p. 5.
11 *Ogonek*, No. 1, 1987, pp. 3-4; *Sovetskaia kultura*, April 18, 1987.
12 *Sovetskaia kultura*, March 31, 1987.

34.   The Springs of Prague and Moscow

1 Vasil Biľak and other Czechoslovak officials repeatedly said that each country's "specific conditions" had to be taken into account when Soviet reforms were considered for implementation outside the USSR and that the Prague Spring experience would not be repeated.   See Czechoslovak Situation Report/3, *RFER*, March 6, 1987, items 1 to 3.   Their anxiety found response in what CPSU CC Secretary Vadim Medvedev told socialist journalists accredited in Moscow on 18 February 1987 as reported by Czechoslovak Television on the same day, 7.30 P.M.

35.   The Ultracautious Reformers

1 See "The Eighth Congress of Soviet Writers: An Appraisal," RL 264/86, July 15, 1986; and

"Manifestations of a 'Thaw" in Soviet Cultural Policy,"
RL 266/86, July 15, 1986.

2 The delegation consisted of CPCS Secretariat member and Editor-in-Chief of *Rudé Právo* Zdeněk Hoření; heads of CC departments and CC members Otto Čmolík and Vasil Bejda; Presidium and Slovak CC member Ľudovít Pezlár; Director of Czechoslovak Radio Jan Riško; Director of Czechoslovak Television Jan Zelenka; and Slovak CC Secretariat member Bohuš Trávníček.

3 All information on the Central Committee session is taken from AP, DPA, and Reuters (Prague), December 5 to 7, 1986, as well as from reports by Radio Prague.

4 See *ibid.*, no. 15, November 14, 1986, item 1.

5 The difference between both approaches can be formulated as follows. The more radical Hungarian and Chinese reforms ultimately aimed at approximating their levels of productivity (and technological levels) to those achieved by the advanced market-based economies; in the pursuit of this objective they were willing to open up their economies and countenance the costs of marketization, such as inflation and unemployment. The "minimalist" approach took no such risks. It did not aim at approximating the productivity levels of the Western economies but desired merely a relative improvement of its own performance. It opened toward the CMEA rather than to the West.

6 Enterprises (and individuals), for example, were to be more severely penalized for producing substandard goods, and quality-control bodies were to get more powers. Also, the availability of funds for investment were to be tightened; and the authorities were contemplating a withdrawal of funds for projects that were particularly poorly managed.

7 Biľak first articulated his attitude toward "restructuring" in his speech to the party ideological commission in February; he then developed his views in an interview with *Rudé právo* February 20, 1987, p. 1). The content of his speech was paraphrased by Moscow's *Pravda* (February 12, 1987, p. 4), and his *Rudé právo* interview was reprinted in the East German party daily *Neues Deutschland*. Biľak's line was also voiced in Moscow by Karel Hoffmann, the Czechoslovak delegate to the Soviet trade unions' congress (see *Pravda* (Bratislava), February 26, 1987, p. 7).

8 Biľak's line did not directly oppose the reformist course; Biľak made it clear in his *Rudé právo* inteview that the "normalization" charter in Czechoslovakia

("Lessons from the Crisis") did sanction the 1968 reforms in principle. Reforms by themselves did not amount to a "counterrevolution," which occurred only when the reforms were abused by enemies of the state and when the party was not vigilant enough and became infected with enemies' ideas.

9 For an analysis, see Czechoslovak Situation Report/2, *RFER*, February 6, 1987, item 2.
10 *Rudé právo*, March 3, 1987.

36.   The Trial of the Jazz Fans

1 The arrested were the section's chairman Karel Srp and six other persons described as musicians: Vladimír Kouřil, Josef Skalník, Čestmír Hunát, Tomáš Křivánek, and the section's treasurer Miloš Drda and his nephew Vlastimil Drda.
2 For a good insight into the history and tribulations of the Jazz Section, see Josef Škvorecký, "Hipness at Noon," *The New Republic*, December 17, 1984.
3 The *Jazzpetit* series, for example, featured an anthology about New York's Living Theater, an anthology on "Minimal + Earth + Concept of Art" edited by Karel Srp, an essay on "The Body, the Thing, and Reality in Contemporary Art" by Petr Rezek, and several monographs on avant-garde artists and musicians. It also carried features on rock musicians, such as John Lennon. *Situace* published unorthodox artwork that the regime found offensive.
4 Škvorecký, *loc. cit.*; and Christine Verity, "Jazz Which Rocks the Eastern Bloc," *The Times*, October 18, 1985.
5 The texts of the letters are available in the West.

37.   Gorbachev's Delayed Visit

1 See paper no. 35 in this volume.
2. A. Jacoviello, "Ligachev Is Gorbachev's 'Slight Cold,'" *La Repubblica*, April 8, 1987.
3 For a summary of Kopecký's speech, see Czechoslovak Situation Report/7, *RFER*, June 12, 1987, item 4.

38.   GDR: Complacency of the Reformed

1 See *Soviet/East European Survey*, *1985-86* (Durham: Duke University Press, 1987), pp 271-74; B. V. Flow and Ronald Asmus, "The Eleventh Party Congress," RAD Background Report/63 (German Democratic Republic), *RFER*, April 30, 1986; and E. Kautsky, "Gorbachev and the GDR," RAD BR/83 (Eastern Europe), *RFER*, December 16, 1986.
2 See *Neues Deutschland*, January 28, 1987.
3 *Ibid.*, January 29, 1987.
4 *Ibid.*, January 31-February 1, 1987.
5 ADN, February 3, 1987.
6 See *Neues Deutschland*, February 3 and 4, 1987.
7 *Ibid.*, February 7-8, 1987.
8 DPA, February 12, 1987.
9 *Neues Deutschland*, February 13, 1987.
10 *Die Welt*, February 10, 1987.
11 Reuters, February 12, 1987. Kvitsinsky said that the East German comrades, if they so desired, could purchase the full text of Gorbachev's speech from the publisher in the FRG.
12 *Neues Deutschland*, April 24, 1987.
13 *Stern*, April 8, 1987; *Neues Deutschland*, April 10, 1987.
14 See, for example, *Neuer Weg*, nos. 4 and 6, 1987; and *Einheit*, nos 3 and 4, 1987.

39.   Hungary: Despondency of the Reformed

1 Flórián Mézes, "Elvételi megfontolások," *Heti Világgazdaság*, July 25, 1987, p.53.
2 *Weekly Bulletin* (MTI), January 23, 1987 and February 27, 1987.
3 Budapest Television, June 6, 1987, 11:35 P.M.
4 For a Soviet effort to praise the Hungarian reforms as support for domestic political purposes, see Pavel Bovin, "What Is Attractive About the Hungarian Experience, and What Should We Beware of?" *Literaturnaia gazeta*, June 10, 1987.
5 See Hungarian Situation Report/4, *RFER*, May 18, 1987, item 3.
6 The KISZ program was published in *Magyar Ifjuság*, May 29, 1987, and the reaction to it was reported in *Ötlet*, June 25, 1987.
7 *A Jövő Mérnöke*, May 15, 1987.
8 György Moldova, *Méhednek Gyümölcse* [Fruit of Your Womb]

(Budapest: Magvető, 1987), p. 87.
9 Sándor Csoóri at the Writers' Union Congress in Budapest on November 29-30, 1986.

41.   Hungarian Experiments Continue

1 *Magyar Közlöny*, no.   28,   July 16, 1986, pp.   622-636. See also *ibid*, Council of Minister's Decree No.   26/1986 pp. 636-638.   Hungary's   previous,   precommunist bankruptcy law was enacted in March 1881.   See also *Ötlet*, August 28, 1986, pp. 10-11.
2 *Magyar Hírlap* September 8, 1986.
3 *Esti Hírlap* September 1, 1986.
4 *Népszabadság*, March 17, 1987.
5 *Heti Világgazdaság*, March 14, 1987.
6 *Ya* (Madrid), June 1, 1987.
7 *Figyelő*, June 11, 1987.
8 Dr. Margit Rodár,   "The   Characteristics   of Hungarian Labor Supply and Demand," *Munkaügyi Szemle*, 1987, no. 5, p. 17.
9 *Népszava*, June 12, 1987.
10 *Népszabadság*, June 17, 1987.
11 *Új Tükör*, June 14, 1987.
12 *Heti Világgazdaság*, May 16, 1987.
13 Béla Bagota and József   Garam: *Mit Kell Tudni a Hetedik Ötéves   Tervről?* [What   Do We Need To   Know About   the Seventh Five-year Plan?] (Budapest: Kossuth, 1986), p. 215.
14 *Figyelő*, September 11, 1986.
15 *Ibid*.
16 *Heti Világgazdaság*, September 20, 1986.
17 *Ibid*.
18 *Ibid*.
19 *Ibid*.
20 *Népszabadság*, November 22, 1986.
21 *Ibid*.
22 *Ibid*.
23 *Statistical Pocket Book of Hungary*, 1985.
24 Hungarian Situation Report/5, *RFER*, March 25, 1986, item 4.
25 Janos Kornai,   *Bürokratikus   és   Piaci   Koordináció*, [Bureaucratic   and Market   Coordination]   (Budapest: Akedémiai Kiadó, 1984).
26 *Heti Világgazdaság*, June 14, 1986.
27 *The 1986 State Budget* (Budapest: Ministry   of Finance,

January 1986).
28 *Heti Világgazdaság*, June 14, 1986.
29 Radio Budapest, August 29, 1986, 6:30 P.M.
30 Radio Budapest, December 1, 1986, 6:30 P.M.; MTI (in English), December 1, 1986.
31 *Népszabadság*, November 22, 1986.
32 *Otlet*, February 7, 1985.
33 *Statisztikai Havi Közlemények* [Statistical Monthly Information], January 1986, p. 21.
34 Albert Racz, "Let Performance and Earnings Be in Accordance!" *Munkaügyi Szemle*, May 1986, p. 1.; *Hungarian Statistical Pocketbook 1985* (Budapest: Central Statistical Office, 1986), p. 31.
35 At *Népszabadság*'s annual public meeting (Radio Budapest, May 1, 1987, 9:10 P.M.).
36 Radio Budapest, May 3, 1987, midday.
37 Interview with Ivan T. Berend in *Figyelő*, March 19, 1987.
38 *Heti Világgazdaság*, March 21, 1987.

42.   Amnesty at Last

1 Radio Warsaw, July 17, 1986, 10:00 P.M.
2 UPI, July 17, 1986.
3 PAP (in English), July 22, 1986.
4 Reuters, July 18, 1986.
5 Radio Warsaw, August 4, 1986, 10:00 P.M.
6 Not all of Poland's political prisoners were immediately released. Deputy Foreign Minister Jan Kinast mentioned 19 people convicted of espionage, sabotage, terrorism, and passing on state secrets who had not been released. They included: the group of youths involved in the accidental shooting of police sergeant Karos in February 1982 and their confessor, Father Sylwester Zych; some of the Lubin miners sentenced in November 1983 for planning "terrorist attacks"; the two Gdańsk policemen, Adam Hadysz and Piotr Siedliński, sentenced in March 1986 for collaborating with the political underground; two conscientious objectors, Wojciech Jankowski and Jarosław Nakielski; and Józef Szaniawski, an historian and journalist with PAP who was accused of writing articles for émigré journals and sentenced to 10 years' imprisonment and the confiscation of all his property. A number of political activists were also being held for criminal offenses not eligible for amnesty. These

included Ryszard Kupczyk, who was sentenced in March 1983 to five years' imprisonment for selling pigs at the behest of underground Solidarity.

7 Michael Kaufman, *The New York Times*, September 15, 1986.
8 Jackson Diehl, *The Washington Post*, September 15, 1986.
9 AP, September 14, 1986.
10 The Italian government had let it be known that the release of political prisoners would greatly improve the chances of the visit to Rome (and, therefore, also in the Vatican) in which Jaruzelski was reportedly very interested.
11 Robert Gillette, interview with Zbigniew Bujak, *Los Angeles Times*, September 22, 1986.

44.   Solidarity Attempts to Regroup

1 Statement by the Chairman of the Independent Self-Governing Trade Union Solidarity dated September 29, 1986, *Tygodnik Mazowsze*, no.182, October 1, 1986.
2 Statement by the Provisional Council of the ISTU Solidarity dated September 29, 1986, *ibid.* See also paper no 42 in this volume.
3 DPA, October 10, 1986.
4 UPI, October 13, 1986.
5 *Ibid.*, October 9, 1986.
6 *Trybuna Ludu*, September 18, 1986.
7 *KOS*, no.106-107, December 8, 1986.
8 UPI, November 24, 1986.
9 *Tygodnik Mazowsze*, no.190, December 3, 1986.
10 *KOS*, *loc.cit.*
11 CDN *Głos Wolnego Robotnika*, December 17, 1986.
12 *Kultura* (Paris), January-February 1987.
13 *Przegląd Wiadomości Agencyjnych*, January 4, 1987; and Reuters and AP, December 22, 1986.

45.   Diplomatic Isolation Broken

1 Reuters, January 12, 1987.
2 RFE Correspondent's Report (Rome), January 12, 1987.
3 PAP (in English), January 14, 1987.
4 Reuters, AP, and UPI, January 13, 1987.
5 Reuters, February 20, 1987.
6 *The Washington Post*, February 18, 1987.

7 In a message to Ronald Reagan (*ibid.*, December 21, 1983.
8 *Ibid.*, September 24, 1986.
9 UPI, February 20, 1987.
10 February 19, 1987, 23.10 P.M.
11 Radio Warsaw, February 29 and 22, 1987, 6:00 A.M. and 12:05 P.M.
12 *Trybuna Ludu*, February 20, 1987.

46.   Special Relationship with Moscow

1 Radio Warsaw, March 10, 1987, and *Trybuna Ludu*, March 11, 1987.   See also UPI, AP, and DPA, March 10, 1987.
2 See Theodore Shabad in *The New York Times*, May 22, 1984.
3 See V. P. Kolesnik, "Sotrudnichestvo prigranichnkh oblastei Sovetskogo Soiuza i voevodstv Polskoi Narodnoi Respubliki (1956-1978 gg.)," in *Porodnennye sotsialisticheskim internatsionalizmom. Druzhestvennye sviazi i sotrudnichestvo porodnennykh oblastei i gorodov USSR i bratskikh stran sotsializma* , Naukova Dumka, Kiev, 1980, pp. 185-220.
4 Włodzimierz Natorf, "Sprostac partnerowi," *Przyjazń*, February 13, 1987, p. 2.
5 See the interview with Messner in Sotsialisticheskaia industriia, February 16, 1986, and the speeches by Messner and Ryzhko in *Pravda*, October 15, 1986.
6 "Vystuplenie tovarishcha Gorbacheva M. S. na X sezde Polskoi obedinennoi rabochei partii 30 iunia 1986 goda," *Partiinaia zhiz*, No. 14, 1986, p. 6; "Komunikat po posiedzeniu Biura Politycznego KC PZPR," *Trybuna Ludu*, October 9, 1986; and *Pravda*, October 10, 1986.
7 "Vstrecha v TsK PORP," *Pravda*, January 25, 1987.
8 Vasyl Hruzin, "Pryami zvyazky-pryama vyhoda," *Silski visti*, March 5, 1987.
9 Radio Warsaw, January 15, 1987.
10 See *Literaturnaia gazeta*, February 4, 1987.
11 AP and Reuters, January 22, 1987.
12 See paper 30 in this volume.
13 See paper 29 in this volume.

47.   The Pope's Visit

1 For details see J.B. de Weydenthal, "The Polish Authorities Prepare for New Stage in Church-State

Relations, RAD Background Report/78 (Poland), *RFER*, May 11, 1987.

2 The text of addresses by General Wojciech Jaruzelski and Pope John Paul II can be found in *Tygodnik Powszechny*, June 14, 1987.

3 The texts of all the papal addresses quoted here can be found in *Tygodnik Powszechny*, June 14 and 21, 1987.

4 For details see Jan Krauze in *Le Monde*, June 16, 1987; Jackson Diehl in *The Washington Post*, June 15, 1987; and Michael Kaufman in *The New York Times*, June 15, 1987.

5 The text of the Pope's statement was published in *Tygodnik Powszechny*, June 21, 1987.

6 The statement was issued following a two-day meeting of the episcopate; see Reuters and AP reports of June 22, 1987; a Polish Press Agency (PAP) report issued on June 21, 1987 was heavily censored and carried no information on the Church's future tasks; but the full text appeared in Slowo Powszechne, June 22, 1987.

7 For details on the Pope's address to the bishops, see Jan Krauze in *Le Monde*, June 16, 1987 and Jackson Diehl in *The Washington Post*, June 15, 1987.

48.   Reform Albanian Style

1 *Zeri i Popullit*, November 4, 1986.

2 *Ibid.*, December 27, 1986.

3 *Ibid.*, March 1, 1987.

4 *Ibid.*, March 24, 1987.

5 ATA, June 23, 1986.

6 February 2, 1987.

7 *Zeri i Popullit*, January 29, 1987.

8 *Rruga e Partise*, January 1987.

9 *Zeri i Popullit*, February 27, 1987.

10 *Ibid.*, April 25, 1987.

11 Michael Kaser, *Albania Under and After Enver Hoxha*, *Country Studies on Eastern Europe and Yugoslavia* (Washington, D.C.: Joint Economic Committee, Congress of the United States, 1986].

12 *Zeri i Popullit*, August 6, 1986.

13 *Ibid.*, August 9, 1986.

14 *Ibid.*, April 23, 1987.

15 Reuters, April 30, 1987.

49.   Ceauşescu and Gorbachev

1 See Romanian Situation Report/4, *RFER*, March 25, 1986, item 1.
2 *Scînteia*, January 27, 1987, p. 1.
3 See Romanian SR/1, *RFER*, February 6, 1987, item 1.
4 Agerpres (in English), February 27, 1987.
5 *Scînteia*, January 28, 1987, p.5.
6 January 30, 1987, p.5; *Lumea*, no. 5, 6 February 1987, p.8.
7 Radio Moscow (in Romanian), February 17, 1987, 5:00 P.M.
8 Ibid., February 18, 1987, 8:00 P.M.
9 *Scînteia*, February 21, 1987, p.3.
10 Petru Panzaru in *Era Socialista*, no. 3, February 10, 1987.
11 Dorel Sandor in ibid., p. 20.
12 Ionel Hagiu in ibid., no. 2, January 25, 1987, pp. 51 and 52.
13 Petru Panzaru in ibid., no. 3. February 10, 1987, p. 11.
14 *Valoság*, no. 29, 1986, pp. 11-12. See Kathrin Sitzler in *Südosteuropa*, no. 1, January 1987, pp. 41-42.

50.   Greek-Bulgarian Friendship Treaty

1 Agerpres (Bucharest) in English, September 11, 1986.
2 RFE Correspondent's Report (Athens), December 10, 1985.
3 BTA (Sofia), September 12, 1986.
4 *Ibid*.
5 *Die Welt*, September 15, 1986; *Stuttgarter Zeitung*, October 7, 1986.
6 Reviewed by *Nova Makedonija*, October 10, 1986.
7 The full text of the declaration was published in
8 TANJUG (Gevgelija), September 10, 1986.
9 RFE Correspondent's Report (Athens), September 9, 1986.
10 See Bulgarian Situation Reports/11, 4, and 1, *RFER*, July 8, 1982, March 25, 1983, and January 16, 1984, items 1, 3, and 5, respectively.
11 *Nova Makedonija*, September 14, 1986.
12 RFE Correspondent's Report (Athens), January 11, 1984 and June 19, 1984.
13 *Financial Times*, October 23, 1984.
14 *Statisticheski Godishnik 1986* [Statistcal Yearbook 1986] (Sophia: Central Statistical Department of the Council of Ministers, 1986) p. 368.

15 RFE Correspondent's Report (Athens), January 5, 1986.
16 *Frankfurter Allgemeine Zeitung*, July 10, 1984.
17 Reuters (Athens), March 6, 1985.

51.   Genocide in Kosovo?

1 *Jugoslovenski   Pregled* [Yugoslav Survey] (Belgrade),
   March 1983; unofficially there were more than 1,500,000
   Albanians and at least 203,000 Serbs and Montenegrins in
   Kosovo in 1987.
2 *Komunist* (Belgrad), June 6, 1986; *Vecernje Novosti*
   (Belgrade), October 24, 1986;
3 *Politika* (Belgrade), September 5, 1983; *Jugoslovenki
   Pregled*, no. 5, May 1984.
4 *Politika*, November 27, 1986. The exchange rate based on
   September 1986 average of 412 dinar = $ 1US.
5 *NIN* (Belgrade), November 9, 1986; *Intervju* (Belgrade),
   November 7, 1986; *Borba* (Belgrade), November 4, 1986.
6 Radio Belgrade, November 16, 1986, 7:00 P.M.
7 *Borba*, June 23, 1987
8 *Jugoslovenski Pregled*, no. 12, December 1986, p.584.
9 TANJUG, November 10, 1986.
10 Spasoje Djakovic,   *Sukosi   na   Kosovu* [Conflicts in
   Kososvo], 2nd editiion, (Belgrad: Narodna Knjiga, 1986),
   p. 305.
11 *Jedinstvo* (Pristina), October 25, 1986.
12 TANJUG, November 11, 1986.
13 *NIN*, November 9, 1986.
14 See Yugoslav Situation Report/3, *RFER*, May 4, 1987, item
   3.
15 *NIN*, May 3, 1987.
16 *Yearbook of the United Nations, 1948-1949* (New York:
   Columbia University Press, 1950), p. 959.
17 *Borba* (Belgrade), April 30, 1987.
18 *Komunist*, June 12, 1987; *Borba* June 23, 1987; see also
   Djakovic, *loc. cit.* p.306.
19 *Komunist*, May 1, 1987.

52.   Yugoslavia's Divided Opposition

1 *NIN* (Belgrade), February 22, 1987.
2 TANJUG, January 30, 1987.
3 *Politika* (Belgrade), January 2, 1987.
4 *Danas* (Zagreb), July 22, 1986.

5 *NIN* (Belgrade), July 20, 1986.
6 *Danas* (Zagreb), December 9, 1986.
7 *Ibid.*
8 See paper no. 50 in this volume.
9 *Borba* (Belgrade), December 19, 1986.

53.   Soviet Dissident's on Glasnost

1 Reuters, June 15, 1987. Sakharov's address was taped in the USSR for showing at commencement ceremonies at the College of Staten Island, New York.
2 AS 5891: Malva Landa and Valeria Novodvorskaia, "Anatoly Marchenko and the Socialist Superstate," December 1986-January 1987.
3 *New York Times*, April 3, 1987.
4 UPI, January 24, 1987.
5 Iurii Orlov's signature appeared on a letter from ten prominent Soviet émigrés entitled "Let Gorbachev Give Us Proof," published in *Moscow News* on March 29, 1987. Most of the ten signatories emigrated many years earlier. For a discussion of this letter, and the Soviet reaction to it, see RL 151/87, "Soviet Press on Émigrés' Attitudes towards Gorbachev," April 16, 1987.
6 *Newsday*, May 5, 1987.
7 "Keine *Glasnost* für politische Häftlinge," *Süddeutsche Zeitung*, June 4, 1987.
8 Gudava, his wife, brother, and mother were granted exit visas in July 1987 and since left the Soviet Union.
9 Koriagin reiterated his statement about the continued abuse of psychiatry in the Soviet Union in an interview on August 12, 1987, in Zurich.
10 AS 5932: Eduard Gudava, "On the Differences Between the Current Release of Political Prisoners, and Genuine Political Amnesty," February 2, 1987.
11 AS 5965: Aleksei Miasnikov, "Open Letter to M. S. Gorbachev," spring 1987

54.   Czechoslovak Opposition Ponders Reform

1 This material is available in the West; it includes "Reconstruction or Changing Clothes?" signed AZ, and an anonymous survey, "Gorbachev's Visit as Reflected in Independent [samizdat] Publications." See also paper no. 37 in this volume.

2 See also Czechoslovak Situation Report/5, *RFER*, 4 May 1987, item 1.

55.   The Fad of Oriental Religions

1 No. 48, April, 1985
2 Juozas Jurevičius, "Emancipation," *Švyturys*, no. 16, August 1985, pp. 12-13 and no. 18, September 1985, pp. 18-19.
3 Jurevičius, "Camps in the Nature Preserve," *ibid.*, no. 6, March 1986, pp. 16-17.
4 Articles in *Literaturnaia gazeta*, 1985, no. 20, p. 13, and no. 30, p. 13 were the first to deal with the story. Articles in *Švyturys*, 1985, nos. 16 and 18 went into greater detail on the Lithuanian aspect of the case. *Tiesa* of August 4, 1985 published a translation of part of the second *Literaturnaia gazeta* article. An article in *Literaturnaia gazeta*, 1986, no. 21, p. 13, was translated completely in *Komjaunimo Tiesa* of May 27, 1986. A later article on the trial was published in *Literaturnaia gazeta*, 1986, no. 41, p. 13.
5 *Sovetskaia Litva*, September 28 and 30 and October 1, 1986.
6 No. 7, April, 1986, pp. 10, 11, and 27.

57.   A Comecon-Common Market Rapprochement

1 *Izvestiia*, March 31, 1972.

58.   East Germany Cultivates European Identity

1 See Honecker's interviews with Dutch journalists, *Neues Deutschland*, June 3, 1987.
2 AP, June 3, 1987.
3 *Neues Deutschland*, June 4, 1987.
4 *Ibid.*, June 3, 1987.
5 For the text of Fischer's speech, see *Neues Deutschland*, November 8-9, 1986.
6 *Soviet/East European Survey 1985-86*, pp. 104-108, 250-56.
7 For the text of Schmidt's speech, see *IPW Berichte*, no.

2/1987.

8 For more on relations between the GDR and the EEC see, Christian Meier, "The GDR and the Relationship between the CMEA and the EEC ," *Aktuelle Analysen* (Bundesinstitut für Ostwissenschaftliche und Internationale Studien), 16/1987.

9 The limits to this policy were, however, equally apparent. In an interview with Dutch journalists, Honecker said that "coexisting in a well-furnished European house" required the recognition that there were "two independent, autonomous German states that belong to two separate alliance systems."

59. Three Faces of Central Europe

1 Timothy Garton Ash, "Does Central Europe Exist?" *The New York Review of Books*, October 9, 1986.

60. Popular Dissatisfaction with Gorbachev

1 Moscow Television, September 18, 1986.
2 Ernst Kux, "Opposition gegen Gorbatschew," *Neue Zürcher Zeitung*, November 19, 1986.
3 Aleksandr Gelman, "Chto snachala, chto potom . . . ," *Literaturnaia gazeta*, September 10, 1986.
4 Radio Moscow, June 17, 1986.
5 Leonid Abalkin interviewed in *l'Unità*, October 25, 1985.
6 Valentin Tolstykh, "Sutdela," *Sovetskaia kultura*, September 16, 1986.
7 *Izvestiia*, December 4, 1986.
8 *The Guardian*, December 15, 1986.
9 Reuters, December 4, 1986.
10 Aleksandr Vasinskii, "Perestroika i perestrakhovshchik," *Izvestiia*, February 15, 1986.
11 *Pravda*, October 1 and 2, 1986.
12 *Ibid.*, Febrauary 26, 1986.
13 Soviet Television, November 1, 1986.
14 Viktor Lishchenko and Anatolii Strelianyi, "Mesiats v derevne," *Literaturnaia gazeta*, December 3, 1986.
15 Vadim Zagladin, "Socialism and the Global Problems of the Contemporary Period," *Politicheskoe samoobrazovanie*, No. 9 (September), 1986, pp. 13-22.
16 Moscow Radio, September 18, 1986. See also what were

purported to be readers' doubts in *Pravda*, September 19
and November 15, 1986, and *Sovetskaia Rossiia*, October 7
and 29, 1986.

17 On October 12, 14, and 22, 1986.

18 Moscow Television, September 18, 1986.

61.   Liberalization and Soviet Jewry

1 See RL 464/86, "Soviet Authors in Dispute over
Ideological Attitude towards Zionism," December 16,
1986; Roman Solchanyk, "In the Soviet Press, Evidence of
a Softer Line on Zionism," *International Herald Tribune*,
March 14-15, 1987.

2 *Sovetskaia Moldaviia*, March 13, 1987.

3 *Literaturnaia Rossiia*, no. 11, 1987, p. 11.

4 *Literaturnaia gazeta*, no. 11, 1987, p. 8.

5 *Nedelia*, no. 4, 1987, p. 9.

6 *Bolshaia Sovetskaia Entsiklopediia*, 3rd ed., Vol. 29,
Moscow, 1978, p. 271.

7 *Izvestiia*, August 29, 1979; *Sovetskaia kultura*, July 21,
1984; *Pravda Vostoka*, October 19, 1986.

8 *Literaturnaia gazeta*, no. 39, 1986; No. 11, 1987.

9 *Izvestiia*, December 3 and 4, 1986.

10 *Komsomolskaia pravda*, May 22, 1987; see also paper 33 in
this volume.

11 *Ogonek*, no. 1, 1987, pp. 3-4; *Sovetskaia kultura*, April
18, 1987; *Moskovskie novosti*, nos. 13 and 20, 1987.

12 *Istoriia SSSR*, no. 4, 1980.

62.   The Growth of "Informal Groups"

1 *Pravda*, March 30, 1987.

2 *Komsomolskaia pravda*, October 10, 1986.

3 *Smena*, No. 4, 1985. For the details on music ensembles,
see AS 5519 and an accompanying comentary.

4 *Pravda*, March 30, 1987; *Smena*, No. 4, 1985;
Komsomolskaia pravda, October 5 and 17, 1986.

5 *Komsomolskoe znamia*, December 6, 1986; *Komsomolskaia
pravda*, August 23, 1985. See also RL 99/87,
"Controversy in Soviet Press over Unofficial Youth
Groups," March 11, 1987.

6 RL 147/82, "Journals of the 'Second Culture' in
Leningrad," March 31, 1982. *Komsomolskoe znamia*, January

18, 1987.

7 *Komsomolskaia pravda*, October 17, 1986.

8 Ibid., January 8, 1986.

9 *Izvestiia*, June 3, 1987; *Ogonek*, No. 20, 1987; *Literaturnaia gazeta*, May 20, 1987.

10 *Pravda*, March 30, 1987.

11 *Komsomolskaia pravda*, October 10, 1987; *Sotsialisticheskaia industriia*, March 25, 1987.

12 *Pravda*, March 30, 1987.

13 *Sotsialisticheskaia industriia*, March 25, 1987; Radio Moscow-1, (9:15 A.M.), January 4, 1987 (talk by the writer M. Antonov on problems of the upbringing of Soviet youth.

14 *Literaturnaia gazeta*, December 25, 1985; Radio "Volga," (12:15 P.M.), March 15, 1987.

15 On "Phantom," for instance, Reuters, September 20, 1985; *Russkaia mysl*, Decmeber 20, 1985; AS 5932.

16 *Komsomolskoe znamia*, January 18, 1987.

17 On the trust group see, for instance, RL 130/84, "The Trial of Olga Medvedkova," March 27, 1984, The USSR News Brief, No. 24, 1986; UPI, February 15, 1987.

18 Radio Moscow-2 (2:30 P.M.), February 26, 1987.

19 *Komsomolskaia pravda*, October 10, 1986.

20 *Ogonek*, No. 5, 1987.

21 *Pravda*, March 30, 1987.

22 See paper no. 33 of this volume.

23 *Vecherniaia Moskva*, May 18, 1987; *Komsomolskaia pravda*, May 22, 1987; *Izvestiia*, June 3, 1987; *Ogonek*, No. 21, 1987.

24 *Izvestiia*, March 27, and April 9, 1987; *Literaturnaia gazeta*, March 25, 1987 and May 20, 1987. In contrast, *Leningradskaia pravda* of March 21, 1987, negatively assessed the activities of the Leningrad informal groups.

25 *Stroitelnaia gazeta*, April 24, 1987.

26 See Thom Shanker in *The Chicago Tribune*, May 18, 1987.

27 *Literaturnaia gazeta*, March 25, 1987; *Izvestiia*, March 27, 1987.

28 *Komsomolskaia pravda*, October 10, 1986. Since 1983, serious efforts have been made to put unofficial music ensembles under the supervision of the USSR's cultural organizations (see the commentary (p. 4) to AS 5519).

29 *Ibid.*

30 *Literaturnaia gazeta*, May 20, 1987.

31 Radio Moscow-1 (3 P.M. and 7 P.M.), December 17, 1986.

32 TASS, June 4, 1987.

63.   The June Plenum: Too Far or Not Far Enough?

1 TASS, June 9, 1987.
2 *Pravda*, June 13, 1987.
3 TASS, June 26, 1987.
4 *Pravda*, June 26, 1987, pp.1-5.
5 Radio Moscow-2, June 26, 1987.
6 *Los Angeles Times*, June 27, 1987.
7 For example, interview with S. Shatalin in *Sobesednik*, No.25, 1987, p. 10.
8 "Zakon   SSSR   o   gosudarstvennom   predpriiatii (obedinenie)," *Pravda*, July 1, 1987.
9 *Ibid.*, June 13, 1987.
10 Gorbachev's phrase, in his speech to the Central Committee plenum, *Pravda*, June 26, 1987.
11 *Izvestiia*, February 8, 1987.
12 Bogomolov at the pre-plenum meeting already cited; Shmelev in *Novyi Mir*, no. 6, 1987 (approved for publication on April 28).
13 Moscow television, 7:00 P.M. CEST, July 10, 1987. Reports of the meeting appeared earlier in the Western press; see *Reuters*, July 13, 1987, and *The Guardian*, July 14, 1987.

The word "pluralism" is known to have appeared only once in the Soviet press in a non-pejorative sense--in a statement by Poland's minister of culture that appeared in 1987 in the popular magazine *Ogonek* (No 7, February 1987). When the Italian Communist Party leader Enrico Berlinguer used the word "pluralism" in his speech to the Twenty-fifth Congress of the CPSU in 1976, *Pravda* refused to publish it and, to the fury of the Italian party, substituted the word "multiformity" instead; see Victor Zorza, "'Pluralism' a Dirty Word to Kremlin," *International Herald Tribune*, March 18, 1976. In an article published in 1981, KGB chairman Viktor Chebrikov charged that hostile Western propaganda advocated the introduction of "political pluralism" to the USSR because that would entail the creation of competeing organizations within the socialist system "that would, of course, be opposed to the Communist Party" (V.M. Chebrikov, "Bditelesnost--ispytannoe oruzhie," *Molodoi kommunist*, No. 4, 1981, pp. 28-34).
15 TASS, May 8, 1985.
16 *Sovetskaya Rossiya*, February 8, 1986.
17 AS 5785.
18 TASS, January 27, 1987.

Index

Abai, Borubaev, chief guru, Mirza (USSR), 350-351

Adamovich, Ales, Belorussian writer, 196

Adelman, Kenneth, head of US Arms Control and Disarmament Agency, 144

Afanasev, Iurii, Soviet historian and director of Moscow State Institute of Historical Archives, 62, 64-67, 398(n9), 399(n19)

Afanasev, Viktor, chief editor of *Pravda* (USSR), 47

Afghanistan, Democratic Republic of: and Vladivostok speech, 8, 157; Soviet criticisms of war in, 68-72; guerrilla attacks on Soviet Union, 72; and drug abuse by Soviet soldiers, 84; and Soviet press, 134; Soviet announcement of troop withdrawals from, 157; and Soviet-Iranian relations, 166-168; and Vienna conference, 178, 181. *See also Glasnost*; Soviet foreign policy

Aganbegian, Abel, Soviet economist, 382

Aitmatov, Chingiz, Soviet writer, 83-84

Akhmadulina, Bella, Soviet poet, 55, 62

Akhmatova, Anna, Soviet poet, 55, 62, 64

Akhromeev, Sergei, chief of General Staff and first deputy minister of defense (USSR), 137

Albania, People's Socialist Republic of: foreign relations, 14, 295-297; and economic reform, 14, 299-301, 303; conflict between Albanians and Serbs in Kosovo, 15, 326-333; relations with Greece, 295; Greek minority in Albania, 295; relations with Italy, 295-296; relations with Turkey, 296-297; Albanian minority in Turkey, 296; ethnic Albanians in Yugoslavia, 296-297, 303; relations with Yugoslavia, 297; and France, 297; and Austria, 297; and Switzerland, 297; and Sweden, 297; and FRG 297, and East European nations, 297; and PRC, 297, parliamentary elections, 297-299; ideology, 299; press/media, 300, 302, 305; population growth rates, 302-303; life expectancy and mortality rate, 302; food production, 302-304; private economic activity, 304-305; foreign influences, 305; youth, 305-306; religion, 306; and Balkan nuclear- and chemical weapons-free zone proposal, 322; and Kosovo conflict, 327, 332. *See also Alia*

Aleksandrov-Agentov, Andrei, former adviser on security issues to general secretary's staff (USSR), 126

Alekseev, Mikhail, Soviet writer, 62

Alia, Ramiz, leader of Albanian communist party: and foreign policy, 295-297; on "party-people" relationship, 298-299, 301; and economic reform, 301; on food production, 302-304; and ethnic Albanians in Yugoslavia, 332

Altunin, General Aleksandr, former chief of civil defense (USSR), 136

Ambartsumov, Evgenii, Soviet journalist, 70

Amelko, Admiral Nikolai N., inspector-adviser to Ministry of Defense (USSR), 174

Ananev, Anatolii, chief editor of *Oktiabr* (USSR), 62

Andropov, Iurii, Soviet general secretary (1982-1984), 4, 28, 110

Aqazadeh, Gholamreza, Iranian petroleum minister, 166

Antonov, Mikhail, Soviet commentator for Radio Moscow, 28

Arbatov, Georgii, head of Institute of the USA and Canada, Academy of Sciences of the USSR, 185, 209

Arsonov, Valerii, Soviet soldier killed in Afghanistan, 69

al-Assad, Hafiz, Syrian president, 171

Association of South East Asian Nations (ASEAN): and Vladivostok speech, 155, 163; and USSR, 163-165

Asylbaev, M., Kazakh citizen convicted for participating in Alma-Ata riots, 193

Australia: and Vladivostok speech, 155

Austria: 346; and Vienna conference, 187; and Albania, 297; and Hungary, 367

Babaian, Eduard, Soviet narcologist, 82

Bácskai, Tamas, former
deputy director-general
of Hungarian National
Bank, 246

Bahr, Egon, West German
Social Democratic Party
member, 49

Bakarič, Vladimir, Cro-
atian communist party
leader   (Yugoslavia),
338, 340

Bauer, William, Canadian
delegate to Vienna CSCE
conference, 181

Beekman, Vladimir, chair-
man of Union of Writers
of the Estonian SSR, 206

Begun, Iosif, Soviet dis-
sident,   178,   184-185,
285

Beil, Gerhard, East German
minister   of   foreign
trade, 297

Bek, Aleksandr, Soviet
writer, 64

Beliaev, Igor, chief of
foreign policy depart-
ment of Literaturnaia
gazeta (USSR), 173

Belov, Vasilii, Soviet
writer, 373

Benda, Václav, Czecho-
slovak   philosopher,
mathematician, and dis-
sident, 345-346

Bender, Peter, West German
journalist, 366-367

Beqeja, Hamit, Albania
psychologist, 305-306

Berecz, János, Hungarian
Politburo member, 244-
245

Berend, Ivan T., president
of Hungarian Academy of
Sciences, 252, 259

Berezovska, S., mother of
two Soviet soldiers: on
Afghanistan, 68-70

Berkhin, Viktor B.,
correspondent for Sovet-
skii shakhter (USSR),
36-38

Bestuzhev-Lada, Igor,
Soviet psychologist,
79-80

Bielecki, Czesław, Polish
publisher, 266

Biľak, Vasil, Czechoslovak
Presidium member, 221,
223, 227, 418(n1), 419
(n7, n8)

Bochevarov, V., Soviet
citizen: criticism of
US-Soviet "telebridge,"
75-76, 400(n10)

Bogomolov, Oleg, Soviet
economist, 386

Bondarev, Iurii, Soviet
writer, 62-63

Bonner, Elena, Soviet dissident and wife of Andrei Sakharov, 342

Borisov, Iurii, Soviet historian, 66

Borisova, Iuliia, Soviet actor, 56

Borusewicz, Bogdan, underground Solidarity leader, 266, 272

Bovin, Aleksandr, Soviet journalist, 134-135

Brailovskii, Viktor, Soviet dissident, 178

Brezhnev, Leonid, Soviet general secretary (1964-1982), 108-109, 123-124, 206, 211-212, 216, 357

British Broadcasting Corporation (BBC), Soviets cease jamming of, 6

Bujak, Zbigniew, underground Solidarity leader, 266, 270, 272

Bulgaria, People's Republic of: Greek-Bulgarian declaration, 14, 318-321, 323; and Yugoslavia and Macedonian issue, 15, 319; mortality rates, 88; and Vienna conference, 180-182, 186; and Turkish minorities in, 181-182, 321, 323; relations with Greece, 323-325; media, 319; and Warsaw Pact, 319, 321; Western reaction to Greek-Bulgarian declaration, 319; and Turkey, 319-320, 323; and Yugoslavia, 319-320; and Balkan nuclear- and chemical weapons-free zone proposal, 321-322; and Soviet "peace" politics, 321; and SDI, 321; and CMEA, 321. See also Czechoslovakia

Burlatskii, Fedor, commentator for Literaturnaia gazeta and head of philosophy department of Institute of Social Sciences, Central Committee of the CPSU: on "democratization," 4, 35; interview with Western correspondents on "democratization," 38-42; on state and cooperative ownership, 111; on global problems, 125; on Soviet arms control proposals, 133; on Sino-Soviet troop reductions, 157

Butenko, Anatolii, Soviet scholar at Institute of Economics of the World Socialist System, 25, 29-30, 110-111

Buturlin, Aleksei, Uzbek prosecutor, 34-35

Canada: and Vienna CSCE conference, 180-181, 187

Carcani, Adil, Albanian prime minister, 296-297

Casaroli, Agostino Card-
inal, Vatican secretary
of state, 278

Ceauşescu, Elena, wife of
Romanian leader, 317

Ceauşescu, Nicolae, leader
of Romanian communist
party: 223, 311, 315;
and reform, 306-308,
312; and Soviet reforms,
308, 312, 317; and CMEA
cooperation, 310, 312;
and Gorbachev's visit to
Romania, 311-318; and
Gorbachev's arms control
initiatives, 312; and
conventional arms con-
trol, 312-313, 318;
on nonuse of force in
international relations,
313; and Gorbachev's
foreign policy posi-
tions, 314, 318; on
minorities in Romania,
316

Central Europe: 16, 364-
367. *See also* Eastern
Europe; FRG

Chagall, Marc, Russian
Jewish painter, 373

Chautauqua Institution-
Eisenhower Institute
Conference on US-Soviet
Relations, Jūrmala, Lat-
via (Chautauqua confer-
ence): 175-177

Chazov, Evgenii, head of
Soviet Academy of
Medical Sciences, 185

Chebrikov, Viktor, KGB
chief, 37

Cherkizov, Andrei, Soviet
journalist, 209-210

Chernavin, Vladimir, com-
mander in chief of
Soviet Navy, 137

Chernichenko, Iurii, Sov-
iet essayist, 55, 60

Chervov, Colonel General
Nikolai, Soviet military
spokesman, 132

Chirac, Jacques, French
prime minister, 141

Chizhov, Liudvig, head of
Pacific Ocean Department
of Ministry of Foreign
Affairs (USSR), 161

Cockburn, Patrick, corre-
spondent for *Financial
Times* (London), 38, 40-
41

Council for Mutual
Economic Assistance
(CMEA, Comecon): 355;
relations with EEC, 16,
356-360; and Hungary,
243, 260; and Romania,
308, 310-313; and
Ceauşescu, 310, 312; and
Bulgaria, 321; and
Gorbachev, 356, 359; and
USSR, 356-359

Committee for State
Security (KGB): 3-4, 75-
76, 136; and Gorbachev,
4; and reforms, 4;

Voroshilovgrad KGB and Berkhin affair, 37; Kazakh KGB, 191

Conference on Security and Cooperation in Europe, Vienna CSCE (Vienna conference): and Jaruzelski arms control proposal, 147; and Jazz Section of Czech Union of Musicians, 226-227. *See also* Afghanistan; Austria; Bulgaria; Canada; FRG; GDR; Hungary; Italy; Netherlands; NATO; Poland; Romania; Shevardnadze; Shultz; Switzerland; Turkey; United Kingdom; United States; USSR; Warsaw Pact

Čosić, Dobrica, Serbian intellectual, 330-331, 333

Craxi, Bettino, Italian prime minister, 269, 277-278, 356, 359

Cyprus: and Balkan nuclear- and chemical weapons- free zone proposal, 322

Czechoslovakia (Czechoslovak Socialist Republic): and Soviet reforms, 10-11, 15-16, 216-218, 222-224, 227, 232; trial of leaders of Jazz Section of Czech Union of Musicians, 10, 224-229; Gorbachev and internal affairs of, 10;

reforms, 11, 212-213, 218-222, 224, 230; and *glasnost*, 11; Gorbachev's visit to, 11, 229-234, 347-348; attitudes toward Gorbachev, 11, 214-216, 346-348; opposition and Gorbachev's reforms, 15; Charter 77, 15-16, 182, 215, 228, 231, 344-348, 354; mortality rate, 88; environmental problems, 113, 115; and Vienna CSCE conference, 180-182, 186; Prague Spring and Soviet reforms, 211-214, 418 (n1); Prague Spring "democratization" compared to USSR's and Gorbachev's, 213; religion, 213, 347; Slovaks, 213; and GDR, 214; and Poland, 214; Prague Spring, 215, 229-230, 234, 348; reforms compared to other socialist nations (Hungary, 216, 219, 419(n5), GDR, 216, 222, Romania, 216, 222, Bulgaria, 216, China, 219, 419(n5); press/media, 216-217, 229; and Gorbachev's reforms, 220-221, 224, 229, 231, 233-234; Jazz Section trial and USSR, 228-229; and Soviet foreign policy, 231; samizdat, 346, 348; and EEC, 360.

Czyrek, Józef, Polish Politburo member and Central Committee secretary, 280

Daniloff, Nicholas, head of Moscow bureau of *US News and World Report*, 175

Davidovich, Vsevolod, Soviet academician at University of Rostov, 25-26

Dedijer, Vladimir, Serbian intellectual, 330-331

Dmitrenko, Vladimir, Institute of History of the USSR, Academy of Sciences of the USSR, 111

Dobrynin, Anatolii, head of International Department, Central Committee of the CPSU: 119, 130; on "new thinking" in foreign and national security policy, 121-122; effect of appointment, 126

Dolanc, Stane, member of Yugoslav Presidium, 320

Donahue, Phil, American talk-show host: and US-Soviet "telebridge," 74-75

Drach, Ivan, Ukrainian poet, 202

Dragosavač, Dušan, Serbian communist leader and member of Central Committee of the Yugoslav communist party, 328-329

Drda, Miloš, member of Jazz Section of Czech Union of Musicians, 228

Drda, Vlastimil, member of Jazz Section of Czech Union of Musicians, 228

Drozd, Volodymyr, Ukrainian writer, 200

Dubček, Alexander, former first secretary of Czechoslovak communist party, 211, 214-215, 230-231

Dudintsev, Mikhail, Soviet writer, 64

Eastern Europe: reforms, 1, 211, 216; and USSR, 1-2, 15-16, 354-356; press/media, 5, 114; environmental problems, 7, 88, 113-115; evolving "pluralism," 14, 16; nationality issues, 14-15, 315-316; dissidents and USSR, 15; dissidents and *glasnost*, 15; and European unity, 16, 356; life expectancy and mortality rates, 87-88; alcohol consumption, 88-89; health care, 89-92; and Chernobyl accident, 91; and AIDS, 91; and drug abuse, 91; comparison of environmental protection under socialism and capitalism, 112-114, 116; and Gorbachev, 232-233, 245; Falin on reforms in, 240;

Kvitsinskii on reforms in, 240; and Albania, 297; and Soviet reforms, 353; and Gorbachev's reforms, 354-355; individual nations and EEC, 358-360; foreign debt, 359; and Central Europe, 365-367. *See also Glasnost;* individual East European nations

Eberstadt, Nicholas, member of Harvard Center for Population Studies, 87-89

Efremov, Oleg, director of Moscow Arts Theater, 56, 209

Egorov, B., Soviet philologist, 58

Eltsin, Boris, first secretary of Moscow City Committee of the CPSU, 103, 208-209, 217

Emelianov, Valerii, Pamiat leader (USSR), 378

Ermakov, N. S., first secretary of Kemerovo Oblast party committee (USSR), 45

Esenin, Sergei, Russian poet (d. 1925), 378

Estonia (Estonian SSR). *See Glasnost;* Soviet nationality issues

European Economic Community (EEC, Common Market): relations with

CMEA, 16, 356-360; and Greece, 321, 323-324; and Gorbachev, 356, 359; and USSR, 356-357; negotiations with individual East European nations, 358-360; and Romania, 358, 360; and Czechoslovakia, 360; and Hungary, 360; and GDR, 363.

Evren, Kenan, Turkish president, 320

Evstafev, Gennadii, Soviet delegate to Vienna conference, 181

Evtushenko, Evgenii, Soviet poet: on Soviet history, 53, 63; and Pasternak, 55; on rejection of Stalinism, 61; on religion, 61

Fadeev, Nikolai, former general secretary of CMEA, 358

Falin, Valentin, head of Novosti Press Agency (USSR), 192

Federal Republic of Germany (FRG, West Germany): and Soviet short-range missiles, 146, 149; and Vienna conference, 180; and Albania, 297; and Central Europe, 366

Fedoseev, Petr, Soviet communist party theoretician, 109

Feofanov, Iurii, corre-
spondent for *Izvestiia*,
35-36

Filonov, Pavel, Russian
avant-garde artist, 52

Fischer, Oskar, East
German foreign minister,
363

Florijančič, Tone, Socialist Alliance leader in
Ljubljana (Yugoslavia),
338

Fojtík, Jan, Czechoslovak
communist party ideo-
logist, 217, 234-235

Fomenko, Mykhailo, Ukrainian minister of educa-
tion, 202-203

France: and US-Soviet arms
control negotiations,
141, 143; reaction to
Polish amnesty, 269; and
Albania, 297; and
Greece, 325

Frasyniuk, Władysław,
underground Solidarity
leader, 266, 272

Garton Ash, Timothy,
foreign affairs editor
for *The Spectator* (Lon-
don), 364, 367

Gelman, Aleksandr, Soviet
playwright, 24, 60

Genscher, Hans-Dietrich,
West German foreign
minister, 146

Gerasimov, Gennadii,
spokesman for Ministry
of Foreign Affairs
(USSR), 171-172, 177,
185; 415(n2)

Geremek, Bronisław, Polish
historian and former
Solidarity adviser, 269

German Democratic Republic
(GDR, East Germany): and
Gorbachev's reforms, 11,
237-242, 361; and Soviet
foreign policy, 11,
362-364; and USSR, 11,
239, 361; and arms
control, 11, 361-363;
extent of *glasnost*, 11;
and FRG, 11, 355, 362;
youth and churches, 11,
247, 249-250; cigarette
smoking, 88; environ-
mental problems, 113,
115; press/media, 237-
238, 240; and Twenty-
seventh Congress of the
CPSU, 237; and January
1987 Central Committee
plenum and Gorbachev's
speech, 237-238;
reforms, 241; revival of
interest in churches,
247-248; church-state
relations, 247, 249-250;
church involvement in
political and ecological
issues, 248-250; rela-
tions with West European
nations, 361-364, 431
(n9); and Netherlands,
361-362; foreign policy
and Gorbachev, 361, 363;
and Vienna conference,
363; and EEC, 363. *See
also* Czechoslovakia;
Glasnost; Honecker

Gheorghui-Dej, Gheorghe, former Romanian leader, 306-307

Ginzberg, Siegmund, Peking correspondent for *l'Unità* (Italy), 158-160

Gjyzari, Niko, chairman of Planning Commission (Albania), 300

Glasnost (in USSR): 4-6, 232, 381, 389; role of, 5, 51-52, 388; and cultural liberalization, 5, 23; and Soviet history (including Stalin and Stalinism), 5-6, 23, 51, 63-64; public reaction to, 6, 50, 371; and disturbances in Baltic republics, 10; comparison of Soviet and East German, 11; and Soviet dissidents, 15, 344; and "democratization," 23, 208; and intelligentsia, 24; and nationality issues, 24, 208, 315-316; and press/media, 47-52, 371; and Chernobyl accident, 49; and local press, 49, 371; and local officials, 50, 371; and Ligachev, 51, 381; and television, 50, 72, 371; and Central Committee meeting with media representatives, 50; opponents in Union of Writers of the RSFSR, 62-63; and Afghanistan war and Shultz, 70-72; and Iakovlev, 73; and prostitution, 82; and

government reports on economic performance, 97; and military issues, 134, 137; and Iazov, 137; and Kazakh press, 192; and Ukrainian language campaign, 202; and Estonian language campaign, 207; openness during Prague Spring compared to, 213; and coverage of Gorbachev's visit to Romania, 311-312; émigré attitudes toward, 342-343; and drug abuse and prostitution, 371; and informal groups, 374-376. *See also* Czechoslovakia; Gorbachev; Eastern Europe

Glatz, Ferenc, deputy directory of Institute of History, Hungarian Academy of Sciences, 315-316

Glemp, Cardinal Józef, Polish primate, 280-281, 283-284

Goncharov, Andrei, Soviet theater director, 56

Gorbachev, Mikhail S., Soviet general secretary (since 1985): 1, 13, 19, 96, 99, 116, 184-185, 187, 209; reforms in general, 2-4, 16; and economic reforms, 6, 20, 380, 382-387; and political reform, 7, 22-23, 387; compared to Khrushchev, 2, 8, 127; and January 1987 Central

Committee plenum, 3, 23, 30-33, 38, 42-43, 51, 61, 63, 387; and Andropov, 4; and KGB, 4; and *glasnost*, 4-5, 23, 32, 49-51, 63, 309; and arms control, 7, 16, 131-132, 134, 139, 141-143, 146, 148-150, 152, 371-372; and Reykjavik summit, 7-8, 130-133, 372; and military, 8; and Rust affair, 8, 136; and foreign affairs, 8, 16, 119-130, 155-160, 172-173, 371; Vladivostok speech, 8, 155-158, 163; and Sakharov, 15, 178, 342; public reaction to reforms, 16, 23; supporters of, 16-17; work discipline campaign, 19; anti-alcohol campaign, 19, 370-371; personnel changes, 19-20, 126; leadership position, 20, 24, 382; and resistance to reforms, 20-24, 27, 41, 369-372, 382, 384, 388-389; on Soviet history, 23, 51, 63-64; Krasnodar speech, 23-24, 39, 369, 372; and "democratization," 23, 32, 39, 232-233, 380, 387-388; on electoral reforms, 23, 32-33, 42-45, 388; on Soviet society, 26-27, 30-33, 387; speech at conference of social scientists, 26-28; on education, 27; and Stalin, 31-33, 389; criticism of Soviet communist party, 32; on party reforms, 32-33;

and Berkhin affair, 38; and June 1987 Central Committee plenum, 48, 382-385, 387; and nationalism, 61; use of television, 72; and "social justice," 99, 105; and Twenty-seventh Congress of the CPSU, 104106, 119-121, 123, 125-126, 380; on cooperatives, 105-106, 383; Khabarovsk speech, 106, 371; on markets, 106; on "developed socialism," 112; on interdependence, 120, 123, 130; on "global problems," 120, 123, 409(n30); on national security, 120-121, 132; on arms control verification measures, 127-128; speech to May 1986 conference of foreign policy officials, 130; and 1985 Geneva summit, 132; and Iazov, 136-138; meetings with Thatcher, 141, 230; Prague speech, 142-143; and Shultz, 143; and Reagan, 172; and Pérez de Cuéllar, 173; and Alma-Ata riots, 206; reforms compared to Dubček's, 211; described by Gromyko, 214; on reform in Czechoslovakia and other socialist nations, 232-233; and Eastern Europe, 232-233, 245; on European unity, 233-234; on Prague Spring, 234; and Jaruzelski, 283-284; in Soviet-Romanian relations, 313; on Soviet reforms during visit to Romania, 314; on Balkan nuclear-free zone, 316; and dissidents and releases of political prisoners, 342-344; and Craxi and EEC, 356, 359; and June conference on economic reforms, 379-380; and law on state enterprises, 380, 382, 384-385; and Iakovlev, 381; and Nikonov, 381; and Sliunkov, 382; and July 1986 meeting with press and creative union officials, 386-388; on "socialist pluralism," 388. *See also* CMEA; Czechoslovakia; GDR; Honecker; Hungary; Ligachev; Poland; Romania; United Kingdom

Gorbunov, Vladimir, Soviet historian, 67

Gorskii, Andrei, Soviet artist, 209

Govorov, Vladimir, chief of civil defense (USSR), 137

Granin, Daniil, Soviet writer, 53, 55, 61, 64

Grebnev, Naum, Soviet translator, 372-373

Greece: Greek-Bulgarian declaration, 14, 318-321; relations with Albania, 295; and Romania, 319; Western reaction to Greek-Bulgarian declaration,

319; and NATO, 319, 321-323, 325; and Turkey, 319, 323, 325; and Yugoslavia and Macedonian issue, 319-320; Yugoslav and Turkish reaction to Greek-Bulgarian declaration, 320; and Balkan nuclear-and chemical weapons-free zone proposal, 321-322; and Soviet "peace" politics, 321-322; and SDI, 321; and EEC, 321, 323-324; economic problems, 322-323; communist party, 323; and Warsaw Pact, 323; and United States, 323, 325; relations with Bulgaria, 323-325; and Turkish minority in Bulgaria, 323; and USSR, 325; military modernization, 325; and France, 325

Grinevskii, Oleg, head of Soviet delegation to Stockholm CSCE conference, 177

Grishchenko, A., chief of Administration for the Struggle against Misappropriation of Socialist Property, Latvian Ministry of Internal Affairs, 81

Grishin, Viktor, former Moscow party chief, 20

Gromov, Vladimir, Soviet librarian, 209

Gromyko, Anatolii, director of Africa Institute,

Academy of Sciences of the USSR, 124, 408(n18)

Gromyko, Andrei, chairman of Presidium of Supreme Soviet of the USSR, 126, 171-172, 214, 407(n6)

Grósz, Károly, Hungarian prime minister, 244-245

Gubenko, Iakov, director of Jewish Studio Theater (Moscow), 373

Guboglo, Mikhail, Soviet ethnolinguist, 201

Gudava, Eduard, member of Georgian Helsinki Group and unofficial rock group (USSR), 343-344

Guerra, Adriano, director of research center for East European studies of the Italian communist party, 353-356

Gumilev, Nikolai S., Soviet poet, 5, 58, 62

Gwiazda, Andrzej, former deputy chairman of Solidarity, 266

Gyurkó, László, Hungarian biographer of Kádár, 253

Hager, Kurt, East German Central Committee secretary for ideology, 241

Hájek, Jiří, Czechoslovak dissident and former foreign minister, 345

Hámori, Csaba, Hungarian Politburo member and first secretary of Communist Youth League, 244

Hamman, Henry, correspondent for Radio Free Europe/Radio Liberty, 38-40, 42

Hankiss, Elemér, Hungarian sociologist, 260

Hasani, Sinan, former head of Yugoslav State Presidency, 332

Havel, Václav, Czechoslovak playwright, 344-346

Hejdánek, Ladislav, Czechoslovak philosopher and dissident, 345

Hilevich, Nil, Soviet poet and literary critic, 198-199

Hint, Mati, Estonian linguist, 206-207

Honchar, Oles, Ukrainian writer, 199

Honcharenko, T. (Goncharenko, B.), first secretary of Voroshilovgrad Oblast party committee (USSR), 37-38

Honecker, Erich, leader of East German communist party: 223, 248; and Shevardnadze, 238; and

GDR economy, 238, 241;
and Soviet foreign
policy, 239, 362, 364;
and Gorbachev's reforms,
238, 240; resistance to
reform, 242; and church,
249-250; and visit to
Netherlands, 361-362;
and WTO, 361; and arms
control, 361

Hoxha, Enver, former
leader of Albanian
communist party, 295,
300-301

Hoxha, Fadil, former head
of Kosovo communist
party and member of
Yugoslav State Presi-
dency, 332

Hübl, Milan, Czechoslovak
dissident, 348

Hungary (Hungarian
People's Republic): 12-
13, 355; and Kádár,
12, 244-245; economic
problems, 12, 242-243,
247, 250, 256-260;
income disparities, 12,
243, 245; crime, 12,
247; and Hungarian
minorities in Romania,
12, 14-15, 182, 308,
315; and USSR, 12, 245;
suicide rate, 12, 245;
economic reforms, 12,
242, 250-252, 254-256;
drug abuse, 85-86; mor-
tality rates, 88; cigar-
ette smoking, 88; and
Vienna CSCE conference,
182, 186; communist
party, 242, 244, 246, 2-
55; declining living

standards, 243, 245; and
CMEA, 243, 260; resis-
tance to government
policies, 244; personnel
changes, 244-245; and
Gorbachev, 245; alcohol-
ism, divorce, and heart-
attack rates, 245; sup-
porters of reform,
245-246; bankruptcy law,
250-252, 258; unemploy-
ment, 252-254; banking
reform, 254-256; and IMF
and World Bank, 255,
257; and EEC, 256, 360;
and Chernobyl accident,
256; wage freeze, 258;
monetary policy, 259-
260; Patriotic People's
Front report on reform,
260-263; and Austria,
367. *See also* Czecho-
slovakia

Husák, Gustáv, leader of
Czechoslovak communist
party, 216, 218, 221-
223, 225, 230, 232-234,
348

Hysa, Zenel, Albanian
Central Committee offic-
ial, 304-305

Iakovlev, Aleksandr,
section head at
Institute of State and
Law, Academy of Sciences
of the USSR, 34-35,
392(n4)

Iakovlev, Aleksandr, Sov-
iet Politburo member and
head of Propaganda
Department, Central Com-
mittee of the CPSU, 52,
138, 209; on *glasnost*,

73; and Gorbachev, 381; and Russian nationalism, 381; and Ligachev, 381

Iakovlev, Egor, editor of *Moscow News*, 30

Ianaev, Gennadii I., head of USSR-USA Society (USSR), 175

Iazov, Dmitrii T., Soviet defense minister: 380-381; and Gorbachev, 136-138; biographical material on, 137; on *glasnost*, 137

India: and Vladivostok speech, 155

International Bank for Reconstruction and Development (IBRD, World Bank): and Hungary; and Poland, 279

International Labor Organization (ILO): and Poland, 275

International Monetary Fund (IMF): and Hungary; and Poland, 279

Iran, Islamic Republic of: relations with USSR, 9, 166-173; relations with USSR and Afghanistan war, 167-168

Iraq: relations with USSR, 9, 166, 169, 171, 173

Isaković, Antonije, deputy to president of the Serbian Academy of Arts

and Sciences (Yugoslavia), 341

Italy: and Vienna CSCE conference, 185-186; and Polish amnesty, 269, 277, 424(n10); Jaruzelski visit to, 277-278; relations with Albania, 295-296

Iurasov, Dmitrii, Soviet historian, 66-67

Jacoviello, Alberto, Moscow correspondent for *La Repubblica*, 230-232

Jankowski, Father Henryk (Poland), 268-269

Japan: and Vladivostok speech, 8, 155; "telebridge" with USSR, 73-74; and Kurile islands dispute with USSR, 74; and US- Soviet arms control negotiations, 139; and Kiribati, 162

Jaruzelski, General Wojciech, Polish communist party first secretary general: 13, 270, 274, 287, 312; arms control proposal, 146-148, 150; and Social Consultative Council, 270-271; visit to Italy, 277-278; and Pope, 278, 287-288; and USSR, 282-283; and Gorbachev, 283-284

Jedynak, Tadeusz, underground Solidarity leader, 266, 272

Jurevičius, Juozas, Lith-
uanian journalist, 349-
350

Kádár, János, Hungarian
communist party secre-
tary, 12, 244-245, 253,
312

Kallas, Teet, Estonian
novelist 204

Kanazir, Dušan, president
of Serbian Academy of
Arts and Sciences (Yugo-
slavia), 341

Kandinsky, Vasilii, Rus-
sian avant-garde artist,
52

Kantůrková, Eva, Czecho-
slovak dissident author,
346

Kapitsa, Mikhail, Soviet
deputy foreign minister,
157, 165

Kapolyi, László, Hungarian
minister of industry,
253-254

Karaduman, Necmettin,
speaker of the Turkish
Grand National Assembly,
296

Kardelj, Edvard, Slovenian
communist party leader
(Yugoslavia), 338, 340

Karpinskii, Len, Soviet
theater critic, 60

Karpov, Viktor, head of
Directorate for Arms

Control and Disarmament
of the Ministry of
Foreign Affairs (USSR),
126

Karpov, Vladimir, first
secretary of Union of
Writers of the USSR, 55,
58

Kashlev, Iurii, head of
Soviet delegation to
Vienna CSCE conference
and head of department
for humanitarian and
cultural contacts of the
Ministry of Foreign
Affairs, 180-181, 183-
184

Kasianenko, V., Soviet
historian, 65

Kaverin, Veniamin, Soviet
writer, 54

Kazakhstan (Kazakh SSR).
See Glasnost; KGB;
Soviet nationality
issues

Kazmin, Ivan, doctor of
law at All-Union
Research Institute of
Soviet Legislation,
35-36

Këllezi, Abdyl, former
Albanian Politburo mem-
ber, 300

Khameini, Ali, Iranian
president, 170

Kharchev, Konstantin,
chairman of Council for

Religious   Affairs
(USSR), 180

Khodasevich,   Vladislav,
Russian émigré writer,
55, 62

Khrushchev,   Nikita S.,
Soviet   leader   (1953-
1964), 2, 8, 41, 65,
136, 214, 307.

Kirata, Babera, Kiribati
minister of   natural
resources and develop-
ment, 162-163

Kiribati: 155;   fishing
agreement with   USSR,
161-163

Kiszczak, Czesław, Polish
minister of   internal
affairs, 268, 270

Klimov,   Elem,   head   of
Union of Cinema Workers
of the USSR, 54

Klymenko,   Oleksandr,
Soviet journalist, 68-70

Kohl, Helmut, West German
chancellor, 146, 149

Kolbin,   Gennadii Vasilevich, first secretary
of   Kazakh   communist
party, 189-190, 193

Koldunov, Aleksandr, for-
mer commander in chief
of Soviet air defense
forces, 136

Kołodziejczyk,   Michal,
vice president of Polish
parliament, 364-365

Kondratev,   Viacheslav,
Soviet writer, 55

Konrad, György, Hungarian
writer, 365

Kopecký,   Miloš,   Czech
actor, 235

Koriagin, Anatolii, Soviet
dissident, 285

Kornai, János, Hungarian
economist, 260

Kornienko,   Georgii M.,
Soviet   first   deputy
foreign   minister   and
deputy chief of the
Department of   Inter-
national   Affairs,
Central Committee of the
CPSU, 166, 175-176

Korotych, Vitalii, editor
of Ogonek (USSR), 55

Kourtis, Antonis, Greece,
320

Kosolapov, Richard, former
chief   editor   of
Kommunist (USSR), 108-
112, 405(n20)

Kouřil, Vladimír, secre-
tary of Jazz Section of
Czech Union of Music-
ians, 228

Kovalev, Aleksei, head of Spasenie [Salvation] and member of Council of Cultural Ecology (USSR), 378

Kovalev, Anatolii, Soviet first deputy foreign minister, 177, 183

Kraja, Osman, rector of Tirana University (Albania), 296

Krawczuk, Aleksander, Polish minister of culture, 283

Kruglei, M. M., Belorussian first deputy minister of education, 195

Król, Krzysztof, Confederation of Independent Poland leader, 266

Kulik, G.I. Marshal of the Soviet Union (d. 1950), 67

Kulikov, Viktor, first deputy minister of defense (USSR), 137

Kunaev, Dinmukhamed, former first secretary of Kazakh communist party, 10, 20, 189-193

Kundera, Milan, Czechoslovak émigré writer, 364-367

Kunitsyn, Georgii, Soviet writer and literary critic, 47-49

Kurowski, Z., deputy secretary of CMEA, 357

Kurón, Jacek, former Solidarity adviser and political analyst, 271, 286

Kuwait: and USSR, 169-170, 173

Kuznetsov, Feliks, first secretary of Moscow City Writers' Organization 54

Kvitsinskii, Iulii, Soviet ambassador to FRG, 240

Lakshin, Vladimir, chief editor of Znamia (USSR), 53, 60, 373

Laliotis, Kostas, Greek official in charge of government propaganda, 322

Landa, Malva, Soviet human rights activist, 342

Larijani, Mohammad Javad, Iranian deputy foreign minister for economic and international affairs, 166, 171

Latsis, Otto, Soviet economist, 60-61

Latvia (Latvian SSR): See Chautauqua conference; Soviet nationality issues; USSR

Lázár, György former

Hungarian prime minister, 244

Lebedev, Major General Iurii, member of General Staff (USSR), 134-135

Lemeshev, first name unknown, member of Pamiat, 209

Lendvai, Paul, Austrian journalist, 367

Ligachev, Egor, Soviet Politburo member and Central Committee secretary for ideology: 209; and speech at social scientists' conference, 26-28, 395(n5); on education, 28; criticism of *Pravda*, 48; and *glasnost*, 51, 381; on the play *Silver Wedding*, 56; on Soviet history, 64; and "conservative" resistance to Gorbachev's reforms, 230-231; and Iakovlev, 381; and Nikonov, 381

Likhachev, Dmitrii, Soviet academician, 55, 62, 378

Likhodeev, Leonid, Soviet writer, 61

Lini, Walter, prime minister of Vanuatu, 163

Lis, Bogdan, underground Solidarity leader, 266, 272

Lisianskii, Mark, Soviet poet, 372-373

Lisichkin, Gennadii, Soviet economist, 104

Liubimov, Iurii, Soviet émigré theater director, 53

Liu Shuqing, Chinese deputy foreign minister, 158

Lizichev, Aleksei, chief of Main Political Administration of the Soviet Army and Navy, 137

Lomeiko, Vladimir, Soviet ambassador-at-large, 124, 177-179, 408(n18)

Losoto, Elena, correspondent for *Komsomolskaia pravda* (USSR), 373

Lubbers, Ruud, Dutch prime minster, 361-362

Lushev, Petr, first deputy minister of defense (USSR), 137

Maksimov, Iurii, commander in chief of Strategic Rocket Forces (USSR), 137

Malevich, Kazimir, Russian avant-garde artist, 52

Malinowski, Roman, chairman of Polish parliament, 274

Markov, Georgii, former first secretary of Union of Writers of the USSR, 55

Maslen, John, head of EEC department for communist nations, 357

Massing, Uku, Estonian poet, 205

Mastnak, Tomas, Slovene sociologist (Yugoslavia), 336-337

Matlock, Jack, senior adviser on Soviet affairs at National Security Council, 176-177

Mazi, Franc, Ljubljana state prosecutor (Yugoslavia), 337

Medgyessy, Péter, Hungarian minister of finance, 259

Meisner, Cardinal Joachim, head of Bishops' Conference of East German Roman Catholic Church, 250

Messner, Zbigniew, Polish prime minister, 282

Merezhkovskii, Dmitrii, Russian émigré writer, 55

Meierkhold, Vsevolod, Soviet theater director (d. 1940), 66-67, 399(n13)

Mezzetti, Fernando, Moscow correspondent for *Il Gioranle* (Milan), 38-41

Miasnikov, Aleksei, Soviet sociologist and former political prisoner, 344

Michnik, Adam, Solidarity leader, 266

Mikhalkov, Sergei, chairman of the Board of Union of Writers of the RSFSR, 55, 62, 398(n64)

Mikhailov, Oleg, Soviet literary critic, 59-60

Mikhoels, Solomon, Russian Jewish actor and director of Jewish State Theater (d. 1948), 373

Mikulić, Branko, Yugoslavian prime minister, 336-337

Milošević, Slobodan, president of Serbian Central Committee Presidium (Yugoslavia), 330

Mints, Isaak, Soviet historian, 65

Mironenko, Viktor, head of Komsomol (USSR), 48, 377

Mirza, Kymbatbaev, guru from Karakalpak ASSR (USSR), 349-351

Misharin, Aleksandr, Soviet playwright, 56

Mitrović, Zagorka, member of Plementine delegation before Federal Assembly (Yugoslavia), 328

Moczulski, Leszek, leader of Confederation of Independent Poland, 266

Molchanov, Vladimir, moderator of Soviet television program "Before and after Midnight," 76-77, 400(n14, n16)

Moldova, György, Hungarian writer, 247

Mongolia: and Vladivostok speech, 156-157

Mousavi, Mir Hossein, Iranian prime minister, 170-171

Mutual and Balanced Force Reduction (MBFR) talks: NATO-Warsaw Pact discussions on replacing, 141-142, 147, 151, 188

Nabokov, Vladimir, Soviet émigré writer, 5, 58, 62

Natorf, Włodzimierz, Polish ambassador to USSR, 282

Natta, Alessandro, Italian communist party leader, 239

Nazarbaev, Nursultan, chairman of Council of Ministers of the Kazakh SSR, 192

Nekrasov, Viktor, Soviet émigré writer, 53

Nenashev, Mikhail, chairman of State Publishing Commission (USSR), 54

Netherlands: and Vienna CSCE conference, 187; and Honecker, 361-362

Nifontova, Rufina, Soviet actor, 56

Nigmatulin, Talgat, Uzbek karate champion, movie actor, and director: murder of, 349-351

Nikonov, Viktor, Soviet Politburo member and Central Committee secretary for agriculture, 381

North Atlantic Treaty Organization (NATO): and US-Soviet arms control negotiations, 8, 146, 148-149, 152; concern over SS-20 deployments, 134; concern over Soviet short-range missiles, 139-149; concern over on-site inspections, 140, 146; and discussions with Warsaw Pact on replacing Mutual and Balanced Force Reductions (MBFR) talks, 141-142, 147, 151, 188; and conventional arms control, 150-151; and Vienna conference, 188; and Greece, 319, 321-323, 325; and Turkey, 322

Novodvorskaia, Valeriia, Soviet human rights activist, 342

Novotný, Antonín, former Czechoslovak leader, 211

Nudel, Ida, Soviet dissident, 178

Nyers, Rezső, Hungarian economist, 246, 253, 260

Obukhov, Aleksei, Soviet arms control negotiator, 145-146

O'Keeffe, Laurence, chief British delegate to Vienna CSCE conference, 185

Okudzhava, Bulat, Soviet poet/balladeer, 55

Olenenko, Yu. O., Ukrainian minister of culture, 199

Oman, Sultanate of: establishment of diplomatic relations with USSR, 169

Onyszkiewicz, Janusz, Polish opposition spokesman, 286

Organization of Petroleum Exporting Countries (OPEC): and USSR, 166, 171

Orlandić, Marko, Montenegrin member of Yugoslavian Central Committee Presidium, 332

Orlov, Iurii, Soviet émigré dissident, 343

Orzechowski, Marian, Polish foreign minister, 147

Osmanczyk, Edmund, former member of Polish parliament, 271

Owen, David, British Social Democratic Party member, 49

Palmer, Mark, US ambassador designate to Hungary, 176

Pałubicki, Janusz, underground Solidarity leader, 272

Pamiat. See Soviet nationality issues

Papandreou, Andreas, Greek prime minister, 318-323, 325

Papandreou, Vassa, Greek deputy minister of industry, 325

Papoulias, Karolas, Greek foreign minister, 319

Pashkov, Evgenii, Soviet geologist, 209

Pasternak, Boris, Soviet writer, 5, 55, 62

Pavlychko, Dmytro, Ukrainian poet, 202

People's Republic of China (PRC): 6, 152, 173; and Vladivostok speech, 8, 155-159; and negotiations with USSR, 158-161; and Albania, 297. *See also* Czechoslovakia

Pérez de Cuéllar, Javier, United Nations secretary general, 173

Petrosiants, Andronik, head of Soviet delegation to Geneva nuclear testing talks, 145

Petrovskii, Vladimir, Soviet deputy foreign minister, 126-127, 169, 171, 175, 409(n37)

Petrushevskaia, Liudmila, Soviet playwright, 57

Piadyshev, Boris, spokesman for Ministry of Foreign affairs (USSR), 150-151, 173

Pigolkin, Albert, doctor of law at All-Union Research Institute of Soviet Legislation, 35-36

Pinior, Józef, underground Solidarity leader, 272

Plachynda, Serhii, Ukrainian writer, 200-201

Plamberger, Vlado, member of Socialist Alliance (Yugoslavia), 338

Poland (Polish People's Republic): press/media, 5, 13, 277, 285; Polish Catholic Church, 13-14, 267-268, 271-272, 276, 281, 290-292; amnesties, 13, 265-268, 273, 275-276, 277, 280, 423(n6); Solidarity, 13-14, 268, 270, 272-277, 281, 289, 354; Social Consultative Council, 13, 270-272, 276; economic relations with USSR, 13, 279-280, 282; and Gorbachev, 13, 282-287; and Soviet-Polish history, 13; opening of consulate in Lvov, USSR, 13, 282-283; ending of diplomatic isolation, 13, 277, 281; and US sanctions, 13-14, 270, 278-281; visit of Pope, 14, 287-293; and relations with USSR, 15, 282-284; drug abuse, 86; mortality rates, 88; cigarette smoking, 88; sewage treatment plants, 90; health care, 91; influence of 1980-81 events on Soviet economic reform debate, 111; and Vienna CSCE conference, 181; reactions to amnesties, 268--270; and ILO, 275; and IMF and World Bank, 279; US-Polish trade, 280; and Soviet Poles, 283; and Russian Orthodox Church, 284; and Soviet reforms, 284-287; and Soviet dissidents, 285; opposition attitude toward

Gorbachev and Soviet reforms, 286. *See also* Eastern Europe; France; Italy; Jaruzelski; Pope John Paul II; United Kingdom; United States

Pope John Paul II: visit to Poland, 14, 287-293; and Polish amnesties, 268; meeting with Jaruzelski at Vatican, 278; and US sanctions on Poland, 281; on Polish-Vatican relations, 291; and Lithuania, 291; and USSR, 291

Ponomarev, Boris, former head of International Department, Central Committee of the CPSU, 126

Potáč, Svatopluk, chairman of State Planning Commission (Czechoslovakia), 218

Potapov, Anatolii, minister of health of the RSFSR, 85

Pozdniakov, Evgenii, senior editor at Novosti Press Agency, 43

Pozner, Vladimir, Soviet television commentator, 50, 74-75

Pozsgay, Imre, general secretary of Hungarian Patriotic People's Front, 246

Primakov, Evgenii, head of Institute for the World Economy and International Relations, Academy of Sciences of the USSR, 127

Prokhanov, Aleksandr, Soviet writer, 70-71

Proskurin, Petr, Soviet writer, 62

Pukk, Holger, Estonian author, 204

Qian Qichen, Chinese deputy foreign minister, 158-160

Raftopoulos, George, former president of the General Confederation of Greek Workers, 322-323

Radio Liberty, 286

Rafsanjani, Ali Hashemi, speaker of Islamic Consultative Assembly (Iran), 169

Rakhmetov, K., former Komsomol secretary in physics department of Kazakh State University, 193

Ramadan, Taha Yassin, Iraqi first deputy prime minister, 171

Rashidov, Sharaf, Uzbek communist party first secretary, 34, 192

Razumovskaia, Liudmila, Soviet playwright, 57

Reagan, Ronald, US president: 323, 345-346, 366; and Reykjavik summit, 7, 131, 372; 1985 *Izvestiia* interview, 76; and Gorbachev, 172; and sanctions on Poland, 278-281

Redman, Charles, US Department of State spokesman, 270

Rekunkov, Aleksandr, Soviet Procurator General, 82-83

Reufi, Kadri, former ethnic Turkish leader in Yugoslavia, 329

Riuitel, Arnold, chairman of Presidium of the Supreme Soviet of the Estonian SSR, 45

Rodos, Boris, Soviet lieutenant general in Ministry of State Security (d.1955?), 66, 399(n14)

Rogachev, Igor, Soviet deputy foreign minister, 158, 160

Rogovin, V. Z., Soviet doctor of philosophical sciences: on "social justice," 99-105

Romania, Socialist Republic of: and Hungarian minorities in, 12, 14-15, 182, 308, 315; mortality rates, 88; health care, 91; and

Vienna CSCE conference, 180, 182; and reform, 306-310, 312, 317; media, 307, 309, 311, 314, 317; and Soviet reforms, 308, 310, 312, 314-316; and CMEA, 308, 310-313; and Gorbachev's speech to January 1987 Central Committee plenum, 309; and Soviet media, 311-312; economic relations with USSR, 309311, 313, 313-314, 318; policy of Soviet leadership toward, 311; and Gorbachev visit to, 311-318; and Greece, 319; and Balkan nuclear-and chemical weapons-free zone proposal, 322; foreign policy, 355; and EEC, 358, 360. *See also* Ceauşescu; Czechoslovakia; Gorbachev

Romanov, Grigorii, former Leningrad communist party chief, 20

Romaszewski, Zbigniew, leader of Commission for Intervention and the Rule of Law (Poland), 275-276

Rosner, Jan, Polish lawyer, 275

Rostropovich, Mstislav, Soviet émigré musician, 53

Rovan, Joseph, French Jewish teacher at the Sorbonne, 366

Rozhdestvenskii, Robert, Soviet party poet, 5

Rozmarynowicz, Andrzej, Polish lawyer, 275

Rusakov, Konstantin, former head of Department for Liaison with Communist and Workers' Parties of Socialist Countries, Central Committee of the CPSU, 126

Runnel, Hando, Estonian poet, 205

Rust, Matthias, West German pilot, 8, 135-136

Rybakov, Anatolii, Soviet writer, 64

Ryzhkov, Nikolai, Soviet Politburo member, prime minister, and chairman of Council of Ministers, 192, 382

Sabitova, Zh. A., Kazakh schoolteacher, 193

Sadouski, P., Belorussian writer, 195

Sakharov, Andrei, Soviet dissident: 9, 15, 178, 184, 285, 342, 344

Salimov, Akil, deputy chairman of Supreme Soviet of the USSR, 163-165

Samsonov, Aleksandr, Soviet historian, 65

Savitskii, S., employee of Kazakh Television Center (USSR): killed in Alma-Ata riots, 193

Schlögel, Karl, West German specialist on Russia, 365, 367

Schönherr, Albrecht, former chairman of Federation of Evangelical Churches (GDR), 248

Schmidt, Max, director of Institute for International Politics and Economics (GDR), 363

Shabanov, Vitalii, Soviet deputy minister of defense, 128, 129

Shakhnazarov, G., deputy to head of Department for Liaison with Communist and Workers' Parties of Socialist Countries, Central Committee of the CPSU, 124

Shatalov, V. P., Voroshilovgrad Oblast public prosecutor, 37

Shatrov, Mikhail, Soviet playwright, 56, 60, 64, 67, 285

Shcharanskii, Natan, Soviet Jewish émigré dissident, 343

Shcherbitskii, Volodymyr, Ukrainian communist

party   leader: and
Berkhin   affair, 37;   on
Pravda   criticism   of
Cherkassy   Oblast
officials, 48

Shevardnadze,   Eduard,
Soviet foreign minister,
130; and US-Soviet rec-
iprocal   nuclear testing
offer, 143-144; and arms
control   negotiations,
153;   and South Pacific
nuclear-free   zone
proposal, 161; and Iran,
168;   and Vienna CSCE
conference, 177, 179; on
"democracy,"   179;
meetings   with   Shultz,
177; and Czechoslovakia,
223, 229;   and GDR and
Honecker, 238

Shikalov,   Viktor,   Soviet
delegate   to   Vienna
CSCE conference, 181

Shmelev,   Nikolai,   Soviet
economist, 386

Shultz, George,   US secretary of state: interview
on Soviet television, 6,
71-72;   Moscow meeting,
143-144,   231;   and
Gorbachev, 143;   Vienna
meetings with Shevard-
nadze, 177

Shundik,   Nikolai,   Soviet
writer, Board Secretary,
RSFR Union   of Writers,
62

Sihanouk, Prince Norodom,
former   leader   of
Cambodian: and   Sino-

Vietnamese   relations,
158

Šik, Ota,   exiled Czechoslovak economist, 214

Silaev,   Ivan,   head   of
Machine-Building   Bureau
and deputy   prime   minister (USSR), 384

Siła-Nowicki,   Władysław,
Polish lawyer, 275

Šimečka,   Milan,   Czechoslovak   dissident, 346

Simonov, Vladimir,   Soviet
journalist: and   television   interview   with
Margaret Thatcher, 76-77

Skóra,   Tadeusz,   Polish
deputy   minister   of
justice, 265-266

Skubiszewski,   Krzysztof,
Polish lawyer, 275

Slepak,   Vladimir,   Soviet
dissident, 178

Sliunkov, Nikolai,   Soviet
Politburo   member   and
Central Committee secre-
tary in   charge   of
civilian economy,   379,
381-382.

Słomka,   Adam,   Confederation of   Independent
Poland leader, 266

Smirnov,   G.   L.,   former
director of Institute of
Philosophy,   Academy of

Sciences of the USSR, 125

Sokolov, Efrem, first secretary of Belorussian communist party, 197-198

Sokolov, Sergei, former Soviet defense minister: dismissal over Rust affair, 8, 136, 138, 380-381; on Soviet defenses, 129

Solarz, Stephan J., US Congressman, 280

Solidarity. *See* Poland

Solomentsev, Mikhail, head of Party Control Committee of the CPSU, 190

Solzhenitsyn, Aleksandr, Soviet émigré writer, 54

Sorokin, Mikhail, chief of Main Inspectorate (USSR), 137

Soviet foreign policy: "new thinking" in foreign and national security policy, 7, 41, 119-130, 407(n7); and arms control negotiations, 7-8, 127-128, 134-135,138-146, 148-153; and Reykjavik summit, 7-8, 130-133, 138, 148, 152; and SDI, 7, 131-134; Vladivostok speech, 8, 155-158, 163; and Afghanistan, 8, 70, 119, 156, 166-168; and PRC, 8, 119, 155-161; and Japan, 8, 155, 164;

and Southeast Asia (ASEAN), 8, 155, 163-165; and Pacific Ocean region, 8, 161; and Iran, 9, 166-173; and Iraq, 9, 166, 169, 171, 173; and Iran-Iraq war, 9, 166, 168-174, 415 (n36); and Vienna CSCE conference, 9, 177-183, 185-188; and human rights, 9, 177-188, 415 (n2); and proposal for human rights conference, 9, 179, 182-184; and GDR, 11, 362-364; opening of Polish consulate in Lvov, 13, 282-283; and internal reforms, 41-42; nuclear testing moratorium, 119; and arms control verification, 119, 127-128, 138-140, 145-146, 153; and Dobrynin, 119, 121-122; comparison of Gorbachev and Brezhnev party congress speeches on, 123-124, 408(n17); Soviet academic writings on, 124-125, 127; organizational and personnel changes in foreign policy apparatus, 126-128, 161; and Nuclear Nonproliferation Treaty, 127; and Stockholm CSCE conference, 128; civil-military relations and defense allocations, 128-129; May 1986 conference of foreign policy officials, 130; military criticism of nuclear testing moratorium, 134; debate over SS-20 deployments, 134-

135; nuclear testing proposals, 143-145; and Australia, 155; and Kiribati, 155, 161-163; and India, 155; and proposal for conference on Asia and Pacific, 155-156; and United States (*see above* for arms control), 156, 164, 166, 169, 172-174, 180; and military bases in Indochina, 156, 165; and Mongolia, 156-157; and Vietnam's occupation of Cambodia, 157, 159-160, 164-165; and Vanuatu, 161, 163; and Cook Islands, 161; and Indonesia, 163-165; and Singapore, 163-164; and Malaysia, 163; and Thailand, 163-165; and Vietnam, 164-165; and OPEC, 166, 171; and UAE, 169; and Oman, 169; and Syria, 168-169, 171; and Kuwait, 169-170, 173; Iranian attack on Soviet freighter, 170; and Israel, 172; and United Nations, 173; and Czechoslovakia, 231. *See also* Chautauqua conference; Gorbachev; GDR; Honecker

Soviet Interview Project: on voter participation in USSR, 44

Soviet journals (publications of): *Literaturnaia gazeta*, 24, 34, 47, 50, 54, 79, 104, 133, 173, 209, 283, 371, 373, 378; *Sovetskaia kultura*, 24, 57-58, 67, 209; *Pravda*, 25, 29, 37, 48-49, 51-52, 72, 92, 112, 127, 192, 217, 285, 316, 371, 375-377; *Moscow News*, 29, 37-38, 45, 61, 62-63, 67, 70, 134-135, 208; *Voprosy filosofii*, 29, 124-125; *Izvestiia*, 35, 46, 52, 65, 75-76, 83, 128, 161, 167, 169, 181, 191, 370, 373, 378; *Radianska Ukraina*, 36; *Teatr*, 51; *Shakhmatnoe obozrenie*, 58; *Literaturnaia Rossiia*, 58-59, 372; *Ogonek*, 58, 63; *Novyi mir*, 58, 64, 83; *Komsomolskaia pravda*, 61, 83, 192, 373-375, 377; *Znamia*, 64; *Druzhba narodov*, 64; *Kommunist*, 64, 120-121; *Argumenty i fakty*, 65, 82, 192; *Molod Ukrainy*, 68-69; *Sobesednik* (weekly supplement to *Komsomolskaia pravda)*, 70, 79; *Sovetskaia Belorussiia*, 80; *Sovetskaia molodezh*, 81; *Novoe vremia*, 82; *Zhurnalist*, 82; *Uchitelskaia gazeta*, 84; *Sotsialisticheskaia industriia*, 85; *MEMO;* 126; *Krasnaia zvezda*, 129, 137; *Literatura i mastatstva*, 194-195; *Kultura i zhyttya*, 199; *Literaturna Ukraina*, 200, 202; *Sirp ja Vasar*, 203-204, 206; *Looming*, 205; *Rahva Hääl*, 205-206; *Noorte Hääl*, 206; *Edasi*, 206; *Moskovskaia pravda*, 208; *Švyturys*, 349, 351;

Sovetskaia Litva, 351; *Nedelia* (supplement to *Izvestiia*), 373; *Molodaia gvardiia*, 374; *Komsomolskoe znamia*, 376; *Stroitelnaia gazeta*, 378

Soviet nationality issues: Crimean Tatar demonstrations, 4; and Soviet reforms, 9; Kazakhstan and Alma-Ata riots, 10, 189-193, 206; and *glasnost*, 10, 208; Baltic republics, 10; Estonia, 10, 203-207, 417(n3); Belorussian language campaign, 10, 194-199; Ukrainian language campaign, 10, 200-203; Russian nationalism, 10, 61; Pamiat, 10, 208-210, 373, 377-378; criticisms of nationalism, 61-62; Iran-Iraq war and Soviet Muslims, 172; and Latvian press/media, 176-177; and Kazakh press, 191-192; Ukrainian cultural liberalization, 199-200; and Ukrainian press, 200; and Estonian press, 203, 205, 207. *See also* Chautauqua conference; Iakovlev

Speakes, Larry, White House spokesman, 269

Srp, Karel, chairman of Jazz Section of Czech Union of Musicians, 226, 228

Stalin and Stalinism. *See* Borisov; Evtushenko;

Glasnost; Gorbachev; Iurasov; Samsonov; Shatrov; Svobodin; Yugoslavia

Stambolič, Petar, former Yugoslav leader, 331

Starodubov, Major General Viktor, head of arms control sector of International Department, Central Committee of the CPSU, 126, 128, 409(n34)

Stelmachowski, Andrzej, Polish lawyer, 275

Strategic Defense Initiative (SDI), 7, 131-134, 184, 321

Štrougal, Lubomír, Czechoslovak prime minister, 220-221, 223

Struchkov, N. A., Soviet specialist on prison system, 285

Sukhorukov, Dmitrii, chief of the Main Personnel Directorate, 137

Suleimenov, Olzhas, head of Union of Writers of the Kazakh SSR, 191

Svobodin, Aleksandr, Soviet theater critic, 60

Sweden: and Albania, 297

Switzerland: and Vienna CSCE conference, 187; and Albania, 297

Sychev, Viacheslav, general secretary of CMEA, 359

Syria: and USSR, 168-169, 171

Tabai, Ieremia, president of Kiribati, 162

Talyzin, Nikolai, candidate Politburo member, chairman of Gosplan, and deputy prime minister (USSR), 158, 384

Tanyuk, Les, chief director of Kiev Youth Theater, 200

Tarasau, Kastus, Belorussian writer, 194

Tarkovskii, Andrei, Soviet émigré filmmaker, 53

Telecommunications Agency of the Soviet Union (TASS), 65, 143-144, 168, 170, 173-174, 184-185, 189-190, 208, 234, 285

Thatcher, Margaret, British prime minister: 323; interview on Soviet television, 6, 76-77; and Gorbachev, 141, 230; and Iran-Iraq war, 172

Theodosi, Koco, former Albanian Politburo member, 300

Titiz, Mustapha Tinaz, Turkish minister of state, 296

Tiutiukin, Stanislav, Soviet historian, 65

Tolstykh, Valentin, senior staff member at Institute of Philosophy, Academy of Sciences of the USSR, 24

Tovstonogov, Georgii, Leningrad theater director, 56-57

Trajković, Momčilo, executive secretary of Priština Presidium (Yugoslavia), 328

Tretiak, Ivan, commander in chief of air defense forces (USSR), 137

Trifonov, Iurii, Soviet writer, 64

Troepolskii, Gavriil, Soviet essayist, 53

Turkey: and Vienna CSCE conference, 181-182; and Turkish minorities in Bulgaria, 181-182, 321, 323; relations with Albania, 296-297; Albanian minority in, 296; and Bulgaria, 319-320; and Greece, 319, 323, 325; reaction to GreekBulgarian declaration, 320; and Balkan nuclearand chemical weaponsfree zone proposal, 322; and NATO, 322

Tvardovskii, Aleksandr, Soviet poet and former

editor of *Novyi mir*, 52-53, 64

Tymchyk, A. I., head of Public Education Board of the Kiev City Executive Committee, 202

Uhl, Petr, Czechoslovak dissident, 345

Ukraine (Ukrainian SSR); language campaign, 10, 200-203; strikes, 22; Ukrainian Central Committee and Berkhin affair, 36-37; cultural liberalization, 199-200; press, 200; language campaign and *glasnost*, 202. *See also* Shcherbitskii

Ulianov, Mikhail, actor and chairman of the board of the Union of Theater Workers of the RSFSR, 56

Union of Soviet Socialist Republics (USSR, Soviet Union): reforms in general, 1-3, 16-17; public reaction to reforms 1, 16, 22, 370; and Eastern Europe, 1-2, 15-16, 354-356; punishment of officials, 3-4, 37, 47; electoral reforms, 4, 23, 32-33, 43-46; "democratization," 4, 23, 32, 38-40, 42- 43, 180, 343, 385; intelligentsia, 5, 17, 24, 61, 84, 108, 191, 369, 389; censorship, 5, 50, 53-54, 58, 205-206; press/

media (*see below* for television), 5, 35, 40, 47-53, 68-72, 79, 82-84, 86, 132, 134, 176-177, 184, 190-192, 200, 203, 205, 207-209, 232, 350-351, 371-379, 386-388; cultural liberalization, 23, 52-63, 199-200, 381; prostitution, 6, 79-82; drug abuse, 6, 47, 82-86; medical system, 6, 47; economic performance, 6, 95-99, 107, 116-118; economic reforms in general, 6, 17, 21; environmental problems, 7, 113; anti-corruption campaign, 7, 34-35, 130; and Rust affair, 8, 135-138, 381; and releases of political prisoners, 9, 23, 185, 342-344; restrictions on foreign travel, 9; attitude of dissidents toward Sakharov, 15, 342; resistance to reforms, 16, 20-25, 27-30, 41, 43, 49, 231, 369-372, 382, 384, 388-389; treatment of Jews, 16-17, 184-185, 372-374; informal groups, 17, 374-379; June 1987 Central Committee plenum, 17, 380, 382-384; law on state enterprises, 17, 21, 380, 382, 384-385; law on "individual labor," 21; campaign against "unearned" or "nonlabor" income, 21, 101-102, 403(n29); Ukrainian and Belorussian strikes, 22;

Chernobyl accident, 23, 49-50, 99, 136, 143; judicial abuses and reforms, 33-38, 60, 186; Politburo, 32-34, 48, 106, 112, 136, 230, 232, 380-382; unpublished directives, 35-36; law against unjust actions of senior officials, 36; Berkhin affair, 36-38; river diversion project, 40, 48; Union of Cinema Workers of the USSR, 40, 52, 54; public opinion, 40, 44, 48; Union of Theater Workers of the RSFSR, 44, 55-57, 60; World War II monument design competition, 48; criticisms of elite privileges, 48, 103; samizdat, 48, 53, 66, 193, 343, 349, 351; television, 49-50, 70-77, 84, 131-133, 176-177, 184, 209, 371-372, 386; sinking of passenger ship in Black Sea, 49; sinking of Soviet nuclear submarine off Bermuda, 49; law on suppression of criticism, 50; Eighth Congress of Union of Writers of the USSR, 52, 54-55; Glavlit, 52; Soviet history, 60, 65-68, 374 (*see also Glasnost*); religion, 61, 180, 185-186, 349; criticisms of war in Afghanistan, 68-72; Twenty-seventh Congress of the CPSU, 82, 103-106, 112, 119-121, 123-126, 129-130; anti-alcohol campaign, 84, 86, 96-97, 370-371; life expectancy, 87, 96; health care, 89; criticisms of rural life in, 92-94; "social justice," 99-105; economic reform debates, 108-112; 1986 party program, 106, 112, 125, 129; defection of Soviet citizen to Sweden in small aircraft, 136; arrest of border guard troops in Moscow, 136; Rust affair and civil-military relations, 136; military personnel changes, 136-137; and Chautauqua conference, 175-177; Moscow international peace forum, 184, 240, 285, 309, 342; attitude of dissidents toward reforms, 342-344; Eastern religions in Lithuania, 349, 351; and CMEA, 356-359; rock groups, 375-377; punks and hippies, 375-377; Liubery, 375, 377; Afghan veterans, 375, 379; June conference on economic reforms, 379-380; personnel changes in Politburo, 380-382. *See also* Afghanistan; Eastern Europe; Gorbachev; Greece; *Glasnost;* Japan; Jaruzelski; Pope John Paul II; Soviet foreign policy; Soviet journals; Soviet nationality issues; Shevardnadze; TASS; United States; individual East European nations

United Arab Emirates (UAE): establishment of diplomatic relations with USSR, 169

United Kingdom (UK, Great Britain): and US-Soviet arms control negotiations, 141, 149; Gorbachev's arms control proposals and Labour Party opposition to nuclear weapons, 143; and Vienna CSCE conference, 180-182, 185, 187; reaction to Polish amnesty, 269

United Nations: and Iran-Iraq war, 172-174; and USSR, 173

United States of America (USA): 161, 166, 169-170, 173; sanctions on Poland, 13-14, 270; 278-281; "telebridges" with USSR, 74-75; and arms control negotiations, 138-146, 148-153; and USSR-Kiribati fishing pact, 162; and Chautauqua conference, 175-177; and Vienna CSCE conference, 180-183, 186-187; reaction to Polish amnesty, 269-270; US-Polish trade, 280; and Greece, 323, 325

Urban, Jerzy, Polish government spokesman, 275, 281-282

Ustinov, A. A.,Department of Propaganda and

Agitation of the Kazakh Central Committee, 192

Uzbekistan (Uzbek SSR): corruption in, 34-35, 192

Vaculík, Ludvík, Czechoslovak dissident, 215-216

Vaitsos, Kostas, Greek deputy minister of economics, 324

Vaksberg, Arkadii, Soviet legal commentator, 60

Vanuatu: establishment of diplomatic relations with USSR, 161, 163; fishing agreement with USSR, 163

Vasilev, Boris, Soviet writer, 61

Vasilev, Dmitrii, Pamiat leader, journalist, and photographer (USSR), 208-209, 378

Vasilev, Ivan, Soviet writer, 92-94

Vasilev, Vladimir, Soviet actor, 56

Velekhova, Nina, Soviet Writer, 373

Velyati, Ali Akbar, Iranian foreign minister, 168

Vetrov, H. M., head of Voroshilovgrad Administration of Internal Affairs (USSR), 37

Vinogradov, Viktor, Soviet architect, 209

Vlasov, Aleksandr, Soviet minister of internal affairs, 85

Voice of America (VOA), Soviets cease jamming of, 6, 228

Volkov, Oleg, Soviet journalist, 48-49, 60

von Weiszäcker, Richard, West German president, 366

Voronin, Lev, chairman of State Supply Committee and deputy prime minster (USSR), 384

Vorontsov, Iulii M., Soviet first deputy foreign minister, 138-140, 171-172

Voznesenskii, Andrei, Soviet poet, 52, 55, 61

Wałęsa, Lech, former leader of Solidarity, 269-273, 275, 280-281

Warsaw Treaty Organization (WTO, Warsaw Pact): 355; and discussions with NATO on replacing MBFR talks, 141-142, 147, 151, 188; March 1987 foreign ministers' meeting, 142; arms control proposals presented at Berlin summit of, 150-151; criticism of NATO call for increased conventional defense spending, 151; creation of "special commission" on arms control, 151; and Vienna CSCE conference, 188; and Bulgaria, 319, 321; and Greece, 323; and Honecker, 361

Wasilkowska, Zofia, former Polish Supreme Court judge and minister of justice, 275

Whitehead, John, US deputy secretary of state, 279

Wójcik, Dariusz, Confederation of Independent Poland leader, 266

Wörner, Manfred, West German defense minister, 146

Yugoslavia, Socialist Federal Republic of: press/media, 5, 330; and Bulgaria and Macedonian issue, 15, 319; and ethnic conflict with Albanians in Kosovo, 15, 326-333, 336, 339, 341; dissent, 15, 335-336, 338; intellectuals, 15, 337; compared to USSR, 15; resistance to reform, 15; relations with Albania, 297; and Bulgaria, 319-320; reaction to Greek-Bulgarian declaration,

320; and Greece and Macedonian issue, 320; and Tito, 331, 336-341; and Balkan nuclear- and chemical weapons-free zone proposal, 322; and Albania and Kosovo conflict, 327, 332; Serbian-Croatian conflict, 335; and Serbians (*see above* for Kosovo conflict), 338-341; economic problems, 339-340; federal system of, 340; and Stalin, 340-341; and "democratization," 341

Yu Zhizhong, Chinese Foreign Ministry spokesman, 158

Zaikov, Lev, Soviet Politburo member and Central Committee secretary for defense sector of economy, 229, 381-382

Zagladin, Vadim, first deputy head of International Department, Central Committee of the CPSU, 125

Zakenfelds, Žanis, chairman of Presidium of the Society for Friendship and Cultural Ties between Latvia and Foreign Lands (USSR), 175

Zakharov, Vasilii, Soviet minister of culture, 283

Zalygin, Sergei, Soviet novelist and chief editor of *Novyi mir* (USSR), 29, 60

Zamiatin, Evgenii, Russian émigré writer, 5, 55, 59-60

Zaslavskaia, Tatiana, Soviet sociologist: on resistance to economic reforms, 25; on "social justice," 99-105, 403 (n26); on reforms, 109

Zhivkov, Todor, leader of Bulgarian communist party, 312, 318-321, 323, 325

Zieliński, Tadeusz, Polish lawyer, 275

Zimmermann, Warren, head of US delegation to Vienna conference, 182-183

Zinoviev, Aleksandr, Soviet émigré writer, 105

Zoshchenko, Mikhail, Soviet writer, 55

Żyta, Józef, Polish prosecutor general, 265